PATTERN RECOGNITION—THEORY AND APPLICATION

NATO ADVANCED STUDY INSTITUTES SERIES

Proceedings of the Advanced Study Institute Programme, which aims at the dissemination of advanced knowledge and the formation of contacts among scientists from different countries.

The series is published by an international board of publishers in conjunction with NATO Scientific Affairs Division

A	Life Sciences	Plenum Publishing Corporation
B	Physics	London and New York
C	Mathematical and Physical Sciences	D. Reidel Publishing Company Dordrecht and Boston
D	Behavioural and Social Sciences	Sijthoff International Publishing Company Leyden, The Neth. and Reading, Mass., USA
E	Applied Science	Noordhoff International Publishing Leyden, The Neth. and Reading, Mass., USA

Series E: Applied Science — No. 22

PATTERN RECOGNITION THEORY AND APPLICATION

edited by

K.S. FU

School of Electrical Engineering,
Purdue University, West Lafayette,
Indiana 47907

and

A.B. WHINSTON

School of Industrial Management,
Purdue University, West Lafayette,
Indiana 47907

Springer-Science+Business Media, B.V. 1977

Proceedings of the NATO Advanced Study Institute
on Pattern Recognition—Theory and Application
Bandol, France
September 1975

ISBN 978-94-011-9690-1   ISBN 978-94-011-9688-8 (eBook)
DOI 10.1007/978-94-011-9688-8

INTRODUCTION

Research in the field of pattern recognition both in theoretical terms and in the area of application continues to flourish.
Pattern recognition is a fairly diverse field involving researchers
whose primary disciplines spread over at least a half dozen
fields. Possibly because of the great diversity of backgrounds
but a common interest in certain broad areas of application,
the field has grown so rapidly and yet seems to promise at least
a similar growth rate for the future.

This book is a collection containing some of the papers that
were presented at the N.A.T.O. Advanced Study Institute held in
Bandol, France, September 1975. The main purpose of the institute
was to present material which would provide a basic background in
the field. Thus, survey papers covering syntactic methods,
picture processing, classification theory, and speech recognition
were presented. This should have provided the listener (and we
hope now, the reader) with an acquaintance with the basic tools, a
look at some of the applications and an appraisal of how each of
the particular topics will evolve. A more recent addition to the
pattern recognition "family" is the work in the areas of economics
and group choice. Since the process of recognizing and interpreting patterns is so fundamental, it probably is no surprise
when a particular discipline is discovered to be amenable to the
already developed techniques. Of course, the hope is that from
the new entrants and the intereaction with the old timers, new
insights will evolve, leading to a general advancement of the
field. We have several papers which consider, from a pattern
recognition viewpoint, several topics in the social sciences.

A second part of the offerings of the Institute consisted of papers reporting on recent research in pattern recognition. Topics generally reflected the subject matter reviewed in the survey papers but were more detailed presentations of a specific problem. A selection of these papers is presented in this volume.

Although the editors have attempted to select material so as to fairly reflect the recent developments in the field of pattern recognition as presented at the Institute, it is regrettable that one aspect of the meetings could not be captured within this book: the spirit and conviviality of the many informal interactions among the participants. The "cultural communication" between individuals with varied orientations towards the field will hopefully lead to continued and increased interdisciplinary applications of pattern recognition in the future.

The editors are indebted to Dr. Kester of the N.A.T.O. Scientific Staff for his support and to the participants of the N.A.T.O. Institute for their cooperation.

K. S. Fu
A. B. Whinston

April 1976

TABLE OF CONTENTS

DECISION-THEORETIC AND RELATED APPROACHES TO PATTERN CLASSIFICATION

Pierre A. Devijver

I. Introduction

Statistically-based classification techniques has been a major theme of theoretical and experimental investigation in Pattern Recognition over nearly two decades. The impetus behind this research work is, to a large extent, to be attributed to C. K. Chow who first formalized the pattern recognition problem as a problem in statistical decision theory. Over the years, an impressive number of statistically-based classification methods have been proposed and a fairly good understanding of the potentialities and limitations of some of these has been gained. However, it is only recently that research works have been oriented toward such ends as evaluating the validity of hypothesized statistical models with respect to actual ones, or providing theoretical guidelines along which competing techniques can be meaningfully compared. It is the purpose of this paper to reflect some of this work.

In the following pages we describe some very basic statistical procedures for pattern classification. Whenever possible, the emphasis is on exhibiting the connections between the various techniques that we examine. From the very beginning we are taking a

Bayesian viewpoint to which we adhere throughout the paper. We start with a brief outline of elementary Bayes decision theory (Section 3) which is complemented, in Section 4, with a discussion of the error and reject tradeoff for the minimum-error-rate decision rule. Next, we go on with the Proportional Prediction technique which is the asymptotic version of the Single-Nearest-Neighbor rule. In Section 6 we introduce various Nearest-Neighbor-type rules including the rules with a reject option, and we exhibit an error and reject tradeoff for these rules. There, the discussion of the relationships between the Bayes and Nearest-Neighbor rules culminates in showing that the former tradeoff is a special case of the latter. In Sections 7 and 8, the discussion of statistically-based classification procedures is extended to cover discriminant procedures commonly employed in practice. There, again, the emphasis is on relating the discriminant procedures to both Bayes and Nearest-Neighbor procedures. The last two sections are concerned with sample-based decision rules and sample-based error-estimates. Since all the results in the previous sections are asymptotic, we exhibit the proper conditions for asymptotic consistency of both sample-based decision rules and error-estimates. Application of the error-reject tradeoff to error-rate estimation is also briefly discussed.

II. Pattern Classification as a Problem in Statistical Decision Theory

Let the pattern X be a random vector with values in R^d, and let $\theta \in \{1,\ldots,m\}$ be designated as the pattern class to be recognized. We shall temporarily assume that (X,θ) has a known distribution which is

$P\{\theta = j\} = P_j, \qquad j=1,\ldots,m,$

$P\{X \leq x|\theta\}$ has a probability density $p_\theta(x)$,

$$\theta=1,\ldots,m. \qquad (1)$$

Unless explicitly stated otherwise, it is assumed that the densities $p_\theta(X)$ are almost everywhere continuous on R^d. On the basis of knowledge, the classification problem is that of deciding the class θ to which an observed and unidentified pattern X belongs.

The solution to the classification problem depends upon the goal that one wants to achieve, and optimal classification procedures are those that enable us to meet the specifications of the chosen goal. Most frequently, the goal is to minimize either the probability of making incorrect decisions or some average measure of the penalty incurred when the decision maker makes an incorrect decision. Expressed in these terms, the classification problem is exactly the same as that of statistical decision theory or statistical hypothesis testing.

Let $\delta(X)$ be some *decision function*, where $\delta(X)=j$ means that the decision is made that the pattern X comes from class $j, j= 1,\ldots,m$. As a safeguard against excessive occurrence of erroneous decisions we can make provision for making *rejects*, i.e., deciding not to classify: $\delta(X)=0$. This interpretation for the term is related to, but should not be confused with that it has in statistical hypothesis testing where some hypothesis is either accepted or rejected on the basis of the information provided by the outcome of some experiment. Suppose that a loss $\lambda_{i,j} = \lambda(\delta=i|\theta=j)$ is incurred when the decision $\delta(X)=i$ is made and $\theta=j$, $i=0,1,\ldots,m$; $j=1,\ldots,m$. Then, conditioning upon X, the *a posteriori conditional risk* $1^i(X)$ of making decision $\delta(X)=i$ is

$$1^i(X) = \sum_{j=1}^{m} \lambda_{i,j} \cdot \pi_j(X) \qquad (2)$$

where
$$\pi_j(X) = \frac{P_j p_j(X)}{\sum_k P_k p_k(X)}$$

is the a posteriori probability of class j. Thus, given some decision rule $\delta(X)$, the conditional risk $1(X)$ is

$$1(X) = \sum_{j=1}^{m} \lambda_{\delta(X),j} \cdot \pi_j(X)$$

and the *unconditional risk* is

$$L = E_X\{ \sum_{j=1}^{m} \lambda_{\delta(X),j} \cdot \pi_j(X)\} \tag{3}$$

where E_X denotes expectation with respect to the unconditional distribution $p(X) = \sum_{k=1}^{m} P_k p_k(X)$. Classically, solving the statistical decision problem calls for determining the decision function $\delta(X)$ that minimizes the risk L as given by Eq. (3).

III. Elementary Bayes Decision Theory

3.1 Minimum-risk classification

From Eqs. (2) and (3), it is clear that we can minimize the overall risk L by assigning $\delta(X)$ the value i such that $l^i(X)$ is as small as possible for every X,[4]. The corresponding decision rule is known as the *Bayes decision rule* $\delta^*(X)$:

$$\delta^*(X) = \begin{cases} i & \text{if } l^i(X) \le l^k(X), \; k=0,\ldots,m, \\ \text{ties are broken arbitrarily.} \end{cases} \tag{4}$$

The resulting unconditional risk L^* is called the *Bayes risk*. It represents the best performance that can be achieved:

$$L^* = E_X \{\min_i \sum_{j=0}^{m} \lambda_{i,j} \cdot \pi_j(X)\}. \tag{5}$$

Our formulation of the Bayes decision rule is not unique: e.g., any transformation that leaves unchanged the ordering of the conditional risks may be used. For example, invoking Bayes rule, we can write

$$l^i(X) = \sum_{j=1}^{m} \lambda_{i,j} \frac{P_j p_j(X)}{p(X)} \qquad i=0,1,\ldots,m.$$

and since the denominator $p(X)$ is independent of i, the decision rule of Eq. (4) can be written

$$\delta^*(X) = \begin{cases} i & \text{if } \sum_{j=1}^{m} \lambda_{i,j} P_j p_j(X) \le \sum_{j=1}^{m} \lambda_{k,j} P_j p_j(X) \\ & \hspace{5cm} k=0,\ldots,m \\ \text{ties are broken arbitrary.} \end{cases} \tag{6}$$

We shall meet another legitimate transformation of the conditional risks in Section 7. In any event, to be optimal in the Bayes sense, the decision rule must be equivalent to the above.

3.2 Minimum-error-rate classification

Suppose all incorrect decisions are equally costly. (We temporarily make no provision for the reject option). We may choose the loss function that assigns no loss to a correct decision and a unit loss to any error:

$$\lambda_{i,j} = \begin{cases} 0 & i=j \\ & \quad i,j = 1,\ldots,m. \\ 1 & i \neq j \end{cases} \tag{7}$$

This is the *symmetrical* or *zero-one* loss function. With this loss function, the risk l^i becomes the *conditional probability of error* e^i since by Eqs. (2) and (7),

$$l^i(X) = \sum_{j \neq 1} \pi_j(X)$$

$$= 1 - \pi_i(X) = 1 - P\{\theta=i|X\} = e^i(X) \tag{8}$$

and $P(\theta=i|X)$ is the probability that $\delta(X)=i$ is the correct decision. Thus, minimum error probability is achieved by the rule that makes decision according to maximum a posteriori probability and the optimal rule becomes:

$$\delta^*(X) = \begin{cases} i & \text{if } \pi_i(X) \geq \pi_j(X), \ j=1,\ldots,m, \\ & \\ \text{ties are broken arbitrarily.} \end{cases} \tag{9}$$

By the same transformation as that used in going from Eq. (4) to Eq. (6) we can also write

$$\delta^*(X) = \begin{cases} i & \text{if } P_i p_i(X) \geq P_j p_j(X), \ j=1,\ldots,m, \\ & \\ \text{ties are broken arbitrarily.} \end{cases} \tag{10}$$

Since the rule δ^* makes decision according to minimum conditional error probability $e^*(X)$, it also achieves minimum average error probability or minimum *error-rate* E^*:

$$E^* = E_X\{e^*(X)\}$$

with

$$e^*(X) = 1 - \max_i \pi_i(X). \tag{11}$$

As Cover and Hart put it [8], E^* represents the limit of excellence beyond which it is impossible to go.

3.3 Two-category classification

When there are only two pattern classes, the optimal decision rules described above reduce to a *likelihood ratio* test. From Eq. (6), it is easily seen that the minimum risk decision rule is

$$\delta^*(X) = \begin{cases} 1 & \text{if } \dfrac{p_1(X)}{p_2(X)} \geq \dfrac{\lambda_{1,2} - \lambda_{2,2}}{\lambda_{2,1} - \lambda_{1,1}} \dfrac{P_2}{P_1} \\[2ex] 2 & \text{otherwise,} \end{cases} \tag{12}$$

where it was assumed that $\lambda_{i,j} > \lambda_{i,i}$; $i \neq j$; $i,j=1,2$. Thus, the rule calls for comparing the likelihood ratio $p_1(X)/p_2(X)$ to a threshold that depends upon the loss function and the pattern class a priori probabilities, but that is independent of the observed pattern X.

For the zero-one loss function, or minimum error-rate decision rule, the rule of Eq. (12) simplifies as follows:

$$\delta^*(X) = \begin{cases} 1 & \text{if } \dfrac{p_1(X)}{p_2(X)} \geq \dfrac{P_2}{P_1} \\[2ex] 2 & \text{otherwise.} \end{cases} \tag{13}$$

IV. Error and Reject Tradeoff for the Minimum Risk Decision Rule

Very often, the actual probability densities $p_i(X)$ that have to be plugged in the expression of the appropriate rule are not easily parameterizable, (as Cover judiciously put it [6]), or it may be nearly impossible to determine their exact analytical expression. In such situations, one may want to substitute mathematically tractable densities to the actual ones and to derive an optimum decision scheme based on this substitution. The same situation occurs when approximate distributions have to be inferred from finite empirical data. We shall presently describe one way to evaluate the validity of the assumed theoretical model with respect to the actual one. Quite unexpectedly, theoretical guidance regarding how to perform such an evaluation is one of the by-products of Chow's analysis of the error and reject tradeoff for the minimum-risk decision rule with a reject option [5].

Let the loss function be chosen as follows: $\lambda_{i,i}=0$, $\lambda_{i,j}=1$, $\lambda_{0,j}=\lambda_r < 1$; $i \neq j$; $i,j=1,\ldots,m$. From Eq. (2), it follows that $l^0(X)=\lambda_r$, and $l^i(X)=1-\pi_i(X) = e^i(X)$ and the optimum decision rule follows from the minimum-risk decision scheme of Eq. (4):

$$\delta^*(X) = \begin{cases} 0 & \text{if } \lambda_r < e^k(X), \quad k=1,\ldots,m \\ i & \text{if } e^i(X) \leq \lambda_r, \; e^k(X), \\ \text{ties are broken arbitrarily.} \end{cases} \qquad (14)$$

Clearly, the reject option is exercised whenever all of the error probabilities $e^i(X)$ exceed the *rejection threshold* λ_r. Thus it converts potential misclassifications into rejections. However, the tradeoff between error and reject rates is seldom one to one: some would-be correct classifications are also converted into rejects.

The decision rule of Eq. (14) divides the pattern space into a *reject region* R_{λ_r} and an *acceptance region* A_{λ_r}:

$$R_{\lambda_r} = \{X \mid \lambda_r < e^k(X), \; k=1,\ldots,m\} \qquad (15)$$

$$A_{\lambda_r} = \{X \mid \exists \; i \text{ such that } e^i(X) \leq \lambda_r\} \qquad (16)$$

In terms of these regions, various probabilities can be defined: The *reject-rate* is

$$R^*(\lambda_r) = \int_{R_{\lambda_r}} p(X) \, dX, \qquad (17)$$

the *acceptance-rate* is

$$A^*(\lambda_r) = \int_{A_{\lambda_r}} p(X) \, dX, \qquad (18)$$

and the *error-rate* is

$$E^*(\lambda_r) = \int_{A_{\lambda_r}} [\min_k e^k(X)] \, p(X) \, dX. \qquad (19)$$

The *correct-classification-rate* $C^*(\lambda_r)$ is related to $R^*(\lambda_r)$ and $E^*(\lambda_r)$ according to

$$R^*(\lambda_r) + E^*(\lambda_r) + C^*(\lambda_r) = 1. \tag{20}$$

Chow has shown [5] that there exists a surprisingly simple and fundamental relationship between E^* and R^*, viz.,

$$E^*(\lambda_r) = - \int_0^{\lambda_r} \lambda' dR^*(\lambda') \tag{21}$$

where the integral is either an ordinary Riemann integral or a Stieltjes integral according to whether or not $R^*(\lambda)$ is differentiable with respect to λ. Chow's method of proof for Eq. (21) was based on an analysis of the incremental change in the reject region as a result of a decremental change in the rejection threshold. An entirely different method of proof will be suggested in Section 6.

Equation (21) is known as the *error-reject tradeoff relation* since the change of the error-rate can be calculated as a function of the change of the reject-rate. Chow has given examples of error-reject tradeoff curves for problems involving unidimensional normal distributions with equal variance, and uniform distributions [5]. One further example is given hereafter.

Example 1. We consider Cover and Hart's two-class example [8] where the unidimensional pattern X has triangular densities on $[0,1]$: $p_1(x)=2x$, $p_2(x)=2-2x$, with prior probabilities $P_1=P_2=1/2$. From Eq. (14) it is clear that there will be no reject if $\lambda_r > 1/2$, and that the effective range for λ_r is $[1,1/2]$ for problems of two classes, (it would be $[0,1-1/m]$ for problems of m classes). It is straightforward to verify that the condition for rejection is equivalent to

$$\frac{\lambda_r}{1-\lambda_r} \le \frac{P_1 p_1(x)}{P_2 p_2(x)} \le \frac{1-\lambda_r}{\lambda_r}. \tag{22}$$

For our example, this becomes:

$$\frac{\lambda_r}{1-\lambda_r} \le \frac{x}{1-x} \le \frac{1-\lambda_r}{\lambda_r}$$

Hence $R^*(\lambda_r) = P\{x\epsilon[\lambda_r, 1-\lambda_r]\} = 1-2\lambda_r$, because $p(x)$ is the uniform distribution. From this and Eq. (21) we derive the error-function $E^*(\lambda_r) = \lambda_r^2$, and the error-reject tradeoff relation is

$$E^*(\lambda_r) = 1/4[1 - R^*(\lambda_r)]^2. \qquad (23)$$

These results are depicted in Figure 1.

Equation (21) gives

$$\frac{dE^*}{dR^*} = -\lambda_r.$$

Thus, the rejection threshold is the differential error-reject tradeoff. In particular, this shows that the tradeoff gets most ineffective as λ_r decreases.

Practical applications of these results lie in the areas of system design, performance evaluation and model validation. In view of Eq. (21), the error-reject tradeoff can be regarded as a characterizing feature of the distributions involved. Moreover, it is possible to calculate the error-rates and, consequently, the tradeoff curve from empirically observed reject-rates. Thus, in situations where, as described above, hypothetical distributions are substituted to the actual ones, the validity of the model can be ascertained by comparing the empirical reject or tradeoff functions with the ones derived from the assumed distributions. Fukunaga and Kessel have noted that this is merely a goodness-of-fit test for the assumed distributions and they have reported theoretical and experimental results on three methods of making this comparison [18].

It should be noted that class-information for test patterns is not being used in calculating reject-rates. There follows that that tradeoff relation provides a simple means of calculating the error-rate without actually identifying the errors. This idea was also pursued by Fukunaga and Kessel who have shown that a significant reduction in the variance of the error-estimate is obtained by ignoring the class identification of test patterns [18], [19]. We shall have more to say on this in the final section of this paper.

V. The Proportional Prediction Procedure

If we examine the conditional distributions induced by the optimal rules described above, viz., $p_{\delta*}(X)$, we notice that they can be very different from the original distributions in the population, viz., $p_\theta(X)$. For some purposes, this might be undesirable. If our goal is to devise a system such that induced distributions are identical to the original ones, then we can resort to the Proportional Prediction technique that was first discussed by Goodman and Kruskal [22] and was attributed by them to W. Wallis, (see also Toussaint, [37]).

The technique simply consists in a) observing an unidentified pattern X, b) throwing an m-sided biased die whose ith side appears with probability $\pi_i(X)$, and c) making decision according to the die showing. In so doing, we are "playing nature against itself" [9], thus if we make infinitely many decisions according to this scheme, it is plain that we shall empirically recover induced distributions that are identical to the original ones. Of course, this is achieved at the price of some sacrifice in system performance as measured by error probability.

Under some mild assumptions concerning the class distributions (specifically, that $p_\theta(X)$ be decomposable into a continuous component plus a series of mass points), the proportional prediction technique is identical to the asymptotic large-sample, single-nearest-neighbor decision rule (1-NN rule) investigated by Cover and Hart [8].

Basically, the finite-sample 1-NN rule works as follows: Being given a sequence $X_d = \{X_i, \theta_i\}_1^{N_d}$ of independent, identically distributed random vectors with the distribution of (X, θ), the 1-NN rule classifies an unidentified pattern X as belonging to the class θ of its nearest-neighbor in X_d.

It is known that when $N_d \to \infty$, the 1-NN error-rate E_1 is [8]

$$E_1 = 1 - E_X \{ \sum_{i=1}^m \pi_i^2(X) \} \tag{24}$$

and is related to the minimum error-rate E^* according to

$$E^* \leq E_1 \leq E^* (2 - \frac{m}{m-1} E^*). \tag{25}$$

When the performance of the rule is to be judged according to the 1-NN risk L_1, it can be shown [12] that

$$L_1 = E_X \{V^t(X) \wedge V(X)\} \tag{26}$$

where $\wedge$ is a square loss matrix $[\lambda_{i,j}]$ and $V(X)$ is an m-vector whose ith component is $\pi_i(X)$, $i,j=1,\ldots,m$. Results similar to those of Eq. (25) also hold but they are somewhat more complicated [12].

Example 2. Independent binary features [28], [15]. Consider a two-class problem with $P_1=P_2=1/2$ and let $X = (x_1,\ldots,x_d)^t$ where the x_i's are conditionally independent, identically distributed, binary-valued random variables, with $p = P\{x_i=1|\theta=1\} = P\{x_i=0|\theta=2\}$, $i=1,\ldots,d$. The distributions $P_\theta(X)$ are

$$P_1(X) = p^{\Sigma x_i} (1-p)^{d-\Sigma x_i}, \quad p > 1/2, \tag{27.a}$$

$$P_2(X) = (1-p)^{\Sigma x_i} p^{d-\Sigma x_i}. \tag{27.b}$$

With $r=\Sigma x_i$, and d odd, the minimum error-rate E^* is, (Cf. [15], p. 43),

$$E^*(p) = \sum_{r=0}^{(d-1)/2} \binom{d}{r} p^r(1-p)^{d-r}. \tag{28}$$

Using Eq. (24) we can calculate the 1-NN error-rate and we find:

$$E_1(p) = p^d(1-p)^d \sum_{r=0}^{d} \binom{d}{r} [p^r(1-p)^{d-r} + p^{d-r}(1-p)^r]^{-1}. \tag{29}$$

The results of the computation of $E^*(p)$ and $E_1(p)$ as functions of p are shown graphically in Figure 2. It is seen that for small values of $E^*(p)$, the proportional prediction technique, or 1-NN rule, performs nearly as well as the optimum decision rule. This, of course, could be expected from Eq. (25).

VI. Error and Reject Tradeoff for Nearest-Neighbor Decision Rule

The performance of the technique of the previous section can be improved if, for any pattern X to be classified, the random experiment is repeated several times, say k times, and the decision is made to classify X in the class that scores the largest number of votes among the outcomes of the die throwings. Equivalently, we may take $\delta(X)$ to be the class that occurs most often among the k Nearest-Neighbors to X (in the asymptotic sense where all k NNs coincide with X). In both cases, ties in voting can be broken at random. (Since we have assumed that the conditional pattern distributions have probability densities, ties in distance for the k-NN rule in the finite-sample case need not be considered for they occur with probability zero).

For this class of rules, the asymptotic error-probabilities E_k satisfy the following inequalities [8].

$$E^* \leq \cdots \leq E_{k+1} \leq E_k \leq E_{k-1} \leq \cdots \leq E_1,$$

and it should come as no surprise that as k grows arbitrary large, the k-NN rule converges to the minimum error-rate decision rule since, by the strong law of large numbers, the frequency of occurrence k_i/k of class i NNs among the k NNs to X converges almost surely to $\pi_i(X)$ as $k \to \infty$.

Hellman has extended this class of rules by introducing the possibility of making rejects: He required that a "qualified majority" of k'/k be attained for a decision to be made, otherwise, the pattern is rejected [23]. When $k'=k$, a decision is reached only when all of the k NNs are of the same class: a very conservative rule indeed.

The error-rate, $E_{k,k'}$, and reject-rate, $R_{k,k'}$, of these (k,k') - NN rules can, again, be related to the error-/and reject-rates of the Bayes procedures. For example, take $k'=k$ and let λ_r be chosen such that $R^*(\lambda_r) = R_{k,k}$. Then, it is known that [23]

$$E^*(\lambda_r) \leq E_{k,k} \leq (1 + k/2) \; E^*(\lambda_r). \tag{30}$$

Hellman also observed that the reject-rate R_{22} of the (2,2)-NN rule is identical to the error-rate E_1 of the 1-NN rule. This was, in fact, as special instance of a more general relationship connecting error-/and reject-rates of (k,k')-NN rules. The following is a brief outline of the derivation of this relationship.

Here, clarity requires that only the two-class case be discussed. However, starting with Eq. (37), our conclusions hold for problems involving an arbitrary number of classes. Let $\pi = \pi_1(X)$ designate the probability that any one of the first k NNs to X belongs to class 1, whereas $1 - \pi = \pi_2(X)$ is the probability that it belongs to class 2. Assuming conditional class-independence, the probability of occurrence of exactly k_1 class 1 NNs among the first k NNs to X is clearly the probability of observing k_1 successes and $k-k_1$ failures in k Bernonilli trials with probabilities π for success and $1-\pi$ for failure. Thus, we can write

$$P\{k_1 | k, \pi\} = b(k_1; k, \pi) = \binom{k}{k_1} \pi^{k_1} (1-\pi)^{k-k_1} \qquad (31)$$

There follows that the probability of occurrence of at least k' class-1 NNs among the first k NNs to X is

$$P\{k_1 \geq k' | k, X\} = S(k'; k, \pi) = \sum_{j=k}^{k} b(j; k, \pi). \qquad (32)$$

Likewise, the probability of occurrence of at most k-k' class-1 NNs (or, equivalently, at least k' class-2 NNs) is

$$P\{k_1 \leq k-k' | k, X\} = B(k-k', k, \pi) = \sum_{j=0}^{k-k'} b(j; k, \pi). \qquad (33)$$

Now, the conditional probability of acceptance for the (k,k')-NN rule is the sum of the probabilities in Eqs. (32) and (33). Thus,

$$A_{k,k'}(X) = S(k'; k, \pi) + B(k-k'; k, \pi) \qquad (34)$$

Note that, in the derivation of Eq. (34) it was implicitly assumed that $k' \geq (k+1)/2$. Invoking again the independence assumption, the conditional probability of correct classification is readily shown to be

$$C_{k,k'}(X) = \pi S(k'; k, \pi) + (1-\pi) B(k-k'; k, \pi), \qquad (35)$$

whereas the conditional probability of error is

$$E_{k,k'}(X) = (1-\pi)\ S(k';k,\pi) + \pi\ B(k-k';k,\pi). \tag{36}$$

Invoking a number of recurrence relations between terms of binomial distributions, it can be shown that [14]

$$A_{k,k'}(X) = C_{k-1,k'-1}(X) + E_{k-1,k'}(X) \tag{37}$$

This, together with $R_{k,k'}(X) = 1 - A_{k,k'}(X)$ yields

$$R_{k,k'}(X) - R_{k-1,k'-1}(X) = E_{k-1,k'-1}(X) - E_{k-1,k'}(X) \tag{38}$$

Eq. (38) exhibits one out of several possible forms for the error-reject tradeoff for (k,k')-NN rules. It is noted that, unlike Chow's result in Eq. (21), it is obtained as a pointwise relation that can be straightforwardly extended in terms of the expected values of the quantities involved. In view of obvious boundary conditions, the overall version of Eq. (38) is equivalent to

$$E_{k,k'} = \sum_{j=k'}^{k} [R_{k+1,j+1} - R_{k,j}]. \tag{39}$$

This shows that, like for the minimum error-rate decision rule, the (unconditional) error-rate $E_{k,k'}$ can be determined from the knowledge of reject-rates. Since, as pointed out earlier, class-information is not being used in determining reject-rates, Eq. (39) makes it possible to calculate the error-rate of any NN-rule without identifying the errors.

The structure of Eq. (39) is somewhat reminiscent of that of Eq. (21). In fact, it can also be shown that the latter is the limit of the former as $k \to \infty$ with $k'/k = 1-\lambda_r$, [14].

Example 3. We consider the class of (k,k)-NN rules, e.g., those rules requiring unanimous votes from the k NNs for making a decision. In view of the boundary condition $E_{k-1,k} = 0$, Eq. (37) becomes

$$A_{k,k} = C_{k-1,k-1}, \tag{40}$$

which establishes an unexpected, simple relationship between acceptance and correct-classification rates. Likewise, from Eq. (38) we obtain

$$R_{k,k} - R_{k-1,k-1} = E_{k-1,k-1} \tag{41}$$

For the two triangular distributions in Example 1, we find

$$R_{k,k} = (k-1)/(k+1), \tag{42}$$

and, by Eqs. (41) and (42),

$$E_{k-1,k-1} = 2/k(k+1), \tag{43}$$

so that the error-reject tradeoff has the form

$$E_{k-1,k-1} = \frac{(1 - R_{k,k})^2}{k + R_{k,k}} = \frac{A_{k,k}^2}{2 - A_{k,k}} \tag{44}$$

Thus, from Eqs. (40) and (44), it is seen that, in this example, the performance of the (k-1,k-1)-NN rule can be completely determined once we know the acceptance-rate of the (k,k)-NN rule.

The interested reader is referred to references 24 and 29 for a number of practical considerations on the use of empirical error-reject tradeoff in pattern classification system design.

VII. Discriminant Functions and Decision Boundaries

There is a number of ways to represent pattern classifiers. Each of these takes advantage of some idiosyncrasie of the problem at hand in order to lay bare the simplest way of synthesizing the corresponding classifying machine. Conceptually, the simplest way of implementing the proportional-prediction technique is via the Nearest-Neighbor type rules. However, this approach suffers from severe limitations in terms of storage requirements. We shall not discuss this point here except for mentioning that some attempts have been made towards reducing the number of possible nearest-neighbors to be searched before applying the rule (Cf. [9] for a series of pertinent references).

One somewhat canonical form of representation for a pattern classifier is in terms of a vector-valued *discriminant function*: $G(X) = [g_1(X), \ldots, g_m(X)]^t$. The corresponding decision rule is to assign a pattern X to class i if $g_i(X) \geq g_j(X)$ for all $j \neq i$. The minimum-risk classifier of Section 2.1 fits quite naturally in the formalism of discriminant functions. It has the general form

16

$G(X) = -\Lambda V(X)$, where Λ and V are as in Eq. (26). For the minimum error-rate discriminant function, we use $G(X) = V(X)$. This formulation in terms of discriminant functions sheds light on the fact that the former simply results from a linear transformation of the latter. It is often convenient to apply order-preserving transformations to the components of the discriminant function in order to gain significant analytical and computational simplifications.

Example 4. The multivariate normal case.

The favoriate example in the pattern recognition literature is that of two classes with multivariate normal distributions with means μ_1 and μ_2 and common covariance matrix $\ddagger$. Taking $g_i(X) = \ln[P_i\, p_i(X)]$, with $p_i(X) \sim N(\mu_i, \ddagger)$, the equation of the *decision boundary* $g_1(X) = g_2(X)$ is [1]

$$[X - 1/2\,(\mu_1+\mu_2)]^t\, \ddagger^{-1}\, (\mu_1-\mu_2) = K, \tag{45}$$

where $K = \ln(P_2/P_1)$ for the minimum-error-rate classifier and

$$K = \ln \frac{\lambda_{12} - \lambda_{11}}{\lambda_{21} - \lambda_{22}} \cdot \frac{P_2}{P_1} \tag{46}$$

for the minimum risk classifier. In this case the optimal decision boundary is a hyperplane, and the classifier may easily be synthesized by a resistive network and a threshold device [15].

Example 5.

Application of the same transformation as in the previous example to the discriminant function for the distributions in example 2 (viz., independent binary features) also leads to a very simple expression for the decision boundary, namely, $\Sigma\, x_i = {}^d/2$. Thus here again, the optimal decision surface is a hyperplane.

VIII. Statistical Criteria for Suboptimal Discriminant Functions.

In real-life problems, the situation is generally far from being as favorable as in the above examples: Very often, optimal decision boundaries have highly complicated functional expressions and would be very costly to synthesize. In such cases we may arbitrarily decide to use simpler ones, but this of course implies some sacrifice in system performance. Besides, determining the minimum error-rate decision boundary with a specified functional form is generally far from trivial [2], [33], [35], [40].

Another possibility is to use an approximation to an optimal discriminant function that is the best one according to some approximation criterion. Here, the error-rate of using the resulting classifier plays no role in our design work. Yet, some recent results make it possible to evaluate the validity of the resulting model without considering the actual error-rate.

Let $G(X)$ be some (generalized) linear discriminant function [15], e.g., $G(X) = [g_1(X),...,g_m(X)]^t$ and $g_i(X)=w_i^t \Phi(X)$ with $w_i = [w_{i,1},...,w_{i,n}]^t$ and $\Phi(X) = [\phi_1(X),...,\phi_{n-1}(X),1]^t$. (See also Nilsson [30] for the development of the ϕ-function approach.) One design approach consists in determining the vectors of coefficients w_i, $i=1,...,m$, for which $G(X)$ is the best approximation to $V(X)$ (i.e., the vector of a posteriori probabilities) in the sense of minimizing the *criterion function*.

$$J = E_X \{||G(X) - V(X)||^2\}. \tag{47}$$

Our purpose here is not to develop the explicit solution to this minimization problem, (such developments can be found in refs. 10 and 41) it is rather to analyze what we can learn from the knowledge of the minimizing $G^*(X)$. From least-square approximation theory [25], we know that $G^*(X)$ is orthogonal to the residual approximation error $J^*(X) = G^*(X) - V(X)$ in the sense that

$$E_X \{G^{*t}(X) [G^*(X) - V(X)]\} = 0. \tag{48}$$

Substituting $G^*(X)$ for $G(X)$ in Eq. (47) and using Eq. (48) the residual error is found to be

$$J^* = E_X\{- V^t(X) [G^*(X) - V(X)]\}. \tag{49}$$

Using Eq. (48) in Eq. (49), we have

$$J^* = E_X\{V^t(X) V(X)\} - E_X\{G^{*t}(X) G^*(X)\}. \tag{50}$$

Noting that $E_X\{V^t(X)\ V(X)\} = E_X\{\sum_{i=1}^{m} \pi_i^2(X)\} = 1-E_1$, we obtain

$$J^* = 1 - E_X\{||G^*(X)||^2\} - E_1, \tag{51}$$

From Eq. (51) and $J^* > 0$, there follows in view of Eq. (25),

$$1 - E_X\{||G^*(X)||^2\} \geq E_1 \geq E^*. \tag{52}$$

The results in Eqs. (51) and (52) call for the following comments. First, if the functional form of $G(X)$ was so chosen that $J^* = 0$, then $G^*(X) = V(X)$, almost everywhere, and the resulting discriminant function achieves Bayes-optimal classification. In other words, $1 - E_X\{||G^*(X)||^2\} = E_1$ is sufficient condition for the optimality of $G^*(X)$. It should be noted however that the condition is not necessary. Second, when $J^* > 0$, we can judge "how closely" $G^*(X)$ approximates the optimal discriminant function $V(X)$ not only by calculating J^*, but also by comparing $1 - E_X\{||G^*(X)||^2\}$ to the 1-NN error-rate E_1. This will be of particular interest in a moment. Third, the quantity $1 - E_X\{||G^*(X)||^2\}$ provides an upper-bound of both the 1-NN and Bayes error-rates. Cases exist where this bound turns out to be simultaneously tight and simple to evaluate, (see Example 6, below).

The above design approach is clearly not applicable when the exact expression for the distributions is not completely known. In that case, we may substitute to J the less demanding criterion function J_1 which is given by

$$J_1 = \sum_{i=1}^{m} P_i\ E_{X/i}\ \{||G(X) - V_i||^2\}, \tag{53}$$

where $V_i = (0,...,0,1,0,...,0)^t$ and the 1 is in ith position. Here, we notice that to compute J_1 we only have to take expectations of a purely algebraic expression. This we shall often be able to do in practical situations by substituting averages to expected values.

It is a quite remarkable fact that both criterion functions J and J_1 yield the same discriminant functions $G^*(X)$ [41]. On the other hand, by applying the same reasoning as above, it can be shown [13] that

$$J_1^* = 1 - E_X\{||G^*(X)||^2\} \qquad (54)$$

Consequently, by Eqs. (52) and (54), we obtain

$$J_1^* \geq E_1 \geq E^*. \qquad (55)$$

We are now in position to transpose, in terms of J_1^* the conclusions we reached in terms of J^*.

a)   A sufficient conditions for Bayes optimality of $G^*(X)$ is that J_1^* be equal to the 1-NN error-rate. This statement exhibits quite clearly that the three techniques that we have been considering thus far are closely interrelated.

b)   From $J^* = J_1^* - E_1$, it is seen that the difference $J_1^* - E_1$ indicates how closely $G^*(X)$ approximates the optimal discriminant function $V(X)$. It can therefore be used to evaluate the appropriateness of the chosen functional form for $G(X)$ with respect to the particular problem to be solved.

c) J_1^* is an upper-bound of both the 1-NN and the Bayes error-rates. It can therefore be used, for example, as a feature evaluation criterion.

Very similar results have been reported in terms of other criteria such as the Fisher discriminant ratio and the analysis of variance criterion, [13], (see also Example 6 below).

Our reasoning can be extended to the case where we want to approximate the optimal minimum-risk discriminant function $\Lambda V(X)$. Since the least-square approximation of a linear transform of the approximating function, the resulting discriminant is $\Lambda G^*(X)$. Results similar to (52) and (55) have also been reported in this more general case [11].

Example 6. Consider a two-class case with $P_1 = P_2$, and let $\Phi(X)$ be the augmented pattern vector [30]. In that case, it is known [13] that $J_1^* = 2(4+\Delta^2)^{-1}$ where Δ^2 is the Mahalanobis distance between

the two pattern classes (viz., $\Delta^2 = (\mu_1-\mu_2)^t (P_1\ddagger_1+P_2\ddagger_2)^{-1} (\mu_1-\mu_2))$.
Let the pattern classes have the triangular distributions of Examples 1 and 3. For these distributions we have $E^* = 1/4$, (see Fig. 1 with $\lambda=0,5$), $E_1 = 1/3$, (by Eq. (43)), and $\Delta^2 = 2$. The inequalities of (55) become

$$2(4+\Delta^2)^{-1} \geq E_1 \geq E^*, \quad 1/3 = 1/3 \geq 1/4. \tag{56}$$

The equality sign indicates that, as could be expected, a linear discriminant is capable of achieving minimum-error and is thus perfectly matched to the problem considered.

IX. Sample-Based Decision Rules

In most of the preceding sections, the probabilistic structure of the classification problem was assumed to be known to the system designer. This is, however, practically never the case and this material can merely be regarded as providing theoretical guidelines as to how we should make use of the information that is actually available.

In practice, decision rules are always *sample-based*, i.e., they have to be inferred from a finite set of sample patterns of known classification: the *design* (training) *sample set* $x_d = \{X_i,\theta_i\}_1^{N_d}$. From the viewpoint of statistical decision theory, sample-based decision rules are substitutes for unknown optimal rules [21]. It should be stressed however that the finiteness of the design sample set dramatically changes and complicates the situation because, except for a few highly constrained problems, the finite-sample behavior of sample-based decision rules is mathematically untractable. It is interesting to ask, however, whether this limitation could be circumvented if an arbitrary large number of samples would be available. Clearly we would like our sample-based decision rules to converge to the theoretical ones as $N_d \rightarrow \infty$. Among other things, this would give us some assurance that results such as those of the previous sections, would apply, at least approximately, once we have collected a large amount of data. This simple argument shows that studying the asymptotic (large sample) behavior of sample-based decision rules is more than of academic interest. The same conclusion can be reached in terms of the error-estimates of the following section.

9.1 Asymptotic optimality of two-steps, sample-based decision rules

Let us a) derive estimates $\hat{P}_\theta$ and $\hat{p}_\theta(X)$ of P_θ and $p_\theta(X)$ from x_d and b) substitute these estimates to the true probabilities and probability densities in the expression of an optimal decision rule such as that of Eq. (10). Sample-based decision rules obtained in this way are called *two-steps procedures*. A very general condition that guarantees asymptotic optimality of two-steps Bayes procedures is as follows [9]: Let

$$E^*(N_d) = P\{\hat{\theta} \neq \theta \mid x_d\} \tag{57}$$

where

$$\hat{\theta} = \begin{cases} i & \text{if } \hat{P}_i\ \hat{p}_i(X) \geq \hat{P}_j\ \hat{p}_j(X), \quad j=1,\ldots,m, \\ \text{ties are broken arbitrarily,} \end{cases} \tag{58}$$

then

$$E^*(N_d) \xrightarrow{N_d} E^* \text{ in probability (with probability one)} \tag{59}$$

if $\hat{P}_\theta$, $\hat{p}_\theta(X)$ are consistent (strongly consistent) estimates of P_θ, $p_\theta(X)$, $= 1,\ldots,m$. Here the notation $\hat{\theta}$ is used in order to emphasize that we are dealing with an estimate of . Since the empirical frequency N_i/N_d of occurrence of class i patterns in x_d is a strongly consistent estimator of P_i, the basic problem lies in the derivation of (strongly) consistent estimators for the probability densities involved.

It is noted that the above condition for asymptotic optimality of two-steps, sample-based Bayes procedures could equally well be written in terms of expected risk, or expected error- and reject-rates.

One result similar to (59) holds in terms of finite-sample k-NN rules: Let $\hat{\theta}$ be the estimate of θ with the k-NN rule based on x_d, and

$$E_k(N_d) = P\{\hat{\theta} \neq \theta \mid x_d\}. \tag{60}$$

Then, [38],

$E_k(N_d) \xrightarrow{N_d} E_k$ in probability, $k=1,2,\ldots$ with the convergence being almost sure convergence for slight assumptions on the densities $p_\theta(X)$. Here, it is seen that the problem of estimating the densities is bypassed since we go directly to the estimation of the decision rule.

The reader is referred to reference 32 for a study of the asymptotic convergence of sample-based (generalized) linear discriminant functions. Of particular interest to us is the fact that the minimum of the empirical criterion function

$$J_1(N_d) = 1/N_d \sum_{i=1}^{m} N_i/N_d \sum_{j=1}^{N_i} [||G(X_j)-V_i||^2], \tag{61}$$

where the second summation extends over those Xs such that $\theta=i$, is, in general, a strongly consistent estimate of J_1.

9.2 Estimation of probability density functions

Following time honored traditions we divide the methods of estimation of probability density functions in two categories according to whether or not it can be assumed that the underlying, unknown densities belong to some parametric family of probability densities. When this assumption is justified the problem simplifies into that of estimating the unknown parameters of the distributions. Here, we need only have (strongly) consistent estimates of the unknown parameters in order to satisfy the asymptotic-optimality requirements. In fact, under quite general regularity conditions on the probability densities $p_\theta(X)$, classical estimation methods such as Maximum Likelihood (ML) estimation or Bayes estimation yield consistent estimators of the distribution parameters. Thus we arrive at the pleasant conclusion that most supervised parametric learning methods currently described in the pattern classification literature [3], [15], [17], [42] yield asymptotically-optimal sample-based decision rules. Yet, it should be kept in mind that the practical usefulness of these rules is significantly

reduced by the number of simplifying assumptions invoked throughout their derivations.

The nonparametric procedures for probability density estimation are appropriate when we do not know the functional form of
the underlying densities. Here, the most effective estimation
schemes are based on a k-NN approach. This is consistent with the
fact that all the information about the underlying statistics is
embodied in the locality of the N_d samples.

Let X_1, ..., X_n be a sequence of independent, identically distributed random variables with unknown density function $f(X)$ and
let it be assumed that, at some point X the information about $f(X)$
is conveyed by the volumes v_i of the hypercubes out to the k_n NNs
to X from $X_1,...,X_n$, $i=1,...,k_n$. Then, assuming continuity of $f(X)$
at X, Fukunaga and Hofstetler were able to show that the ML estimator $f_n(X)$ of $f(X)$ is [20]

$$f_n(X) = \frac{k_n}{n \cdot V_n} ,$$ (62)

where V_n stands for v_{k_n}. If this estimate is to satisfy our consistency requirement, three conditions appear to be required, viz.,
$\lim_{n \to \infty} V_n = 0$, $\lim_{n \to \infty} k_n = \infty$, and $\lim_{n \to \infty} k_n/n = 0$. Since the definition of our
estimate leaves us with one "degree of freedom", we can either
specify V_n as a function of n and let $k_n = k(V_n)$ or specify k_n as
some function of n and let $V_n = V(k_n)$. The former approach yields
the Parzen-window method [31] whereas the latter yields the estimate of Loftsgaarden and Quesenberry [27]. For the Parzen estimate
of $f(X)$, we have

$$f_n = \frac{1}{n} \sum_{i=1}^{n} \frac{1}{V_n} K\left(\frac{X-X_i}{h_n}\right)$$ (63)

where h_n is the length of an edge of the hypercube V_n and K is
some appropriately chosen bounded kernel function such as $K(u) =$
$(1/2e^{-|u|}$, $K(u) = (1/\sqrt{2\pi}) e^{-u^2/2}$, and $K(u) = (xin^2 u)/u^2$. Letting
$K(u)$ be the Rosenblatt kernel $K(u) = 1$ for $|u| < 1/2$, and zero elsewhere, the estimator of (63) is easily seen to be identical to

that of (62). With the additional conditions $|u \, K(u)| \to 0$ as $|u| \to \infty$, and $\int K(u) \, du = 1$, the Parzen estimator $f_n(X)$ is a consistent estimator of $f(X)$ at every point of continuity of $f(X)$ if $h_n \to 0$ and $nh_n \to \infty$ as $n \to \infty$, [15], [7]. From this and the general condition for asymptotic optimality, it follows at once that the sequence of two-steps sample-based decision rules obtained by using the Parzen estimator yields a sequence of probabilities of error converging to the minimum error-rate in the limit as N_s tends to infinity. Under appropriate conditions, similar conclusions can be made for two-steps procedures based on the estimator of Loftsgaarden and Quesenberry.

X. Sample-Based Error-Estimates

Although the results from the previous section give us some reasonable assurance that our sample-based rule will perform well when classifying new patterns, they do not enable us to predict the future performance of the rule since in general we cannot calculate the error-probabilities of Eqs. (57) and (60). Estimating such error-probabilities is another topic that has received considerable attention in the pattern recognition literature. In this section we discuss two common ways of obtaining *error-estimates*.

10.1 Error-estimates based on error-count

The most straightforward approach to error-estimation is to test the classifier experimentally and to determine its empirical error-rate. This approach raises the embarrassing question of how we should partition the available data, viz. x_d into a design set and a test set. Toussaint has compiled an extensive bibliography on various methods for doing this [36].

The *resubstitution estimate* obtained by using x_d for both designing the rule and testing it is often ruled out on the basis of its excessive optimistic bias in the small sample case. Yet, it is an asymptotically unbiased consistent estimate of the Bayes error-probability E^* for the class of Bayes two-step procedures of the previous section [16].

Wagner has extensively studied the *deleted-estimates* of the error-rates [38], [39]. These are obtained by a) designing the rule with x_d, X_i being deleted, b) testing it with X_i, and c) repeating the process for $i=1,\ldots,m$. For a wide class of rules for which there exists an E such that $\lim_{N_d \to \infty} E(N_d) = E$ (with convergence in probability), Wagner shows that the deleted-estimate $\hat{E}(N_d)$ is a consistent estimate of E, [39]. For rules based on a k-NN approach, Rogers and Wagner exhibit the following distribution-free upper-bound on the mean-square estimation error [34].

$$E\{[E(N_d) - \hat{E}(N_d)]^2\} \leq \frac{2k+1/4}{N_d} + 2k \frac{\sqrt{2k+1/4}}{N_d^{3/2}} + \frac{k^2}{N_d^2} \qquad (64)$$

In addition, for the 1-NN rule, the bound of (64) can be tightened to yield [34]

$$E\{[E_1(N_d)\hat{E}_1(N_d)]^2\} \leq \frac{9m-8}{4m\,N_d} + \frac{1}{m.\,N_d}\,[(9m-8)(m-1)/N_d]^{1/2}$$
$$+ \frac{m-1}{m\,N_d^2} \qquad (65)$$

These results can be used in a straightforward manner to derive confidence intervals for the deleted-estimate of $E(N_d)$, [34].

Error-rate estimation is obviously one of the problem-domains where the error and reject tradeoff, offer new prospects. As the following example shows, identical estimation schemes yield estimators having different properties according to whether they are based on error-count or on reject-count.

Example 7. Estimation of the 1-NN error-rate.

It is known from Section 6 that $E_1 = R_{22}$. Consequently, any estimate of R_{22} is also an estimate of E_1 and vice versa. The resubstitution method always yields an overly optimistically-biased estimate of zero for E_1. At the contrary, the resubstitution-estimate of R_{22} is easily seen to be identical to the unbiased and consistent deleted-estimate of E_1. Whether other reject-estimates will exhibit some peculiar behavior still remains to be investigated.

As pointed out previously, particular advantage can be taken of the error and reject tradeoffs in those cases where, in addition to x_d, the designer has available a set $x_t = \{X_i\}_1^{N_t}$ of sample patterns whose class identification may be unknown. Then a reasonable approach is to use x_d for designing the rule and x_t for testing it. In those situations where the class information is very costly, this may be of great economic importance [26].

10.2 Error-estimates based on the apparent error-probability

For designing the two-step procedures of the previous section, we first derived estimates $\hat{P}_\theta$ and $\hat{p}_\theta(X)$ of P_θ and $p_\theta(X)$. If we now substitute these estimates in the expression of the error probability,

$$E = \int e(X)\ p(X)\ dX \tag{66}$$

we obtain

$$\hat{E} = \int \hat{e}(X)\ \hat{p}(X)\ dX \tag{67}$$

where $\hat{e}(X)$ and $\hat{p}(X)$ are based on $\hat{P}_\theta$ and $\hat{p}_\theta(X)$. $\hat{E}$ is known as the *apparent error-probability*. Glick has proved that the apparent error-probability of the Bayes two-step procedure of Eq. (58) with respect to (strongly) consistent estimates is a (strongly) consistent estimate of E^* [21].

A fairly simple and elegant idea has been developed by Fukunaga and Kessel for using unclassified sample patterns (such as those in x_t) in estimating E, [19]. They observed that the class information is necessary for estimating the conditional error-rate $e(X)$, and is not used in estimating $p(X)$. Thus they suggested to estimate $e(X)$ with x_d and $p(X)$ with x_t.

Example 8. [20].

In the two-class case we can write

$$e^*(X) = \frac{1}{2} - \frac{1}{2} \frac{|P_1 p_1(X) - P_2 p_2(X)|}{P_1 p_1(X) + P_2 p_2(X)} . \tag{68}$$

Suppose we use ML estimators for P_θ and $p_\theta(X)$, viz.

$$\hat{P}_\theta = N_\theta / N_d \tag{69}$$

and
$$\hat{P}_\theta = \frac{k_{\theta, N_d}}{N_d, V_{N_d}} \tag{70}$$

(Cf. Eq. (62)). Let us take V_{N_d} to be the volume out to the kth NN to S from x_d. We obtain

$$\hat{P}_\theta = \frac{k_\theta}{N_d V} \tag{71}$$

where k_θ is the number of class-θ NNs among the k NNs to X from x_d. Substituting these estimates in Eq. (68) yields the ML estimate $\hat{e}^*(X)$ of $e^*(X)$

$$\hat{e}^*(X) = \frac{1}{2} - \frac{1}{2} \frac{|k_1 - k_2|}{k} \tag{72}$$

Since $\hat{e}^*(X)$ does not use the class-information at X, it can be averaged over the unclassified test set x_t to provide the minimum error-rate estimate $\hat{E}^*$:

$$\hat{E}^* = \frac{1}{N_t} \underset{X \epsilon x_t}{\Sigma} \hat{e}^*(X) \tag{73}$$

Results on the asymptotic behavior of this type of error-estimates are reported in reference 20.

One chief characteristic of the error-estimates obtained by the technique just described is a substantial reduction in the variance of the estimate as compared to the variance of the estimate based on error-count [18]. This is a somewhat paradoxical result since we are getting a better estimate by ignoring the class information of test samples. This peculiar behavior has been attributed to the fact that error-counting techniques give a (0-1) quantization of $e^*(X)$ while an estimate such as that of Eq. (72) allows the assignment of a real value [18], [26]. Fukunaga and Kessel conjecture that an even better estimate might be found if the class information of test samples could be used adequately [18].

Acknowledgement

It is the author's pleasant duty to express thanks to his colleagues Drs. P. Delsarte and J. M. Goethals who contributed several fine points in the derivation of the material in Section 6.

28

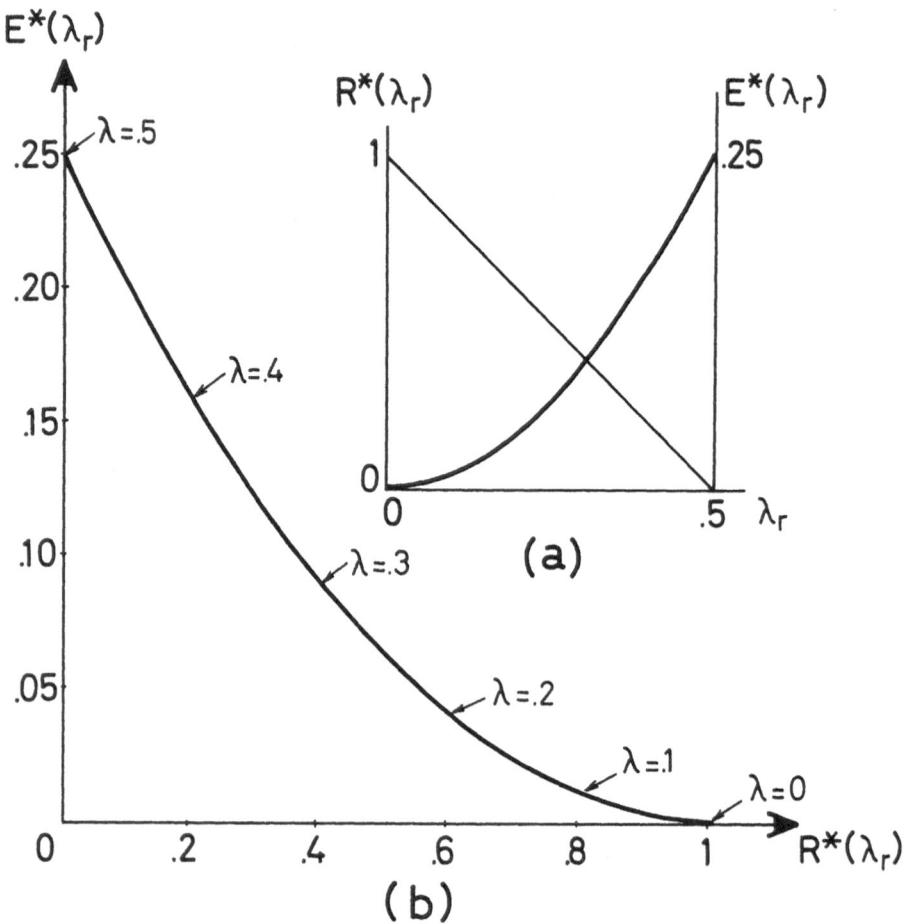

Figure 1. Error and Reject Tradeoff for the distributions in
Example 1. (a) Reject and Error curves.
(b) Error-Reject Tradeoff curve.

29

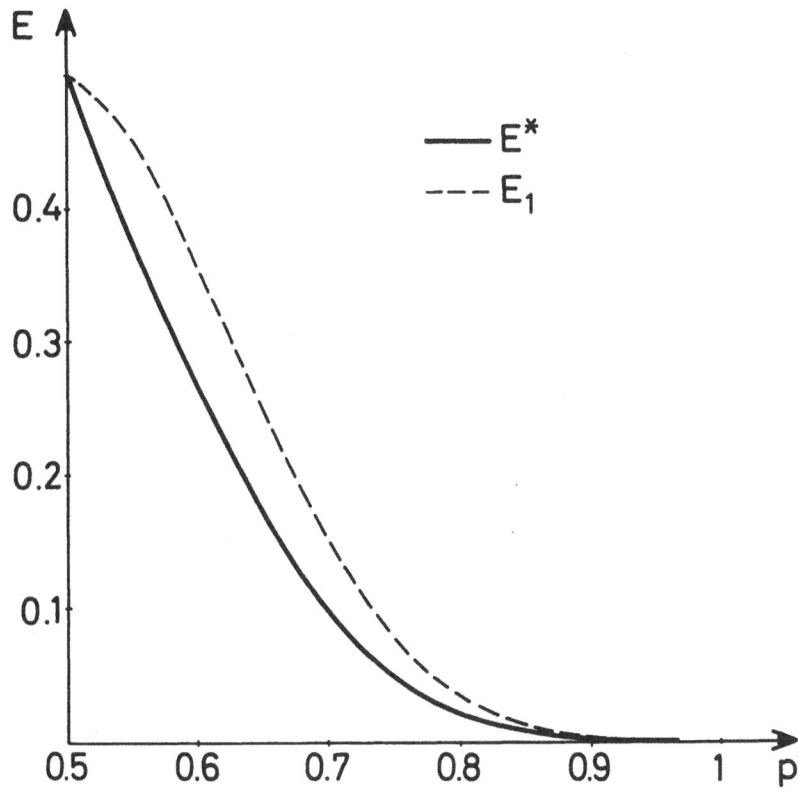

Figure 2. Error-rates for the distributions in Example 2.

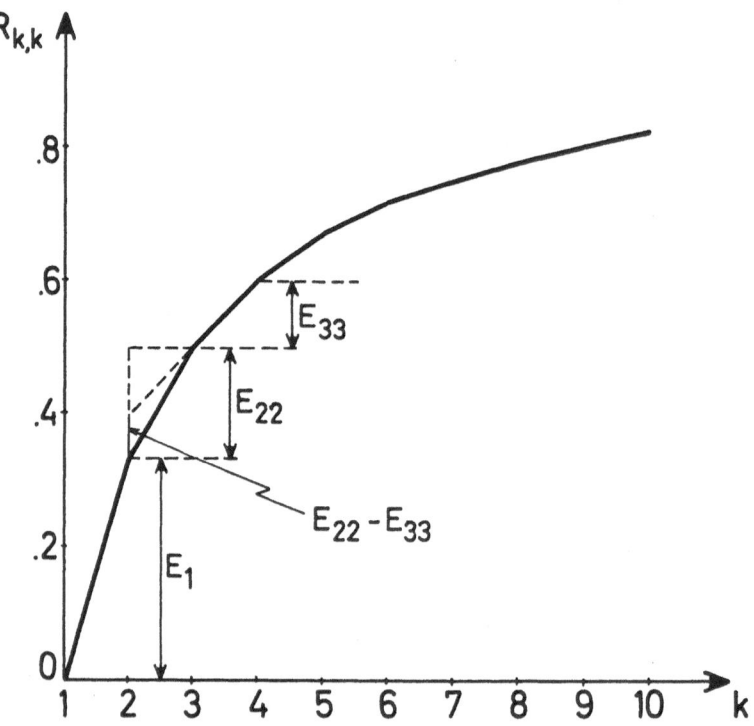

Figure 3. Reject curve, $R_{k,k}$ vs k, for the triangular
distributions in Example 1.

References

1. Anderson, T. W., An <u>Introduction to Multivariate Statistical Analysis</u>, New York: Wiley, 1958.

2. Anderson, T. W. and Bahadur, R. R., "Classification into two multivariate normal distributions with different covariance matrices", <u>Ann. Math. Stat.</u>, Vol. 33, pp. 422-431, June 1962.

3. Chen, C. H., <u>Statistical Pattern Recognition</u>, Rochelle Park: Spartan, 1973.

4. Chow, C. K., "An optimum character recognition system using decision functions", <u>IRE, Trans. Electronic Computers</u>, Vol. EC-6, pp. 247-254, Dec. 1957.

5. Chow, C. K., "An optimum recognition error and reject trade-off", <u>IEEE Trans. Inform. Theory</u>, Vol. IT-16, pp. 41-46, Jan. 1970.

6. Cover, T., "Learning in pattern recognition", in <u>Methodologies of Pattern Recognition</u>, S. Watanabe Ed., New York: Academic Press, 1969, pp. 111-132.

7. Cover, T., "A hierarchy of probability density function estimates", in <u>Frontiers of Pattern Recognition</u>, S. Watanabe Ed. New York, Academic Press, 1972, pp. 83-98.

8. Cover, T. M. and Hart, P. E., "Nearest neighbor pattern classification", <u>IEEE Trans. Inform. Theory</u>, Vol. IT-13, pp. 21-27, 1967.

9. Cover, T. M. and Wagner, T. J., "Topics in statistical pattern recognition", in <u>Recent Advances in Pattern Recognition</u>, K. S. Fu Ed., Berlin: Springer-Verlag, in press.

10. Devijver, P. A., "On the asymptotic property of the least-mean-square error design criterion in pattern recognition", <u>Philips Res. Repts.</u>, Vol. 28, pp. 37-49, Feb. 1973.

11. Devijver, P. A., "Relationships between statistical risks and the least-mean-square-error design criterion in pattern recognition", <u>Proc. 1st Int. Joint Conf. Pattern Recognition</u>, IEEE Special Publication CHO 821-9c, 1973, pp. 139-148.

12. Devijver, P. A., "The generalized Bayesian distance", <u>MBLE Res. Rept.</u> R232, Oct. 1974.

32

13. Devijver, P. A., "Entropie quadratique et reconnaissance des formes", in Computer Oriented Learning Processes, J. C. Simon Ed., Leyden: Noordhof, in press.

14. Devijver, "Error and reject tradeoff for Nearest-Neighbor decision rules", in preparation.

15. Duda, R. O. and Hart, P. E., Pattern Classification and Scene Analysis, New York: Wiley, 1973.

16. Fralick, S. C. and Scott, R. W., "Nonparametric Bayes-risk estimation", IEEE Trans. Inform. Theory, Vol. IT-17, pp. 440-444, 1971.

17. Fukunaga, K., Introduction to Statistical Pattern Recognition, New York: Academic Press, 1972.

18. Fukunaga, K. and Kessel, D. L., "Application of optimum error-reject functions", IEEE Trans. Inform. Theory, Vol. IT-18, pp. 814-817, Nov. 1972.

19. Fukunaga, K. and Kessel, D. L., "Nonparametric Bayes error estimation using unclassified samples", IEEE Trans. Inform. Theory, Vol. IT-19, pp. 434-440, July 1973.

20. Fukunaga, K. and Hofstetler, L. D., "k-Nearest-Neighbor Bayes-risk estimation", IEEE Trans. Inform. Theory, Vol. IT-21, pp. 285-293, May 1975.

21. Glick, N., "Sample-based classification procedures derived from density estimators", J.A.S.A., Vol. 67, pp. 116-122, March 1972.

22. Goodman, L. A. and Kruskal, W. H., "Measures of association for cross-classifications", J.A.S.A., Dec. 1954, pp. 732-764.

23. Hellman, M. E., "The Nearest-Neighbor classification rule with a reject option", IEEE Trans. Syst. Sci. Cybern., Vol. SSC-6, pp. 179-185, 1970.

24. Hennis, R. B., "The IBM 1975 optical page reader, Part I: System design", IBM J. Res. and Develop., Vol. 12, pp. 346-353, Sept. 1968.

25. Ho, H. S., "Mean convergence of approximation to a function by general finite sums", Quat. Applied Math., Vol. 31, pp. 177-184, July 1973.

26. Kanal, L. N., "Patterns in Pattern Recognition: 1968-1974", IEEE Trans. Inform. Theory, Vol. IT-20, pp. 697-722, Nov. 1974.

27. Loftsgaarden, D. O. and Quesenberry, C. P., "A nonparametric estimate of a multivariable density function", Ann. Math. Statist., Vol. 38, pp. 1261-1265, 1965.

28. Minsky, M., "Steps toward artificial intelligence", Proc. IRE, Vol. 49, pp. 8-30, Jan. 1961.

29. Nadler, M., "Error and reject rates in a hierarchical pattern recognizer", IEEE Trans. Computers, Vol. C-20, pp. 1598-1601, Dec. 1971.

30. Nilsson, N. J., Learning Machines: Foundations of Trainable Pattern Classifying Systems, New York: McGraw-Hill, 1965.

31. Parzen, E., "On the estimation of a probability density function and the mode", Ann. Math. Statist., Vol. 33, pp. 1065-1076, 1962.

32. Patterson, J. D., Wagner, T. J., and Womack, B. F., "A performance criterion for adaptive pattern classification systems", IEEE Trans. Autom. Control, Vol. AC-12, pp. 195-197, April 1967.

33. Peterson, D. W. and Mattson, R. L., "A method of finding linear discriminant functions for a class of performance criteria", IEEE Trans. Inform. Theory, Vol. IT-12, pp. 380-387, July 1966.

34. Rogers. W. H., and Wagner, T. J., "A finite-sample distribution-free performance bound for local discrimination rules", submitted to Ann. Statis., 1974.

35. Smith, F. W., "Design of minimum-error optimal classifiers for patterns from distributions with Gaussian tails", IEEE Trans. on Inform. Theory, Vol. IT-17, pp. 701-707, Nov. 1971.

36. Toussaint, G. T., Bibliography on estimation of misclassifications", IEEE Trans. Inform. Theory, Vol. IT-20, pp. 472-479, July 1974.

37. Toussaint, G. T., "On the divergence between two distributions and the probability of misclassification of several decision rules", Proc. 2d Int. Joint Conf. Pattern Recognition, IEEE Special Publication CHO 885-4C, 1974, pp. 27-34.

38. Wagner, T. J., "Convergence of the Nearest-Neighbor rule", IEEE Trans. Inform. Theory, Vol. IT-17, pp. 566-571, 1971.

39. Wagner, T. J., "Deleted estimates of the Bayes risk", Ann. Statist., Vol. 1, pp. 359-362, 1973.

34

40. Wassel, G. W., "Training a linear classifier to optimize the error probability", Rept. Univ. of California, Irvine, Ca., Dec. 1972.

41. Wee, W. G., "Generalized inverse approach to adaptive multi-class pattern classification", IEEE Trans. Computers, Vol. C-17, pp. 1157-1164, Dec. 1968.

42. Young, T. Y. and Calvert, T. W., Classification, Estimation and Pattern Recognition, New York: Elsevier, 1974.

PATTERN RECOGNITION TECHNIQUES FOR BINARY DATA

Tzay Y. Young

Department of Electrical Engineering
University of Miami
Coral Gables, Florida 33124

Abstract: Statistical pattern recognition techniques specifically designed for binary data are considered. Previous works
on approximating probability distributions are discussed briefly.
An optimal modulo-2 linear transformation is introduced, which
minimizes an entropy criterion. It yields a set of better feature
vectors, and improves the approximation of probability distributions. A numerical example is presented and compared with previous works.

I. Introduction

In recent years there has been substantial progress in pattern recognition and feature extraction techniques. Most of the
works deal with continuous-valued pattern vectors. In some medical and social science problems, the pattern vectors and feature
vectors are binary-valued. It is believed that for this type of
problems, pattern recognition techniques should be designed that
take advantage of the special properties of the binary data.

Many pattern recognition problems may be formulated as a
problem of approximating probability distributions. For binary
data, the problem has been investigated by several authors [1]-
[6]. The approximation include first-order and second-order

product approximations, and the dependence tree approximation.

The application of modulo-2 linear transformation to binary data is investigated. For the class of generalized binomial distributions, it is shown that linear transformations exist that will yield statistically independent binary-valued random variables. An optimal transformation minimizes an entropy criterion, and improves the approximation of probability distributions. It gives us a coordinate system for a simpler and more meaningful representation of binary data, and hence it is in this sense, similar to the Karhunen-Loeve trnasformation for continuous-valued random variables. A numerical example is presented and compared with previous works.

II. Approximating Probability Distributions

Let $\underline{x} = [x_1, x_2, \ldots x_n]$ be a binary-valued random row vector with a probability distribution $p(\underline{x})$. A first-order product approximation of $p(\underline{x})$ is

$$\hat{p}_1(\underline{x}) = \prod_{i=1}^{n} p_i(x_i), \tag{1}$$

where $p_i(x_i)$ is a first-order marginal distribution of $p(\underline{x})$. If we let $p_i = p_i(1)$,

$$\hat{p}_1(\underline{x}) = \prod_{i=1}^{n} p_i^{x_i} (1 - p_i)^{1-x_i} \tag{2}$$

The distribution in (2) is called a multi-variate binomial distribution.

A second-order product approximation may be written as

$$\hat{p}_2(\underline{x}) = \prod_{i=1}^{n} \prod_{j>i} v_{ij}(x_i, x_j), \tag{3}$$

Subject to the constraint that the second-order marginals of $\hat{p}_2(\underline{x})$ are the same as those of $p(\underline{x})$. The values of v_{ij} can be obtained by iterative procedures only. Higher-order product approximations can be defined in a similar manner. The significance and optimality of product approximations have been discussed in detail by previous authors [1]-[6].

A dependence-tree approximation is a product of first-order conditional distributions. The optimal tree structure and the approximation, $\hat{p}_t(\underline{x})$, can be found by comparing the $n(n-1)/2$ pairwise mutual information $I(x_i, x_j)$ [5].

The approximation criterion commonly used is the information error criterion,

$$J(p;\hat{p}) = \sum_{\underline{x}} p(\underline{x}) \, [\log p(\underline{x}) - \log \hat{p}(\underline{x})]. \qquad (4)$$

It is well known that $J(p;\hat{p}) \geq 0$, and it equals zero if and only if $\hat{p}(\underline{x}) = p(\underline{x})$ for all $\underline{x}$. It has been shown that [6]

$$J(p; \hat{p}_1) \geq J(p; \hat{p}_t) \geq J(p; \hat{p}_2). \qquad (5)$$

III. <u>Linear Transformations of Binary-Valued Random Vectors</u>

Let $\underline{A}$ be an $n \times n$ matrix of zeros and ones, and

$$\underline{y} = \underline{x} \, \underline{A}, \qquad (6)$$

where all operations are modulo-2 operations with addition defined by

$$0 + 0 = 0, \qquad 0 + 1 = 1,$$
$$1 + 0 = 1, \qquad 1 + 1 = 0. \qquad (7)$$

We ask the following question. When does a nonsingular $\underline{A}$ exist which makes the components of $\underline{y}$ in (6) independent?

<u>Theorem</u> A nonsingular $\underline{A}$ exists which yields a set of statistically independent components of $\underline{y}$, if and only if linearly independent basis vectors $\underline{b}_1, \underline{b}_2, \ldots \underline{b}_n$ and numbers, $q_1, q_2, \ldots q_n$, $0 \leq q_j \leq 1$, exist such that

$$p(\underline{x}) = \prod_{j=1}^{n} (q_j)^{\zeta_j} \, (1 - q_j)^{1-\zeta_j} \qquad (8)$$

where

$$\underline{x} = \sum_{j=1}^{n} \zeta_j \, \underline{b}_j \qquad (9)$$

Proof:

Suppose there exists a set of linearly independent vectors $\underline{b}_1, \underline{b}_2, \ldots \underline{b}_n$. Let us define a matrix $\underline{B}$ that consists of the n

basis vectors as its row vectors, and its inverse A. Then

$$\underline{y} = \underline{x} \, \underline{A} = \sum_{j=1}^{n} \zeta_j \, \underline{b}_j \, \underline{A} = [\zeta_1, \, \zeta_2, \ldots \zeta_n], \qquad (10)$$

since $\underline{A} = \underline{B}^{-1}$. In other words, $y_j = \zeta_j$ and the random vector $\underline{y}$
is binomial distributed. It follows from the definition of a
binomial distribution that the random variables, $y_1, y_2, \ldots y_n$, are
statistically independent. The converse can be shown by reversing
the arguments.

The above result carries over to random vectors whose values
lie in an arbitrary finite field. The distribution of the random
vector $\underline{x}$ given by (8) and (8) is called a generalized binomial
distribution for obvious reasons.

Modulo-2 linear transformation may be applied to binary data
with an arbitrary distribution $p(\underline{x})$. Consider the nonsingular
transformation in (6), and let $q(\underline{y})$ be the distribution of the
random vector $\underline{y}$. We wish to find a new coordinate system so that
the binary random variables, $y_1, y_2, \ldots y_n$, are "least dependent".
Let us generalize the concept of mutual information to n random
variables,

$$I(\underline{y}) = \sum_{\underline{y}} q(\underline{y}) \, [\log q(\underline{y}) - \log \prod_{j=1}^{n} q_j(y_j)] \qquad (11)$$

where $q_j(y_j)$ is the j-th first-order marginal distribution of $q(\underline{y})$.
Since $I(\underline{y}) \geq 0$ and equals zero if and only if the random variables
are statistically independent, it is a measure of mutual dependence of the n random variables. An optimal linear transformation
is defined as the one that yields a minimum $I(\underline{y})$. Clearly this
definition includes the transformation in the theorem as a special
case.

For an arbitrary nonsingular linear transformation, $q(\underline{y}) = p(\underline{x})$ and the first term in (11) is independent of the transformation. The second term is obviously equivalent to an entropy cri-
terion,

$$H = \sum_{j=1}^{n} H_j = - \sum_{j=1}^{n} \sum_{y_j=0}^{1} q_j(y_j) \log q_j(y_j), \tag{12}$$

and minimizing $I(\underline{y})$ is equivalent to minimizing H. It is interesting to note that minimum entropy is one of the major properties of the Karhunen-Loève transformation for continuous random variables [7]-[10].

To find an optimal $\underline{A}$, one may first consider exhaustively the 2^n-1 non-zero binary column vectors $\underline{\alpha}^j$, and calculate the probability distribution of $\underline{x}\,\underline{\alpha}^j$ and the corresponding H_j. The optimal $\underline{A}$ consists of those column vectors that yield minimum H, subject to the constraint of linear independence. This approach is obviously not feasible when n is relatively large. An iterative procedure is being developed, using Hamming distance and the entropy criterion.

IV. Approximation in the Transformed Space

With a linear transformation $\underline{y} = \underline{x}\,\underline{A}$, the information error criterion becomes

$$J(q;\hat{q}) = J(p;\hat{q}) = \sum_{\underline{y}} q(\underline{y})\,[\log q(\underline{y}) - \log \hat{q}(\underline{y})]. \tag{13}$$

We use $\hat{q}_1(\underline{y})$, $\hat{q}_2(\underline{y})$ and $\hat{q}_t(\underline{y})$ to denote product and dependence-tree approximations in the y-space.

Consider the first-order product approximation

$$\hat{q}_1(\underline{y}) = \prod_{j=1}^{n} q_j(y_j). \tag{14}$$

A substitution of (14) into (13) shows that in this case $J(q;\hat{q}_1) = I(\underline{y})$ of (11). Therefore the optimal $\underline{A}$ that minimizes (13) is the minimum entropy transformation and

$$J(q;\hat{q}_1) \le J(p;\hat{p}_1). \tag{15}$$

The method may be interpreted as an optimal approximation by a generalized binomial distribution. It is conceivable that there are generalized binomial distributions which can not be represented exactly by low-order product approximations in the x-space; and hence $\hat{q}_1(\underline{y})$ is not necessarily inferior to $\hat{p}_2(\underline{x})$.

The situation for $\hat{q}_t(\underline{y})$ and $\hat{q}_2(\underline{y})$ is not clear; however we expect that in many cases an approximation in the y-space will be better than the corresponding approximation in the x-space. It is possible to define an optimal transformation as the one yielding an optimal $\hat{q}_t(\underline{y})$ or $\hat{q}_2(\underline{y})$, but the computation will be more complicated.

Example.

This is the same example considered by previous authors, and the results are tabulated in Table 1. The true probability distribution, $p(\underline{x})$, is listed in the third column of the table, and $\hat{p}_1(\underline{x})$, $\hat{p}_t(\underline{x})$ and $\hat{p}_2(\underline{x})$ are taken directly from Chow and Liu [5] and Ku and Kullback [6].

To find the optimal transformation $\underline{A}$, we consider all non-zero binary column vectors $\underline{\alpha}^j$, j=1, 2,...15, and calculate H_j for each random variable $\underline{x}\,\underline{\alpha}^j$. The results in natural logarithm are as follows with the $\underline{\alpha}$'s listed in row-vector form:

$H_j = 0.500$ for $\underline{\alpha}_j = 0110$,

$H_j = 0.610$ for $\underline{\alpha}_j = 1100$

$H_j = 0.687$ for $\underline{\alpha}_j = 0010, 0011, 0100, 0101,$

                           $1000, 1001, 1110,$ or 1111

$H_j = 0.692$ for $\underline{\alpha}_j = 0001, 0111, 1010, 1011,$

                          or $1101.$

Thus according to the discussions in Section III, we choose

$$\underline{A} = \begin{bmatrix} 0 & 1 & 0 & 0 \\ 1 & 1 & 0 & 0 \\ 1 & 0 & 1 & 1 \\ 0 & 0 & 0 & 1 \end{bmatrix}$$

where the last two column vectors are chosen more or less arbitrarily. The first-order marginal distributions of $q(\underline{y})$ are 0.800, 0.200; 0.700, 0.300; 0.450, 0.550; 0.450, 0.550, and $\hat{q}_1(\underline{y})$ is the product of these marginals. We note from Table 1 that $\hat{q}_1(\underline{y})$ is a substantially better approximation than $\hat{p}_1(\underline{x})$, and in fact almost as good as $\hat{p}_t(\underline{x})$. The values of the information error listed in

TABLE I

x	y	p(x)=q(y)	$\hat{p}_1(x)$	$\hat{q}_1(y)$	$\hat{p}_t(x)$	$\hat{q}_t(y)$	$\hat{p}_2(x)$
0000	0000	.100	.04556	.11340	.130	.01937	.09977
0001	0001	.100	.04556	.13860	.104	.01937	.10000
0010	1011	.050	.05569	.04235	.037	.05000	.04958
0011	1010	.050	.05569	.03465	.030	.05000	.04927
0100	1100	.000	.05569	.01215	.015	.00000	.00051
0101	1101	.000	.05569	.01485	.012	.00000	.00026
0110	0111	.100	.06806	.07260	.068	.11250	.10011
0111	0110	.050	.06806	.05940	.054	.05625	.05035
1000	0100	.050	.05569	.04860	.053	.04375	.05027
1001	0101	.100	.05569	.05940	.064	.08750	.09996
1010	1111	.000	.06806	.01815	.015	.00000	.00039
1011	1110	.000	.06806	.01485	.018	.00000	.00076
1100	1000	.050	.06806	.02835	.033	.05000	.04945
1101	1001	.050	.06806	.03465	.040	.05000	.04978
1110	0011	.150	.08319	.16940	.149	.14063	.14992
1111	0010	.150	.08319	.13860	.179	.14063	.14962
J(p;p) or J(q;q)			.3687	.0988	.0952	.00338	.00186*

*This value is substantially smaller than the one given in Ku and Kullback. It is evaluated directly by substituting $\hat{p}(x)$ and $\hat{p}_2(x)$ of the table into (4), and it is more reasonable in view of the information errors of other approximations.

the last line of the table substantiate this fact.

Now let us calculate the pairwise mutual information,

$I(y_1,y_2) = 0.0816$

$I(y_1,y_3) = I(y_1,y_4) = 0.00195,$

$I(y_2,y_3) = 0.00177,$

$I(y_2,y_4) = 0.0119$

$I(y_3,y_4) = 0.00012$

These values are measures of pairwise dependence of the random variables. Since $I(y_1,y_2)$, $I(y_2,y_4)$ and $I(y_1,y_3)$ are the largest quantities, we have a dependence-tree approximation [5],

$$\hat{q}_t(\underline{y}) = q_1(y_1)q_{21}(y_2|y_1)q_{31}(y_3|y_1)q_{42}(y_4|y_2),$$

where the double subscripts denote conditional probabilities. The values of $\hat{q}_t(\underline{y})$ and $J(q;\hat{q}_t)$ are tabulated in the seventh column of the table. Again $\hat{q}_t(\underline{y})$ is a much better approximation than $\hat{p}_t(\underline{x})$, the corresponding approximation in the x-space, but it is somewhat less accurate than $\hat{p}_2(\underline{x})$.

References

1. P. M. Lewis, "Approximating Probability Distributions to Reduce Storage Requirement", Information and Control, Vol. 2, pp. 214-225, 1959.

2. D. T. Brown, "A Note on Approximations to Discrete Probability Distributions", Information and Control, Vol. 2, pp. 386-392, 1959.

3. I. J. Good, "Maximum Entropy for Hypothesis Formulation Especially for Multidimensional Contingency Tables", Ann. Math. Statistics, Vol. 34, pp. 911-934, 1963.

4. C. T. Ireland, and S. Kullback, "Contingency Tables with Given Marginals", Biometrika, Vol. 55, pp. 170-188, 1968.

5. C. K. Chow, and C. N. Liu, "Approximating Discrete Probability Distributions with Dependence Trees", IEEE Trans. Information Theory, Vol. IT-14, pp. 462-467, 1968.

6. H. H. Ku and S. Kullback, "Approximating Discrete Probability Distributions", IEEE Trans. Information Theory, Vol. IT-15, pp. 444-447, 1969.

7. S. Watanabe, "Karhunen-Loève Expansion and Factor Analysis - Theoretical Remarks and Application", Proc. 4-th Conf. Information Theory, Prague, pp. 635-660, 1965.

8. Y. T. Chien and K. S. Fu, "Selection and Ordering of Feature Observations in a Pattern Recognition System", Information and Control, Vol. 12, pp. 395-414, 1968.

9. J. T. Tou and R. P. Heydorn, "Some Approaches to Optimum Feature Extraction", Computer and Information Science II, ed. J. T. Tou, pp. 57-89, Academic Press, New York, 1971.

10. T. Y. Young, "The Reliability of Linear Feature Extractors", IEEE Trans. Computers, Vol. C-20, pp. 967-971, 1971.

ON THE USE OF DISTANCE AND INFORMATION MEASURES IN PATTERN
RECOGNITION AND APPLICATIONS*

C. H. Chen

Southeastern Massachusetts University
North Dartmouth, Massachusetts 02747

Abstract: In the development of pattern recognition theory
during the past few years, there has been active interest in comparing the relative merits of various distance and information
measures by evaluating the error bounds. Normally the tighter the
error bounds a distance or information measure can provide, the
better features it can select. There are now at least fifteen
different measures available. They have two main advantages.
(1) They are generally easier to calculate than the error probability itself which normally cannot be computed exactly. These
measures can provide good upper and/or lower bounds of the error
probability. (2) Features can be selected and ordered to maximize
(or in some cases minimize) the measures in order to minimize indirectly the error probability. Linear transformation for dimensionality reduction can also be derived from these measures. This
paper is concerned with the theoretical problems and the applications of these measures. The paper begins with a survey of distance and information measures, relationships among the error
bounds, and then examines the finite sample size effects, and
other theoretical problems. The applications considered are the

*This work was supported by Grant AFOSR 71-2119.

signal selection in communication and radar, and feature extraction in imagery pattern recognition.

I. Introduction

Due to the continuing efforts among the pattern recognition researchers especially in the past few years, there is now a better understanding of the relative merits of various distance and information measures for feature extraction and selection. Recently Kanal [1] provided a fairly complete list of distance measures and the relationships among the error bounds. Such understanding, however, is still not adequate to make effective use of these measures in pattern recognition and related applications. The advantages and problems with these measures can be summarized as follows. These measures offer two main advantages. (1) They are generally easier to calculate than the error probability itself which normally cannot be computed exactly. They can provide good upper and/or lower bounds of the error probability. (2) Features can be selected and order to maximize (or in some cases minimize) the measures in order to minimize indirectly the error probability. The practical and theoretical problem with the measures are the following.

1)   Almost all available error bounds are based on the unrealistic assumptions of finite sample size and known probability distributions. In practice, the number of samples is finite. What kind of feature selection method should then be used for a given set of pattern recognition data? How can we relate the information and distance measures with the sample size? The probability density is not known or only partially known in practice. The distance measures using estimated probability density may not perform as effectively as theoretically predicted. In fact, experimental (computer) results have not been available to support the theoretical relationships among the error bounds. Thus the basic problem here is the gap between theory and practice.

2) Error bounds which are tight for two classes may be very loose for multiple pattern classes. Feature selection criteria which are tight for multiple pattern classes are much needed.

3) Without specifying the probability density, error bounds for the existing feature selection criteria are as tight as possible. So far the "best" feature selection criteria tend to agree on minimizing the "mean-square error." This appears to be the result of the "distance" oriented measure and implies an emphasis on the second order statistics which may be quite inadequate for some patterns. With a few exceptions, closed form expressions for the distance and information measures for important probability densities remain to be derived or are simply not available.

4) Vector samples are very much dependent in practice such as in image recognition. All the studies thus far on distance measures did not take such contextual information into consideration.

5) The computational difficulty of some of the existing feature selection criteria is almost as bad as the error probability itself.

In spite of the problems listed above, the information and distance measures such as the equivocation, divergence, and Bhattacharyya distance have played an important role in feature selection. In this paper, we are concerned with both the theoretical problems and various applications of these measures.

II. A Survey of Distance and Information Measures

Notations in this paper will be similar to those in the paper by Kanal [1]. Let $\Omega = (\omega_i, i = 1,2,\ldots,m; 2 \leq m \leq \infty)$ be a set of pattern classes; P_i be an a priori probability of class ω_i, x be an n dimensional vector random variable; s_x be a sample space of x; $p(x/\omega_i)$ be a conditional probability density function; $P(\omega_i/x)$ be the a posteriori probability of class ω_i conditioned on x;

$p(x) = \sum\limits_{i=1}^{m} P_i p(x/\omega_i)$ be the mixture density. Also let E be an expectation over s_x with respect to $p(x)$, R_{kNN} be the k nearest neighbour risk. The Bayes error probability defined by

$$P_e = 1 - \int\limits_{s_x} \max_i [P_i p(x/\omega_i)] dx \qquad (1)$$

is rarely available in pattern recognition problems. The information and distance measures are used to minimize the error probability by tight error bounds which are expressed in terms of such measures. Equation (1) implies a (0, 1) loss function in the Bayes risk. There has been some recent effort to generalize the distance measure to minimize the Bayes risk with any loss function [2]. Our discussion will be limited to (0, 1) loss function, i.e. Bayes error probability as it is the most realistic measure of the recognition performance. The following is a list of expressions for distance and information measures.

(1)   Equivocation or Shannon entropy
$$H(\Omega/x) = E [- \sum\limits_{i=1}^{m} P(\omega_i/x) \log P(\omega_i/x)] \qquad (2)$$

Closely related to this is the mutual information
$$I(\Omega/x) = H(\Omega) - H(\Omega/x) \qquad (3)$$

(2)   Average conditional quadratic entropy (Vajda [3], [4]) or Bayesian distance (Devijver [5], [6]).
Average quadratic entropy
$$h(\Omega/x) = E \{ \sum\limits_{i=1}^{m} P(\omega_i/x) [1 - P(\omega_i/x)] \} \qquad (4a)$$

Bayesian distance
$$B(\Omega/x) = E \{ \sum\limits_{i=1}^{m} [P(\omega_i/x)]^2 \} = 1 - h(\Omega/x) \qquad (4b)$$

Note that $h(\Omega/x)$ can be obtained from $H(\Omega/x)$ by replacing $-\log P(\omega_i/x)$ with $1 - P(\omega_i/x)$.

(3)   Average conditional cubic entropy (proposed by this author)
$$h_3(\Omega/x) = 1 - E \{ \sum\limits_{i=1}^{m} [P(\omega_i/x)]^3 \} \qquad (5)$$

which obtained by replacing $\log P(\omega_i/x)$ with $P(\omega_i/x) - 1 + \frac{1}{2}(P(\omega_i/x) - 1)^2$.

(4) Divergence (see e.g. Kullback [7])

$$J(\Omega/x) = \int_{S_x} [p(x/\omega_1) - p(x/\omega_2)] \log \frac{p(x/\omega_1)}{p(x/\omega_2)} \, dx \quad (6)$$

(5) Transformed divergence (Swain, et.al [8], [9])

$$J_T = 2[1 - \exp(-J/8)] \quad (7)$$

(6) Bhattacharyya coefficient (see e.g. Kailath [10])

$$b(\Omega/x) = E\{[P(\omega_1/x)P(\omega_1/x)P(\omega_2/x)]^{1/2}\} \quad (8)$$

(7) Minkowski measure of nonuniformity (Toussaint [11])

$$M_k(\Omega/x) = E\{\sum_{i=1}^{m} |P(\omega_i/x) - \frac{1}{m}|^{2(k+1)/2k+1}\} \quad (9)$$

(8) Chernoff bound (see e.g. Kailath [9])

$$C(\Omega/x, s) = E\{[P(\omega_1/x)^{1-s} P(\omega_2/x)^2]\} \quad (10)$$

(9) Kolmogorov variational distance (see e.g. Kailath [10])

$$K(\Omega/x) = \frac{1}{2} E\{|P(\omega_1/x) - P(\omega_2/x)|\} \quad (11)$$

(10) Generalized separability measure (Lissack and Fu [12])

$$J_\alpha(\Omega/x) = E\{|P(\omega_1/x) - P(\omega_2/x)|^\alpha\}, \, 0 < \alpha < \infty \quad (12)$$

(11) A family of approximating functions (Ito [13])

$$Q_n(\Omega/x) = \frac{1}{2} - \frac{1}{2} E\{[P(\omega_1/x) - P(\omega_2/x)]^{2(n+1)/2n+1}\} \quad (13)$$

(12) The Matusita distance (see e.g. Kailath [10])

$$\gamma = [\int_{S_x} p(x/\omega_1) - p(x/\omega_2)^2 \, dx]^{1/2} \quad (14)$$

(13) f-divergence as defined by Csiszar [12], [13]

$$H_f(\Omega/x) = \int_{S_x} f(\frac{p(x/\omega_1)}{p(x/\omega_2)})p(x/\omega_2)dx \quad (15)$$

where f is a real valued function defined and convex on [0, + ∞) includes the divergence given by Eq. (6) as a special case. An important class of f-divergence is called, X^α-divergence (Vajda [16]),

$$\chi^\alpha(\Omega/x) = \int_{S_x} \left| 1 - \frac{p(x/\omega_1)}{p(x/\omega_2)} \right|^\alpha p(x/\omega_2)dx, \quad \alpha \geq 1 \quad (16)$$

(14) Generalized distancemmeasure (Trouborst, et.al [17])

$$B_n(\Omega/x) = E\left\{ \sum_{i=1}^m P(\omega_i/x)^n / \sum_{i=1}^m P(\omega_i/x)^{n-1} \right\} \quad (17a)$$

$$B_{n'}(\Omega/x) = E\left\{ \left[\sum_{i=1}^m P(\omega_i/x)^n \right]^{1/n} \right\} \quad (17b)$$

For $n = 2$, Eq. (17a) is identical to the Bayesian distance as introduced by Devijver [5][6]. It was shown [17] that Eqs. (17a) and (17b) provide upper and lower bounds respectively to the error probability.

(15) Fisher's criterion, defined as the ratio of interclass distance to the square root of the sum of square of intraclass distances. A closely related measure is the scatter ratio from discriminant analysis [18] defined as

$$L = \log \frac{\det(B + W)}{\det W} \quad (18)$$

where B is the average between-class covariance matrix, W is the average within-class covariance matrix, and "det" denotes the determinant. This measure has been shown to be effective experimentally [19] and is nonparametric because the probability density is not used.

(16) Mahalanobis distance

$$M = (\mu_1 - \mu_2), W^{-1}(\mu_1 - \mu_2) \quad (19)$$

where μ_1 and μ_2 are the mean vectors of classes 1 and 2 respectively. Again this measure is nonparametric in nature.

The above list is by no means exhaustive. Any well-behaved function which provides some measure of the distance between two probability densities or pattern classes may be proposed for the distance measure. Features selected according to the distance and information functions listed above tend to have strong discrimination capability. Different measures do not necessarily select the same set of "good" features. In addition to the theoretical study, a great deal of experimental results are much needed to compare various measures.

A few additional remarks on the above list should be made here. For two classes, The Kolmogorov variational distance is identical to the error probability. γ gives the same bound as $b(\Omega/x)$. Other useful properties are:

$$Q_o = 1 - B(\Omega/x), \quad Q_{n+1} \leq Q_n \tag{20}$$

$$h(\Omega/x) = R_{NN} = \frac{m-1}{m} - M_o(\Omega/x) \tag{21}$$

$$h(\Omega/x) = \frac{1}{2} [1 - J_2(\Omega/x)] \tag{22}$$

$$B_{n+1} \geq B_n; \quad B'_{n+1} \leq B'_n$$

Also for two classes, $h(\Omega/x)$ and $h_3(\Omega/x)$ are same if $h_3(\Omega/x)$ is normalized to 0.5 at $P(\omega_1/x) = 0.5$.

III. Relationships Among the Error Bounds

In this section, the inequalities which bound the (Bayes) error probability are examined. A detailed discussion of this subject was presented in Ref. 20. A number of new error bounds were published in the last two years. For m pattern classes, i.e. $m \geq 2$,

$$\frac{1}{2} [1 - B(\Omega/x)] \geq [1 - \sqrt{B(\Omega/x)}] \leq \frac{m-1}{m} \left[1 - \sqrt{\frac{mB(\Omega/x) - 1}{m - 1}} \right]$$

$$\leq \frac{h(\Omega/x)}{1 + \sqrt{1 - 2h(\Omega/x)}} \leq P_e \leq h(\Omega/x)$$

$$= R_{NN} \leq \frac{1}{2} H(\Omega/x) \tag{24}$$

$$P_e \leq R_{NN} \leq R_{kNN} \quad \text{for finite sample size} \tag{25}$$

The equivocation, average conditional quadratic entropy, nearest neighbour risk, average conditional cubic entropy, and Minkowski measure are defined directly for m classes, and thus provide better bounds than other measures which are difined for two classes only. In the latter case, the error probability for m-class is bounded as

$$P_e \leq \sum_{i=1}^{m} \sum_{j=i+1}^{m} P_e(\omega_i, \omega_j) \tag{26}$$

The following are useful relationships for m = 2,

$$\frac{1}{2} \{1 - [J_\alpha(\Omega/x)]^{1/\alpha}\} \leq P_e \leq \frac{1}{2} \{1 - J(\Omega/x)\}, \quad \alpha \geq 1; \tag{27}$$

$$P_e \leq Q_n(\Omega/x) \leq Q_o(\Omega/x) \leq \frac{1}{2} H(\Omega/x) \leq \frac{1}{2} b(\Omega/x) \qquad (28)$$

A slightly more general definition of divergence replacing $p(x/\omega_i)$ by $P_i \, p(x/\omega_i)$, $i = 1,2$, is

$$J(\Omega/x) = \int_{S_x} [P_1 \, p(x/\omega_1) - P_2 \, p(x/\omega_2)] \log \frac{P_1 p(x/\omega_1)}{P_2 p(x/\omega_2)} \, dx \qquad (29)$$

A tight lower bound of error probability in terms of divergence given by Eq. (29) is [21],

$$J(\Omega/x) \geq 2(2P_e - 1)\log[P_e/(1 - P_e)] \qquad (30)$$

which is much tighter than an earlier bound [10],

$$P_e \geq \frac{1}{4} \exp(-J/2) \qquad (31)$$

The transformed divergence was shown experimentally to perform better than the divergence and Bhattacharyya coefficient [8], [9]. The nonlinear functional relationship between J and J_T, overcomes some disadvantages of the divergence. The Chernoff bound which is the same as the Bhattacharyya coefficient for $s = 1/2$ does not in general provide tighter error bounds than the Bhattacharyya coefficient [13].

Even with the Bayesian distance the difference between the upper and lower error bounds can be as large as 0.125 for $m = 2$, which unacceptably high in most pattern recognition applications. As m increases the maximum difference also increases up to 0.25 for $m = \infty$. To get closer upper and lower error bounds needs better distance and information measures. However, further improvement would be very small if the probability density is not specified. Closed form expressions for $M_k(\Omega/x)$, $k > 0$; $Q_n(\Omega/x)$, $n > 0$; $J_\alpha(\Omega/x)$, $\alpha > 2$ are not available even for Gaussian distribution, although these measures may provide tighter bounds. The χ^α-divergence suffers the same difficulty for $\alpha > 2$, and it would be better to replace $p(x/\omega_i)$ by $P_i \, p(x/\omega_i)$.

The upper error bound in terms of average conditional cubic entropy is

$$P_e \leq k(m) \, h_3(\Omega/x) \qquad (32)$$

where $k(m)$ is the normalizing constant depending on the number of classes. $k(m)$ is chosen to make the upper bounds equal for $h(\Omega/x)$ and $h_3(\Omega/x)$ when $P(\omega_i/x) = 1/m$. Thus $k(2) = 2/3$, $k(3) = 3/4$, etc. It can be seen that the upper bounds in terms of $h(\Omega/x)$ and $h_3(\Omega/x)$ are nearly the same. $h_3(\Omega/x)$ however takes into consideration the third order statistics and should be more effective in practice.

The measures using the ratio of inter to intra-class distances (items 15 & 16 in the previous section) should provide good performance for finite sample size if the inter-class distance is large. Error bounds for such measures, however, are not available for comparison.

IV. The Finite Sample Size Effects

To examine the finite sample size effects, consider first the case of two univariate Gaussian densities with means m_1 and m_2 and the same variance σ^2. Let "$^{\wedge}$" denote the quantity evaluated by using the sample estimates. Then the difference in divergence between infinite sample and finite sample sizes is

$$J - \hat{J} = \frac{1}{\sigma^2} [(m_1 - m_2)^2 - (\hat{m}_1 - \hat{m}_2)^2] \qquad (33)$$

where we have assumed that σ^2 is known in both cases. The expected value of the difference can be shown as

$$E(J - \hat{J}) = -\frac{1}{N_1} - \frac{1}{N_2} < 0 \qquad (34)$$

where N_1 and N_2 denote the numbers of samples for classes 1 and 2 respectively. It is also assumed that all samples are statistically independent. Equation (34) indicates that the expected error is inversely proportional to the sample sizes. The negative error further indicates that the divergence evaluated by using finite number of samples can lead to an over optimistic estimate of the error probability.

As a second example, consider the above Gaussian case again with zero means instead and the variances σ_1^2 and σ_2^2 are estimated from samples in the finite sample case for which the divergence is

$$J = \frac{\hat{\sigma}_1^2}{2\hat{\sigma}_2^2} + \frac{\hat{\sigma}_2^2}{2\hat{\sigma}_1^2} - 1 \qquad (35)$$

The ratio $\omega = \hat{\sigma}_1^2/\hat{\sigma}_2^2$ has the F-distribution, with (N_1, N_2) degree of freedom, given by

$$p(\omega) = \begin{cases} C\omega^{N_1/2-1} \dfrac{\sigma_2^{N_1} \sigma_2^{N_2}}{(N_2\sigma_1^2 + N_1\sigma_2^2)^{N/2}} & ; \ \omega \geq 0 \\ 0, \omega < 0 \end{cases} \qquad (36)$$

where $N = N_1 + N_2$, and

$$C = \frac{\Gamma(\frac{N}{2}) \ N_1^{N_1/2} \ N_2^{N_2/2}}{\Gamma(\frac{N_1}{2}) \ (\frac{N_2}{2})}$$

The expected error due to the finite sample size is

$$E(J - \hat{J}) = J + 1 - \frac{1}{2} \int (\omega + \frac{1}{\omega}) p(\omega) d\omega$$

$$= \frac{1}{2} \frac{\sigma_1^2}{\sigma_2^2} (1 - \frac{N_2}{N_2-2}) + \frac{1}{2} \frac{\sigma_2^2}{\sigma_1^2} \left[1 - \frac{N_1(N_2 + 2)(N_2 + 4)}{(N_1 - 2)(N_1 - 4)(N_1 - 6)} \right];$$

$$N_1 > 2, \ N_2 > 2 \qquad (37)$$

which approaches zero as N_1, N_2 approach ∞. However, for small sample size the error is always negative when $N_1 \leq N_2 + 8$. Equations (34) and (37) indicate that the sample estimates of divergence are always biased. It may also be proved that the estimates are consistent.

Although the above discussion is based on very simple and special cases, it does indicate the ineffectiveness of the distance measures when the sample size is small. To obtain more useful results for recognition system design use, the above discussion must be extended to vector sample case as well as other measures and distributions.

V. Other Theoretical Problems

Computational recognition complexity is considered as one of the ten problem areas in statistical pattern recognition [22] for which the solution is most wanted. Just to consider the difficulty

in computing the distance measures, the divergence and Bhattacharyya coefficient are the easiest to compute; next in line are
the mutual information (up to second order dependence), the inter
to intra-class distance ratio; and the Bayesian distance and
Komogorov variational distance are the most difficult to compute
and numerical integration is almost always necessary. To select
the features using the distance and information measures, sequential recursive algorithm requires the least amount of computer
memory and computation time [23]. To make effective use of the
measures, more computationally efficient algorithms are much
needed.

To study the error bounds, it is most logical to specify the
probability densities. All the available published results [24],
[25], [26] based on the assumed probability densities are for one-
dimensional measurements only. Except for perfectly separable
cases, the maximum deviation between the upper and lower error
bounds so far available is at least 12% for any distance measure
even with the assumption of probability density. This implies
that the distance measures can provide useful error bounds only
when the classes are well separated.

Distance measures are also useful for feature space transformation so that effective transformed feature set of smaller
dimensionality can be derived. Furthermore, the nonparametric
methods in distance measures deserve much study as the nonparametric statistics is designed for finite (or even small) sample
size.

VI. Signal Selection and Parameter Estimation

Divergence, Bhattacharyya distance, and mutual information
have been useful in signal selection and estimation of signal
parameters (for recent literature see e.g. [27]). They do not
necessarily select the same signals. The basic results in [27] a
are the following.

1. For detection of known signal in additive (colored) Gaussian noise, the signal energy should be concentrated on the direction corresponding to the smallest eigenvalue of the noise covariance matrix.

2. For noncoherent detection of signal of unknown amplitude and phase, the Bhattacharyya distance is better than divergence or mutual information when integration with respect to the unknown parameter must be performed.

3. The measures provide a good and nearly the same solution on signal energy distribution for diversity reception.

4. The measures provide the same solution for radar parameter estimation at high signal-to-noise ratio.

5. In both signal selection and parameter estimation, solution is much needed at low signal-to-noise ratio.

In general the distance and information measures provide a good alternative approach to the signal selection and parameter estimation which typically use the criteria of minimum error probability and minimum mean square estimation error respectively.

VII. Feature Extraction in Imagery Pattern Recognition

An important class of features extracted for imagery pattern recognition is the so called textural features. A number of textural features have been proposed and examined (e.g. [28][29]). The number of available textural features is usually large, many of those are redundant or of little value in separating the classes. For a classifier to work successfully, these features must be removed. Divergence was ·found to be very effective for selecting a small set of features out of a large set of textural features for recognition of chest radiographs [30]. Divergence was also very effective for feature selection in multispectral images in space applications (see an extensive list of references in [31]). The main reason here is that the measurements can be adequately described by Gaussian densities with distinct means between pattern classes. The Bhattacharyya distance and mutual information should have similar capability in these applications. For a set of aerial photographs, the following texture measure [32] has been very effective with the aid of spatial relationship among the subpictures,

$$t_m = \sum_k \sum_j |i - j|^3 \log(n_{ij} + 1) \qquad (38)$$

where n_{ij} is the number of co-occurrence of ith and jth levels between the adjacent picture elements. t_m has a good distance measure interpretation [32].

It should be noted that in addition to pictorial patterns, the distance and information measures have been used extensively in speech recognition, character recognition, etc.

References

1. L. Kanal, "Patterns in pattern recognition: 1968-1974", IEEE Trans. on Information Theory, Vol. IT-20, No. 6, pp. 697-722, November 1974.

2. P. A. Devijver, "The generalized Bayesian distance", MBLE Research Report R232, October 1974.

3. I. Vajda, "Bounds of the minimal error probability on checking a finite or countable number of hypotheses", Information Transmission Problems, Vol. 4, pp. 9-19, 1968.

4. I. Vajda, "Note on discrimination information and variation", IEEE Trans. on Information Theory, Vol. IT-16, pp. 771-773, November 1970.

5. P. A. Devijver, "On a new class of bounds on Bayes risk in multihypothesis pattern recognition", IEEE Trans. on Computers, Vol. C-23, pp. 70-80, January 1974.

6. P. A. Devijver, "The Bayesian distance, a new concept in statistical decision theory", Proc. of 1972 IEEE Conference on Decision and Control, pp. 543-544, 1974.

7. S. Kullback, "Information Theory and Statistics", Dover Publications, Inc., New York, 1968.

8. P. H. Swain, T. V. Robertson, and A. G. Wacker, "Comparison of the divergence and B-distance in feature selection", Information Note 020871, Laboratory for Applications of Remote Sensing, Purdue University, Lafayette, Indiana, February 1971.

9. P. H. Swain and R. C. King, "Two effective feature selection criteria for multispectral remote sensing", Proceedings of the First International Joint Conference on Pattern Recognition, Washington, D. C., October 30-November 1, 1973, IEEE Catalog #73 CHO 821-9C.

10. T. Kailath, "The divergence and Bhattacharyya distance measures in signal selection", IEEE Trans. on Communication Technology, Vol. COM-15, pp. 52-60, February 1967.

11. G. T. Toussaint, "Feature evaluation criteria and contextural decoding algorithms in statistical pattern recognition", Ph.D. dissertation, University of British Columbia, Vancouver, Canada, 1972.

12. T. Lissack and K. S. Fu, "A separability measure for feature selection and error estimation in pattern recognition", Purdue University, TR-EE 72-15, May 1972.

13. T. Ito, "Approximate error bounds in pattern recognition", in Machine Intelligence, Vol. 7, Edinburgh, Scotland; Edinburgh University Press, pp. 369-376, November 1972.

14. I. Csiszar, "Information-type distance measures and indirect observations", Studia Sci. Math, Hungar. Vol. 2, pp. 299-318, 1967.

15. I. Csiszar, "A class of measures of informativity of observation channels", unpublished report, also presented at MIT, EE Department Seminar, May 1971.

16. I. Vajda, "X^{α}-divergence and generalized Fisher's information", Trans. of the Sixth Progue Conference on Information Theory, Statistical Decision Functions Random Process, 1971 published by Academia, publishing house of the Czechoslovak Academy of Sciences, Prague 1973.

17. P. M. Trouborst, E. Backer, D. E. Boekee and I. J. Moxma, "New families of probabilistic distance measures", pp. 3-5, Record of Second International Joint Conference on Pattern Recognition, August 1974.

18. S. S. Wilks, "Mathematical Statistics", pp. 564-581, Wiley, New York 1962.

19. M. Michael and W. C. Lin, "Experimental study of information measure and inter-intra class distance ratios on feature selection and ordering", IEEE Trans. on Systems, Man and Cybernetics, pp. 172-181, Vol. SMC-3, No. 2, March 1973.

20. C. H. Chen, "Statistical Pattern Recognition", Hayden Book Co., Rochelle Park, New Jersey, Chapter 4, February 1973.

21. G. T. Toussaint, "On the divergence between two distributions and the probability of misclassification of several decision rules", Proceedings of the Second International Joint Conference on Pattern Recognition, Copenhagen, Denmark, August 1974.

22. C. H. Chen, "Statistical pattern recognition-review and outlook", TR-EE 75-4, prepared for Grant AFOSR 71-2119D, June 1975.

60

23. C. H. Chen, "On a class of computationally efficient feature selection criteria", Pattern Recognition Journal, Vol. 7, No. 1, 1975.

24. D. G. Lainiotis and S. K. Park, "Probability of error bounds", IEEE Trans. on Systems, Man, and Cybernetics, Vol. SMC-1, No. 2, pp. 175-178, April 1971.

25. T. Ito, "Approximate bounds of misrecognition and their computational evaluation", Second International Joint Conference on Pattern Recognition, Copenhagen, Denmark, August 1974.

26. C. H. Chen, "On information and distance measures, error bounds, and feature selection", Information Sciences Journal, to appear.

27. C. H. Chen, "On signal selection using distance measures", National Tellecommunications Conference, New Orleans, December 1-3, 1975.

28. R. M. Haralick, K. Shanmugam, and I. Dinstein, "Textural features for image classification", IEEE Trans. on Systems, Man, and Cybernetics, Vol. SMC-3, No. 6, pp. 610-621, November 1973.

29. J. S. Weszka and A. Rosenfeld, "A comparative study of texture measures for terrain classification", Fifth Annual Sympsoium on Automatic Imagery Pattern Recognition, University of Maryland, April 1975.

30. R. P. Kruger, W. B. Thompson, and A. F. Turner, "Automated diagnosis of pneumoconiosis from posterior-anterior chest radiographs", Hawaii Conference on Systems Science, January 1973.

31. C. H. Chen, "Theory and applications of image pattern recognition", TR-EE 75-3, prepared for Grant AFOSR 71-2119, April 1975.

32. C. H. Chen and P. C. C. Chen, "A comparative evaluation of texture measures", TR-EE 75-9, prepared for Grant AFOSR 71-2119E, September 1975.

FEATURE SELECTION METHODS BASED ON THE KARHUNEN-LOEVE EXPANSION

Josef Kittler

SRC Research Fellow, Department of Electronics
The University, Southampton S09 5NH, England

Abstract: Eleven feature selection procedures based on the
Karhunen-Loeve expansion are reviewed. These include the Selfic
feature selection technique which is suitable for feature selction
in nonsupervised pattern recognition. The method of Chien and Fu
is suitable for selecting features from patterns containing discriminatory information in second order statistical moments.
Healy and Parrish's feature selection method on the other hand
lays emphasis on the discriminatory information containted in the
class mean vectors. The method of Kittler and Young in addition
compresses this first order discriminatory information into the
smallest possible number of features. The ordering criterion in
the feature selection technique of Fukunaga and Koontz is the ratio
of the average projection onto a candidate coordinate axis of data
from one class to that of all the other classes. The feature selection procedure of Heydorn and Tou yields features with minimum
population entropy. Finally, the subspace methods (Clafic, non-
orthogonal retrenched subspace method, orthogonal subspace method)
proposed by Watanabe, which combine the role of feature selection
and pattern classification are discussed.

I. Introduction

In many pattern recognition problems it is relatively easy to
acquire a large number of measurements for a detailed representation of the data. In such situations we are faced with the problem of extracting from the representation pattern vectors the useful discriminatory information about the patterns and compressing
it into a small number of features by removing the redundant and
irrelevant information [1]. The common denominator of these methods is that the information compression is achieved by a linear
mapping of pattern representation vectors from the measurement
space into a low dimensional feature space. The transformation
matrix which defines the mapping depends, of course, on the ob-
jectives of the designer.

One of the most important approaches to feature selection in
the transformed space is that based on the Karhunen-Loeve expansion. The attractiveness of this method for feature selection
purposes derives from the following numerous properties of the
expansion: first, the expansion maximizes information compression;
it minimizes approximation error; it minimizes representation
entropy; it minimizes population entropy; it decorrelated pattern
vector components.

To date eleven feature selection procedures which utilize
these properties have been suggested [6-15]. This paper reviews
all these feature selection methods and discusses their fundamental differences, advantages and shortcomings.

II. Properties of the Karhunen-Loeve Expansion

Expansion of pattern vectors $\underline{x}$,

$$\underline{x} = [x_1, x_2, \ldots \ldots \ldots, x_N]^T \tag{1}$$

into the orthonormal system of the Karhunen-Loeve coordinate
functions $\underline{\phi}_j$, $j=1,2,\ldots N$, i.e.

$$\underline{x} = \sum_{j=1}^{N} y_j \underline{\phi}_j \tag{2}$$

where y_j are the coefficients of the expansion, has the following very interesting properties for feature selection purposes [2-6].

A. <u>Minimum Approximation Error</u>

Suppose that pattern $\underline{x}$ is approximated by the first n terms of the Karhunen-Loeve expansion in (2), i.e.

$$\hat{\underline{x}} = \sum_{j=1}^{n} y_j \underline{\emptyset}_j \tag{3}$$

Then the mean square error, e, between pattern $\underline{x}$ and its approximation $\hat{\underline{x}}$ averaged over the elements of all the classes ω_i, i=1, 2,...,m, i.e.

$$e = \sum_{i=1}^{m} P(\omega_i) \, E\{(\underline{x}-\hat{\underline{x}})^T(\underline{x}-\hat{\underline{x}})\} \tag{4}$$

is minimal with respect to the corresponding error associated with the expansion of $\underline{x}$ into any other system of orthonormal functions.

B. <u>Minimum Representation Entropy</u>

Let λ_j be the variance of coefficient y_j of an expansion, i.e.

$$\lambda_j = \sum_{i=1}^{m} P(\omega_i) \, E(y_j^2) \tag{5}$$

Then the entropy function, H, of the distribution of variances λ_j, i.e.

$$H = \sum_{j=1}^{N} \lambda_j \log \lambda_j \tag{6}$$

Which is a measure of representation entropy (uncertainties) associated with the system of expansion functions is minimal for the Karhunen-Loeve coordinate system.

C. <u>Uncorrelated Coefficients</u>

The coefficients y_j of the K-L expansion are uncorrelated, i.e.

$$\sum_{i=1}^{m} P(\omega_i) \, E\{y_j y_k\} = \begin{cases} 0 & j \neq k \\ \lambda_j & k=j \end{cases} \tag{7}$$

D. <u>Relationship with the Fourier Transform</u>

When patterns $\underline{x}$ are weakly stationary the Karhunen-Loeve coordinate axes are sinusoidal functions. In other words, the

Karhunen-Loeve expansion is identical with the Fourier series.

E. Minimum Population Entropy

Under the assumption of Gaussian probability distribution of classes in an n-dimensional feature space A the population entropy, H_p, of the data set, defined as

$$H_p(A) = -E\{\log p\ (A^T \underline{x}|\omega_i)\} \tag{8}$$

is maximized for A composed of the last n axes of the Karhunen-Loeve coordinate system, i.e.

$$A = [\underline{\phi}_N, \underline{\phi}_{N-1}, \ldots \ldots \underline{\phi}_{N-n+1}] \tag{9}$$

It is apparent that the first three properties, although different in nature, are not unconnected, since all of them show the ability of the expansion to compress information about patterns into a few terms of the expansion. In fact they simply provide a basis for three different concepts of information compression. Thus, for instance, the minimum mean square error property implies that very little information is projected onto the axes of the Karhunen-Loeve coordinate system with high indices since the effect of the omission of these components from the expansion on the accuracy of pattern representation is negligible. Similarly the minimum representation entropy implies that the magnitudes of variances of the expansion coefficients, which are measures of information content in each term of the expansion, are maximally dispersed. As a result information about patterns will be concentrated in a few coefficients with large magnitudes. Finally, it seems reasonable to argue that by decorrelating individual components of the pattern vector a certain information compression will inevitably be achieved, for a number of pattern descriptors are likely to be simply linear combinations of other measurements and, naturally these can be discarded after the decorrelation process.

The last two properties of the Karhunen-Loeve expansion listed above do not demonstrate, of course, the information compression capabilities of the expansion. However, as we shall see in the following section they have been utilized in some feature selection procedures.

So far we have discussed the Karhunen-Loeve expansion in the context of pattern representation. It should be noted that while the Karhunen-Loeve basis functions are essential for representation of data, these functions are deterministic and, therefore, all the discriminatory information about patterns must be contained in the coefficients of the expansion. Thus, for classification purposes it is sufficient to work with a set of these coefficients, y_j, $j=1,2.....n$, which constitute a feature vector $\underline{y}$, i.e.

$$\underline{y} = [y_1, y_2, ... y_n]^T \tag{10}$$

Needless to say, these basis functions are needed for determining feature vector $\underline{y}$. Broadly speaking these functions are formed by a system of eigenvectors of an appropriate covariance matrix defined on the pattern set. The type of the matrix depends on the particular objective of feature selection and the various possibilities will be discussed in the following section.

Once the transformation matrix A is acquired the feature vector $\underline{y}$ is then given as

$$\underline{y} = A^T \underline{x} \tag{11}$$

III. Feature Selection Procedures

A. Method of Chien and Fu

The goal of the feature selection procedure proposed by Chien and Fu [7] is to compress optimally the discriminatory information contained in the second order statistical moments of the pattern vectors. This means that the class mean vectors, $\underline{\mu}_i$, are removed from patterns $\underline{x}$ prior to any analysis. Thus only centralized pattern vectors, $\underline{z}_i$

$$\underline{z}_i = \underline{x}_i - \underline{\mu}_i \quad \underline{x}_i \in \omega_i \tag{12}$$

are utilized for obtaining the Karhunen-Loeve coordinate system. In other words, the K-L coordinate system is determined irrespective of its effect on the class mean information contained in patterns.

The K-L coordinate axes Φ,

$$\Phi = |\underline{\phi}_1, \underline{\phi}_2, \ldots\ldots\ldots\underline{\phi}_N| \qquad (13)$$

are in this case the eigenvectors of covariance matrix C_1 defined as

$$C_1 = \sum_{i=1}^{m} P(\omega_i) \; E\{\underline{z}_i \underline{z}_i^T\} \qquad (14)$$

Since coefficients y_j associated with eigenvectors $\underline{\phi}_j$ with large indices do not contain much information, provided the eigenvectors are ordered in the descrnding order of the corresponding eigenvalues, it will be sufficient if matrix A in (11) is composed of the first n eigenvectors $\underline{\phi}_j$ only, i.e.

$$A = [\underline{\phi}_1, \underline{\phi}_2, \ldots\ldots\underline{\phi}_n] \qquad (15)$$

The omission of the insignificant axes results in dimensionality reduction of the pattern space.

B. <u>Procedure of Heydorn and Tou</u>

If the objective of feature selection is to transform patterns into a feature space where the spread of class clusters is minimal [6] (minimal population entropy), only centralized pattern vectors $\underline{z}_i$ in (12) should be considered for determining the appropriate Karhunen-Loeve coordinate system. Thus, in this method transformation matrix A is once again constructed from eigenvectors of covariance matrix C_1 in (14). But in contrast with previous method, here A is composed of n eigenvectors with the largest indices, i.e.

$$A = [\underline{\phi}_N \underline{\phi}_{N-1}, \ldots\ldots\ldots\underline{\phi}_{N-n+1}] \qquad (16)$$

C. <u>Selfic</u>

Selfic feature selection procedure [8] makes no distinction between the first and second order statistical information about patterns. The method has been designed to compress all this information as efficiently as possible. To take both the first and the second order information into consideration, the appropriate covariance matrix, C_2, from which the optimal coordinate system can be determined, is defined in terms of the original pattern representation vectors $\underline{x}$, i.e.

$$C_2 = \sum_{i=1}^{m} P(\omega_i) \, E\{(\underline{x}_i - \underline{\mu})(\underline{x}_i - \underline{\mu})^T = E\{(\underline{x} - \underline{\mu})(\underline{x} - \underline{\mu})^T\} \quad (17)$$

where vector $\underline{\mu}$ is the mean of the mixture sample set. As in the first method, feature selection transformation A is formed by n eigenvectors of the covariance matrix (17) associated with the largest eigenvalues. It should be noted that no a priori information is required for computation of covariance matrix C_2 and thus the method can be used for feature selection in nonsupervised pattern recognition problems.

D. Method of Healy and Parrish

The goal of the method of Healy and Parrish [14] is to select from the K-L coordinate axes, $\underline{\emptyset}_j$, defined by covariance matrix C_1 in (14) those which convey most of the first order discriminatory information inherent in the data. The criterion of optimal ordering in this case is the Fisher linear discriminant, γ_j, which is defined in terms of the class mean vectors $\underline{\mu}_i$, i=1,2....m and eigenvalues λ_j of matrix C_1 as

$$\gamma_j = \frac{\sum_{i=1}^{m} (\underline{\emptyset}^T_j \, \underline{\mu}_i)^2}{\lambda_j}$$

Then the optimal N x n transformation matrix A is composed of the first n K-L axes $\underline{\emptyset}_j$ arranged in the descending order of magnitude of the indicators γ_j, i.e.

$$\gamma_1 \geq \gamma_2 \geq \cdots \gamma_n \geq \cdots \gamma_N$$

E. Kittler and Young Method

The feature selection procedure of Kittler and Young also lays emphasis on the discriminatory information contained in the class mean vectors [9]. However, in contrast to the method of Healy and Parrish which selects optimal axes in the space defined by eigenvectors of matrix C_1, the objective of this method is to determine the best set of axes in the space where the class mean infor-

mation is compressed onto the smallest number of basis vectors.
In order to compress this information it is necessary to normalize
the second order statistical information contained in the patterns.
The normalization process involves, first of all, decorrelation of
the data which is achieved by transforming pattern vectors into
the coordinate system formed by eigenvectors Φ in (13) of the covariance matrix C_1 defined in (14). Subsequently the variances of
the pattern vectors arennormalized to unity by a diagonal matrix
$\Lambda^{-1/2}$ where Λ is the matrix of eigenvalues of C_1. The class mean
information in pattern vectors is then compressed into a small
number of features by a third linear N x n mapping, B, whose columns are those eigenvectors of matrix C_3,

$$C_3 = I + \sum_{i=1}^{m} P(\omega_i) \Lambda^{-1/2} \Phi^T (\underline{\mu}_i - \underline{\mu})(\underline{\mu}_i - \underline{\mu})^T \Phi \Lambda^{-1/2} \tag{18}$$

which are associated with eigenvalues of C_3 with magnitude greater
than unity. Thus, the overall feature selection transformation A
is given as

$$A = \Phi \Lambda^{-1/2} B \tag{19}$$

F. A Feature Selection Method for High Dimensional Problems

This method, which is suitable only for pattern vectors satisfying the condition of weak stationarity [4], is essentially the
same as the previous method but here the first transformation
matrix Φ in (13) is replaced by the Fourier transform operator,
F [10]. In this special case, the element λ_j of the normalizing
transformation Λ is the expected value of the corresponding components of the power spectrum, i.e.

$$\lambda_j = \sum_{i=1}^{m} P(\omega_i) E\{(\underline{x}_i - \underline{\mu}_i)^T F_j F_j (\underline{x}_i - \underline{\mu}_i)\} \tag{20}$$

The advantage of this technique is that the computationally involved eigenvalue analysis of matrix C_1 in the first stage of the
feature selection procedure is not required.

G. Fukunaga-Koontz Method

In the method of Fukunaga and Koontz [13] the feature selection matrix is determined in a completely different manner. First of all, the mixture correlation matrix of pattern vectors, C_2, defined in (17) is transformed into the identify matrix by a normalizing transformation B, i.e.

$$B^T C_2 B = I$$

After this normalization process the correlation matrices G_i, i=1,2....m, of individual classes defined as

$$G_i = P(\omega_i) \ B^T E\{(\underline{x}_i - \underline{\mu}) \ (\underline{x}_i - \underline{\mu})^T\}B$$

have very interesting properties. In particular, the system of eigenvectors of G_i is identical with the eigenvectors of matrix D_i formed by the correlation matrices of all the other classes, i.e.

$$D_i = \sum_{\substack{l=1 \\ l \neq i}}^{m} P(\omega_l) \ G_l$$

Moreover, the matrices of eigenvalues Λ_{G_i} and Λ_{D_i} of matrices G_i and D_i respectively satisfy

$$\Lambda_{G_i} + \Lambda_{D_i} = I \tag{21}$$

Thus, the coordinate axes associated with large eigenvalues of of G_i are very important for representing patterns in class ω_i and, at the same time, they are least significant for representation of elements from all the other classes. It follows that if matrix A is composed of eigenvectors $\underline{\emptyset}_j$, j=1,...n_i, i=1,...m, of matrices G_i corresponding eigenvalues close to unity, i.e.

$$A = [\underline{\emptyset}_{11}, \ldots \underline{\emptyset}_{kn_i}, \ldots \ldots \ldots , \underline{\emptyset}_{mn_m}]$$

the resulting feature vector will have discriminatory potential. The main disadvantage of this method is, however, that it will completely ignore axes equally suited for representation of several classes even if these axes contain discriminatory information.

H. Clafic

The following methods differ conceptually from the procedures reviewed thus far in that here the process of feature selection and classification are not considered separately but instead they are viewed as one operation. In practical terms the most significant difference of this approach is that the information compression operation is carried out for each class separately. Pattern vectors can then be classified using a simple function of the resulting class conditional feature vectors. In this way the subsequent design of a classifier required by all the previous methods is obviated.

The procedure Clafic is the seminal method in this category. It has been introduced by Watanabe in two versions, namely as a dispersion method and as a subspace method [8]. The former version now has only a historical value. Although the practical potential of the subspace version of Clafic is also very limited, the method deserves some attention here for it led to the development of more sophisticated procedures.

In this method the K-L expansion is applied to the paradigms of individual classes separately. In other words the i-th class K-L axes are the eigenvectors of correlation matrix C_i defined on a set of patterns belonging to class ω_i, i.e.

$$C_i = E\{\underline{x}\underline{x}^T\} \quad \underline{x} \in \omega_i$$

Thus, for each class ω_i the method yields a coordinate system A_i,

$$A_i = [\underline{\phi}_{i1}, \cdots \underline{\phi}_{in_i}] \tag{22}$$

composed of those n_i axes of the K-L expansion which contain most of the information about the class.

An unknown pattern is then classified by comparing the magnitudes of its projection into the subspaces defined by A_i.

I. Orthogonal Subspace Method

The main disadvantage of Clafic procedure is that the subspaces of individual classes may overlap. It is, therefore, desirable to form matrix A_i only by those axes of class ω_i which are orthogonal to the basis vectors of systems $A_j, \forall\ j \neq i$ [12]. Matrix A_i in (22) must, therefore, be amended by all those columns $\underline{\emptyset}_{ij}$ for which there exist $l \neq i$ and r such that

$$\underline{\emptyset}_{ij} - |sgn(\underline{\emptyset}_{ij}^T \underline{\emptyset}_l)|\ \underline{\emptyset}_{ij} = 0 \tag{23}$$

J. <u>Nonorthogonal Retrenched Subspace Method</u>

The orthogonal subspace method discussed in the previous subsection is very restrictive because often it will be impossible to find non-empty orthogonal subspaces for individual classes even in cases where the data classes are separable. It is, therefore, reasonable to remove from each class subspace only that part which coincides with any other class subspace [12]. Determination of these retrenched subspaces A_i is rather difficult. Their constituent axes e_{ij}, $j=1,2....q_i$, are the eigenvectors of matrix B_i

$$B_i = \Phi_i\ D_i$$

Here Φ_i is defined in terms of the columns of A_i in (22) as

$$\Phi_i = \sum_{j=1}^{n_i} \underline{\emptyset}_{ij} \underline{\emptyset}_{ij}^T$$

and matrix D_i is given as

$$D_i = \sum_{j=1}^{q_d} \underline{f}_{ij}\ \underline{f}_{in}^T$$

where $\underline{f}_{ij}$ is an eigenvector associated with eigenvalue equal to $m-1$ of matrix F_i and q_d is the number of these eigenvectors. Finally, matrix F_i is defined as

$$F_i = \sum_{\substack{l=1 \\ l \neq i}}^{m} [I - \sum_{j=1}^{q_1} \underline{h}_{lj} \underline{h}_{lj}^T]$$

where $\underline{h}_{lj}$ are eigenvectors associated with unity eigenvalues of matrix $1/2[\Phi_i + \Phi_1]$.

K. <u>Method Based on the Fukunaga-Koontz Procedure</u>

Although the method of Fukunaga and Koontz is not very reliable in selecting features for the conventional model of pattern recognition system, it is ideally suited for construction of class subspaces in the subspace approach to pattern recognition [15]. The relationship (21) implies that if a diagonal element of Λ_{G_i} approaches unity the corresponding element in Λ_{D_i} is negligible. In other words, no information about pattern vectors belonging to classes ω_1, ∇ l≠i is projected onto the associated eigenvectors. Thus, all the eigenvectors e_{ij}, j=1,2...q_i, of matrix G_i associated with eigenvalues close to unity can be considered to constitute a subspace occupied by class ω_1, i.e.

$$A_i = [e_{i1}, \ldots \underline{e}_{i_{q_i}}]$$

By analogy, subspaces of all the other classes can be determined in this manner.

In this method, the overlap of class subspaces can be controlled by varying the threshold of admissible magnitudes of eigenvalues of Λ_{G_i}. As a result, the method is more flexible than the previous techniques.

IV. Conclusions

Eleven feature selection procedures which utilize properties of the Karhunen-Loeve expansion have been discussed. These include, first of all, the seminal feature selection techniques of Watanabe known as Selfic which is suitable for feature selection in nonsupervised pattern recognition. The method suggested by Chien and Fu is suitable for selecting features from patterns containint discriminatory information in second order statistical moments. The feature selection procedure of Heydorn and Tou yields features with minimum population entropy. Healy and Parrish's feature selection method lays emphasis on the discriminatory information contained in the class mean vectors. The method of Kittler and Young in addition compresses this first order discriminatory information into the smallest set of features. The ordering criterion in the feature selection technique of Fukunaga and Koontz is the ratio of the average projection onto a

candidate axes of data from one class to that of all the other
classes.

The discussion has also included the subspace methods of
pattern recognition (Clafic, orthogonal subspace method, nonortho-
gonal retrenched subspace method) proposed by Watanabe, which combine the role of feature selection and pattern recognition. Finally, the method for determining class subspaces, based on the feature selection technique of Fukunaga and Koontz has been reviewed.

References

1.   Kittler,J., "Mathametical methods of feature selection in
     pattern recognition", Internat. Jnl. of Man-Machine Studies,
     7, pp. 609-637, 1975.

2.   Mendel, J. M. and Fu, K. S., Adaptive, learning and pattern
     recognition systems, Academic Press, New York, 1970.

3.   Watanabe, S., Karhunen-Loeve expansion and factor analysis,
     Trans. 4th Prague Conf. on Information Theory, 1965.

4.   Fukunaga, K., Introduction to statistical pattern recognition,
     Academic Press, New York, 1972.

5.   Watanabe, Knowing and guessing, Wiley, New York, 1969.

6.   Tou, J. T. and Heydorn, R. P., "Some Approaches to Optimum
     Feature Extraction", Computer and Information Sciences II,
     pp. 61-89, Academic Press, New York, 1967.

7.   Chien, Y. T. and Fu, K. S., "On the generalized Karhunen-
     Loeve expansion", IEEE Trans. Inf. Theory, IT-13, pp. 518-
     520, 1967.

8.   Watanabe, S. et al., Computer and Information Sciences II,
     Academic Press, New York, 1967.

9.   Kittler, J. and Young, P. C., "A New Approach to Feature
     Selection Based on the Karhunen-Loeve Expansion", Pattern
     Recognition, 5, pp. 335-352, 1973.

74

10. Kittler, J., A method of feature selection for high dimensional pattern recognition problems, Proc. 2nd Int. Conf. on Pattern Recognition, Denmark, 1974.

11. Kittler, J., Practical aspects of the Karhunen-Loeve feature selection procedure for high dimensional pattern recognition problems, Proc. Int. Compt. Sympos., Taipei, 1975.

12. Watanabe, S. and Pakvase, N., Subspace method in pattern recognition, Proc. 1st Int. Conf. on Pattern Recognition, Washington, 1973.

13. Fukunaga, K. and Koontz, W. L. G., "Application of the Karhunen-Loeve Expansion to Feature Selection and Ordering", IEEE Trans. Comput., C-19, pp. 826-829, 1970.

14. Healy, M. P. and Parrish, E. A., An optimal method of ordering the basis vectors in the truncated Karhunen-Loeve expansion using the Fisher linear discriminant, (Submitted to IEEE Trans. on Computers.)

15. Kittler, J., A method for determining class subspaces, (Submitted to Information Processing Letters.)

FEATURE EXTRACTION IN THE TIME DOMAIN: APPLICATION TO THE
ANALYSIS OF FINANCIAL DATA AND STRATEGIES OVER TIME

L. F. Pau

Telecommunications, 46 rue Barrault
75013 Paris, France

Abstract: The purpose of this applications-oriented paper
is to describe those relations found to be actually useful between
feature extraction theory, financial data banks, and display systems for sectorwise differential financial analysis or security
selection. After having reviewed some economic applications of
pattern recognition, it is shown how correspondence analysis has
been implemented into the time domain for the purpose of display-
ing multidimensional time series as oriented trajectories in a
lower dimensional space. Three case studies are given, with the
corresponding financial interpretations (European companies, and
8 Danish banks over a five year time period).

I. Introduction

To evaluate and compare the performances of certain sets of
companies or stocks, a number of authors from the economic area
have tried to set up rules governing a typology for these companies
or stocks. The goal is to divide such sets and isolate the features which could explain differential performances among such
companies/stocks; as pointed out by Blin [5], Smith [23], this
question of deciding collectively on a number of various financial results, can be modeled as a pattern recognition problem.

The first section of the paper is devoted to a brief review of some economic literature about typology for companies/stocks. The second section of the paper references some nonparametric linear feature extraction methods (normalized principal component analysis, correspondence analysis), and indicates how they can be implemented in the time domain. In addition, the classical proximity analysis or clustering procedures can be extended in order to apply in this time=domain, thus leading to a causality analysis used in support of financial analysis. The third section is a collection of three applications of correspondence analysis to the analysis of financial data and strategies:

1. Using readily available raw data in limited number about the growth of a fairly large number of multinational European companies, we show that our methods provide quite straightforward typologies, compatible with the ones obtained independently from features provided by complicated accounting rules.

2. Using raw accounting data about 8 major Danish banks over the period from 1967-1971, we have validated the idea of correspondence analysis in the time-domain; because about 70% of the discriminating information was contained in the vector basis of the two first functional features extracted, it has been possible to represent the evolutions over time of each bank or of each account as trajectories in a two-dimensional display space.

3. Raw accounting data about 8 major Danish banks, are used together with precise statistical information on the Danish monetary market and public finances; we have again applied correspondence analysis in the time-domain but here to a set of ratios deduced from the previous internal and exogeneous informations. Precise qualitative results are obtained for differential analysis in the banking sector; the consequences of some legal

measures and of some agreements among banks can easily
be identified visually.

A. Typology of Companies or Stocks

1. The general concepts of taxonomy, learning, and
clustering have been known for a long time in statistical
circles working on economic or sociological data. This appears clearly in the works of Henryson [27], Zagoruiko-
Zaslavska [25,26] and others. A number of straightforward
applications of clustering or of discriminant analysis techniques have been made in the applied economic field: typology of countries according to their foreign trade (Plassard-
Soum [21]), discriminant analysis of financial ratios and
prediction of bankruptcy (Altman [1]), classification of
investment securities (Smith [23]), learning of buyer behavior (Fogler [11]), classification of applications for
small consumer loans (Levasseur et. al. [28]).

2. Specializing to the field of financial analysis, two
new aspects appear: first, the time factor necessary for
forecasts and portfolio selections, and next the elimination
of market/conjuncture trends. Except the research reported
in the following, there is only very little evidence known
to us about pattern recognition applied to financial time
series. In classical financial analysis, two kinds of
typologies of evolutions are considered: either into absolute organizational stages (Stich [24]), or into relative
development stages vs. the growth rate of the major market
segment (Bijon [3]), Goronzy [12]).

3. Because there is a need for tools able to ease the
differential analysis of stocks from a given sector or portfolio, we will in the following show how appropriate feature
extraction methods implemented into the time-domain may provide the analyst with decision charts, eventually weighted
according to estimated factor loadings or to a priori selected
priorities.

B. <u>Feature Extraction in the Time-Domain</u>

Using appropriate feature extraction methods, it is possible to display on a scopy measurements related to a stochastic process, or a set of scalar time series, <u>via an oriented trajectory</u>. Differential diagnosis may then be based on <u>a visual examination of the similarities (proximity and orientation) between a number of such trajectories</u> (Pau [16,19]). In the following we assume the measurements to be carried out at discrete successive instants.

  1. <u>Principle for the compression of sampled signals</u>. Let $X(t) \triangleq [X_1(t)....X_n[t])$ be the measurement vector at time t; the common property of most linear signal compression methods is to consider any such vector $X(t)$ as the result of a weighted summation of a limited number of basis vectors f_1 $1 = 1,...,r$; these basis vectors are ranked by order of decreasing importance, in such a way that neglecting those of least importance in a given synthesis of $X(t)$, will preserve the most useful variance characteristics of this measurement vector; discrete unsupervised Karhunen-Loeve expansion and unsupervised alternatives (Watanabe [29], Fukunaga [10], Chapters 4, 8, 11), as related to principal components analysis (Kendall [15]), or correspondence analysis (Benzecri [2], Pau [16,18]).

  2. <u>Two-dimensional display of a n-dimensional signal $X(t)$</u>. Select for example the two first-basis vectors f_1 and f_2. According to the previous principle, any measurement vector $X(t)$ can be approximated by a two-dimensional vector $Y(t) \triangleq [Y_1(t), Y_2(t)]$ in the (f_1, f_2)

Consider now the signal $X(t)$ over a bounded time-horizon $0 \leq t \leq \zeta$; the image of this signal in the (f_1, f_2) plane will be the curve:

  $S(X, 0, \zeta) = [Y(t); 0 \leq t \leq \zeta]$

oriented by increasing values of time t. Assuming f_1, f_2 to be known, this curve $S(X,0,\zeta)$ can be drawn in real time, on a scope, thanks to a simple analog or digital circuitry synthesizing the formulas (1) and (2). By selecting the vectors f_1 and f_2 in an adequate way one will be able to extract different significant features from $X(t)$. One of the most useful unsupervised multi-variate analysis methods is sketched out in subsection B.3, and can be applied to the matrix $A(o,T) = [X(n\Delta t)\ 0 \leq n\ \Delta\ t \leq T]$, and thus implemented into the time-domain like signal compression methods such as the Karhunen-Loeve expansion.

More generally, we may consider N different records $A^i(0,T)$ i=1,...,N, corresponding to N different processes $X^i(t)$ i=1,...,N taking place over the interval $0 \leq t \leq T$. The above mentioned multivariate analysis methods may then be applied globally to the matrix

$$B(o,T) = [A^i\ (0,T),\ i=1,...,N]\quad \text{(Figure 1)}$$

This will yield a trajectory $Y^i(t)$ for any such process $X^i(t)$, i=1,...,N, all the trajectories being displayed in the same fea-ture space (f_1, f_2), and computed taking into account the cross-correlations among the individual processes $X^i(t)$.

3. Correspondence analysis in the time-domain (Pau [17])

Assume that $A(0,T)$ is non-negative, and define succes-sively:

a. the contingency table:

$$P = [p(i,j);\ i=1,\ T;\ j=1,n]\ ;\ P(I,.) = [p(i,.)] \cdot P(.,J)= [p(.,j)]$$

$p(i,j) = a(i,j)/ \underset{1,k}{\Sigma}\ a(1,k)$ with marginal probabilities
$p(i,.)$,
$p(.,j)$

b. the transformed tableau:

$$Z = [Z(i,j) = \frac{p(i,j)}{p(i,.)p(.,j)} = 1;\ i=1,T;j=1,n]$$

Correspondence analysis can then be presented or summarized as being the result of the application of principal component analysis to the tableau Z, the least-squares criterion being replaced by the following distance functions:

$$d_i^2(t_1,t_2) = \sum_{j=1,n} p(.,j) \, [Z(t_1,j) - Z(t_2,j)]^2$$

$$d_j^2(j_1,j_2) = \sum_{i=1,T} p(i,.) \, (Z(i,j_1) - Z(i,j_2))^2$$

One may prove that the normalizations (a) and (b), which keep the symmetry between rows and columns in Z, provide almost scale-independent features maximizing the CHI-2 norm of $[P - P(I,.) \otimes P(.,J)]$, which represents the dependence between the samples $t = 1,..,T$ and the measurements $j = 1,...,n$. For more details about correspondence analysis, see Benzecri [2], Pau [16,18]. Implemented into the time-domain as indicated above, (see also Pau [16,17]), and applied to the matrix B(0,T), this method is useful for the comparison of the individual trajectories $Y^i(t)$ $0 \leq t \leq T$, $i=1,...,N$, almost regardless of the scale of the individual measurements $x_j^i(t)$ $i=1,...,N$, $j=1,...,n$.

C. <u>Feature Extraction by Correspondence Analysis: Applications to the Analysis of Financial Data</u>

We will successively describe three case studies; the first one is a static analysis of financial growth data; the last two ones are concerned with feature extraction in the time-domain and representations via trajectories.

1. <u>Multinational European companies</u>; research done in 1970. (Figure 1)

Using the financial growth data provided by [9] (growth rates, balances for turnover and profits, profits/equity capital, profits/sales) correspondence analysis has been applied directly to these measurements, each company being described by one single measurement vector of dimension 14. These 77 companies belong to various sectors such as: steel, cement, chemicals, drugs, electrotechnical equipment, department stores, food. The goal of the financial analyst is to express in the financial terms used for the definition of those n=14 measurements, the associations between companies and ratios, corresponding to geometric proximities on the maps of decreasing weights (B.2) [18]. The (f_1,f_2) plane contains 44+14=58% of all discriminating information, and the main result is that the clustering here confirms the typology described in (Bijon [3]) and superimposed to Figure 1. Notice that the clustering-based typology has not requested any estimation of the equilibrium growth rates t_e, which are too difficult to evaluate in practice.

2.   Danish banks: raw accounting data 1967-1971 ; research was done in 1972-73 . (Figure 2)

Correspondence analysis is here considered in the time-domain, for 8 Danish banks of various sizes (Figure 2). The annual measurements used for each bank are all those raw accounting data given in Greens [13], and based solely on annual reports for which the same presentation and definitions of the financial results are requested (this is a legal obligation for the banks). Each bank is represented by 5 successive measurement vectors of dimension 24. The trajectories obtained represent the evolutions over time of all synthesized accounting time series (Figure 2); each account is simultaneously represented by one single point for the 5 years.

We see how the larger banks cluster together to the right (Privatbanken, Landmandsbanken, Handelsbanken, Privinsbanken), while the smaller banks cluster together in the upper left corner (Amagerbanken, Slagelse bank, Midtbank, Jysk bank). This can be explained by looking at those accounts the trajectories are closest to; the major banks are close to "13" (liquidity + securities held) and "2" (revenues from securities and foreign exchange); this can be confirmed by the fact that the

ratio: "7" (liquidity/balance of assets) is in the average higher for the 4 larger banks (20-35%) than for the
4 smaller ones (12-20%).

   We may also observe that the trajectories of all
smaller banks are oriented in the direction going from
"1" ((financial revenues-financial expenses)/assets) to
"13" (reserves/paid-in capital) which can be confirmed
by increasing ratios "1" (and "7" liquidity/assets) from
1967 to 1971; this is especially true for Slagelse Bank
for which a large jump takes place between the 1969 and
1970 accounts (ratio "7" jumping from 17.0% to 30.1%).
Most smaller banks remain close to "1"; here again the
ratio: (Financial revenues/total assets) is higher for
the smaller banks (5-7%) than for the larger ones (4-5%),
with an increasing tendency over 1967-1971. For further
details, see: Drud, Valstorp-Frederiksen [8].

3.   Danish banks: financial ratios and monetary data 1969-
     1973; research completed in 1975.
     Each of 8 Danish banks (Figure3) is here described by
     5 measurement vectors corresponding to the successive
     values taken in the accounting years 1969-1973 by a set
     of 33 ratios. The corresponding raw data about these
     banks are taken from [14], while the figures about the
     Danish monetary market are provided by the National Bank
     [7]. All size dependent figures for the banks have been
     scaled down via the amount of the balance of assets
     held each year.

     a.   Interpretation of the feature axes f_1, f_2 (Figure
          3): Let $F(j,1)$ j=1,33 1=1,2 be the coordinate of
          the ratio j on the feature axis 1. By selecting
          those ratios having the largest positive or nega-
          tive contribution: $(p(.,j) [F(j,1)]^2$. Sign
          $[F(j,1)])$ to the variance of an axis 1 (Pau [16]),
          one may interpret the feature axis 1:

1. Axis 1 ranks the instantaneous bank balances and
    trajectories by decreasing correlations to the
    variations of the money supply M_2 (ratio 30), and
    by increasing correlations to a set of ratios (28,
    2,21) expressing reduced relative rates of invest-
    ment in bonds, shares and increased portfolios of
    loans.

2. Axis 2 ranks the banks according to the growth and
    reinvestment policy for profits; negative ordinates
    indicate strong correlations with investor preferred
    high-yield securities (ratios 19, 17, 20), while
    positive ordinates indicate an increased relative
    importance of cautions (thus higher committments
    to the rapidly increasing market for foreign and
    industrial loans) (ratios 31, 9, 28). Correspond-
    ingly, positive ordinates indicate relatively small
    dividends compared to net profits.

b. Differential analysis of the evolutions achieved by
    the individual banks (Figure 3)

1. The fact that all 8 trajectories have very similar
    shapes can be explained by the first axis M_2 and
    ratio-8-related governmental restrictions on loans
    (ratio 8 = lending/assets).

2. Throughout 1969-1973 two of the major banks (Handels-
    banken, Privatbanken) have had very similar evolu-
    tions, initially strongly growth oriented, with
    later consolidations; the third "major" has had
    a more stable evolution, also from the point of
    view of yield; Provinsbanken has followed a similar
    policy.

3. Among the minor banks: Slagelse Bank, Amager Bank,
    Djurslands Bank, Midtbank, have on the average all
    favored distribution to the shareholders; this is

especially true for Slagelse Bank and Amager Bank, while Djurslands Bank and Midtbank have showed growth oriented policies after relatively sharp rises in the prices of their shares in 1970.

4. The strong similarity among the 1972 balances is largely due to ceilings on bank lending and excellent bank liquidity, as a result of a sharp increase in governmental deficit cash position (M_2: + 15%).

The above analysis can be supplemented by detailed statements of all casuality relations among represented ratios and banks.

D. Conclusion

Experiments such as the above tend to indicate that feature extraction methods, such as correspondence analysis in the time domain, may be useful as general non-parametric procedures for aggregating financial data in differential analysis of company accounts. Bayesian Correspondence analysis [16] allows for an a-priori weighting of the measurement ratios or accounts, and leads therefore to security selection. By comparing the shapes and orientations of the trajectories, it is possible easily to apprehend the trend effects and to eliminate them in comparative analysis.

The procedures described above have actually been implemented in a financial institution, using remote time-shared graphic display terminals in connection with a joint data bank with accounting information. The results were found more useful than those screening methods selecting securities having specified ratios.

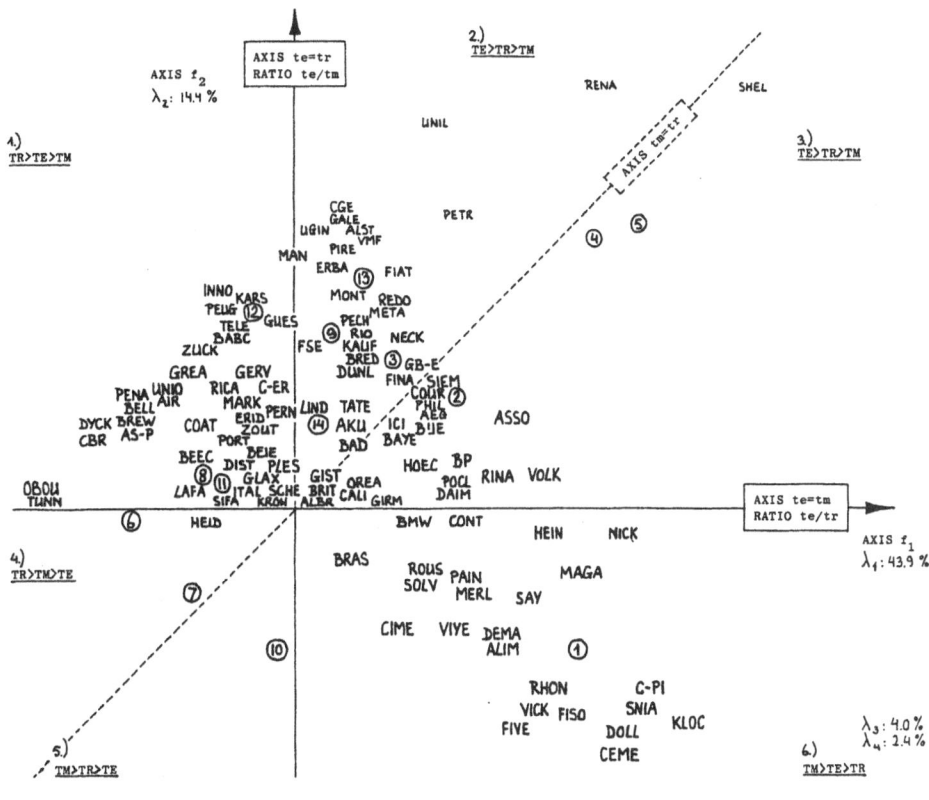

Figure 1.
EUROPEAN COMPANIES FROM DIFFERENT SECTORS
Relative Financial Growth 1967 - 1968.

TR/tr = growth rate for after-tax sales turnover

TM/tm = growth rate for the major market segment

TE/te = equilibrium growth rate which is the upper limit beyond which the financial structure must change

1.) growth companies with likely financial disequilibrium

2.) companies growing faster than the average market

3.) companies living mostly on their previous financial assets

4.) companies in bad financial and commercial situation

5.) declining companies

6.) companies requiring a rapid change in management policy or product line

The companies and the individual measurements i used for each company are listed in [9].

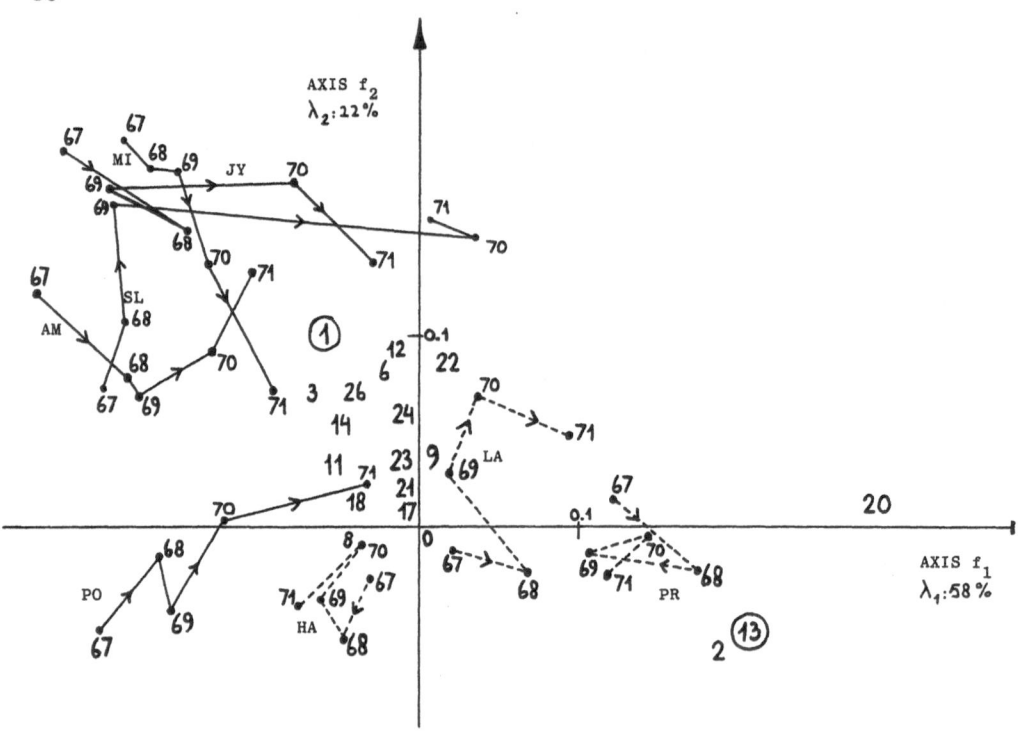

INDIVIDUAL ACCOUNT AND NATURE
 1 = financial revenues
     (interests, etc.)
 2 = earnings on securities
     and foreign exchange
 3 = commissions earned
 6 = financial charges
     (interests paid)
 8 = taxes
 9 = write-offs
11 = nett profits
12 = amount of dividends
13 = cash, securities, and
     other liquid assets
14 = lending
17 = balance of assets
18 = deposits
22 = capital
23 = reserves
26 = market value, 31.12

BANK AND SYMBOL
HA - Handelsbanken (major)
LA - Landmansbanken (major)
PR - Privatbanken (major)
PO - Provinsbanken (major)
AM - Amagerbanken
JY - Jydske Bank
SL - Slagelse Bank
MI - Midtbank

The evolutions of the three major
banks are represented by dotted
lines.

Figure 2.
DANISH BANKS 1967 - 1971, Based on Raw Accounting Data.

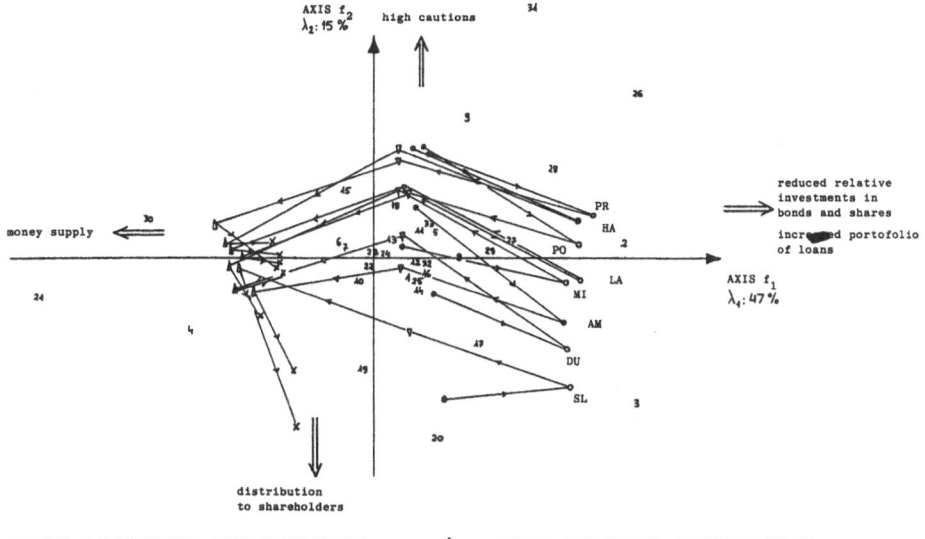

BANK ACCOUNTS AND NATIONAL DATA FOR

	YEAR-TO-YEAR INCREASE M_2
1969 = ●	1969 : 10,4 %
1970 = ○	1970 : 2,9 %
1971 = ▽	1971 : 8,8 %
1972 = △	1972 : 15,0 %
1973 = ✕	1973 : 12,7 %

BANKS AND SYMBOLS	BALANCE OF ASSETS bounds for 1969 and 1973
HA - Handelsbanken	12.9 - 18.2 billions Kr
PR - Privatbanken	7.9 - 11.2 billions Kr
LA - Landmansbanken	10.7 - 15.6 billions Kr
PO - Provinsbanken	4.3 - 6.2 billions Kr
MI - Midtbank	591 - 1,483 millions Kr
SL - Slagelse Bank	222 - 338 millions Kr
AM - Amagerbanken	717 - 1,032 millions Kr
DU - Djurslands Bank	154 - 279 millions Kr

Figure 3.
DANISH BANKS 1969 - 1973, Simultaneous Representation of the Evolutions and of the Financial Ratios.

References

It was considered interesting to list references mostly of applied nature, related to pattern recognition approaches in microeconomy.

1. Altman, E. I., Financial ratios, discriminant analysis and the prediction of corporate bankruptcy, Journal of Finance, September 1968.

2. Benzecri, J. P. et al, L'analyse des données, Dunod, Paris, 1973.

3. Bijon, C., Recherche d'une typologie des entreprises face au developpement, Hommes et Techniques, n° 317, March 1971, 224-226.

4. Blin, J. M., Fu, K. S. and Whinston, A. B., Applications of pattern recognition to some problems in economics, in: Techniques of Optimization (A. V. Balakrishnan Ed.), Academic Press, New York, 1972.

5. Blin, J. M., Patterns and configurations in economic science, D. Reidel Publ. Co. Dordrecht - Cambridge, 1973.

6. Blin, J. M., Whinston, A. B., Pattern recognition in the social sciences, in: Special issue, IEEE Trans. on Social Systems Engineering, March 1975.

7. Danmarks National Bank, Monetary review, issued quarterly; used here: Vol. 13, no°13, November 1974.

8. Drud, A., Valstorp-Frederiksen, P., Regnskabsanalyse (in Danish), pp. 34-65, in: L. F. Pau (Ed.), Topics in Pattern Recognition, IMSOR, Technical University of Denmark, Lyngby, September 1973, p. 159.

9. Expansion, Numero special, Europe-Expansion, 1969 and 1970.

10. Fukunaga, K., Introduction to statistical pattern recognition, Academic Press, New York, 1972; and W. L. G. Koontz: Application of the Karhunen-Loeve expansion to feature selection and ordering, IEEE Trans. Computers, Vol. C-19, 1970, p. 826-829.

11. Fogler, H. R., Pattern recognition model for forecasting, Management Science, Vol. 20, n° 8, April 1974, 1178-1189.

12. Goronzy, F., A factor analysis of selected variables of manufacturing business enterprises, Management Internation, Rev. (Germany), n° 6, 1969, 71-96.

13. Green's, Danske fonds og aktier, Børsens Forlag, Copenhagen, 1971 and 1972.

14. Haandbogen om Dansk Erhvervsliv, Forlaget Børsen, Copenhagen, 1974.

15. Kendall, M. G., A course in multivariate analysis, Hafner Publ. Co., New York, 1957.

16. Pau, L. F., Methodes statistiques de reduction et de reconnaissance des formes, Dr. Thesis, Paris University, 1972; and: Analyse des correspondances bayesienne, in: "Classification automatique et perception par ordinateur", Coll. Seminaires IRIA, IRIA, Rocquencourt, February 1975.

17. Paul, L. F., Statistical reduction and recognition of speech patterns, Conf. on Machine Perception of Patterns and Pictures, Conf. Publ. Book n°13, Institute of Physics, London, 1972, 126-133.

18. Pau, L. F., Applications of pattern recognition to the diagnosis of equipment failures, Pattern Recognition, Vol. 6, pp. 3-11, 1974.

19. Pau, L. F., Shape dependent similarity measure for oriented line patterns, Computer Graphics and Image Processing J., December, 1975.

20. Pau, L. F., La Bourse de Copenhague, Analyse financiere, n° 15, Vol., 1973-4, 36-45; and T. R. Sag 953, IMSOR, Technical University of Denmark, Lyngby, June 1972.

21. Plassard, F., Soum, D., L'analyse typologique, Section recherches, Institut des estudes economiques, 15, quai Claude Bernard, 69007, Lyon, November 1971.

22. Seashore, S. E., Yuchtman, E., Factorial analysis of organizational performance, Administrative Science Quarterly, December 1967, 337-395.

23. Smith, K. V., Classification of investment securities using multiple discriminant analysis, Krannert Research Institute, Purdue University, WP n° 101, January 1969.

24. Stich, R. S., How well do multinational companies perform?, Management International Review (Germany), Vol. 11, 1971-4/5, 33-44.

90

25. Zagoruiko, N. G., Zaslavska, T. I. (Ed.), Raspoznavanie obrazov v sotsial'nykh issledovaniakh (pattern recognition in social research) Institute of Economics, and Institute of Mathematics of the Siberian Department of the USSR Academy of Sciences, Novosibirsk, Nauka Press, 1968.

26. Zagoruiko, N. G., Zaslavska, T. I., On the possibility of pattern recognition methods utilization in sociological research, Quality and Quantity, Vol. 4, n°2, December, 1970, 365-373.

27. Henryson, S., Applicability of factor analysis in the behavioural sciences, Stockholm Studies in Educational Psychology, Vol. I, Asquist and Wicksell, Stockholm, 1957.

28. Levasseur, M., Margain, M., Schlosser, M., Vernimmen, P., Attribution automatisee des credits a la consommation, Revue Banque, n° 308, June 1972, 581-594.

29. Watanabe, S. et al, Computer and Information Sciences II, Academic Press, New York, 1967.

NOTE: All data related to the three case studies of Section C are available upon request from the author; the same applies to the full results, symbol lists, and feature defnitions.

CONSIDERATION OF THE DATA UNCERTAINTY WITH REGARD TO THE
SEQUENTIAL DECISION SCHEME

M. Terrenoire & D. Tounissoux

Universite Lyon 1 - FRANCE

I. Introduction

A classical approach for a pattern recognition problem can
be expressed as follows [3],[2],[8]:

Let (Ω, a, p) be a probability space, we consider a partition
of Ω into two measurable sets T_1 and T_2.

Let (ξ_n) $n \varepsilon$ IN, be a sequence of random variables, independent for the probability laws p_1 and p_2 defined by:

$$p_1(\cdot) = p(\cdot/T_1)$$
$$p_2(\cdot) = p(\cdot/T_2)$$

For a given experiment $\omega* \varepsilon$ Ω, we observe the values of all
the variables ξ_n and we want to decide which of the two hypothesis
$\omega* \varepsilon$ T_1 or $\omega* \varepsilon$ T_2 is true. RENYI [3] shows that the mean error
resulting from the Bayesian decision procedure when observing the
values of the n random variables $\xi_0, \ldots, \xi_{n-1}$ tends to zero when
n tends to infinite, if and only if:

$$\lim_{n \to \infty} \prod_{k=0}^{n-1} \int_{-\infty}^{+\infty} \sqrt{f_k(x) \, g_k(x)} \, dx = 0$$

where f_k and g_k are the density functions of random variables ξ_k
for the probability laws p_1 and p_2 respectively.

When the random variables ξ_n only take on a finite number of values, we can consider them as finite partitions $q = (q_1,\ldots,q_{a(q)})$ ($a(q)$ integer ≥ 2) of Ω, called questions.

The usual data of the problem are the quantities $p(q_i/T_j)$, probability of observing the issue q_i of the question q under the hypothesis T_j. From this point of view and generalizing to the case when we must distinguish n patterns, we have introduced the Pseudoquestionnaires [4], pattern recognition procedure in which the considered question at the mth stage depends on the issues of the $(m-1)$ preceding questions. Such a process may be represented by an arborescent graph:

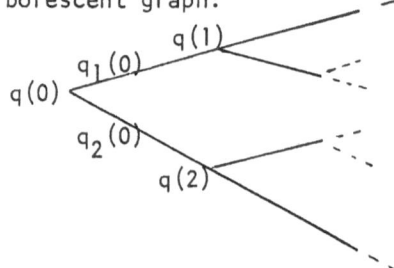

We use a notion of convergence to describe the fact that one can almost surely decide in a Pseudoquestionnaire, with an arbitrarily reduced error risk. Thus, we obtain the following result [7]:

Proposition 1:

> We can construct a convergent Pseudoquestionnaire if and only if there exists a sequence $\{q(r)\}$, r IN, of questions such that:
>
> $$\forall\ j \in \{1,\ldots,n\}, \quad \forall\ k \in \{1,\ldots,n\}\ \ j \neq k \tag{1}$$
>
> $$\lim_{R \to \infty} \prod_{l=0}^{R} \sum_{i=1}^{a(q(l))} [p(q_i(l)/T_j)\ p(q_i(l)/T_k)]^{1/2} = 0$$

In this paper, we will deal with the uncertainty with which the conditional probabilities are usually known. We do not intend to discuss any learning process, but we want to know if these uncertainties allow to decide accurately.

Then, we will suppose that we only have an estimation $\rho(q_i/T_j)$ of the unknown quantity $p(q_i/T_j)$ with an uncertainty $\delta_i^i(q)$.

> We show that we can construct a convergent Pseudoques-
> tionnaire if there exists a sequence of questions $q(r)$,
> $r \in \mathbb{N}$, such that:
>
> $$\lim_{R \to \infty} \prod_{\ell=0}^{R} \sum_{i=1}^{a(q(\ell))} \left[\frac{(q_i(\ell)/T_j) \ (q_i(\ell)/T_k)}{(1 - \delta_i^j(q(\ell))) \ (1 - \delta_i^k(q(\ell)))} \right]^{1/2} = 0$$
>
> $\nabla \ j \ \epsilon\{1,\ldots,n\} \quad \nabla \ k \ \epsilon\{1,\ldots,n\} \qquad j \neq k$

II. A Pattern Recognition Procedure: The Pseudoquestionnaires

A. A short description of the Pseudoquestionnaires [4],[5],[6].

Given a probability space (Ω, a, p) we consider:

- a finite complete system of events $T = (T_1,\ldots,T_n)$ on (Ω, a).
- a set D of complete systems of events on (Ω, a), independent
  for the probability laws $p(./T_j)$. We note by $q_1,\ldots,q_{a}(q)$
  integer ≥ 2) the elements of such a system q, and we say
  that q is a question with issues $q_1,\ldots,q_{a}(q)$.

A Pseudoquestionnaire (abbreviated form Pq) constructed on D
is a triplet $K = (A,u,B)$ where:

- $A = (X,\Gamma)$ is an arborescent graph, finite or infinite
- u is an application of the set Y of non terminal vertices
  of A into D such that:
  - (i) $|\Gamma_y| = a(u(y)) \ \nabla \ y \ \epsilon \ Y$
  - (ii) The restriction of u to the set of vertices of each
    path in A is injective
- $B = \{b_y | y \ \epsilon Y\}$ where b_y is a bijection between the set of
  arcs going from y and the set of issues of the question
  $u(y)$.

III.   Probabilities attached to the vertices of Pq

Given a Pq $K = (A,u,B)$; let us consider a vertex x of K and
the ordered set $(x_o,\ldots,x_k)$ of its ancestors in K (with $x_{k+1} = x$).
We note:

$$\begin{cases} q(\ell) = u(x_\ell) & \ell \in \{0,\ldots,k\} \\ b_{x_\ell}((x_\ell, x_{\ell+1})) = q_{i_x}(\ell) \\ \varepsilon(x) = \bigcap_{\ell=0}^{k} q_{i_x}(\ell) \end{cases}$$

We call rank of x in K, and we note it by r(x) the number of the ancestors of x in $\acute{A}$ (here r(x) = k+1). We define the probability of the vertex x in K to be the quantity p (ε(x)), noted by p(x).

We define the probability vector associated with x to be the element $P(T/x)$ of IR^n having as components $p(T_j/\varepsilon(x))$, noted by $p(T_j/x)$. We will note by π the probability vector associated with the root x_o of the Pq.

IV. Convergence of Pq

Given a Pq K constructed on D, we note, for any vertex y in K:

$$Pe(y) = 1 - Max [p(T_j/y) \mid j \in \{1,\ldots,n\}]$$

and we consider the quantities:

$$\forall R \in IN \quad Pe(K,R) = \sum_{r(y)=R} p(y) \, Pe(y)$$

$$Pe(K) = \lim_{R \to \infty} Pe(K,R)$$

We say that K is convergent if Pe(K) = 0

A. Convergence and decision rule

In practice, one can use the following decision rule: given a threshold $\varepsilon > 0$, we decide to choose T_j at a vertex x of K if:

$$p(T_j/x) \leq 1 - \varepsilon$$

Let us note by $E(R,\varepsilon)$ (R interger > 0) the set of the vertices x of rank R in K such that:

$$\forall y \in [x_o, x] \forall j \in \{1,\ldots,n\} \quad p(T_j/x) < 1 - \varepsilon$$

($[x_o, x]$ denotes the set of ancestors of x in K, x included). Then we have the following property:

$$K \text{ convergent} \Longleftrightarrow \forall \varepsilon > 0 \quad \lim_{R \to \infty} p(E(R,\varepsilon)) = 0$$

V. Stable Convergence

A. Introduction

We suppose that the conditional probabilities $p(q_i/T_j)$ are estimated by quantities $\rho(q_i/T_j)$ and are known with an uncertainty $\delta_i^j(q)$; more precisely we do the following hypothesis:

$$\left. \begin{array}{l} \forall\, q\, \in D, \forall\, j\, \in \{1,\ldots,n\}\,,\, \forall\, i\, \in \{1,\ldots a(q)\} \\[4pt] (1 - \delta_i^j(q))\, \rho(q_i/T_j) \le p(q_i/T_j) \le \dfrac{1}{1-\delta_i^j(q)}\, \rho(q_i/T_j) \end{array} \right\} (2)$$

We will aim to find decision rules and convergence conditions which concern only the estimated quantities $\rho(q_i/T_j)$.

B. Decision rule and S - convergence

Given a Pq K and an error probability ε, at a vertex x of K, we will decide to choose T_j if:

$$\sum_{\substack{k=1 \\ k\neq j}}^{n} \frac{\pi_k}{\pi_j} \prod_{\ell=0}^{r(x)-1} \frac{\rho(q_{i_x}(\ell)/T_k)}{\rho(q_{i_x}(\ell)/T_j)} \times \frac{1}{(1 - \delta_{i_x}^j(q(\ell)))\,(1 - \delta_{i_x}^j(q(\ell)))} \le$$

$$\frac{\varepsilon}{1 - \varepsilon} \tag{3}$$

Let us note the condition (3) implies, according to (2):

$$\sum_{\substack{k=1 \\ k\neq j}}^{n} \frac{\pi_k}{\pi_j} \prod_{\ell=0}^{r(x)-1} \frac{p(q_{i_x}(\ell)/T_k)}{p(q_{i_x}(\ell)/T_j)} - \frac{\varepsilon}{1 - \varepsilon} \tag{4}$$

The condition (4) is equivalent to:

$$p(T_j/x) \ge \frac{1}{1 + \dfrac{\varepsilon}{1 - \varepsilon}} = 1 - \varepsilon$$

Thus, the decision rule (3) gives us satisfaction since it only deals the quantities $\rho(q_i/T_j)$ and it leads to an error risk arbitrarily small. It is to be compared to the Sequential Probability Ration Test [1].

Given an integer R > 0, we note by $G(R,\varepsilon)$ the set of vertices x of rank R in K such that at any vertex y of the path $[x_o, x]$ we cannot decide according the criterion (3), that is to say:

$$\forall y \in [x_o, x], \quad \forall j \in \{1,\ldots,n\}$$

$$\sum_{\substack{k=1 \\ k \neq j}}^{n} \frac{\pi_k}{\pi_j} \prod_{\ell=0}^{r(y)-1} \frac{\rho(q_{i_y}/T_k)}{\rho(q_{i_y}/T_j)} \times \frac{1}{(1 - \delta_{i_j}^{i}(q(\ell)))(1 - \delta_{i_y}^{k}(q(\ell))} >$$

$$\frac{\varepsilon}{1 - \varepsilon}$$

Definition

A Pq is S - convergent (stable convergence) if:

$$\forall \varepsilon > 0 \lim_{R \to \infty} \sum_{x \in G(R,\varepsilon)} \rho(x) = 0$$

with $\rho(x) = \sum_{j=1}^{n} \pi_j \prod_{\ell=0}^{r(x)-1} \rho(q_{i_x}(\ell)/T_j)$

C. **Sufficient condition of S - convergence**

Proposition 2:

We can construct a S. convergent Pq if there exists a sequence $\{q(\ell)\}$, $\ell \in \mathbb{N}$ in D such that:

$$\forall j \in \{1,\ldots,n\}, \forall k \in \{1,\ldots,n\}, j \neq k$$

$$\lim_{R \to \infty} \prod_{\ell=0}^{R} \sum_{i=1}^{a(q(\ell))} \left[\frac{\rho(q_i(\ell)/T_j) \, \rho(q_i(\ell)/T_k)}{(1 - \delta_i^{j}(q(\ell)))(1 - \delta_i^{k}(q(\ell)))} \right]^{1/2} = 0$$

The proof being too long, we cannot give it here.

VI. **Numerical Reflexions**

We suppose that the number of patterns to distinguish is equal to 2. The general theorem concerning the convergence of Pq (Proposition 1) shows that we can measure the quality of a question q by the quantity:

$$\Phi(q) = \sum_{i=1}^{a(q)} [\rho(q_i/T_1) \, \rho(q_i/T_2)]^{1/2}$$

The question q is the more discriminant as $\Phi(q)$ is closer to zero and the less discriminant as $\Phi(q)$ is closer to 1.

In practical applications (feature selection) the first idea consists in assimilating the quantities $\rho(q_i/T_j)$ with their estimation $\rho(q_i/T_j)$ and so, in measuring the power of discrimination of q by the quantity:

$$\phi(q) = \sum_{i=1}^{a(q)} [\rho(q_i/T_1) \, \rho(q_i/T_2)]^{1/2}$$

In fact and when the uncertainties $\delta_i^i(q)$ can be evaluated, $\phi(q)$ must be replaced by:

$$\tilde{\Phi}(q) = \sum_{i=1}^{a(q)} \left[\frac{\rho(q_i/T_1) \, \rho(q_i/T_2)}{(1 - \delta_i^1(q)) \, (1 - \delta_i^2(q))} \right]^{1/2}$$

So, a "good question" according to the measure $\phi(q)$ may be a question the discrimination power of which is null ($\tilde{\Phi}(q) \geq 1$).

As a numerical example, let us consider a question q with two issues such that:

$$\rho(q_1/T_1) = 0.25 \qquad \rho(q_1/T_2) = 0.75$$
$$\rho(q_2/T_1) = 0.75 \qquad \rho(q_2/T_2) = 0.25$$
$$\delta_i^1(q) = 0.1 \qquad i = 1,2$$
$$\delta_i^2(q) = 0.05 \qquad i = 1,2$$

According to these date, we have

$$\phi(q) \not{\#} 0.866$$

while:

$$\tilde{\Phi}(q) \not{\#} 0.93$$

Let us note that in the case of n patterns, $\Phi(q)$ becomes a vector of $IR^{\frac{n(n-1)}{2}}$.

References

1. K. S. Fu, "Sequential Methods in Pattern Recognition and Machine Learning", Academic Press, New York and London, 1968.

2. Kakutani, "On Equivalence of Infinite Product Measure", Ann. of Math, Vol. 49, p. 214-226, 1948.

3. A. Renyi, "On Some Basic Problems of Statistics from the Point of View of Information Theory", Proc. 5th Berkeley Symposium, Math. Stat. and Prob., University of California Press, p. 531-543, 1967.

4. M. Terrenoire, "Un Modèle Mathématique Pour les Processus d'interrogration: les Pseudoquestionnaires, Thèse Grenoble, 1970.

5. M. Terrenoire, "An Evaluation of Algol 68 for Interrogation Process Algorithms", Journal on Computer and Information Sciences, March 1972.

6. M. Terrenoire, "Convergence of Heuristics for Some Inter-rogation Processes", 1st Int. Joint Conf. on Pattern Recognition, October 1973.

7. D. Tounissoux, "Utilisation de la distance de Bhattacharyya dans les Pseudoquestionnaires", C. R. Acad. Sc. Paris, t 280, Série A p. 1241, 1975.

8. Vajda, "Limit theorems for total variation of cartesian project measures", Studia Scientiarum Mathematicarum Hunganica 6, p. 317-333, 1971.

SYNTACTIC METHODS IN PATTERN RECOGNITION

K. S. Fu

Purdue University, West Lafayette, Indiana

Abstract: This paper provides a brief overview of the syntactic (structural) pattern recognition. Languages are used to describe patterns, and syntax analysis procedures are employed as recognition procedures. Methods for the selection of pattern primitives are presented. Both one-dimensional (string) and high dimensional grammars and their applications are discussed. An example of fingerprint pattern recognition is given for illustration. Problems for further research are suggested.

I. Syntactic (Structural) Approach to Pattern Recognition

Most of the developments in pattern recognition research during the past decade deal with the decision-theoretic approach [1-11] and its applications. In some pattern recognition problems, the structural information which describes each pattern is important, and the recognition process includes not only the capability of assigning the pattern to a particular class (to classify it), but also the capacity to describe aspects of the pattern which make it ineligible for assignment to another class. A typical example of this class of recognition problem is picture recognition or more generally speaking, scene analysis. In this class of recognition problems, the patterns under consideration are usually quite complex and the number of features required is often very large which make the idea of describing a complex pattern in terms of a (hierarchical) composition of simpler subpatterns very attractive. Also, when the patterns are complex and the number of possible descriptions is very large it is impractical to regard each description as defining a class (for example in fingerprint and face identification problems, recognition of continuous speech, Chinese characters, etc.). Consequently, the requirement of recognition can only be satisfied by a description for each pattern rather than the simple task of classification.

In order to represent the hierarchical (tree-like) structural information of each pattern, that is, a pattern described in terms of simpler subpatterns and each simpler subpattern again be described in terms of even simpler subpatterns, etc., the linguistic or structural approach has been proposed [12-16]. This approach draws an analogy between the (hierarchical, tree-like) structure of patterns and the syntax of languages. Patterns are specified as building up out of subpatterns in various ways of composition just as phrases and sentences are built up by concatenating words and words are built up by concatenating characters. Evidently, for this approach to be advantageous, the simples subpatterns selected, called "pattern primitives", should be much easier to recognize than the patterns themselves. The "language" which provide the structural description of patterns in terms of a set of pattern primitives and their composition operations, is sometimes called "pattern description language". The rules governing the composition of primitives into patterns are usually specified by the so-called "grammar" of the pattern description language. After each primitive within the pattern is identified, the recognition process is accomplished by performing a syntax analysis or parsing of the "sentence" describing the given pattern to determine whether or not it is syntactically (or grammatically) correct with respect to the specified grammar. In the meantime, the syntax analysis also produces a structural description of the sentence representing the given pattern (usually in the form of a tree structure).

The syntactic approach to pattern recognition provides a capability for describing a large set of complex patterns using small sets of simple pattern primitives and of grammatical rules. As can be seen later, one of the most attractive aspects of this capability is the use of recursive nature of a grammar. A grammar (rewriting) rule can be applied any number of times, so it is possible to express in a very compact way some basic structural characteristics of an infinite set of sentences. Of course, the practical utility of such an approach depends upon our ability to recognize the simple pattern primitives and their relationships represented by the composition operations.

An alternative representation of the structural information of a pattern is to use a "relational graph" [12]. Since there is a one-to-one corresponding relation between a linear graph and a matrix, a relational graph can certainly also be expressed as a "relational matrix". In using the relational graph for pattern description, we can broaden the class of allowed relations to include any relation that can be conveniently determined from the pattern. (Notice that (i) the concentenation is the only natural operation for one-dimensional languages, and (ii) a graph, in general, contains closed loops whereas a tree does not.) With this generalization, we may possibly express richer descriptions than we can with tree structures. However, the use of tree structures does provide us a direct channel to adapt the techniques of formal language theory to the problem of compactly representing and analyzing patterns containing a significant structural content.

II. Syntactic Pattern Recognition System

A syntactic pattern recognition system can be considered as consisting of three major parts; namely, preprocessing, pattern

description or representation, and syntax analysis.[†] A simple
block diagram of the system is shown in Fig. 1. The functions of
preprocessing include (i) pattern encoding and approximation, and
(ii) filtering, restoration and enhancement. An input pattern is
first coded or approximated by some convenient form for further
processing. For example, a black-and-white picture can be coded
in terms of a grid (or a matrix) of 0's and 1's, or a waveform can
be approximated by its time samples or a truncated Fourier series
expansion. In order to make the processing in the later stages of
the system more efficient, some sort of "data compression" is often applied at this stage. Then, techniques of filtering, restoration and/or enhancement will be used to clean the noise, to re-
store the degradation, and/or to improve the quality of the coded
(or approximated) patterns. At the output of the preprocessor,
presumably, we have patterns with reasonably "good quality". Each
preprocessed pattern is then represented by a language-like structure (for example, a string or a graph). The operation of this
pattern-representation process consists of (i) pattern segmentation, and (ii) primitive (feature) extraction. In order to represent a pattern in terms of its subpatterns, we must segmentize the
pattern and, in the meantime, identify (or extract) the primitives
and relations in it. In other words, each preprocessed pattern is
segmentized into subpatterns and pattern primitives based on prespecified syntactic or composition operations; and, in turn, each
subpattern is identified with a given set of pattern primitives.
Each pattern is now represented by a set of primitives with specified syntactic operations. For example, in terms of "concatenation" operation, each pattern is represented by a string of (concatenated) primitives. More sophisticated systems should also be
able to detect various syntactic relations within the pattern.

[†]The division of three parts is for convenience rather than necessity. Usually, the term "linguistic pattern recognition" refers
primarily to the pattern representation (or description) and the
syntax analysis.

The decision on whether or not the representation (pattern) is syntactically correct (i.e., belongs to the class of patterns described by the given syntax or grammar) will be performed by the "syntax analyzer" or "parser". When performing the syntax analysis or parsing, the analyzer can usually produce a complete syntactic description, in terms of a parse or parsing-tree, of the pattern provided it is syntactically correct. Otherwise, the pattern is either rejected or analyzed on the basis of other given grammars, which presumably describe other possible classes of patterns under consideration.

Conceptually, the simplest form of recognition is probably "template-matching". The string of primitives representing an input pattern is matched against strings of primitives representing each prototype or reference pattern. Based on a selected "matching" or "similarity" criterion, the input pattern is classified in the same class as the prototype pattern which is the "best" to match the input. The hierarchical structural information is essentially ignored. A complete parsing of the string representing an input pattern, on the other hand, explores the complete hierarchical structural description of the pattern. In between, there are a number of intermediate approaches. For example, a series of tests can be designed to test the occurrences or non-occurrence of certain subpatterns (or primitives) or certain combinations of subpatterns or primitives. The result of the tests (for example, through a table look-up, a decision tree, or a logical operation) is used for a classification decision. Notice that each test may be a template-matching scheme or a parsing for a subtree representing a subpattern. The selection of an appropriate approach for recognition usually depends upon the problem requirement. If a complete pattern description is required for recognition, parsing is necessary. Otherwise, a complete parsing could be avoided by using other simpler approaches to improve the efficiency of the recognition process.

In order to have a grammar describing the structural information about the class of patterns under study, a grammatical inference machine is required which can infer a grammar from a given set of training patterns in language-like representations[†] [72]. This is analogous to the "learning" process in a decision-theoretic pattern recognition system [1-11,17-20]. The structural description of the class of patterns under study is learned from the actual sample patterns from that class. The learned description, in the form of a grammar, is then used for pattern description and syntax analysis. (See Fig. 1). A more general form of learning might include the capability of learning the best set of primitives and the corresponding structural description for the class of patterns concerned.

Practical applications of syntactic pattern recognition include the recognition of English and Chinese characters, spoken digits, and mathematical expressions, the classification of bubble chamber and spark chamber photographs and chromosomes and fingerprint images, and the identification of machine parts [21-37].

III. Selection of Pattern Primitives

As was discussed in Section 3.1, the first step in formulating a syntactic model for pattern description is the determination of a set of primitives in terms of which the patterns of interest may be described. This will be largely influenced by the nature of the data, the specific application in question, and the technology available for implementing the system. There is no general solution for the primitive selection problem at this time. The following requirements usually serve as a guideline for selecting pattern primitives.

(i) The primitives should serve as basic pattern elements to provide a compact but adequate description of the data in terms of the specified structural relations (e.g., the concatenation relation).

[†]At present, this part is performed primarily by the designer.

(ii) The primitives should be easily extracted or recognized by existing non-linguistic methods, since they are considered to be simple and compact patterns and their structural information not important.

For example, for speech patterns, phonemes are naturally considered as a "good" set of primitives with the concatenation relation[+]. Similarly, strokes have been suggested as primitives in describing handwriting. However, for general pictorial patterns, there is no such "universal picture element" analogous to phonemes in speech or strokes in handwriting[++]. Sometimes, in order to provide an adequate description of the patterns, the primitives should contain the information which is important to the specific application in question. For example, if the size (or shape or location) is important in the recognition problem, then the primitives should contain information relating to size (or shape or location) so that patterns from different classes are distinguishable by whatever method is to be applied to analyze the descriptions. This requirement often results in a need for semantic information in describing primitives [12].

A set of primitives commonly used to describe boundaries or skeletons is the chain code given by Freeman [43,44]. Under this scheme, a rectangular grid is overlaid on the two-dimensional pattern, and straight line segments are used to connect the grid points falling closest to the pattern. Each line segment is assigned an octal digit according to its slope. The pattern is thus represented by a chain (or string) or chains of octal digits. Fig. 2 illustrates the primitives and the coded string describing a

---

[+]The view of continuous speech as composed of one sound segment for each successive phoneme is, of course, a simplification of facts.

[++]It is also interesting to see that the extraction of phonemes in continuous speech and that of strokes in handwriting are not a very easy task with respect to the requirement (ii) specified above.

curve. This descriptive scheme has some useful properties. For example, patterns coded in this way can be rotated through multiples of 45° simply by adding an octal digit (modulo 8) to every digit in the string (however, only rotations by multiples of 90° can be accomplished without some distortion of the pattern). Other simple manipulations such as expansion, measurement of curve length, and determination of pattern self-intersections are easily carried out. Any desired degree of resolution can be obtained by adjusting the fineness of the grid imposed on the patterns. This method is, of course, not limited to simply-connected closed boundaries; it can be used for describing arbitrary two-dimensional figures composed of straight or curved lines and line segments.

Notable work using Freeman's chain code include efforts by Knoke and Wiley [45] and by Feder [46]. Knoke and Wiley attempted to demonstrate that linguistic approaches can usually be applied to describe structural relationships within patterns (hand-printed characters, in this case). Feder's work considers only patterns which can be encoded as strings of primitives. Several bases for developing pattern languages are discussed, including equations in two variables (straight lines, circles and circular arcs, etc.), pattern properties (self-intersections, convexity, etc.), and various measures of curve similarity. The computational power (automaton complexity) required to detect the elements of these pattern languages is studied. However, this problem is complicated considerably by the fact that (i) these languages are mostly context-sensitive and not context-free, (ii) the chain code yields only a piecewise linear approximation of the original pattern, and (iii) the coding of a typical curve is not unique, depending to a degree on its location and orientation with respect to the coding grid.

Other applications of the chain code include description of contour maps [47], "shape matching" [48], and identification of high energy particle tracks in bubble chamber photographs [49].

Contour lines can be encoded as chains. Contour map problems may involve finding the terrain to be flooded by a dam placed at a particular location, the water shed area for a river basin, the terrain visible from a particular mountain-top location, or the determination of optimum highway routes through mountainous terrain. In shape matching, two or more two-dimensional objects having irregular contours are to be matched for all or part of their exterior boundary. For some such problems the relative orientation and scale of the objects to be matched may be known and only translation is required. The problem of matching aerial photographs to each other as well as to terrain maps falls into this category. For other problems either orientation, or scale, or both may be unknown and may have to be determined as part of the problem. An example of problems in which relative orientation has to be determined is that of the computer assembly of potsherds and jigsaw puzzles [50].

Other syntactic pattern recognition systems using primitives with the emphasis on boundary, skeleton or contour information include systems for hand-printed character recognition [51-53], bubble chamber and spark chamber photograph classification [27,28,54, 55], chromosome analysis [29,56,57], fingerprint identification [30-32,58,59], face recognition [60,61], and scene analysis [62-64].

A set of primitives for encoding geometric patterns in terms of regions has been proposed by Pavlidis [65]. In this case, the basic primitives are halfplanes in the pattern space[+] (or the

---

[+]This could be generalized to halfspaces of the pattern space. Another approach to the analysis of geometric patterns using regions is discussed primarily in the problem of scene analysis [9,63]. Minsky and Papert [69] have considered the direct transformation of a gray scale picture to regions, bypassing the edge-finding, line-fitting procedures. Regions are constructed as the union of squares whose corners have the same or nearly the same gray scale. The method proposed by Guzman [70] assumes that a picture can be reduced by preprocessing to a list of vertices,

field of observation). It can be shown that any figure (or arbitrary polygon) may be expressed as the union of a finite number of convex polygons. Each convex polygon can, in turn, be represented as the intersection of a finite number of halfplanes. By defining a suitable ordering (a sequence) of the convex polygons composing the arbitrary polygon, it is possible to determine a unique minimal set of maximal (in an appropriate sense) polygons, called primary subsets, the union of which is the given polygon. In linguistic analogy, a figure can be thought of as a "sentence", the convex polygons composing it as "words" and the halfplanes as "letter". It is noted that this approach provides a formalism for describing the syntax of polygonal figures and more general figures which can be approximated reasonably well by polygonal figures. The analysis or recognition procedure requires the definition of suitable measures of similarity between polygons. The similarity measures considered so far are quite sensitive to noise in the patterns and/or are difficult to implement practically on a digital computer. A somewhat more general selection procedure of pattern primitives based on regions has been recently proposed by Rosenfeld and Strong [66].

---

lines and surfaces. Various heuristics, based on the analysis of types of intersections of lines and surfaces, are applied to this list to compose its elements inti two- or three-dimensional regions. Some candidate pattern recognition schemes have been investigated, all of which involve methods for matching the reduced pattern descriptions against a prototype dictionary. The procedure studied by Brice and Fennema [71] decomposes a picture into atomic regions of uniform gray scale. A pair of heuristics is used to join these regions in such a way as to obtain regions whose boundaries are determined more by the natural lines of the scene than by the artificial ones introduced by quantization and noise. Then a simple line-fitting technique is used to approximate the region boundaries by straight lines and finally, the scene analyzer interprets the picture using some simple tests on object groups generated by a Guzman-like procedure.

IV. Pattern Grammar

Assume that a satisfactory solution of the "primitive selection" problem is available for a given application. The next step
is the construction of a grammar (or grammars) which will generate
a language (or languages) to describe the patterns under study.
Ideally, it would be nice to have a grammatical inference machine
which would infer a grammar from a given set of strings describing
the patterns under study. Unfortunately, such a machine has not
been available except for some very special cases [72]. In most
cases so far, the designer constructs the grammar based on the a
priori knowledge available and his experience. It is known that
increased descriptive power of a language is paid for in terms of
increased complexity of the analysis system (recognizer or acceptor). Finite-state automata are capable of recognizing or accep-
ing finite-state languages although the descriptive power of finite-state languages is also known to be weaker than that of context-free and context-sensitive languages. On the other hand,
non-finite, nondeterministic devices are required, in general, to
accept the languages generated by context-free and context-sensitive grammars. Except for the class of deterministic languages,
nondeterministic parsing procedures are usually needed for the
analysis of context-free languages. The trade-off between the
descriptive power and the analysis efficiency of a grammar for a
given application is, at present, almost completely justified by
the designer. (For example, a precedence language may be used for
pattern description in order to obtain good analysis efficiency;
or, on the other hand, a context-free programmed grammar generating a context-sensitive language may be selected in order to describe the patterns effectively.) The effect of the theoretical
difficulty may not be serious in practice, as long as some care
is exercised in developing the required grammars. This is especially true when the languages of interest are actually finite-
state, even though the form of the grammars may be context-sensitive

or when the languages may be approximated by finite-state languages.

Although many classes of patterns appear to be intuitively context-sensitive, context-sensitive (but not context-free) grammars have rarely been used for pattern description simply because of their complexity. Context-free languages have been used to describe patterns such as English characters [21], chromosome images [29], spark chamber pictures [27], chemical structures [73], fingerprint patterns [30], and spoken digits [33].

In addition to (i) the trade-off between the language descriptive power and the analysis efficiency, and (ii) the compromise sometimes necessary between the primitives selected and the grammar constructed, the designer should also be aware of the need to control the excessive strings generated by the constructed grammar. The number of pattern strings available in practice is always limited. However, in most cases, the grammar constructed would generate a large or infinite number of strings[†]. It is hoped that the excessive strings generated are similar to the available pattern strings. Unfortunately, this may not be true since the grammar, in many cases, is constructed heuristically. The problem may become very serious when the excessive strings include some pattern strings which should belong to other classes. In this case, adjustments should be made to exclude these strings from the language generated by the constructed grammar.

Recently, probably due to their relative effectiveness in describing natural language structures, transformational grammars have been proposed for pattern description [74-77]. Transformational grammars would allow the possibility of determining from

---

[†]It may be argued that, in practice, a pattern grammar can always be finite-state since it is contructed from a finite number of pattern strings. However, the finite-state grammar so constructed may require a large number of productions. In such a case, a context-free or a context-free programmed pattern grammar may be constructed for the purpose of significantly reducing the number of productions.

the pattern generative mechanism a simple base grammar (deep structure) which generates a certain set of patterns and a problem-oriented set of transformations. Through the base grammar and the transformations, the original set of patterns can be described.

From the above discussion, it might be concluded that, before efficient grammatical inference procedures are available, a man-machine interactive system would be suitable for the problem of construction. The basic grammar and the various trade-off's and compromises have to be determined by the designer. The results of any adjustment on the grammar constructed can be easily checked and displayed through a computer system.

V. High-Dimensional Pattern Grammars

In describing patterns using a conventional string grammar, the only relation between subpatterns and/or primitives is the concatenation; that is, each subpattern or primitive can be connected only at the left or right. This one-dimensional relation has not been very effective in describing two- or three-dimensional patterns. A natural generalization is to use a more general formalism including other useful relations [21,76-81]. Let R be a set of n-ary relations ($n \geq 1$). A relation r R satisfied by the subpatterns and/or primitives $X_1,...,X_n$ is denoted $r(X_1,...,X_n)$. For example, TRIANGLE (a,b,c) means that the ternary relation TRIANGLE is satisfied by the line segments a, b, and c, and ABOVE (X,Y) means that X is above Y.

A simple two-dimensional generalization of string grammars is to extend grammars for one-dimensional strings to two-dimensional arrays [84,85]. The primitives are the array elements and the relation between primitives is the two-dimensional concatenation. Each production rewrites one subarray by another, rather than one substring by another. Relationships between array grammars and array automata (automata with two-dimensional tapes) have been studied recently [85].

Shaw, by attaching a "head" (hd) and a "tail" (tl) to each

112

primitive, has used the four binary operators +, x, - and * for
defining binary concatenation relations between primitives [86,
87].

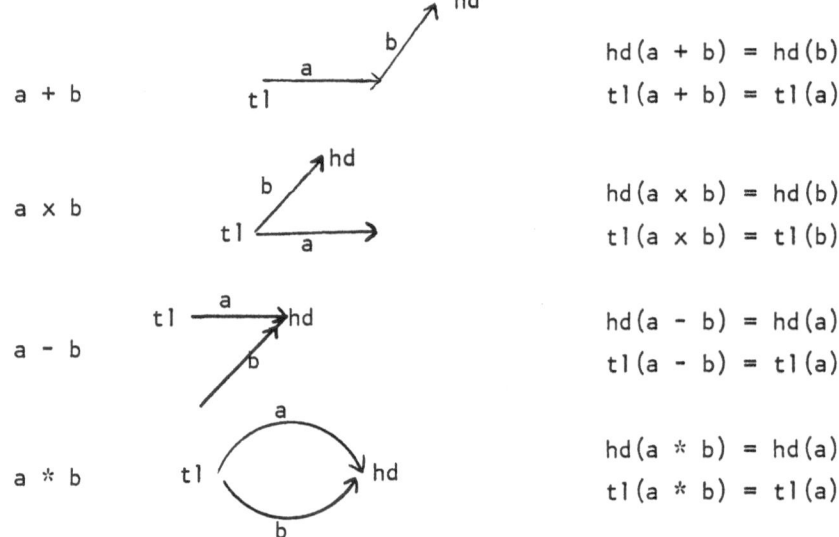

a + b

hd(a + b) = hd(b)
tl(a + b) = tl(a)

a x b

hd(a x b) = hd(b)
tl(a x b) = tl(b)

a - b

hd(a - b) = hd(a)
tl(a - b) = tl(a)

a * b

hd(a * b) = hd(a)
tl(a * b) = tl(a)

For string languages, only the operator + is used. In addition,
the unary operator ~ acting as a tail/head reverser is also defined; i.e.,

~ a

hd(~ a) = tl(a)
tl(~ a) = hd(a)

In the case of describing patterns consisting of disconnected subpatterns, the "blank" or "don't care" primitive is introduced.
Each pictorial pattern is represented by a "labelled branch-ori-
ented graph" where branches represent primitives.

The grammar which generates sentences (PDL expressions) in
PDL (Picture Description Language) is a context-free grammar

$$G = (V_N, V_T, P, S)$$

where

$V_N = \{S, SL\}$
$V_T = \{b\} \cup \{+, x, -, /, (,)\} \cup \{\ell\}$, b may be any primitive (including the "null point primitive" λ
which has identical tail and head)

and

$$S \rightarrow b, \; S \rightarrow (S \; \phi_b \; S), \; S \rightarrow (\sim S), \; S \rightarrow SL, \; S \rightarrow (/SL),$$
$$SL \rightarrow S^{\ell}, \; SL \rightarrow (SL \; \phi_b \; SL), \; SL \rightarrow (\sim SL), \; SL \rightarrow (/SL),$$
$$\phi_b \rightarrow +, \; \phi_b \rightarrow \times, \; \phi_b \rightarrow -, \; \phi_b \rightarrow *$$

ℓ is a label designator which is used to allow crossreference to the expressions S within a description. The / operator is used to enable the tail and head of an expression to be arbitrarily located. A top-down parsing procedure was used for the recognition of PDL expressions describing pictorial patterns [87].

Once we include relations more than just contenations, the description of a pattern may be more conveniently represented by a relational graph, where nodes represent subpatterns or primitives and branches denote (binary) relations[†]. When n-ary relations are involved, a graph-representable description can be obtained by transforming all relations into binary ones. A unary relation $r(X)$ can be changed to a binary one $r'(X,\lambda)$ where λ denotes the "null" primitive. $r(X_1,\ldots,X_n)$ (n > 2) can be transformed into a composition of binary relations, such as

$$r_1(X_1,r_2(X_2,\ldots,r_{n-1}(X_{n-1},X_n))),$$

or into a conjunction of binary relations

$$r_1(X_{11},X_{12}) \wedge r_2(X_{21},X_{22}) \wedge \cdots \wedge r_k(X_{k1},X_{k2}),$$

or into a combination of these. For example, the ternary relation TRIANGLE (a,b,c) could be transformed into either one of the following equivalent binary relations:

$$CAT(a,b) \wedge CAT(b,c) \wedge CAT(c,a)$$

or

$$\Delta(b,CAT(a,c))$$

where $CAT(X,Y)$ means that $hd(X)$ is concatenated to $tl(Y)$, i.e., $CAT(X,Y) = X + Y$, and $\Delta(X,Y)$ means that the line X is connected to form a triangle with the object Y consisting of two concatenated segments. In general, replacement of an n-ary relation with

---

[†]This straightforward representation is called a "labelled node-oriented directed graph."

binary ones using composition requires the addition of more levels
in the description.

Based on an idea in [51], Feder has formalized a "plex" grammar which generates languages with terminals having an arbitrary
number of attaching points for connecting to other primitives or
subpatterns [73]. The primitives of the plex grammar are called
N-Attaching Poing Point Entity (NAPE). Each production of the
plex grammar is in context-free form in which the connectivity of
primitives or subpatterns is described by using explicit lists of
labelled concatenation points (called joints lists). While the
sentences generated by a plex grammar are not directed graphs,
they can be transformed by either assigning labelled nodes to
both primitives and concatenation points as suggested by Pfaltz
and Rosenfeld [88] or by transforming primitives to nodes and concatenations to labelled branches.

Pfaltz and Rosenfeld have extended the concept of string
grammars to grammars for labelled graphs called webs. Labelled
node-oriented graphs are explicitly used in the productions. Each
production describes the rewriting of a graph α into another graph
β and also contains an "embedding" rule E which specifies the connection of β to its surrounding graph (host web) when α is rewritten. A web grammar G is a 4-tuple

$$G = (V_N, V_T, P, S)$$

where V_N is a set of nonterminals; V_T is a set of terminals; S is
a set of "initial" webs; and P is a set of web productions. A
web production is defined as[†]

$$\alpha \rightarrow \beta \, , \, E$$

where α and β are webs, and E is an embedding of β. If we want
to replace the subweb α of the web ω by another subweb β, it is
necessary to specify how to "embed" β in ω in place of α. The
definition of an embedding must not depend on the host web ω since

---

In a most general formulation, the contextual condition of the
production is added.

we want to be able to replace α by β in any web containing α as a subweb. Usually E consists of a set of logical functions which specify whether or not each vertex of ω - α is connected to each vertex of β.

It is noted that web grammars are vertex - or node-oriented compared with the branch - or edge - oriented grammars (e.g., PDL, Plex grammars, etc.). That is, terminals or primitives are represented as vertices in the graph rather than as branches. Some applications of web grammars for picture description can be found in [90,91].

An important special case of a web grammar is that in which the terminal set Σ consists of only a single symbol. In this case, every point of every web in the language has the same label, so that we can ignore the labels and identify the webs with their underlying graphs. This type of web grammar is called a "graph grammar", and its language is called graph language [92]. Pavlidis [92,94] has generalized string grammars to graph grammars by including nonterminal symbols which are not simple branches or nodes. The formalism of web grammars has been rather extensively analyzed [88,90]. The relations among PDL grammars, plex grammars and web grammars have been discussed by Shaw [89] and Rosenfeld [93].

By extending one-dimensional concatenation to multi-dimensional concatenation, strings are generalized to trees. Tree grammars and the corresponding recognizers, tree automata, have been studied recently by a number of authors [95,96]. Naturally, if a pattern can be conveniently described by a tree, it will easily be generated by a tree grammar. Applications of tree grammars to syntactic pattern recognition are described in [97,98].

VI. An Application Example - Fingerprint Pattern Recognition

Recently, the syntactic approach has been applied to the fingerprint classification problem [30,31,98]. Each fingerprint impression is first divided into 16 x 16 sampling squares. The orientation of the ridge in each sampling square, expressed by a

directional code, is used as the basic features for the fingerprint pattern. Feature combinations' in a 2 x 2 sampling-square
window are the pattern primitives. Figure 3 shows the sampling
matrix of the "plain arch", "whorl" and "loop" fingerprint patterns.
Figure 4 gives the 69 canonical feature combinations with their
code representations. Each fingerprint pattern is then described
by a three-level tree as shown in Figure 5. The leaves or terminals of the tree are the pattern primitives. With this description, each fingerprint is represented by a string of 64 primitives.

Context-free grammars were constructed to generate strings
describing fingerprints from seven major classes. A sequential
syntax analyzer was implemented to classify each fingerprint impression into one of the seven classes. Further subclassification
from the seven major classes to about forty classes required probabilistic information to resolve some ambiguities, that is, to use
stochastic context-free grammars. This technique of using context-
free and stochastic context-free languages basically classifies
the fingerprint patterns according to their global configurations.
The resulting classifier appears to be quite simple in structure
and efficient in syntax analysis.

A significant expansion in the number of classes was achieved
by directly using minutial as features. Instead of being represented by a string, each fingerprint pattern is represented by a
set of trees. Each tree provides a rather detailed structural
description of the ridges in a 4 x 4 sampling-square window. Tree
grammars are used to generate trees representing fingerprint impressions, and the corresponding tree automata are used for the
recognition. A grammatical inference procedure was suggested to
automatically infer new tree grammars from new fingerprint patterns. This technique has the potential of generating about 2 x
10^{34} classes for fingerprint patterns. The recognition procedure
is quite simple since tree automata are basically finite-state
automata.

VII. Concluding Remarks

In this paper, we have demonstrated that languages can be used to describe complex patterns. Consequently, syntax analysis procedures can be used to implement the pattern recognition process. It should be noted that, for many practical applications, often both syntactic and decision-theoretic approaches are used [12,101]. For example, decision-theoretic approaches are usually effective in the recognition of pattern primitives. This is primarily due to the fact that the structural information of primitives are sensitive to noise and distortion. On the other hand, in the recognition of subpatterns and the pattern itself which are rich in structural information, syntactic approaches are therefore required. Also, in some practical applications, a certain amount of uncertainty exists in the process under study. For example, due the presence of noise and variations in the pattern measurements, ambiguities often occur in the languages describing real-data patterns. In order to describe and recognize noisy patterns under possible ambiguous situations, the use of stochastic languages has been recently suggested [102-108].

A stochastic grammar is a 4-tuple $G_s = (V_N, V_T, P_s, S)$ where P_s is a finite set of stochastic productions and all the other symbols are the same as defined in nonstochastic grammars. For a stochastic context-free grammar, a production in P_s is of the form

$$A_i \xrightarrow{\quad p_{ij} \quad} \alpha_j \, , \qquad A_i \in V_N, \ \alpha_j \in (V_N \cup V_T)*$$

where p_{ij} is called the production probability. The probability of generating a string x, called the string probability $p(x)$, is the product of all production probabilities associated with the productions used in the generation of x. The language generated by a stochastic grammar consists of the strings generated by the grammar and their associated string probabilities.

By associating probabilities with the strings, we can impose a probabilistic structure on the language to describe noisy pat-

terns. The probability distribution characterizing the patterns
in a class can be interpreted as the probability distribution associated with the strings in a language. Thus, statistical decision rules can be applied to the classification of a pattern under
ambiguous situations (for example, use the maximum-likelihood or
Bayes decision rule). Furthermore, because of the availability of
the information about production probabilities, the speed of syntactic analysis can be improved through the use of this information [108,109]. Of course, in practice, the production probabilities will have to be inferred from the observation of relatively
large numbers of pattern samples [72,103].

Other approaches for the recognition of distorted or noisy
patterns using syntactic methods include the use of transformational grammar [74] and the application of error-correcting parsing
techniques [110]. In the use of error-correcting parsing as a
recognition procedure, different types of primitive extraction
error (substitution, deletion and insertion) are introduced. The
original pattern grammar is modified by taking these errors into
consideration. The recognition process is then based on the parser designed according to the modified grammar. The error-correcting capability of this class of parsers can be achieved by using
either a minimum-distance or a maximum-likelihood decision criterion [110,111].

Acknowledgements

This work was supported by AFOSR Grant 74-2661.

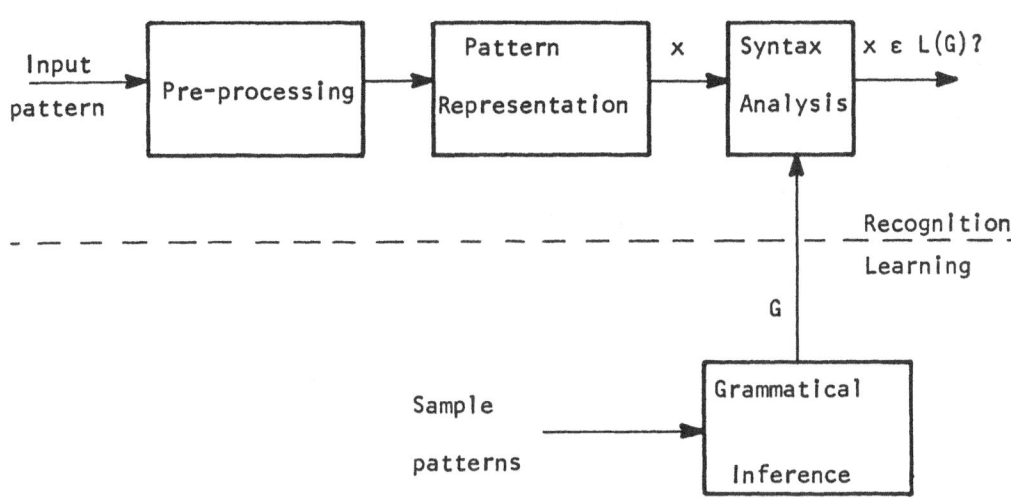

Figure 1. Block Diagram of A Linguistic Pattern Recognition System

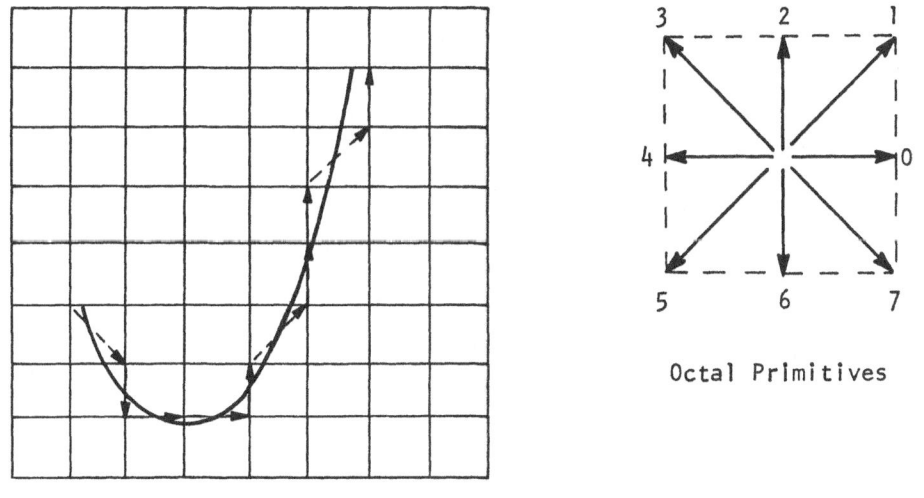

Coded String of the Curve = 7600212212

Figure 2. Freeman's Chain Code

120

(a)

(b)

(c)

Figure 3. The Sampling Matrices of Arch (a), Loop (b),
and Whorl (c)

Figure 4.   Cononical Combinations

122

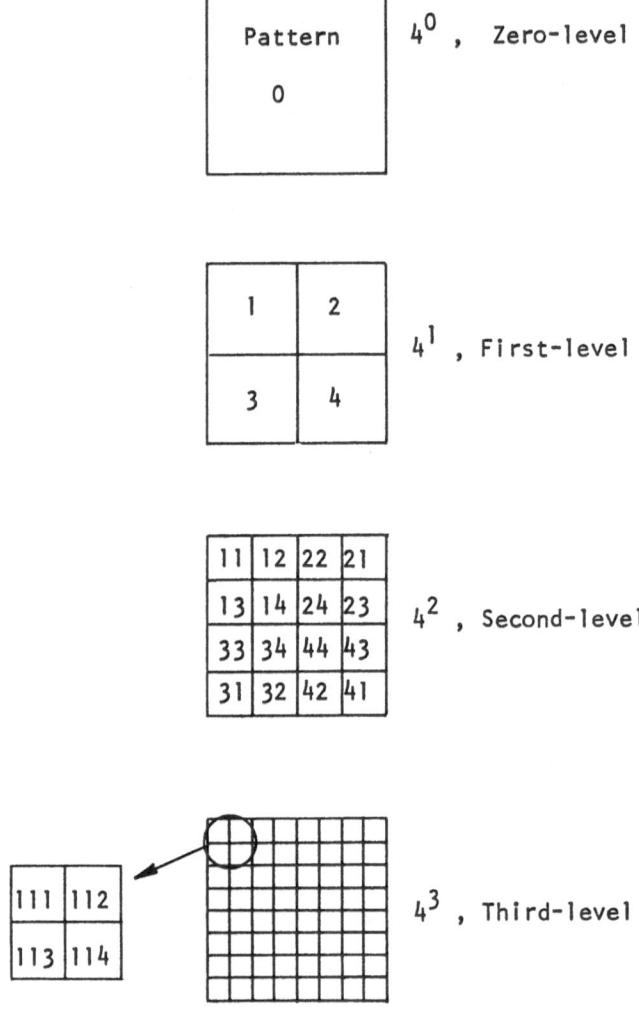

Figure 5.   (a) Multilevel Sampling Matrices

123

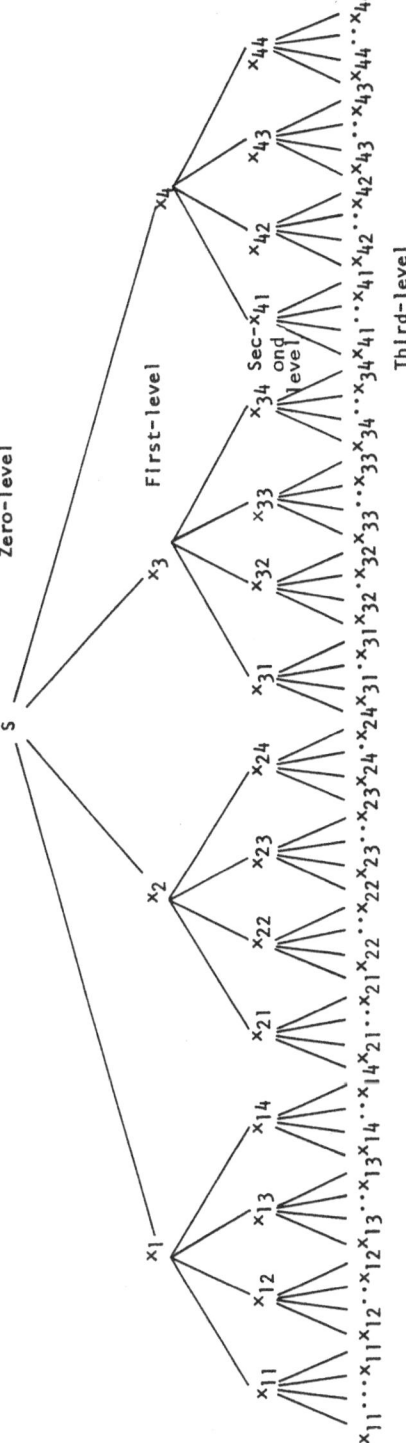

Figure 5. (b) Derivation Tree

124

Bibliography

1. K. S. Fu: <u>Sequential Methods in Pattern Recognition and Machine Learning</u>, (Academic Press, 1968).

2. G. S. Sebestyen: <u>Decision Processes in Pattern Recognition</u>, (Macmillan, New York, 1962).

3. N. J. Nilsson: <u>Learning Machines-Foundations of Trainable Pattern-Classifying System</u>, (McGraw-Hill, 1965).

4. J. M. Mendel and K. S. Fu: <u>Adaptive, Learning and Pattern Recognition Systems</u>: Theory and Applications, (Academic Press, 1970).

5. W. Meisel: <u>Computer-Oriented Approaches to Pattern Recognition</u>, (Academic Press, 1972).

6. K. Fukunaga: <u>Introduction to Statistical Pattern Recognition</u>, (Academic Press, 1972).

7. E. A. Patrick: <u>Fundamentals of Pattern Recognition</u>, (Prentice-Hall, 1972).

8. H. C. Andrews: <u>Introduction to Mathematical Techniques in Pattern Recognition</u>, (Wiley, 1972).

9. R. O. Duda and P. E. Hart: <u>Pattern Classification and Scene Analysis,</u> (Wiley, 1973).

10. C. H. Chen: <u>Statistical Pattern Recognition</u>, (Hayden Book Company, Washington, D. C., 1973).

11. T. Y. Young and T. W. Calvert: <u>Classification, Estimation, and Pattern Recognition</u>, (Americal Elsevier, 1973).

12. K. S. Fu: <u>Syntactic Methods in Pattern Recognition</u>, (Academic Press, 1974).

13. W. F. Miller and A. C. Shaw: Proc. AFIPS Fall Joint Computer Conference (1968).

14. R. Narasimhan: Report 121, (Digital Computer Laboratory, University of Illinois, Urbana, Illinois, 1962).

15. Special Issues of PATTERN RECOGNITION on Syntactic Pattern Recognition, Vol. 3, No. 4, 1971 and Vol. 4, No. 1, 1972.

16. N. V. Zavalishin and I. B. Muchnik: Automatika i Telemekhanika, 86 (1969).

17. Ya. Z. Tsypkin: <u>Foundations of the Theory of Learning System,</u> (Nauka, Moscow, 1970).

18. M. A. Aiserman, E. M. Braverman, L. I. Rozonoer: <u>Potential Function Method in Theory of Learning Machines</u>, (Nauka, Moscow, 1970).

19. K. S. Fu: <u>Pattern Recognition and Machine Learning</u>, (Plenum Press, 1971).

20. A. G. Arkadev and E. M. Braverman: <u>Learning in Pattern Classification Machines</u>, (Nauka, Moscow, 1971).

21. R. Narasimhan: On the Description, Generation, and Recognition of Classes of Pictures, in <u>Automatic Interpretation and Classification of Images</u>, (Academic Press, 1969) ed. by A. Grasselli.

22. W. Stallings: Computer Graphics and Image Processing <u>1</u>, 47 (1972).

23. T. Sakai, M. Nagas and H. Terai: Information Processing <u>10</u>, 10 (1970).

24. S. K. Chang: IEEE Trans. on Systems, Man and Cybernetics, <u>SMC-3</u>, 257 (1973).

25. R. H. Anderson: Syntax-Directed Recognition of Hand-Printed Two-Dimensional Mathematics, Ph.D. Thesis, (Harvard University, Cambridge, Mass., Jan. 1968).

26. S. K. Chang: Information Sciences, <u>2</u>, 253 (July 1970).

27. A. C. Shaw: Rept. SLAC-84, Stanford Linear Accelerator Center, Stanford, California (March 1968).

28. B. K. Bhargava and K. S. Fu: "Application of Tree System Approach to Classification of Bubble Chamber Photographs", Techn. Rept. TR-EE 72-30, School of Elec. Eng., Purdue University, W. Lafayette, Indiana, Nov. 1972.

29. R. S. Ledley, L. S. Totolo, T. J. Golab, J. D. Jacobsen, M. D. Ginsburg, and J. B. Wilson: <u>Optical and Electro-Optical Information Processing</u>, (ed. by J. T. Tippett, D. Beckowitz, L. Clapp, C. Koester and A. Vanderburgh, Jr., MIT Press, Cambridge, Mass.) 591 (1965).

30. B. Moayer and K. S. Fu: "A Syntactic Approach to Fingerprint Pattern Recognition", <u>Pattern Recognition</u>, Vol. 7, No. 1, 1975.

126

31. B. Moayer and K. S. Fu: "An Application of Stochastic Languages to Fingerprint Pattern Recognition", Pattern Recognition, Vol. 8, 1976.

32. W. J. Hankley and J. T. Tou: Automatic Fingerprint Interpretation and Classification via Contextural Analysis and Topological Coding.

33. R. DeMori: A Descriptive Technique for Automatic Speech Recognition, IEEE Trans. on Audio and Electroacoustics, Vol. AU-21, 89 (April 1973).

34. A. Kurematsu, M. Takeda and S. Inoue: A Method of Pattern Recognition Using Rewriting Rules, Second International Joint Conference on Artificial Intelligence, London, September 1971, pp. 248-287.

35. R. H. Anderson: "Syntax-Directed Recognition of Hand-Printed Two-Dimensional Mathematics", Interactive Systems for Experimental Applied Mathematics, ed. by M. Klerer and J. Reinfelds, Academic Press, 1968.

36. T. Vamos and Z. Vassy: "Industrial Pattern Recognition Experiment - A Syntax Aided Approach", Proc. First International Joint Conference on Pattern Recognition, Washington, D. C. October 30 - November 1, 1973.

37. A. W. Laffan and R. C. Scott: "A New Tool for Automatic Pattern Recognition: A Context-Free Grammar for Plane Projective Geometry", Proc. Second International Joint Conference on Pattern Recognition, Lyngby-Copenhagen, Denmark, August 13-15, 1974.

38. R. L. Grimsdale, F. H. Summer, C. J. Tunis and T. Kilburn: Proc. IEEE, Vol. 106, Part B, No. 26, March 1959, pp. 210-221; reprinted in Pattern Recognition (Wiley, 1966) pp. 317-338.

39. M. Eden and M. Halle: Proc. 4th London Symposium on Information Theory, (Butterworth, London 1961) pp. 287-299.

40. L. D. Earnest: Information Processing, ed. by C. M. Poplewell, (North Holland Publishing Co., Amsterdam, 1963) pp. 462-466.

41. P. Mermelstein and M. Eden: Information and Control, 7, 255 (1964).

42. M. Eden and P. Mermelstein: Proc. 16th Annual Conference on Engineering in Medicine and Biology, (1963) pp. 12-13.

43. H. Freeman: IEEE Trans. Elec. Comp. EC-10, 260 (1961).

44. H. Freeman: Proc. National Electronics Conf. 18, 312 (1962).

45. P. J. Knoke and R. G. Wiley: Proc. IEEE Comp. Conf., 142 (1967).

46. J. Feder: Information and Control, 13, 230 (1968).

47. H. Freeman and S. P. Morse: J. of Franklin Inst. 284, 1 (1967).

48. J. Feder and H. Freeman: IEEE International Convention Record, Part 3, 1966, pp. 69-85.

49. C. T. Zahn: SLAC Rpt. 72, (Stanford Linear Accelerator Center, Stanford, Calif. 1966).

50. H. Freeman and J. Garder: IEEE Trans. on Elec. Comp. EC-13, 118 (1964).

51. R. Narasimhan: Comm. ACM 9, 166 (1966).

52. R. J. Spinrad: Information and Control 8, 124 (1965).

53. J. F. O'Callaghan: "Problems in On-Line Character Recognition", Picture Language Machines (ed. by S. Kaneff, Academic Press, 1970).

54. M. Nir, "Recognition of General Line Patterns with Application to Bubble-Chamber Photographs and Hand-Printed Characters", (Ph.D. Thesis, Moore School of Electrical Engineering, University of Penn., Dec. 1967).

55. R. Narasimhan: Information and Control 7, 151 (1964).

56. J. W. Butler, M. K. Butler and A. Stroud: "Automatic Classification of Chromosomes", Proc. Conference on Data Acquisition and Processing in Biology and Medicine, New York, 1963.

57. H. C. Lee and K. S. Fu: "A Syntactic Pattern Recognition System with Learning Capability", Proc. COINS-72, Dec. 1972.

58. A. Grasselli: "On the Automatic Classification of Fingerprints", in Methodologies of Pattern Recognition (ed. by S. Watanabe, Academic Press, 1969).

59. G. Levi and F. Sirovich: Info. Sciences 4, 327, (1972).

128

60. M. Nagao: "Picture Recognition and Data Structure", in Graphic Languages, (ed. by F. Nake and A. Rosenfeld, North-Holland Publishing Co., Amsterdam, London, 1972).

61. M. D. Kelley: "Visual Identification of People by Computer", Ph.D. Thesis Dept. of Computer Science, Stanford University, Stanford, Calif., June 1970.

62. L. G. Roberts: Optical and Electro-Optical Information Processing, (ed. by J. T. Tippett, D. Beckowitz, L. Clapp, C. Koester and A. Vanderburgh, Jr., MIT Press, Cambridge, Mass.) 159 (1965).

63. R. O. Duda and P. E. Hart: "Experiments in Scene Analysis", Proc. First National Symposium on Industrial Robots, Chicago, April 1970.

64. J. A. Feldman, et al: "The Stanford Hand-Eye Project", Proc. First International Joint Conference on Artificial Intelligence, Washington, D. C., May 1969.

65. T. Pavlidis: Pattern Recognition $\underline{1}$, 165 (1968).

66. A. Rosenfeld and J. P. Strong: "A Grammar for Maps", Software Engineering ($\underline{2}$, ed. by J. T. Tou, Academic Press, 1971).

67. T. Pavlidis: Pattern Recognition $\underline{4}$ 5 (1972).

68. T. Pavlidis: "Structural Pattern Recognition: Primitives and Juxta-position", Frontiers of Pattern Recognition (ed. by S. Watanabe, Academic Press, 1972).

69. M. L. Minsky and S. Papert: Project MAC Progress Rept. IV, MIT Press, Cambridge, Mass., 1967.

70. A. Guzman: Proc. AFIPS FJCC $\underline{33}$, Pc. 1, 291 (1968).

71. C. R. Brice and C. L. Fennema: Artificial Intelligence $\underline{1}$, 205 (1970).

72. K. S. Fu and T. L. Booth: "Grammatical Inference - Introduction and Survey", Part I and Part II, IEEE Trans. SMC, $\underline{SMC-5}$, (Jan. and July, 1975).

73. J. Feder: Information Sciences $\underline{3}$, 225 (July 1971).

74. M. C. Clowes: "Transformational Grammars and the Organization of Pictures", in Automatic Interpretation and Classification of Images, (ed. by A. Grasselli, Academic Press, 1969).

75. Laveen Kanal and B. Chandrasekaran: "On Linguistic, Statistical and Mixed Models for Pattern Recognition", in Frontiers of Pattern Recognition, (ed. by S. Watanabe, Academic Press, 1972).

76. R. Narasimhan: "Picture Languages", in Picture Language Machines, (ed. by S. Kaneff, Academic Press, 1970).

77. W. E. Underwood and L. N. Kanal: "Structural Description, Transformational Rules and Pattern Analysis", Proc. First International Joint Conference on Pattern Recognition, Washington, D. C., October 30 - November 1, 1973.

78. T. G. Evans: "A Formalism for the Description of Complex Objects and Its Implementation", Proc. Fifth International Congress on Cybernetics, Namur, Belgium, Sept. 1967.

79. M. L. Minsky: Proc. IRE 49,88 (1961).

80. M. B. Clowes: "Pictorial Relationships - A Syntactic Approach", in Machine Intelligence IV, (ed. by B. Meltzer and D. Michie, American Elsevier, New York, 1969).

81. T. G. Evans: "Descriptive Pattern Analysis Techniques", in Automatic Interpretation and Classification of Images, (ed. by A. Grasselli, Academic Press, 1969).

82. H. G. Barrow and J. R. Popplestone: Machine Intelligence 6, (ed. by B. Meltzer and D. Michie, Edinburgh University Press, 1971) pp. 377-396.

83. R. A. Kirsch: IEEE Trans. on Elec. Comp. EC-13, 363 (1964).

84. M. F. Dacey: Pattern Recognition 2, 11 (1970).

85. D. M. Milgram and A. Rosenfeld: IFIP Congress 71, (North-Holland, Amsterdam, August 1971, Booklet TA-2) pp. 166-173.

86. A. C. Shaw: Information and Control 14, 9, (Jan. 1969).

87. A. C. Shaw: J. ACM 17, 453 (June 1970).

88. J. L. Pfaltz and A. Rosenfeld: Proc. First International Joint Conference on Artificial Intelligence, (May 1969, Washington, D. C.) pp. 609-619.

89. A. C. Shaw: "Picture Graphs, Grammars, and Parsing", in Frontiers of Pattern Recognition, (ed. by S. Watanabe, Academic Press, 1972).

130

90. J. L. Pfaltz: "Web Grammars and Picture Description", Technical Report 70-138, Computer Science Center, University of Maryland, College Park, Maryland (1970).

91. J. M. Brayer and K. S. Fu: Web Grammars and Their Application to Pattern Recognition", Technical Report 75-1, School of Electrical Engineering, Purdue University, W. Lafayette, Indiana 47907 (1975).

92. T. Pavlidis: Jour. of ACM 19, No. 1, 11 (1972).

93. A. Rosenfeld: "Picture Automata and Grammars: An Annotated Bibliography", Proc. Symposium on Computer Image Processing and Recognition, Vol. 2, Aug. 24-26, 1972, Columbia, Mo.

94. T. Pavlidis: "Graph Theoretic Analysis of Pictures", in Graphic Languages, (ed. by F. Nake and A. Rosenfeld, North-Holland, Amsterdam) 1972.

95. W. S. Brainerd: Information and Control 14, 217 (1969).

96. J. E. Donar: "Tree Acceptors and Some of Their Applications", Jour. of Computer and System Sciences 4, (1970).

97. K. S. Fu and B. K. Bhargava: "Tree Systems for Syntactic Pattern Recognition", IEEE Trans. on Comp., C-22, 1087 (Dec. 1973).

98. B. Moayer and K. S. Fu, "A Tree System Approach for Fingerprint Pattern Recognition", IEEE Trans. on Computers, Vol. C-25, March 1976.

99. J. M. Foster: Automatic Syntactic Analysis, (American Elsevier) 1970.

100. A. V. Aho and J. D. Ullman: The Theory of Parsing, Translation, and Compiling, Vol. 1, Parsing (Prentice-Hall) 1972.

101 F. W. Blackwell: "Combining Mathematical and Structural Pattern Recognition", Proceeding Second International Joint Conference on Pattern Recognition, Aug. 13-15, 1974, Copenhagen, Denmark.

102. V. Grenander: "Syntax-Controlled Probabilities", Tech. Rept. Division of Applied Math., Brown University, Providence, Rhode Island, 1967.

103. K. S. Fu: "Syntactic Pattern Recognition and Stochastic Languages", in Frontiers of Pattern Recognition, (ed. by S. Watanabe, Academic Press) 1972.

104. V. A. Kovalevsky: "Sequential Optimization in Pattern Recognition and Pattern Description", Proc. IFIP Congress, Amsterdam 1968.

105. K. S. Fu: "Stochastic Languages for Picture Analysis", U.S.-Japan Seminar on Picture and Scene Analysis, July 23-27, 1973, Kyoto, Japan.

106. L. W. Fung and K. S. Fu: "Stochastic Syntactic Classification of Noisy Patterns", Proc. Second International Joint Conference on Pattern Recognition, Aug. 13-15, 1974, Copenhagen, Denmark.

107. V. Dimitrov: "Multilayered Stochastic Languages for Pattern Recognition", Proc. First International Joint Conference on Pattern Recognition, Washington, D. C., October 30-November 1, 1973.

108. H. C. Lee and K. S. Fu: "A Stochastic Syntax Analysis Procedure and Its Application to Pattern Classification", IEEE Trans. on Computers, C-21, 660 (1972).

109. T. Huang and K. S. Fu: "Stochastic Syntactic Analysis for Programmed Grammars and Syntactic Pattern Recognition", Computer Graphics and Image Processing, 1, 257 (Nov. 1972).

110. A. V. Aho and T. G. Peterson: "A Minimum Distance Error-Correcting Parser for Context-Free Languages", SIAM J. Compt. 1, No. 4, 305 (Dec. 1972).

111. L. W. Fung and K. S. Fu: "Stochastic Syntactic Decoding for Pattern Classification", IEEE Trans. on Computers, vol. C-24, June 1975.

112. M. G. Thomason and R. C. Gonzalez: "Classification of Imperfect Syntactic Pattern Structures", Proc. Second International Joint Conference on Pattern Recognition, Aug. 13-15, 1974, Copenhagen, Denmark.

113. R. Bajcsy and L. I. Lieberman: "Computer Description of Real Outdoor Scenes", Proc. Second International Joint Conference on Pattern Recognition, Aug. 13-15, 1974, Copenhagen, Denmark.

114. K. Hanakata: "Feature Selection for Compact Pattern Description", Proc. First International Joint Conference on Pattern Recognition, Washington, D. C., October 30-November 1, 1973.

132

115. S. L. Horowtiz and T. Pavlidis: "Picture Segmentation by a Directed Split-and-Merge Procedure", Proc. Second International Joint Conference on Pattern Recognition, Aug. 13-15, 1974, Copenhagen, Denmark.

116. T. Pavlidis: "Structural Pattern Recognition: Primitives and Juxta-position Relations", in Frontiers of Pattern Recognition (ed. by S. Watanabe, Academic Press) 1972.

117. S. Kaneff (ed.): Picture Language Machines (Academic Press) 1970.

118. A. Rosenfeld: "Isotonic Grammars, Parallel Grammars, and Picture Grammars", Machine Intelligence VI, (Edinburgh University Press) 1971.

119. K. Tanaka, J. Toyoda and N. Abe: "Some Studies on Web Grammars", Proc. First International Joint Conference on Pattern Recognition, October 30-November 1, 1973, Washington, D. C.

120. F. Nake and A. Rosenfeld (eds.): Graphic Languages, (North-Holland, Amsterdam) 1973.

121. Y. E. Cho: "The Generating Properties of Context-Free Picture Grammars", Proc. Second International Joint Conference on Pattern Recognition, Aug. 13-15, 1974, Copenhagen, Denmark.

122. R. S. Ledley: Programming and Utilizing Digital Computers, (McGraw-Hill, 1972).

123. John Albus: "Electrocardiogram Interpretation Using a Stochastic Finite-State Model", Proc. Conference on Computer Graphics, Pattern Recognition and Data Structure, May 14-16, 1975, Los Angeles.

124. S. L. Horowitz: Communications of ACM, 18, 281 (1975).

125. H-Y. F. Feng and T. Pavlidis: IEEE Trans. on Computers, C-24, 636 (1975).

126. K. S. Fu (ed.): Pattern Recognition, Communication and Cybernetics, Vol. 10, Springer-Verlag, 1976.

FEATURE SELECTION AND EXTRACTION FOR DECISION THEORETIC APPROACH AND STRUCTURAL APPROACH

K. Hanakata

University of Stuttgart
West Germany

I.   Introduction

The significance of feature selection and ordering is widely recognized in dealing with pattern recognition problems in practice. The relation between feature selection and classification is twofold. One is related to the recognition power of a recognition system and the other the cost performance. A good feature selection generally means the higher correct recognition rate for a given classification meahcnism on the one side. On the other, it means the lower cost of recognition processing which includes not only the measurement cost of features but also classification time and memory space as well. For example, in the case of classification of remotely sensed data we need one band-filter for each feature to be measured; or in the case of Zip-code recognition we need to process 3 or 5 digit numerals within the range of milliseconds.

With regard to the design of a whole recognition system, this means that if the construction of a good classifier is very expensive, we may eventually reduce the classification capability as low as possible, and instead, by enhancing the feature selection capability without losing the global recognition power. In dealing with the real recognition data we frequently encounter the cases where the classification part itself becomes so trivial by means of appropriate feature selection. Thus we try to design the optimal recognition system in terms of cost and performance by trading off the capability between the two subsystems.

These two subsystems are illustrated in Fig. 1.1. This procedural separation of feature selection from classification is due to a convenient self-explanation and not essential. This is particularly true when the Bayes decision rule is applied for feature selection and classification (see Section II.1) or sequential adaptive methods are used.

Corresponding to the variety of existing pattern recognition problems, a large number of strategies are developed in terms of general characteristics of the pattern space concerned. For instance, patterns are represented by a set of numerical measurements which are characterized by statistics of corresponding classes, or patterns are given as a set of elements which are related to each other by an underlying structure, and so on.

According to the rough classification of existing recognition approaches as pointed out in "Syntactic methods in pattern recognition" by K. S. Fu in this issue, methods of feature selection, extraction and ordering are also divided into two categories:

1) Feature selection in decision theoretic approach (decision categorizer model)

2) Feature selection in structural approach (syntactic approach, description-based approach, linguistic approach)

This rough classification of pattern recognition methods is due to the simple overview of the seemingly heterogeneous strategies of existing pattern recognition methods. There are also such methods which are not uniquely classified into one of the above categories but are based on both characteristics.

The function of feature selection in connection with a given
classification system may consist of the following three sub-
functions.

    a)   Specification of attributes (or property names)

    b)   Search of the specified attributes in a pattern descrip-
         tion

    c)   Measurement of property value.

The specification of attributes has been intensively investigated in the decision theoretic approach where the model of pattern information and category information are represented as a
simple form of a set. However, under some circumstances of complicated patterns such as picture patterns, or linguistic patterns,
the search of the specified property names and their values in the
depth of an implied structure is not trivial.

In the following, a brief review of methods of feature selection and ordering in the decision theoretic approach is discussed
firstly, and then followed by a method of feature selection and
generation for the structural approach.

II.   Feature selection, extraction and ordering in decision theoretic approach (review)

The existing methods of pattern recognition in the so-called
decision theoretic approach are based upon the simple representation model of patterns and categories. Patterns to be recognized
are represented in the form of vectors, and categories, to which
a given pattern is classified, are represented by a set of identi-
fiers. This representation model of pattern vector has proved to
be eligible in practice for a significant amount of existing recognition problems. This is partly because of the easiness and completeness of mathematical handling of vectors, (often it is tinged
with its aesthetics) and partly because of its fairly natural
generalization of real pattern data which sequentially occur as
time proceeds.

The function of a pattern recognition system generally consists thus on the whole in a mapping λ of the pattern vector space

R into the category space

$$\lambda : R \to \Omega \qquad\qquad\qquad (2.0.1)$$

In the practical implementation of this simple model of pattern recognition, the mapping function λ is divided into two mapping functions as shown in Fig. 1.1. The first function is designed to select the best subset of measurements with regard to some recognition performance criterion. As was mentioned earlier, if a given classification function exhibits its behaviour in a dynamic decision process, the selection function corresponds to the ordering one. It should be noted that if a class identifier is considered as a feature, then the second classification function is also interpreted as a special selection function which specifies only one feature, namely a class identifier in the category space.

In the following sections, for conceptual understanding of the relation between feature selection and classification, the feature selection in Bayes classification decision is explained. Then the existing methods of feature selection based on the representation criterion and separability criterion are briefly reviewed.

2.1 Feature-subset selection in Bayes classification decision

As is mentioned in the introduction, the function of feature selection is closely related to the function of classification with regard to classification power and cost. In decision theoretic approach conceptually the most intuitive way of dealing with both feature selection and classification may be to define a loss function in terms of classification decision and feature subset to be selected.

Let $L(\omega_i, d_j, X_\ell)$ be the loss which occurs if the classification decision d_j is made for the feature subset X_ℓ (ϵX) when the pattern X really belongs to the class ω_i. The a posteriori conditional expected risk is given for the selection $X_\ell (\epsilon X \sim \omega_i)$

$$r_X(P;d,X_\ell) = \sum_{i=1}^{m} L(\omega_i,d,X_\ell) \frac{P(X|\omega_i)P(\omega_i)}{P(X)} \qquad (2.1.1)$$

where P is a set of a priori probabilities of each class:

$$P = \{p(\omega_i) | i=1,2,\ldots m\}$$

For the given pattern X the problem is to decide the optimal d* and X_ℓ^* which minimize the a posteriori conditional expected risk (2.1.1), that is

$$r_X(P,d*,X_\ell^*) = \min_{d,X_\ell} \{r_X(P,d,X_\ell)\} \qquad (2.1.2)$$

An intuitive way of designing a loss function may be such that the function value increases along with the increasing number of features.

The Bayes' method of feature selection is conceptually simple to understand how feature selection and classification should be coordinated, however, practically it is difficult to find the optimal subset among the combinatorial number of subsets of a given large measurement set. This computational complexity may be avoided to some extent by applying the method of dynamic programming (see Section II.4).

2.2 Feature selection based on a representation criterion

The idea is that a good recognition with the lower cost postulates the good representation of the original pattern with a small number of measurements.

There are a large number of publications on this topic, therefore in this review a standard interpretation is given. For further details readers are recommended to refer to such introductory articles as Fukunaga [2, 1972] (Chapter 8,9), Fu [1, 1968] (Chapter 2), Watanabe [3, 1967], Tou [4, 1967].

The simplest form of a representation criterion is the minimum mean-square error. In the following, a version of generalized Karhunen-Loeve expansion is briefly given.

Let a stochastic pattern of class ω_i be

$$X_i = \begin{matrix} x_{i1} \\ x_{i2} \\ \cdot \\ \cdot \\ \cdot \\ x_{iN} \end{matrix} \qquad i = 1,2,\ldots m \qquad (2.2.1)$$

and be represented without error in terms of a set of orthonormal basis vectors $\{\psi_i | i=1,2,\ldots n\}$

$$\psi_i = [\xi_{i1}, \xi_{i2}, \ldots, {}_{iN}] \qquad (2.2.3)$$

$$X_i = \phi^T V^*_i$$

where the matrix ϕ consists of orthonormal column vectors.

$$V_i = \begin{matrix} v_{i1} \\ v_{i2} \\ \cdot \\ \cdot \\ v_{iN} \end{matrix} \qquad (2.2.4)$$

and

$$\phi = \begin{matrix} \psi_1 \\ \psi_2 \\ \psi_n \end{matrix} \qquad (2.2.5)$$

and * indicates complex conjugate. The covariance matrix of stochastic pattern vectors of m classes can be expressed as

$$K = E_i \{ E_{X_i} (X_i \, X_i^{*T}) \} \qquad (2.2.6)$$

Where E_i and E_{xi} denote class expectation of ω_i and pattern expectation X_i respectively.

By substitution of X_i given in (2.2.4) into (2.2.6) we have the form

$$K = E_i \{ E_{V_i} (\phi^T V_i (\phi^T V_i)^{*T})$$
$$= \phi^T E_i \{ E_{V_i} (V_i V_i^{*T}) \} \phi^* \qquad (2.2.7)$$

Suppose $\{X_i \; i=1,2,\ldots m\}$ have zero means without loss of generality, and

$$E_i \{ E_{V_i} (V_i V_i^{*T}) \} = \Sigma_V \hat{=} \{ \delta_{ij} \lambda_i \} \quad i=1,2,\ldots n \qquad (2.2.8)$$

i.e. the <u>uncorre</u>lated stochastic coefficients of <u>interclass</u> basis vectors with factor $\{\lambda_i\}$ and <u>corre</u>lated stochastic coefficients of each innerclass basis vector. Under these conditions for basis vectors the covariance matrix of (2.2.7) can be rewritten as

$$K = \Phi^T \Sigma_V \Phi^* \qquad (2.2.9)$$

The set of basis vectors and their coefficient vectors used for the expansion can be obtained from the equation followed from (2.2.3) and (2.2.9).

It is well-known that if we expand the original X_i by a subset of Φ say,

$$\hat{\Phi} = \begin{matrix} \psi_{\ell 1} \\ \psi_{\ell 2} \\ \cdot \\ \cdot \\ \psi_{\ell m} \end{matrix} \qquad m < n$$

$$\hat{X}_i = \hat{\Phi}^T \hat{V}_i^* \quad , \qquad \hat{V}_i = \begin{matrix} v_{i\ell_1} \\ v_{i\ell_2} \\ v_{i\ell_3} \\ \cdot \\ \cdot \\ v_{i\ell_m} \end{matrix}$$

so the mean-square error becomes

$$E_i\{E_{x_i}(|X_i - \hat{X}_i|^2)\} = 1 - tr(\hat{\Phi}^T \Sigma_{V_i} \hat{\Phi}^*) = 1 - \sum_{k=1}^{} \lambda_{\ell_k} \qquad (2.2.10)$$

under the condition (2.2.8) for $(i = \ell_1, \ell_2, \ldots \ell_m)$. Therefore, we conclude that in order to minimize the representation error we should select those m features that correspond to the upper m largest eigenvalues, i.e.

$$X_\ell^* = \{x_{ij} | j \epsilon \{\ell_k\} \text{ for } \lambda_{\ell_1} \geq \lambda_{\ell_2} \geq \ldots > \lambda_\ell > \lambda_\ell; \nabla_{\ell \notin} \{\ell_1 \ell_2 \ldots \ell_m\}\} \qquad (2.2.11)$$

Watanabe [5.1965] proved that this set of features selected by minimum mean-square error also minimizes <u>the entropy function</u> defined in terms of a normalized set of eigenvalues.

According to Chen [6.1967], if we normalize the original vectors

$$X_i^T X_i^* = 1 \qquad \text{therefore } V_i^T V_i^* = 1$$

then $\{\lambda_k\}$ for which

$$\sum_{k=1}^{n} \lambda_k = 1, \ 0 \leq \lambda_k \leq 1 \qquad (2.2.12)$$

minimize the entropy

$$H(\Phi) = - \sum_{k=1}^{n} \lambda_k \log \lambda_k \qquad (2.2.13)$$

This means that the weight coefficients of each class are more or less "sharply concentrated on a few coordinates which are to be considered as most informative for the corresponding class". From this result we can imagine that the larger the distance between two concentrations of weight coefficients and the more condensed each concentration, the easier the classes are separable.

2.3 Feature selection based on a separability criterion

In the last section it is shown that the feature selection based on the representation criterion also displays one aspect of separability of classes. There is no such general feature selection method which produces the optimal subset of features in all aspects of criteria related to any classification methods. Therefore, the separability criteria for the feature selection are fairly heuristic depending upon the proposed classification method. For this reason preferable conditions pertinent to the selection criteria to be established are roughly proposed, for example (Fu [1, 1968], Fukunaga [2, 1972]).

(a) Monotonic relationship between the percentage of correct recognition and features to be selected,

(b) Consistent with the classification transformation,

(c) Additive and metric properties, etc.

Which properties are more critical for a given feature selection method may depend on the situation where a specific classification method is adopted.

So far, a number of feature selection criteria based on the separability between classes are proposed. For instance, from the

informational point of view, <u>a measure of conditional entropy</u> may
well represent the separability between classes in terms of a
feature to be selected. According to Lewis [7, 1962], the average
conditional entropy for a feature f_j with the given feature measurements X_n is written as

$$T(f_j|X_n) = - \sum_{i=1}^{m} P(f_j,\omega_i,X_n) \log \frac{P(f_j,\omega_i,X_n)}{P(f_j)P(\omega_i)P(X_n)}$$

where

$$X_n = (x_1,x_2,\ldots x_n)$$
$$f_j \in F_r = F_N - F_n$$
$$F_N = (f_1,f_2,\ldots f_N)$$
$$F_n = (f_{t_1},f_{t_2},\ldots f_{t_n}) \qquad\qquad (2.3.1)$$

This conditional entropy measure, as is pointed out by Watanabe
[5, 1965] earlier, shows how much the feature f_j contributes to
strengthen the local concentration of measurements in an orthogonal coordinate space. Therefore, at n-th stage of feature ordering that feature f_j is selected from the remaining feature set
F_n which minimizes $T(f_j|X_n)$. Note that the large entropy means
the evenness of distribution.

Because of the sequential characteristics of this method, it
is appropriate for sequential classification (refer section 2.4.1).

Another approach to the general feature selection problem is
directly to relate the separability criterion to the distance between centers of local concentration of measurements. We select
those subsets of features for which the sample representations of
classes are located as far as possible.

The so-called divergence criterion between two classes (Green
et al [8, 1963]) are defined as difference between the two likelihood ratios of logarismic expectations, i.e.

$$J(\omega_i,\omega_j) = E(I_{ij}|\omega_i) - E(I_{ij}|\omega_j) \qquad\qquad (2.3.2)$$

where

$$I_{ij} = \log \frac{P(X|\omega_i)}{P(X|\omega_j)}$$

It is shown by Fu et al [9, 1970] that for the given two classes the error probability of classification decision in Gaussian distributions monotomically depends on the divergence measure $J(\omega_i, \omega_j)$. This means that in order to minimize the error probability, those features are selected which maximize the divergence measure.

As a simple extension to the case with more than two classes, a subset of features is found such that the minimal divergence of any pairs

$$J(\omega) = \sum_{i=1}^{m} \sum_{j=1}^{m} J(\omega_i, \omega_j) P(\omega_i) P(\omega_j) \qquad (2.3.3)$$

are maximized.

2.4 Feature selection and ordering in sequential classification decision

Non-sequential feature selection methods so far discussed in the preceding sections are general in the sense that they specify a set of features to be measured, independent of individual patterns, at most class-dependent (Watanabe) or class-independent (Fu, Chien). However, from the view point of classification performance this generality doesn't necessarily mean any advantage under certain circumstances, especially, in the case where the information of a specific pattern is sequentially available. In such a situation, feature selection mechanism can be so designed as to effectively use the sequential information of preceding measurements to exhibit an adaptive process for each individual pattern.

2.4.1 Application of Wald's sequential probability ratio test

Application of sequential decision procedures to pattern classification (Fu [1, 1968]) is directly motivated for reducing the number of features to be measured. Each time after one additional feature is measured, the sequential probability ratios

$$U_n(X_n | \omega_i) = \frac{P_n(X_n | \omega_i)}{[\sum_{q=1}^{m} P_n(X_n | \omega_q)]^{\frac{1}{m}}} \qquad i = 1, 2, \ldots m \qquad (2.4.1)$$

are computed and compared with the prespecified stopping boundaries for corresponding classes

$$A(\omega_i) = \frac{1 - e_{ii}}{[\prod\limits_{q=1}^{m} (1-e_{iq})]^{\frac{1}{m}}} \qquad i = 1,2,\ldots m \qquad (2.4.2)$$

where e_{ij} denotes the error probability for decision d_i while $X \sim \omega_j$. By this comparison all those classes are eliminated for which

$$U_n(X_n|\omega_i) < A(\omega_i) \qquad (2.4.3)$$

By lowering the boundaries appropriately depending upon the increasing number of measurements, we can advance the terminal classification decision. In this method, however, the order of feature sequence is assumed to be predetermined.

Another approach to accelerate the terminal decision is to combine this sequential method with a method of feature ordering based on a separability criterion, e.g. divergence (2.3.3) or conditional entropy (2.3.1). In this case, among the available features f_j (ϵF_r) after having measures $X_n = \{x_1,x_2,\ldots x_n\}$ that feature f_j^* is selected which maximizes $T(f_j|X_n)$ of (2.3.1), because f_j^* is on average most informative for the next decision.

2.4.2   Application of Gill's sequential decision tree

Application of conditional entropy measure to the modified generalized sequential ratio test (GSPRT) (Fu [1, Section 3.4, 1968]) may accelerate the termination of sequential feature measurement on the basis of the mutual information (2.3.1) or divergence criterion (2.3.3). However, it doesn't necessarily mean that it supplies the optimal sequence of features in terms of the sequential decision rule (2.4.3). The procedure for the state identification of a finite state machine may give us an appropriate formalism for forward sequential pattern classification and feature ordering. In the methodology of pattern recognition we generally tend to consider the recognition mapping λ in (2.0.1) as an assignment of a given pattern X to an unknown class ω_i. Most of the existing pattern recognition approaches are based on this

pattern-to-class direction, and quite a few are based on the other
way round. Theoretically this doesn't mean any difference, however, this attitude may well be reflected to the design of feature
selection and classification mechanism.

According to the procedure of state identification in a finite
automaton (Gill [10, 1962], Ginsburg [11, 1958]), a set of admissible states A(M) is defined as a collection of those states which
possibly includes the unknown initial state to be found. Suppose
that the state transition graph is known. The problem is then to
find an input sequence of the minimal length with which we can
specify the initial state among the given admissible states. With
the help of a state transition graph we divide the set of subsequent unknown states from the admissible states into a set of subsets, every one of which consists of subsequent states with the
same output symbol.

A decision tree for the initial state identification can be
built up by putting the given admissible set at the top of the
tree, i.e. root, assigning a branch to every input symbol, and a
subdivision of the subsequent states forms a node which follows
from the preceding node via an input branch. The following figure
(Fig. 2.4.2.1) (Gill [10, 1962]) illustrates an example of decision
tree with the admissible set

$$A(M) = \{S_2, S_3, S_4, S_5\} \tag{2.4.2.1}$$

for an automaton M Algorithm to construct the decision tree from
a given state transition graph is given in Gill [10, 1962].

Any unknown initial state S_i ($\varepsilon A(M)$) can be identified by any
one of the input sequences which lead from the root A(M) to those
terminal nodes in the decision tree which consist of a set of subsets each containing only one element.

In the above example, any one of unknown initial state in
$\{S_2, S_3, S_4, S_5\}$ can be identified by observing the output sequence
by the input sequence $\alpha\alpha\alpha$:

Table 2.4.2.2   Output sequence of $\alpha\alpha\alpha$ for each
possible initial state

Initial State	$\alpha\alpha\alpha$/output
S_2	000
S_3	010
S_4	101
S_5	100

It is known, that if the given identification problem is solvable
at all, then the maximal length of the input sequence ℓ is given
by

$$\ell \leq (m-1) \cdot n^m \tag{2.4.2.2}$$

where n and m denote the number of states in M and A(M), respectively. We notice that if we observe "0" output of the first
input, then we need only another input symbol   to identify the
initial state S_2 or S_3 depending upon the second output "0" or "1",
respectively.   From this example, it can be seen that the state
identification procedure by means of a decision tree can be applied
to the pattern classification and feature ordering problem.   An
automaton can be considered as a model of the hypothesis test
mechanism which takes as the input symbol a pair of class hypothesis and a feature specification.   When the automaton takes an
input pair (ω_i, f_j^t) then it makes a decision whether ω_i is acceptable with regard to the measurement of f_j^t, X_j^t and $(X_{j1}^1, X_{j2}^2, \ldots$
$X_{jn}^{t-1})$ so far measured and stored in the memory (capacity N).   If
it is acceptable, then it gives the output "1", otherwise "0".
This means that the automaton can restrict the number of possible
classes more strongly based on the additional feature measurement
X_j^t eliminating those classes for which X_j^t is improbable.

The decision tree (see an example in Fig. 2.4.2.2) of the
given hypothesis test mechanism consists of a set of possible
classes as the root, a set of branches each corresponding to a
range of a feature measurement, and a set of nodes denoting the

class subdivisions. Each subset of classes at a node indicates
that the elements of the subset are not distinguishable from each
other by means of the sequence of feature measurements given by the
route from the root to the present node. The class of a given
pattern can be identified by comparing the actual output sequence
with that of the decision tree for a specified input sequence. The
following steps describe the procedure to recognize the class of
a given pattern under the assumption that the decision tree for
the recognition problem is given.

    (1) Give all pairs of admissible classes and the first fea-
         ture specification and then observe each output.

    (2) Find the subsequent branch whose node corresponds to the
         set of binary outputs, and define those classes as an
         admissible set.

    (3) If the present admissible set consists of only one class,
         then the pattern belongs to the class. Otherwise repeat
         steps (1) and (2).

The above procedure can be improved to shorten the feature
sequence in the following way:

    (2)´ After giving one feature specification to the automaton
         and getting the resulting subset of possible classes,
         look for such a node which satisfies the following con-
         ditions,
         (a) it contains the same resulting subset,
         (b) it leads to a terminal node consisting of one ele-
              ment subset
         (c) the expected distance from this node to the termi-
              nal node is the shortest among those nodes which
              satisfy the conditions (a) and (b).

    (2)´´ change route from the present node to that node speci-
         fied by step (2) and (2)´ with the new feature sequence
         which follows the new node and its descendant terminal
         node.

An admissible set of classes at any node can principally be considered as a new problem with a restricted number of possible classes and still available features, and therefore any feature selection and classification methods may independently applied for the problem. However, because of the correlation between the preceding features so far measured and the remaining, and because of the uniformity it may be better to consistently use the same decision rules.

In the case that the sequential probability ratio test is applied for the admissible set of each node of a decision tree, the range of a feature measurement or combination of feature measurements which corresponds to a branch of a decision tree is to be calculated from (2.4.1) and (2.4.2). In order to find the expected shortest route from the root to a terminal node of one element subset, we generally order those features in the higher levels which contain the measurement ranges generating the accep-table subsets with the least number of class elements. In other words, the expected number of classes accepted by selecting the feature $f^*_{t_n}$ should be minimized:

$$E(N(\{\omega_k\}|X_n,F_{t_n})) = \min_{f_{t_n} \varepsilon F_{n\Omega_{X_n}}} \int N(\{\omega_k\}|X_n,F_{t_n})dP(x_n|X_{n-1},F_{t_{n-1}},$$
$$f_{t_n},\omega_k) \qquad (2.4.2.3)$$

$$F_{t_{n-1}} = f_{t_1},f_{t_2},\ldots f_{t_{n-1}} \quad : \text{ set of features selected so far}$$

$$F_n = F_N - F_{t_N} \qquad\qquad : \text{ set of features which are still}$$
available for selection

$$X_n = \{x_1,x_2\ldots x_n\}N(\{\omega_k\}|X_{n_1}F_{t_n}) =$$

$\{\omega_k|U_n(X_n|\omega_k) \geq A(\omega_k)\}$: Number of possible classes accepted after the observation of f_{t_n}

The feature sequence

$$F^*_{t_n} = (f^*_{t_1} \quad f^*_{t_2}\ldots f^*_{t_n}) \qquad\qquad (2.4.2.4)$$

148

which is ordered by (2.4.2.3) expectively minimizes the sum

$$\sum_{i=1}^{m} N(\{\omega_k\}|X_i,F_{t_i}) \qquad (2.4.2.5)$$

but doesn't necessarily achieve the strict optimum in the sense that the expected transition

$$E\{A(M) \to \omega_k|F_{t_n}\} \qquad (2.4.2.6)$$

is minimized. Therefore, the feature ordering given by (2.4.2.3) is suboptimal in the sense of (2.4.2.6). The alternative way to achieve the transition with the minimum length from the initial state to such a goal state that satisfies certain conditions, in this case

$$N(\{\omega_k\}|X_i,F_{t_i}) = 1 \qquad (2.4.2.7)$$

is discussed in Hanakata [12, 1970]. However, from the viewpoint of the computational complexity, it is much easier to obtain the suboptimal feature sequence given by (2.4.2.3) than the strict optimum by the backward procedure employed in this reference.

2.4.3 Application of Bayes' sequential test by dynamic programming methods (Chien et al [13, 1967])

The feature-subset selection by means of Bayes' decision mentioned in section 2.1 can be formulated in a sequential procedure. In this sequential procedure the Bayes loss function given in (2.1.1) is modified separating the cost of measurements X_n obtained so far $C(X_n)$ and the loss of decision in terms of ω_i and X_n. Therefore, the equation (2.1.1) can be written as

$$r_{X_n}(P,d,X_n) = \sum_{i=1}^{m} [C(X_n) + L(\omega_i,a,X_n)]P(\omega_i|X_n) \qquad (2.4.3.1)$$

Then, the average risk is expressed as

$$R(P,d) = \sum_{i=1}^{m} P(\omega_i) \cdot \int_{\Omega_{X_n}} r_{X_n}(P,d,X_n)aX_n \qquad (2.4.3.2)$$

Application of dynamic programming methods to this problem is proposed by Chien, et al [13, 1967].

According to the methods of dynamic programming, the expected risk for the measurement continuation at the n-th stage is calculated in terms of cost of continuation and the minimal expected risk at (n+1)th stage. That is,

$$\rho_n(X_n|F_{t_n}) = \min \begin{aligned} \min\{C(X_n, F_{t_n}) + \int \rho_{n+1}(X_{n+1}|F_{t_{n+1}})dP(x_{n+1}; \\ f_{t_{n+1}}|X_n, F_{t_n})\} \end{aligned}$$

$$\min R(X_n, d_i|F_{t_n})$$

(2.4.3.3)

where ρ_n : the minimum expected risk at the n-th stage

$R(X_n, d_i|F_{t_n})$: the expected risk of terminal decision d_i based on the measurements X_n for F_{t_n}

$C(X_n|F_{t_n})$: the cost of the decision for measurement continuation.

The maximal number of available features is predetermined as N, so $R(X_N, d_i|F_{t_N})$ can be obtained as a constant which is equal to $\rho_N(X_n|F_{t_N})$.

III. Feature selection, extraction and generation in structural approach

3.1 Structures in pattern space, category space and problem space

In the decision theoretic approach the recognition problem is generally formulated in terms of simple models of pattern representation, i.e. pattern vector, and category. A set of attributes is explicitly given, and the problem of feature selection consists in specifying a subset of these predetermined attributes such that a given recognition criterion is optimized. The subset of attributes which we call (or even define as) feature-set is supposed to characterize a class of patterns most effectively with respect to the given recognition mission, that is to say classification.

In the structural approach, on the other hand, objects with which we are concerned are characterized not only by their constituents but also by internal and/or external relations amongst them. These kinds of objects cannot be represented in a simple form of vectors without losing any basic information which is indispensable for the solution of recognition problems. Those pattern recognition experiments which have been ventured in the past in dealing with these kinds of structural patterns by means of decision categorizer model, are either unsatisfactory with respect to its recognition power (Kirsch [14, 1965]) or unsuccessful because of its overwhelming computational complexity.

One exception may be the case where the given recognition requirement is so moderate that rough categorization suppresses occurrences of bad results.

As is implicated in this exceptional case, the structural approach in general is also characterized by its complicated model of recognition mission in comparison with the simple model of classification in the decision theoretic approach. In the structural approach there is no such well-formed but rigid inflexible set of categories (Rosenfeld [17, 1969]). Instead, if we may accept this concept of category set and try to make it applicable to the structural approach, we have to introduce into the category model a kind of relationships among categories with respect to the existing relations within the space of recognition problems of our concern. One category may be independent of others on the same level or includes them as its subcategories etc. And corresponding to this structure a given recognition problem (or mission) may be related to a subcategory on a lower level such as a detailed question about a property contained in a pattern. Or it may be concerned with a category on a higher level such as a concept being specified by a set of properties.

The importance of features in the same sense as used in the decision theoretic approach is also pertinent to the recognition problem-solving in the structural approach. As the criterion of feature selection and ordering are formulated based on the model

of categorical information in the decision theoretic approach, a
certain kind of significance scheme may be built up within the
given structured pattern on the basis of the structured category
space. This, of course, means that such a significance scheme
should, for the reason mentioned above, reflect indirectly the
importance of features with respect to the recognition problems to
be given. In other words, it shows how "meaningful" a part of
the pattern, that is, constituents including relations, is with
regard to the present recognition problem. Therefore, the significance measure of features is expected to supply enough information for controlling the process of recognition problem solving,
i.e. structure analysis.

   3.2 <u>Top-down and bottom-up of recognition and description</u>
       <u>process</u>

   In dealing with structures of patterns, problems and categories, the whole process of recognition problem-solving cannot help
being similar in a certain aspect to that of human cognition. In
this respect there are a great deal of works done in the fields
of cognitive psychology, physiology and artificial intelligence.
Although the biological aspect of the whole perceptive and cognitive process is of intrinsic interest, it is left untouched in
the context under discussion.

   One point which seems to be of importance in connection with
the feature selection and extraction may be the duplex characteristics of top-down and bottom-up in the recognition and description process. In processing pictorial patterns which are considered as the representative type of structural patterns, following two characteristics are generally recognized:

    (1) the more complicated a given pattern becomes, the smaller
         is the ratio between a part of the pattern information
         which has direct relevance ot the present recognition
         problem versus the whole information the pattern conveys.
         Otherwise the complex recognition problem can be analyzed

into a set of subproblems, for each of which the above principle is valid.

(2) The lower the constituents of a given pattern become, the more common they are also in other patterns. The same type of lower constituents (e.g. in the extreme case, picture primitives) are more frequently found in patterns of given pattern space.

This is a practical reason why such lower-level constituents as edges, arcs, corner, intersection or curvatures of contour lines are extracted as most "meaningful" features (Uhr [15, 1973]) regardless of what kind of specific problem is presently given. That is to say, with very little risk a given complicated pattern can usually be preprocessed only with very global knowledge about the whole pattern space and problem space under consideration, instead of every detail of particular problems. In this respect, the preprocessing may be considered on the one hand, as for general-purpose, though it is restricted only to the lower level. On the other hand, for this very reason the preprocessing may be non-puposive because it still takes a risk of resulting in a higher-level discrepancy with respect to a particular problem in the context of problem-dependent structure in categorical space (Rosenfeld [17, 1969]). The resulting lower-level features may be considered in some aspects as a bottom-up clustering process from the lowest level of raw pattern data to a certain level of features. In picture patterns, for example, a small set of neighbour-ing image points (of the lowest level) are connected to each other in some direction so as to form a lower-level feature such as a line segment or an arc, etc. (Rosenfeld [17, 1969]). The result-ing lower-level features, which are mostly simple, are "supposed" to be used as a basis for constructing a set of higher-level fea-tures (Muchnik [18, 1966]) which are more problem-dependent (Hanakata [19, 1973]).

The boundary of these lower levels to the higher-levels is vaguely and very heuristically defined depending upon the allowable risk of possible discrepancies in the higher-level structure analysis.

More significantly, it may depend also upon the level of the general knowledge about problem space and category space. In other words, the lower the level of general knowledge becomes, the higher the low-level feature extraction. This means in turn that the problems to be treated with the given pattern are not much varied with respect to their levels.

Contrary to the bottom-up process of feature extraction (or generation in the sense of synthesis), the analysis process of problem structure, which is considered as a part of recognition process, is a kind of top-down way by means of the structural information in category space. Descriptions of given problems are analyzed according to the structure of the category space into a set of subproblems which may be in some intricate relationships. The problem of feature selection and ordering in the category space is then to find from the reduced subproblems an appropriate set of attributes (property names, see section I(a)) and relational predicates so that these subproblems are effectively solved by finding their corresponding values in a pattern description

The following scheme (Fig. 3.2.1) illustrates the relationship between pattern description, problem description and categorical representation.

The crucial analysis of the whole recognition process, namely the subproblem-solving takes place on intermediate levels where structured features of the given pattern from the bottom-up side meet subproblems of the given recognition problem from the top-down side.

3.3 Representation and description of structural patterns, problems and categories

The topics related to the representation of general structures are often fundamentally rooted to such an elemental theory as mathematical logic, theory of graphs and so on. Even in the

various fields of applied sciences themes are centered on this
topic in connection with data structure, linguistic structure, for
example.

Within the framework of structural approach there are a number of significant pioneer works which tried intentionally to express implicit or explicit structures of patterns as a description
base for recognition.

They can be classified roughly into the following two types:

(a)   Interpretation of pattern structure into a linguistic
      structure (linguistic approach)

(b)   Representation of pattern structure in a computer-based
      data structure.

In the first approach hierarchic relations within the pattern
structure is emphasized by introducing a kind of production operators or labels. There are many research works of these methods,
for example Kirsch [21, 1964], Ledley et al [22, 1965], Narasimhan
[23, 1966], Rosenfeld [24, 1969], Fu [25, 1972], etc.

The second representation method is closely related to the
techniques developed for computer graphic systems. In this method
consideration is made with respect to the effective memory organization of line-drawings, compatibility to the control mechanisms
of structure analysis, etc. Very little is based on some formal
theories, instead, rather the practical side of computer implementation is emphasized. On the other hand, it is very difficult to
clarify its general characteristics such as its description power
which has been well studied in the first method. A subarea of
artificial intelligence, namely computer vision in connection with
Robotics may be considered to have emerged from this approach. It
should be also noted that this is one of the methods in which an
inference mechanism based on the structured categorical information plays a significant role in the recognition process (Sutherland [26, 1963], Guzman [27, 1969], Whinston [28, 1973]).

So far, representation and description of structural patterns have been briefly mentioned. As far as these recognition problems or categories are concerned, very little has been done in the field of pattern recognition, but a lot of very ambitious works are being done in artificial intelligence. This ia partly because both substances involve the semantic structures of users to whom the whole recognition system is designed to serve. The processing of natural languages with semantic background, is one of the central themes of artificial intelligence. Another reason is that in dealing with complicated structures of patterns, problems and concepts, we cannot solve the whole problem complex only within the framework of classification function, but we need more powerful means such as an inference mechanism, with which we are going to challenge a fundamental problem of structural complexity.

A comprehensive discussion on the functions of pattern recognition from the point of view of artificial intelligence is beyond the scope of this paper and two introductory books Minsky [29, 1968] and Feigenbaum et al [30, 1963] are referred.

As is indicated in section 3.1 various problems of different levels are to be given in connection with a given structural pattern. It may refer to the texture feature or a diameter of the cardiac silhouette of lower levels, or it may ask the name of the disease of higher levels which is ascribed to a set of intricately structured diagnostic features. However, the knowledge about the range of problems gives the direction of importance and meaningfulness of lower level features.

The representation formalism of problems and category space may be greatly motivated by that of Question-Answering systems. At present there are basically two different methods for representing the structural knowledge. One is the representation method based on the predicate calculus (Sandwall [31, 1972]) and the other is procedural method (Hewitt [32, 1973]). Characteristic features of these methods are well described in Winograd [33,

1974]. In the area of artificial intelligence processing of natural language is centered on the representation of knowledge, which is considered as a model of structural category space in the framework of pattern recognition.

The model of category space contains general knowledge of subjects, for instance, inner structure, functional relation of constituents, properties and so on. A given pattern is considered as one sample, a realization of one particular Gestalt of subject. In connection with the processing of natural language a semantic network (Simmons [34, 1973]) is used as a model of large scale structure for a recognition base. Recently, Minsky proposed a new model of representing general knowledge called "Frame" combining the various advantages of different methods so far developed (Minsky [35, 1974]). Following is an example of a part of a Frame.

```
        NOSE is a part of FACE
            FUNCTION:   smell, breathe
            SHAPE:      vertical RIDGE a pair of NOSTRILS
                        at the bottom-triangle
                        at the bottom    in parallel
            LOCATION:   middle, vertical
            TEXTURE:    SKIN
            RELATION:   Under, between EYES
                        Above MOUTH
                        between CHEEKS
```

Fig. 2.3.1 A Frame for nose (part)

A Frame can be thought of as a collection of features and its further specifications (i.e. values) which may be again features or predicates in lower levels. The structural description of a given pattern is compared with a part of this complex of frames with regard to the specifications of a given recognition problem. For a recognition problem, whether the given object pattern is acceptable as a nose, feature values of a description of the pattern are checked against those of corresponding features of frames.

The following questions are crucial to the recognition power of
the system.

    (i)   In what order should the features be checked in order to
make the final decision as early as possible? (ref.
section 3.4).

    (ii) How detailed should the specifications of features in
frames be described? For example, a recognition question
whether it is a nose of a European or an Asian, cannot
be dealt with the above example of a frame.

3.4 Feature generation and extraction of intermediate levels

In section 3.2 importance of low-level features such as edges,
arcs, textures or intersections are discussed. These low-level
features are so general as to be almost independent of the problem
space of interest. An arc is as meaningful for chromosome patterns
as for fingerprint patterns. However, from the point of view of
description and recognition efficiency, they are not enough effective. It may generally be an accepted fact that the more general
the set of features becomes in terms of which a given pattern is
characterized or described, the more redundant is the description
and the less effective proceeds the description analysis. For
this reason, features should be as specific as possible for a
given class of patterns to the extent that they don't become very
inflexible.

For example, in natural languages, we have an alphabet which
is very general in nature (it is used for various languages!) and
corresponds to a set of pattern primitives (the lowest-level features). Words are intermediate-level features which specify a
given sentence to some extent. This is why the method of sentence
analysis by means of key-words works to some extent. Key words
are carefully selected so that they characterize a given subject.
The next higher level features may be idioms, etc. It is easy to
imagine how bad the performance of Key-letters system which iden-
tifies the semantics of a sentence by a carefully selected set of

letters, instead of Key-words of Key-idioms. In the structural
approach of pattern recognition, a set of pattern primitives is
very intuitively introduced, for example Freeman's octal codes
(Freeman [36, 1961]) or a set of primitive curves for chromosomes
(Ledley [22, 1965]), or a set of strokes for handwritten characters (Narasimhan [23, 1966]), or a set of vertex types for geometrical 3D-patterns (Guzman [37, 1967]).

Because of the reason mentioned above, a set of intermediate-
level features are introduced in some works. For example, a set
of horizontal features in terms of 7 stroke segment directions
i.e. primitives (Genchi [39, 1968]) are used for description of
handwritten zip code [see Fig. 3.4.1].

Another example of intermediate-level features is given for
the recognition of fingerprints in a syntactic approach (Fu [38,
1975]). In this method 69 canonical combinations in terms of 4
pattern primitives are formed (see Fig. 3.4.2).

Interesting is, that the authors say 'frequencies of occurrence of some combinations such as .... are high, and some others
may have zero expected value of occurrence. In fact, some combinations may be used as discriminating criteria between fingerprint
patterns and any other line-type configurations ...'. 'It is
obvious that 256 features are too many for any grammar, ...
Hence, a set of 17 features are chosen to represent 69 canonical
combinations: i.e. feature extraction is developed to make the
number of features feasible for the grammars'.

In both examples, the decision criterion for selection of
intermediate-level features is very heuristic. From the second
example we see a possibility to use the frequency measure as a
selection criterion for intermediate-level features. Hanakata [40,
1973] proposed to use entropy measure for this purpose. The
lower-level features are connected to each other hierarchically
building up the higher-level features, and those resulting higher-
level features are eliminated whose entropy is larger than the

upper boundary specified for the corresponding level. That means, those combinations of lower-level features are not eligible for membership of higher-level features, if their frequencies of occurrence within the pattern space are less than some threshold specified for each level. Features of each level which are generated in this way are identified by a feature name with a set of state parameters. A given pattern is <u>described</u> in terms of these features in the usual way of hierarchical connections of features and substructures. The entropy measures of features are used to control the matching process between the pattern description and the representation of the category space (Frames). If more than one feature is to be checked at any stage of the matching process, features are checked <u>in the order of their entropy measures</u> so that the number of "<u>back-ups</u>" caused by mismatchings which are inherent in nature are minimized (see the point (i) of section 3.3). An example of Tangram is programmed along this scheme (Hanakata [41, 1976]).

3.5 <u>Concluding remarks</u>

Feature selection, extraction, ordering and generation in both decision theoretic approach and structural approach are discussed. While a great deal of works have been done in the first approach on the basis of a simple model of patterns, recognition problem (i.e. classification) and categories, feature selection problem in the second approach has been studied very little, partly because of the complexity of problems in nature and partly because of the lack of proper models. In this paper the first two chapters are devoted to a brief survey of feature selection in decision theoretic approach and the third chapter is contributed to the same topic in the structural approach. In this chapter it is emphasized that feature selection should be performed not only from the original pattern, but also on the basis of the information about problem space to be handled and category space i.e. knowledge-base of the given pattern space. It is also emphasized that features are not only the pattern primitives but also their compositions. For a generation of an appropriate set of features, a hierarchical connection of continuous levels should be performed for the optimal pattern descriptions and structure analysis. Because of the limited space and the range of the subject the latter structure analysis was not discussed very much, although it is indispensable to discuss the feature selection in its context.

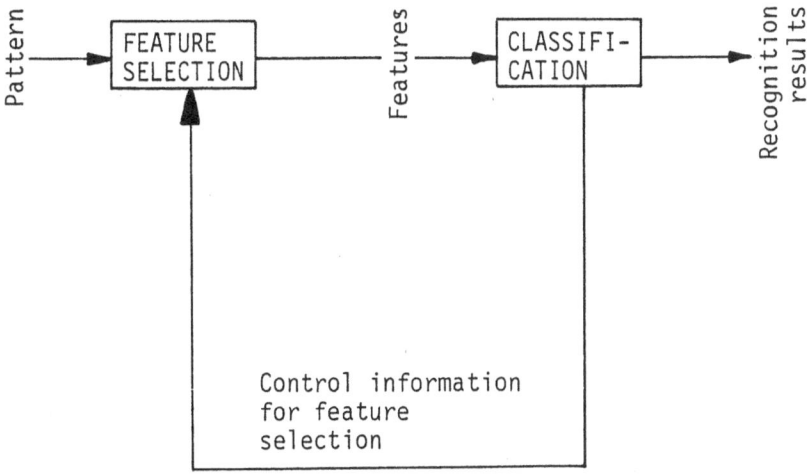

Figure 1.1

Table 2.4.2.1
State transition matrix (Input / Output)

State t+1 \ State t	S_1	S_2	S_3	S_4	S_5
S_1	α/o			β/1	
S_2	α/o				β/1
S_3	β/1				α/o
S_4			α/1	β/1	
S_5		α/1			β/1

162

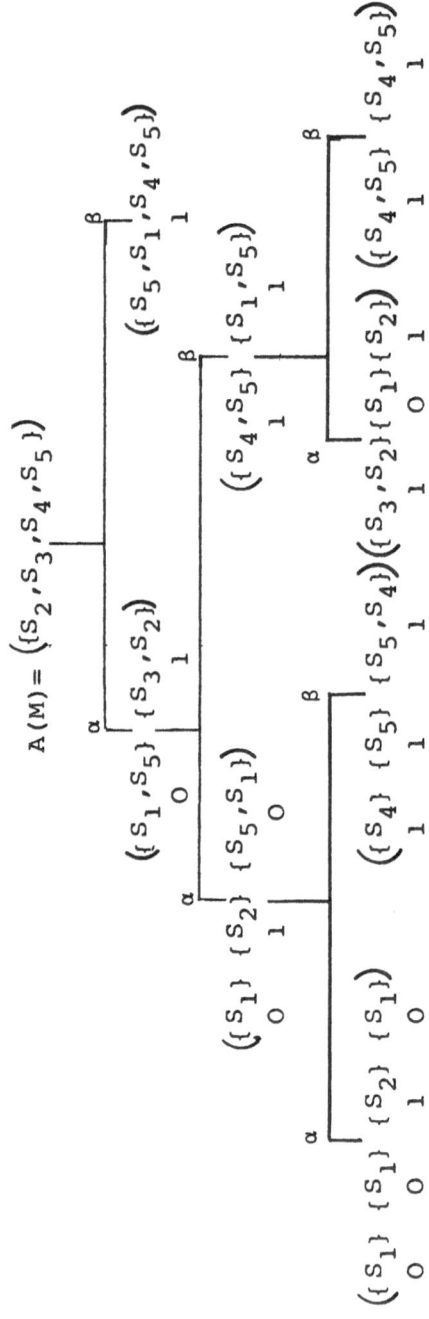

Figure 2.4.2.1
Decision tree for A(M) in M.

163

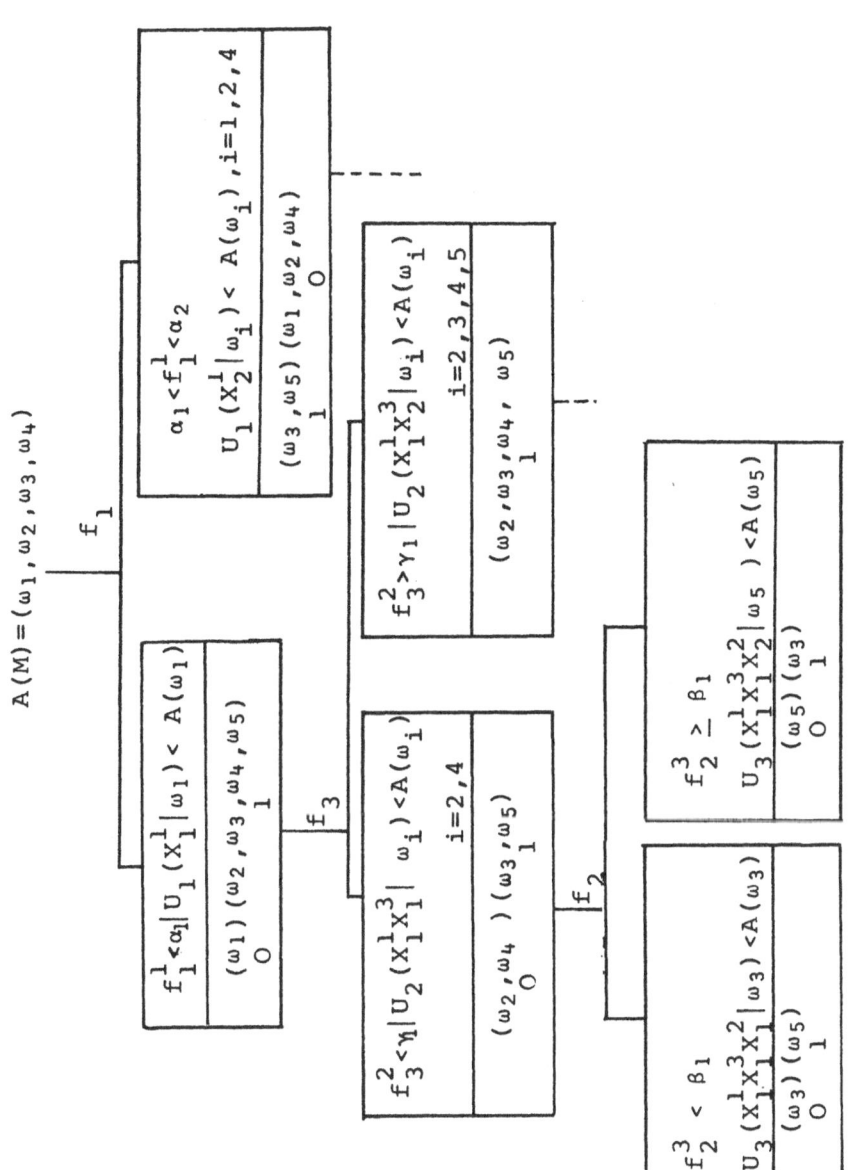

Figure 2.4.2.2

164

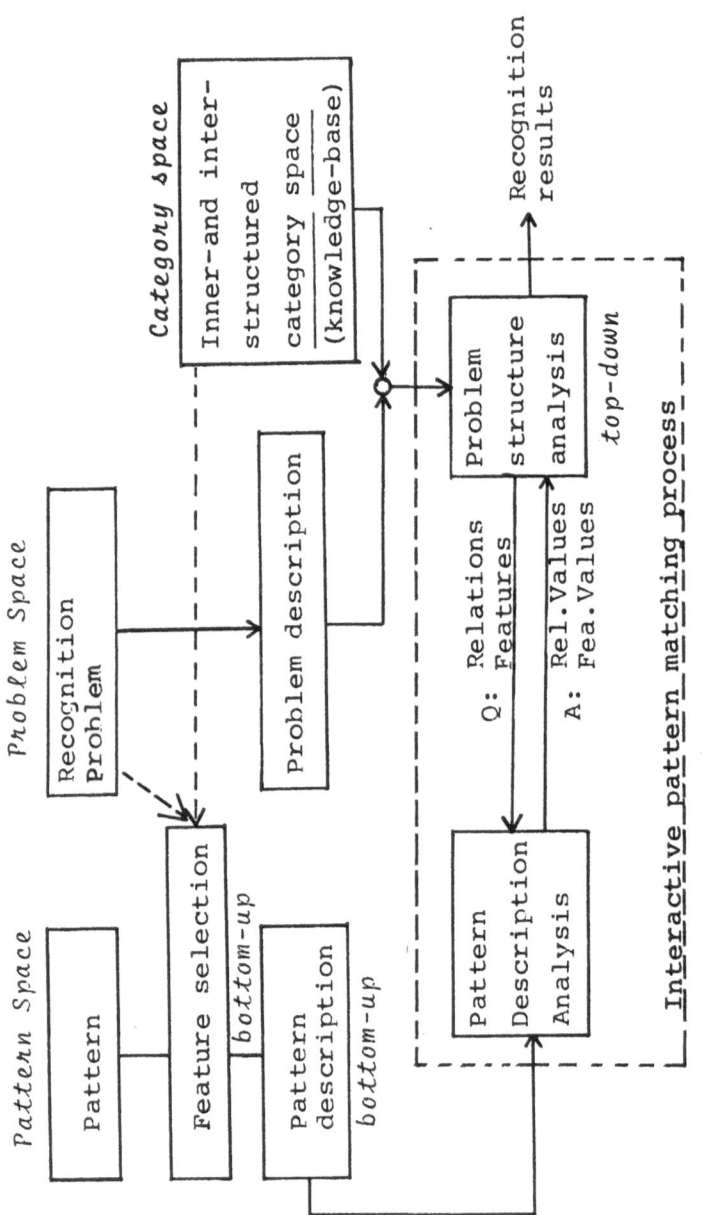

Figure 3.2.1

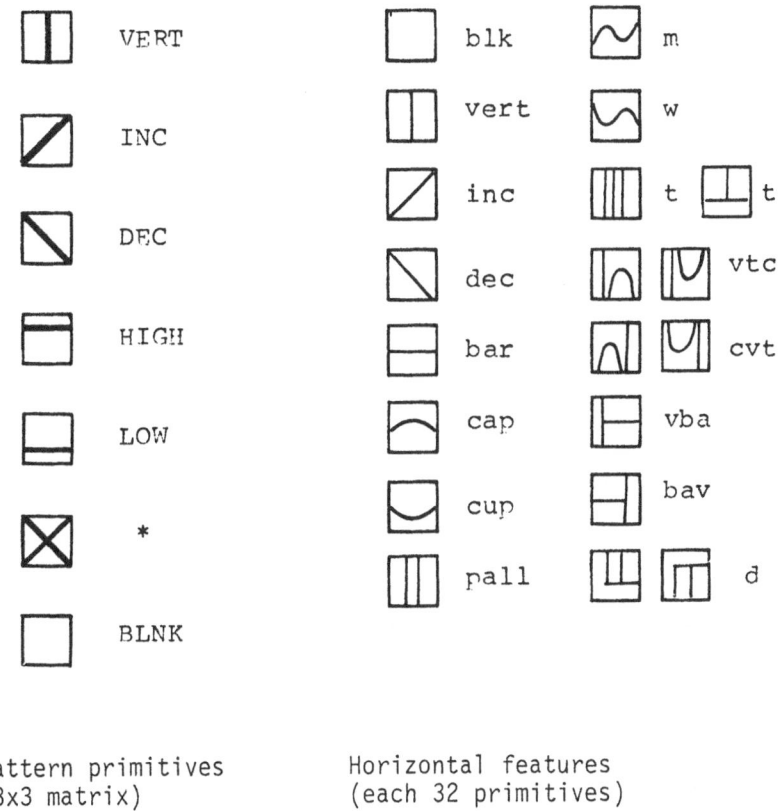

Pattern primitives   Horizontal features
(3x3 matrix)   (each 32 primitives)

Figure 3.4.1
A set of pattern primitives and intermediate-level features
(Genchi et al. [39, 1968]) for handwritten zip code.

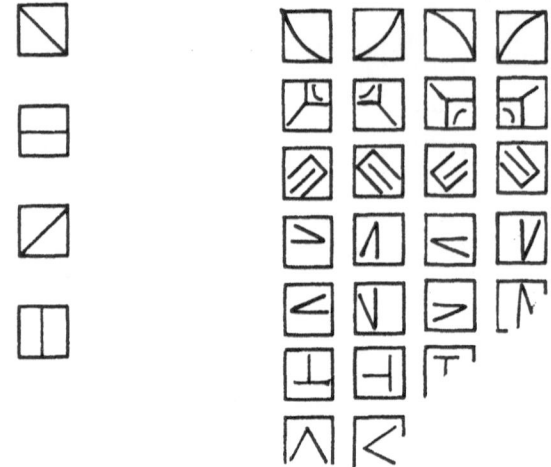

Pattern
primitives

Seventeen features for each direction
for representation of 69 canonical
combinations

Figure 3.4.2
Pattern primitives and intermediate-level features for
fingerprints (Fu et al. [38, 1975]).

References

Fu, K. S., Sequential methods in pattern recognition and machine learning, Academic Press, 1968.

Fukunaga, K., Introduction to statistical pattern recognition, Academic Press, 1972.

Watanabe, S., Evaluation and selection of variables in pattern recognition, in Computer and information sciences - II, J. T. Tou (ed.), Academic Press, 1967, pp. 91-122.

Tou, J. T. et al, Some approaches to optimum feature extraction, in Computer and information sciences - II, J. T. Tou (ed.), Academic Press, 1967, pp. 57-89.

Watanabe, S., Karhunen-Loeve expansion and factor analysis - Theoretical remarks and application - Proc. 4th Conf. Information theory, Prague, 1965.

Chen, Y. T., On the generalized Karhunen-Loeve expansion, IEEE Trans. on Information Theory, Vol. 13, No. 2, pp. 518-520.

Lewis, P. M., The characteristic selection problem in recognition systems, IRE Trans., IT-8, 1962.

Green, D. M.and Maril, T., On the effectiveness of receptors in recognition systems, IEEE Trans., IT-9, 1963.

Fu, K. S. and Min, P. J., Feature selection in pattern recognition, IEEE Trans. SSC-6, No. 1, Jan. 1970.

Gill, A., Introduction to the theory of finite-state machines, McGraw-Hill, 1962.

Ginsburg, S., On the length of the smallest uniform experiment which distinguishes the terminal state of a machine. JACM, Vol. 5, 1958, pp. 266-280.

Hanakata, K., Ein adaptive und lernfahiges System fur diskrete stochastische Prozesse I, II, Kybernetik, Nr. 7, 1970, pp. 196-200, 201-206.

Chien, Y. T., Cardilo, G. T. and Fu, K. S., A dynamic programming approach to sequential pattern recognition, IEEE Trans. Elect. Computer, EC-16, No. 6, 1967.

14. Kirsch, R. A., Lipkin, L. E., and Watt, W. C., The analysis, synthesis and description of biological images, Ann. New York Acam. Science, Vol. 128, 1965, pp. 984-1012.

15. Uhr, L., Pattern recognition, learning and thought, Prentice-Hall, Inc,. Englewood Cliffe, 1973.

16. Rosenfeld, A., Non-purpose perception in computer vision, Fachtagung "Cognitive Verfahren und Systeme", in Lecture Notes Nr. 83, 1973.

17. Rosenfeld, A., Picture processing by computer, Academic Press, New York, 1969.

18. Muchnik, I. B., Local characteristic formation algorithms for visual patterns, Automation and Remote Control, Vol. 27, No. 10, 1966, pp. 1737-1747.

19. Hanakata, K., Feature selection for sompact pattern description, Proc. of 1st Intern. Joint Conference on Pattern Recognition, Washington, D. C., 1973.

20. Nilsson, N., Problem-solving methods in artificial intelligence, McGraw-Hill, 1971.

21. Kirsch, R. A., Computer interpretation of English text and picture patterns, IEEE Trans. Elek. Computers, Vol. 13, No. 4, 1964, pp. 363-376.

22. Ledley, R. F., et al, Fidac; Film input to digital automatic computer and associated syntax-directed pattern recognition programming system, Optical and Elec.-Optical Inform. Processing, M.I.T. Press, Cambridge, Massachusetts, 1965.

23. Narasimhan, R., Syntax-directed interpretation of class of pictures, Commun. ACM, Vol. 9, No. 3, 1966, pp. 166-173.

24. Rosenfeld, A., Pfaltz, J. L., Web grammars, Proc. of 1st Intern. Joint Conference on Artificial Intelligence, Washington, D. C., 1969, pp. 609-619.

25. Fu, K. S., On syntactic pattern recognition and stochastic languages, Frontiers of Pattern Recognition, (S. Watanabe, Ed.), New York Academic Press, 1972.

26. Sutherland, I. E. Sketchpad, A man-machine graphical communication system, Lincoln Lab, M.I.T., TR-296, 1963.

27. Guzman, A., Computer recognition of three-dimensional objects in a visual scene, MAC-TR-59, M.I.T., Cambridge, Massachusetts, 1969

28. Winston, P., (Ed.), Progress in vision and robotics, M.I.T., AI-Lab, TR-281, Cambridge, Massachusetts, 1973.

29. Minsky, M., (Ed.), Semantic information processing, Cambridge, M.I.T., Massachusetts, 1968.

30. Feigenbaum, E. A., Feldman, J. (Ed.), Computer and thought, McGraw-Hill, New York, 1963.

31. Sandwall, E., PCF-2, A first-order calculus for expressing Conceptual information, University of Uppsala, Computer Science, Department, February 1972.

32. Hewitt, C., Procedural embedding of knowledge in PLANNER, Proc. of 2nd Intern. Joint Conf. on Artificial Intelligence, September 1971, London, pp. 167-182.

33. Winograd, T., Five lecture notes on Artificial Intelligence, Stanford University, Artificial Intelligence Lab. MEMO AI-246.

34. Simmons, R., Semantic networks in Computer models of thought and language, Schank and Colby (Ed.), San Francisco, 1973.

35. Minsky, M., A framework for representing knowledge, M.I.T., AI-Memo 306, 1974.

36. Freeman, H., On the encoding of arbitrary geometric Configurations, IRE Trans. Electronic Computers, EC-10, 1961, pp. 260-268.

37. Guzman, A., Decomposition of a visual scene into bodies, Project MAC, MAC-M-357, M.I.T., Cambridge, Massachusetts, 1967.

38. Fu, K. S., A syntactic approach to fingerprint pattern recognition, Pattern Recognition, Vol. 7, No. 1/2, 1975, pp. 1-23.

39. Genchi, H. et al, Recognition of handwritten numerical characters for automatic letter sorting, Proc. of the IEEE, Vol. 56, No. 8, 1968, pp. 1292-1301

40. Hanakata, K., Feature selection for compact pattern recognition, Proc. of 1st International Joint Conference on Pattern Recognition, Washington, D. C., 1973, pp. 416-422.

41. Hanakata, K., TANGRAM: A computer simulation of Tangram play by means of a deductive system (in preparation).

SOME OBSERVATIONS AND EXPERIMENTS ON THE
ELEMENTS FOR A PICTURE LANGUAGE

T. Kasvand

Computer Graphics Section, Electrical Engineering
National Research Council of Canada
Ottawa, Ontario K1A 0R8 CANADA

Summary:

Numerous linguistic and syntactic procedures have been proposed for scene analysis but the features in terms of which a
real scene can be modelled have not been defined comprehensively.
In the processing of the image of a realistic scene a profusion
of ad hoc "features" can be obtained. To find a predefined combination of features from such a collection, even on a proba-
balistic basis, results in a combinatorial explosion.

In the literature on psychology of vision, on the effects
of brain damage, on how to draw pictures, etc., there is a wealth
of hints on how "biological systems" appear to solve the scene
analysis problem. To biological systems scene analysis "comes
naturally"; one is not even aware that problems exist. In this
article an attempt is made to compare observational results from
these fields with our computational procedures. Even though the
results are rather preliminary, the following overall impressions
may be worth noting:

    i) In analysis of images, the biological system uses
        numerous (organization rules" which reduce the com-
        binatorial problem to manageable proportions or may
        even largely eliminate it.

172

    ii) The observed processing strategies in biological image
analysis differ greatly from our present computational
procedures.

By the studying the biological processing strategies, it is
hoped that greater understanding is achieved on a problem which
at present appears insoluble. The present article is a highly
condensed version of a report (1) and somewhat complementary to
a previous article (2).

I. Introduction

The author has programmed several practical but restricted
pattern recognition programs (3,4). As usual, after considerable
programming effort, a specialized system is obtained which can
neither be generalized conceptually nor practically. This led to
the development of a so-called "picture language" system, to
which, one hoped, the different specific problems could be taught
(5). Even though this language was quite primitive compared to
present-day theories (6), one could teach it a practical problem
in a few hours compared to several months of programming required
to solve the same problem as a specific case. On simple objects
the program behaved quite intelligently. However, on more complicated objects, the principle of building up a total description from indentifiable fragments was found inadequate.

In light of these experiences and those of others one is
forced to conclude that some rather fundamental principles
necessary for the solution of the pattern recognition and scene
analysis problem have been ignored. To solve the present impasse
attempts are made to extract results, observations and theories
from any field of endeavour which relates to the problem of scene
analysis and pattern recognition. The author is well aware of
the dangers in trying to interpret such findings as hints to the
nature of the underlying algorithms and claims no special expertise in all the fields from which material has been obtained.
However, to quote from KNOWING AND GUESSING by Dr. S. Watanabe,

"Yet an amateur has a fresh sense of 'amazement', a balanced bird's-eye view of tremendous scope, and a direct contact with the world of common sense which is the mother earth of all knowledge."

II. Biological vs. Algorithmic Information Processing

Human and animal information processing systems have evolved to facilitate survival and orientation in space. They supply quick answers to questions of the type: What might it be? What is it doing? These systems form hypotheses and make decisions based usually on very sparse evidence. They do not represent the world "as it really is" in the sense of engineering, physics and mathematics (7). The senses operate in a unitary fashion (8a) as exemplified by the frequent confusion of smell and taste. Nor do the principles of logic or mathematics correspond to our instinctive understanding (8b) of these problems, as, for example, portrayed in everyday language. Thus 1 man + 1 man = 2 men, but 1 man + 1 horse = 1 rider. Serious thought has been given to the integration of the senses (9), and somehow our algorithmic treatments of such problems will have to be reconciled with these facts.

Reason for Studying Biological Systems:

The solution of the scene analysis and pattern recognition proglem is so natural to us that it does not even appear as a problem until we try to solve a similar problem with a computer. One reason for studying the "biological solution method" is thus obvious: there is a procedure to be discovered that actually works. The other, and much more important reason is that the algorithmic (computerized) solution will have to give similar results on the same problem as the biological one. How else are we to agree with our machines as to what a particular object is or what a scene depicts? Our opinion as to what a scene represents is the standard to which the algorithmic solution will have to conform. This constraint, of course, does not apply in situations where our own inate capabilities are insufficient (for example in image enhancement or in reconstruction of the original from multiple projections).

A Paradox:

On the assumption that identification or recognition requires some form of prior knowledge in terms of which the unknown input (object, scene) is to be interpreted, one encounters in the general case a rather basic paradox. To identify an as yet unknown object in an unknown scene, the object will have to be extracted, described and compared with previously stored (known) descriptions. The unknown object, however, cannot be extracted before its identity is known, unless all possible combinations of features have been tried. This fundamental difficulty is further complicated by our own superbly developed ability to abstract the significant descriptors of a scene and to elaborate on them in terms of our stored knownledge and "built-in" reactions. The well-drawn caricature of a face, for example, is only in remote (mathematical) correspondence with a photograph of the same face.

This paradox can be sidestepped in numerous ways in particular situations. If for example, the objects are distinct from the background, known to be non-touching and unbroken, contour following is often used, yet we ourselves are not aware of this paradox, i.e. we experience no apparent difficulties with the "combinatorial problem". Our abilities to solve such combinatorial problems, however, are actually quite poor.

Image Input and Preprocessing:

The "biological pattern recognition systems" have two eyes and are mobile. The computerized approach to scene analysis in most cases uses a single gray level photograph or a TV image. In so doing a large part of the information available to the biological system has been degraded or lost. For example, Table I gives 13 cues to depth perception. The effects due to motion of the observer and the correlation of the images in the two eyes figure prominently. Consequently, on the "feature detector" (retinal field) level (10,11) many of the feature detectors react to change in space and time. Algorithms for detection of these features do not appear to be very difficult, but they have not been studied very intensively (12,13). In general, however, the profusion of results obtained from these operations are not as easy to use as was initially believed.

Local Organization of Features:

In a general case, the number of local features that can be obtained algorithmically is very large. All the expected features will not be present while there are many extraneous ones. To try all the possible combinations becomes impossible in practice.

Biological information processing systems seem to avoid the combinatorial problem by having evolved a set of processing strategies according to which individual feature elements are to be combined. Such a procedure naturally reduces the number of possible combinations that need to be compared against some model (i.e. related to previous knowledge). Even though the experiments from which the underlying procedures (the so-called Gestalt laws) have been elucidated have been done on simple figures, presumably the results carry over into scene analysis (see Appendix A). Systematic computer simulations of these laws seem not to have been undertaken (14).

Selective Search for Information:

In computerized procedures each processing step is normally carried to completion over the entire picture before the next computing step is started, even though selective processing reduces the computational load significantly (15,16). The procedures according to which the biological system samples a scene may be inferred from the studies of eye motion. Much pertinent information which computer programming requires is still lacking, but it is known that a person neither scans the scene nor does he sample it it random. Very elegant strategies are involved. It is found that a person looks at (fixates) regions in the picture which carry most information for the given problem that he is faced with (see Appendix B). Some computer simulations exist (17,28).

Scene Segmentation:

The evidence on how or whether a biological system actually segments a scene needs qualifications as to what is meant by segmentation. If segmentation is to mean separation of a scene into meaningful objects, then there is a definite possibility that scene segmentation in the biological system is obtained after the analysis has been completed. A superficial analysis of the scene is completed very rapidly and without an apparent fixed strategy (18), but whether this results in "segmentation" is open to question. On the feature level, for example, moving and flickering "things" catch our attention immediately, but whether this is called segmentation or an input for selective search is uncertain.

Structural Descriptions:

The, to linguists, most interesting aspect of the human information processing system concerns the existence of a picture language. There are hints that such a language exists. The clearest indications of its nature are obtained from studies on damaged systems where various aspects of the information processing strategy or some "preprocessors" have failed, (see Appendix C), and from the studies on developing systems when the structural descriptions are being formed, (see Appendix D).

Additional evidence on structure may be found in the works of artists. They reduce a complex scene to a rather limited set of lines, colour combinations and so on. The caricature or cartoon artist in particular, specializes in representing a scene in a minimal set of lines. In the majority of cases we are satisfied with these representations. The few lines drawn by the artist apparently closely approximate the information we normally extract during examination of the original scene.

III. Strategies for Scene Analysis and Recognition

At the start the scene will be assumed to be totally unknown, i.e. no prior information of any kind is available regarding the contents of the scene. Under this assumption, the processing of the scene can only proceed in stages where the results of one calculation may indicate which calculates are expected to be appropriate in the second stage, etc. This poses the question: What can be computed from the picture in the absence of any prior knowledge?

A specific object can be assumed to be a unique combination of measurable spatial as well as temporal characteristics. However, in general it cannot be assumed that an object possesses measurable characteristics which are unique to this object alone and which can be extracted in the absence of any prior knowledge. Not even a class of objects, it seems, can be defined in terms of uniquely measurable characteristics without prior knowledge. The exceptions occur on the "simple" feature level, where a class may be defined as "anything moving", all flickering things", "areas of given colour", etc. Scene analysis resembles an investigation by a detective where, it is claimed, quickest progress is made by finding answers to the following questions: i) What to look for? ii) How to look for it? iii) Where to look for it? Three approaches are proposed, one on the global, the second on the macro and the third on the micro level.

Global Computations:

The purpose of the global calculations is only to determine the general nature of the scene. Answers to questions of the following type are sought:

a. Is the picture representing a world of straight edges? ("Block world", office scene, etc.)

b. How are the details in the picture distributed? (If there uniform areas, where are they? Which areas are full of detail? Etc.)

c.   Is there periodicity to the data in the picture?

d.   Where are the more pronounced contours?

e.   Any areas of uniform texture?

The above list is only intended as an illustration of the nature of the questions to which answers can be found without need to know what the scene represents (1,2). It is likely that somewhat similar operations are carried out by peripheral vision (18). The scene can be segmented according to the nature of the information obtained from such calculations. However, the information derived and the resulting segmentation is in general not specific to any particular object in the scene, even though a classification of these scene segments is now feasible.

Computations on Micro Level:

On the micro or local level in the scene a profusion of "features" are available from the local operations. The operation that produced a given local feature (for example, gradient, contour) has of course, automatically identified it. The local features can thus be considered recognized and the scene can be segmented based on the micro-level results. But, as in the global case, generally the segments are not unique objects. The local features are, however, too unreliable and far too numerous to be formed into all possible combinations for the purpose of matching against known data.

Computations on Macro Level:

It is felt that the macro-level computations are the links that tie the global and micro-level computations together. The algorithms which produced the micro-level results have identified (recognized) the local features. Likewise, the global computations have identified the nature of the regions in the picture. Neither procedure, however, will locate or identify an object in the scene, except in some exceptional case.

It is believed that the macro-level results should be "coherent" collections of micro-level results which allow computer manipulations, such as size normalization, rotation, etc. It is desirable and likely that the computational algorithms at the macro level also produce automatic identification of the results. There are two problems, however, that need to be clarified, namely, the variability and the combinatorial problem.

Table II lists the more obvious changes that an object in (or a segment of) a scene can undergo. It is clear that a procedure (such as mask matching) which requires a search through the entire variability space is totally impractical. The alternative is to arrange the form of the fragment description and to use parameters (features, primitives) that go into the description such that the description becomes:

a) invariant with respect to the entries in Table II. If this fails for all or some of the table entries, then it should be

b) separable, i.e. the effect of each variability dimension should be decoupled. This allows a search only along the particular variability-axis, rather than through the entire space.

If neither of these conditions on the fragment description can be satisfied, the description is useless in a general case. To repeat, the primitives as well as the form of the gragment description have to be normalizable before any comparison operation is attempted. At least limited adherence to (a) and (b) is feasible experimentally (5).

Biological systems have, of course, encountered the combinatorial problem and rather than trying to form all the possible combinations of features, they have evolved a set of organization rules (see Appendix A). These rules operate on "extended-local" or "semiglobal" level, compete among each other and are overruled by any combination of features that makes up a meaningful object. In psychology literature these organization rules go under the name of "good continuation", "grouping by proximity and similarity", etc. Computer simulations of these "rules" do not seem to have been done, except possibly in following a contour or line which contains gaps.

IV. Conclusions

The computations for "global features" should be used to help the attempts to organize the features from the micro-level. However at present, the results of these calculations are too numerous and there are too many methods. These procedures will have to be guided by a picture language as soon as the first hypothesis can be formulated as to what an area in a scene might represent. The picture language will have to use primitives that are computable from a scene: (a) in the absence of prior information and (b) in the presence of hypotheses provided by the language. The picture language must be able to guide the search by providing tentative answers to the three questions: What to look for? How to look for it? and, Where to look for it? It is not certain, however, whether we are at present capable of putting such a system together.

The enormous amount of information available on "biological pattern recognition systems" has some relevance to computerized procedures. The few parallels drawn in this paper are tentative. The only real need to study biosystems is to make sure that computer interpretation of, for example, a scene, agrees with our own understanding of it. However, it may also be interesting to know what the research and development on biological systems (evolution) has achieved in the last 10^9 years.

The observations in the present article and the more detailed comparisons between human and computer vision (19,20) are essentially pointing out that a realistic picture language should try to employ the principles found in biological information processing systems. At present only specific instances of the operation of these principles are observed, some of which have been described. The situation is similar to trying to elucidate (or formulate) the laws of aerodynamics by observing birds in flight. Furthermore,

it is to be expected that biological information processing procedures are greatly influenced by the nature of the underlying "hardware", which is so different from the conventional computer hardware.

Figures A1 to A10: Some examples of "the laws of organization".
(After P.A. Kolers [7, M. Wertheimer])

```
x  o  x  o  x  o          x  o    x  o    x  o
x  o  x  o  x  o          x  o    x  o    x  o
x  o  x  o  x  o          x  o    x  o    x  o
x  o  x  o  x  o          x  o    x  o    x  o
x  o  x  o  x  o          x  o    x  o    x  o
x  o  x  o  x  o          x  c    x  o    x  o
x  o  x  o  x  o          x  o    x  o    x  o
x  o  x  o  x  o          x  o    x  o    x  o
```

Figure A1
Grouping by similarity.
Columns of x's and o's may
be seen easier than rows
of xoxoxo.

Figure A2
Grouping by proximity.
Three columns of xo's may be
seen easier than other combinations.

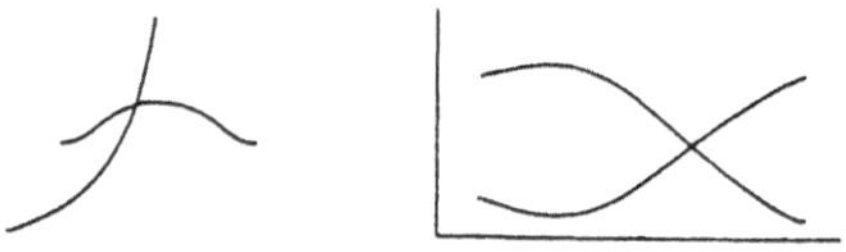

Figure A3
Principle of good continuation. Two crossing smooth curves may be
seen easier than two v-shaped curves joined at apices.

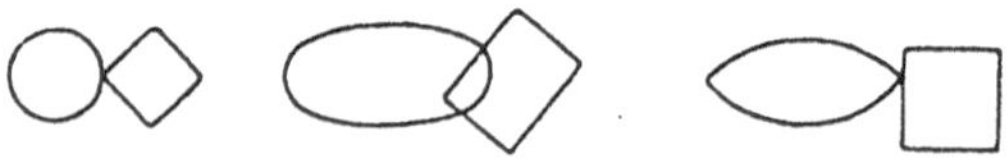

Figure A4
Law of closure. Closed contours or "complete objects" appear as
"wholes".

Figure A5
Cooperation and conflict between grouping by similarity and
proximity.

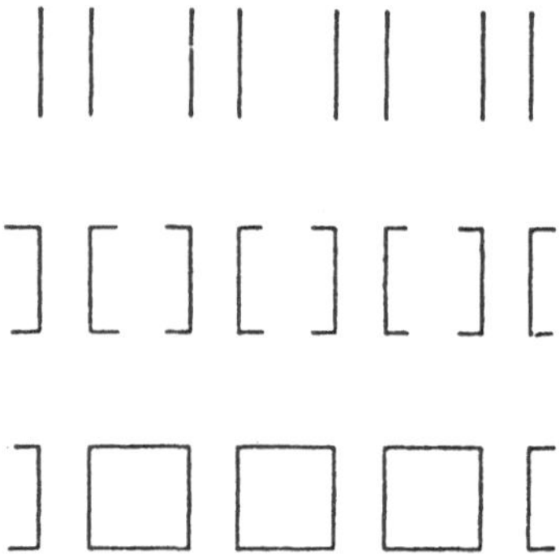

Figure A6
Law of closure overrides grouping by
proximity and similarity.

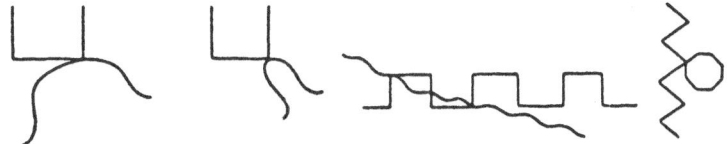

Figure A7
Law of closure overrides the principle of good continuation.

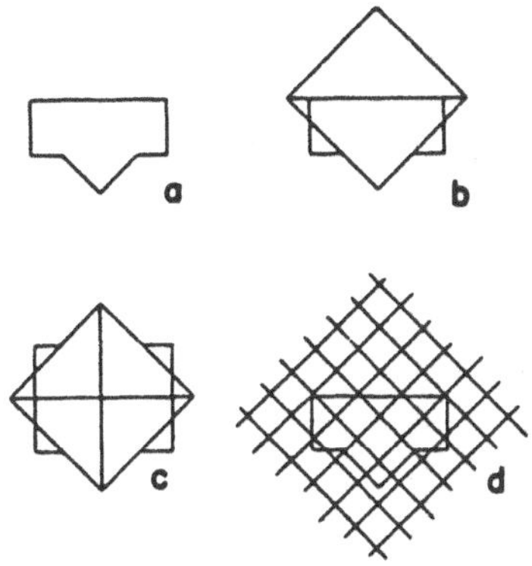

Figure A8
Proper (b,c) and improper (d) methods of camouflaging an object (a). Use of grouping, continuation and closure laws to hide the original object. "Principle of camouflaging".

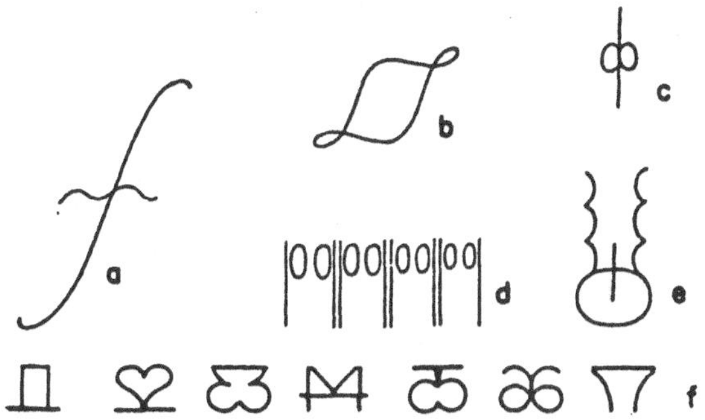

Figure A9
Examples of camouflage:
(a,b) combinations of script I and L;
(c) combination of b and q;
(d) of many p's and q's;
(e) of script 3,4,E and S;
(f) what is the next term in this series ?

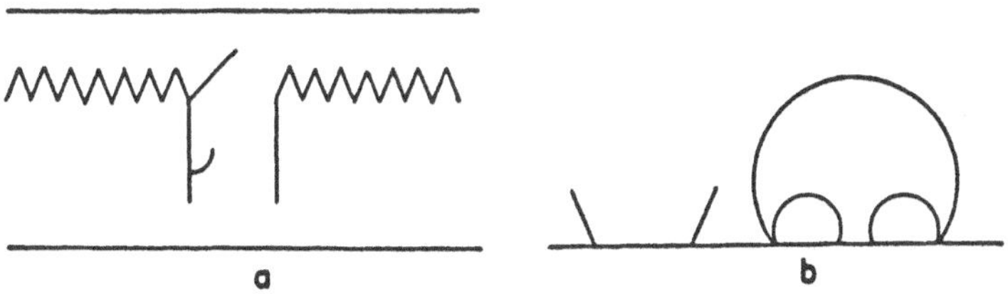

Figure A10
Organization impressed by meaning:
(a) A soldier and his dog passing by a hole in a picket fence;
(b) A washerwoman cleaning the floor.

Figures B1 to B3: Some examples of eye motion during observation
of pictures. (After A.L. Yarbus [26])

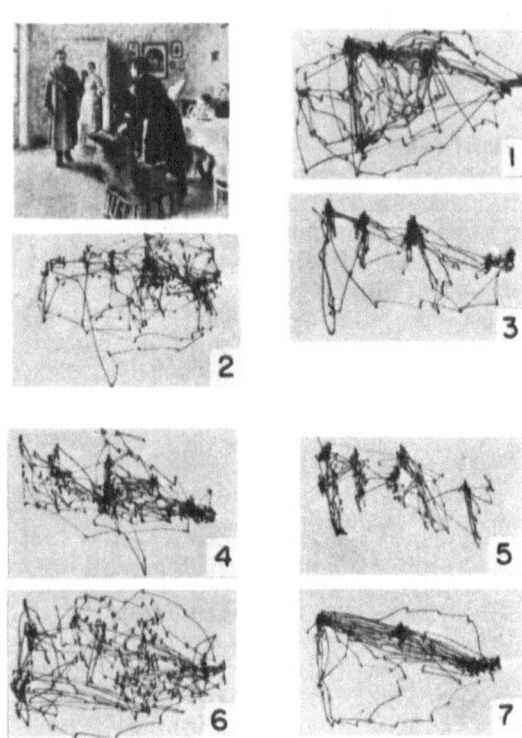

Figure B1
Eye movement dependence on the information to be extracted from
the picture in upper left corner during 3-minute observation:
(1) free observation, no instruction
(2) "Tell me, is the family poor or wealthy ?"
(3) "How old are the people in the picture ?"
(4) "What were they doing before the man entered the room ?"
(5) "Try to memorize the clothing the people are wearing."
(6) "Try to memorize the placement of the furniture."
(7) "How long had the man been away from his family ?"

 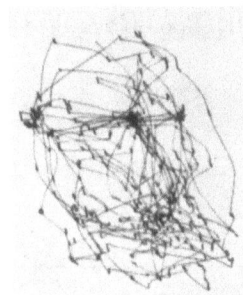

Figure B2
Eye motion (fixation pattern) for a black and white picture.

Figure B3
Eye motion pattern for a line drawing (contours only).

186

<u>Figures D1 and D2</u>: Some examples of children's drawings. (After
H. Schaeffer - Simmern 35)

Figure D1
Horizontal-vertical relationships obeying the greatest contrast
of direction rule.

Figure D2
Diagonal relationships which are more interesting and allow
representation of movement.

Table I: Cues to Depth (21)

Perspectives of position: (The observer is stationary, effect
visible with one eye)

1.   Texture perspective. (Texture gradient)

2.   Size perspective. (Object size vs. distance)

3.   Linear perspective. ("Parallel lines meet at infinity")

Perspectives of parallax:

4.   Binocular perspective. (The skew of the image in one eye
with respect to that in the other, stationary observer)

5.   Motion perspective. (The change in binocular perspective
when eyes are moved and the change in relative displace-
ments of objects due to moving observer). Several aspects of the motion perspective are also observable by
the moving one-eyed observer.

Perspectives independent of observer's motion or position:

6.   Aerial perspective. (The haziness, blueness and desatura-
tion of colours as a function of distance)

7.   The perspective of blur. (Variation in the quality of
blur as a function of displacement from the center of
clear vision)

8.   Relative upward location in the visual field. (The angular extent of background between the lower margin of the
visual field and the object)

"Depth at a contour":

9.   Shift of texture density or linear spacing. (Sudden
change of texture or texture gradient)

10. Shift in the amount of double imagery. (Sudden change in
the skew of texture over distance)

11. Shift in the rate of motion. (Change in the displacement
of texture elements on one side of a contour with respect to the other due to motion of the head)

Depth due to object shape:

12. Completeness or continuity of outline. (Complete objects
appear closer)

188

Depth effects due to lighting:

    13. Transition between light and shade.

Table II: "Variability dimensions"

Type of Variability	Number of search dimensions	
	2D case	3D case
1. Number of objects	n	n
2. Position in space (translation)	2	3
3. Rotation in space	1	3*
4. Size	1	1
5. Distortion (of shape)	?	?
6. Partial view (objects obscure each other)	$(n-1)^{n**}$	$(n-1)^{n**}$
7. Gray level	1	1
8. Texture	?	?
9. Colour	3	3
10. Object flexibility (the relation between parts of a flexible or jointed object)	?	?
11. "Noise" (variability in smaller details, poor illumination in parts, etc.)	?	?

    *6 faces minimum

    **for fixed overlap between any two objects

Acknowledgments

The author would like to express his sincere thanks to the Computer Graphics Section of NRC and the following publishers in particular: Oxford University Press, MIT Press, Plenum Publishing Company, Basic Books Incorporated, Springer-Verlag, University of Chicago Press and University of California Press for making this study possible.

APPENDIX A: THE GESTALT LAWS

To quote from the writings of the originator of Gestalt theory (8c): "The fundamental 'formula' of Gestalt theory might be expressed in this way: There are wholes, the behaviour of which is not determined by that of their individual elements, but where the part-processes are themselves determined by the intrinsic nature of the whole. It is the hope of Gestalt theory to determine the nature of such wholes...This problem cannot be solved by listing possibilities for systematization, classification and arrangement."

Examples of Gestalt Laws in vision (7,8d,22,23,24)

1) Grouping by similarity. (Objects which look similar tend to be grouped together, fig. A1).

2) Grouping by proximity. (Close objects of approximately similar size but differing shape are grouped together, fig. A2).

3) Principle of good continuation. (A line or contour which has been cut (interrupted) is seen as a whole if the pieces form a smooth curve, fig. A3).

4) The law of closure. ("Closed objects are whole", fig. A4).

5) Many other laws are discussed in the texts on Gestalt psychology.

The interaction between these laws is illustrated in figures A5 and A9. An amusing example of how a model impresses organization onto even a few lines, or that conclusions are based on very sparse evidence, is given in fig. A10.

APPENDIX B: EYE MOTION DURING OBSERVATION OF PICTURES
(18,25,26,27)

It is assumed that the points on a picture where an observer focuses his eyes and the duration of that observation are related to the mental processes in identifying what the scene depicts. It is found that the observer neither scans the picture like a TV camera, nor does he sample it at random. Rather, the sampling process is driven by picture content as well as the question to which an answer is sought in the picture, fig. B1. Areas which carry information for solution of a given problem are carefully observed while those which are not related to the problem at hand are practically ignored. Within any one observation, an area of high interest is not inspected until exhausted of information, but

rather, the attention alternates between the areas of high interest,
with occasional excursions outside of these areas. Blank and
uniformly textured areas are seldom looked at. Crude attempts at
contour following are apparent in some cases, but even in the case
of written text the line of text is not followed systematically.
Colour does not significantly alter the overall eye motion statistics. Neither is the gray level per se of particular significance.
Qualitative studies indicate that the fixation pattern does not
differ even if the picture is a black and white (silhouette) or
a line (contour) drawing. See figures B2 and B3.

APPENDIX C: HANDICAPPED SYSTEMS (29,30,31,32,33)

The brain operates as a unit. Consequently damage to any of
its parts may cause extremely varied disturbances in visual perception. This form of blindness is called "mental blindness" since
the picture processing strategies disintegrate to some degree.
Some of the observed phenomena are very suggestive of a "picture
language" which is failing in various ways. These observed failures
in perception are tantalizingly easy to interpret as, for example,
a missing feature detector, a transformation not carried out, an
incorrect classification, a forgotten positional relationship,
analysis terminated too early, etc. On the assumption that such
"algorithmic" interpretations are meaningful, the observed failures
may be viewed as confirmations that the operational procedures
used by the visual system are well within our computational knowhow.
The observed phenomena, however, do not reveal how the now failing
operations were used by the intact visual system.

The man who was a contour follower (8e)

In this case of brain damage the unfortunate victim's preprocessing consisted basically of contour following. He was not
able to see the "wholeness" of objects, i.e. the Gestalt laws were
inoperative.

Basically, he traced the contours of letters in order to read.
If a letter was traced the "wrong" way, (i.e. contrary to his

customary starting point or direction) he did not recognize the letter. If the letters were obscured by extraneous lines (of about equal thickness to the letters) his tracing became derailed. There was no "plan" to guide his tracing. The tracing consisted of hand or head movements. If these movements were inhibited, he was not able to identify the letters. He had no impression of straight or curved lines. Circles, squares, triangles, etc. were blobs to him which had to be traced. If the presentation of the object was too short for the tracing to be completed, the object was not recognized. He could not see motion, nor could he see "depth" in pictures of three-dimensional scenes.

However, he was able to "get around" in his environment quite well. To quote from the article:

Question: "How do you distinguish men from vehicles?"

Answer: "Men are all alike--narrow and long, vehicles are wide."

Problem: The shadow of a large tree.

Question: "What is it?"

Observation: The patient looked up at the tree then down at the shadow.

Answer: "That's a shadow."

Question: "How do you know?"

Answer: "Well, there is a tree and there it is dark."

APPENDIX D: DEVELOPING SYSTEMS

There is an enormous amount of observations and experiments on children's problem solving procedures in the writings of Jean Piaget. The present short expose, however, is limited to Britsch's theory on how the "data structures" in children's drawings develop (34,35). According to this theory, children's drawings follow a well-defined development sequence which parallels the child's understanding of his visual surroundings. To quote (35): "The drawings reflect the mental activity that transforms the multiplicity of visual impressions into self-created visual unities

which leads to visual cognition. Visual cognition is the result
of an immediate mental digestion of visual experience into a visual
synthesis of form; it is not the result of an accumulation, regis-
tration, or reproduction of mere facts by means of conceptual activity."

The following steps in the development may be observed:
(a) Scribble: The discovery of being able to bring something about
    that was not there before. It is not a representation of anything.
(b) Circles: The circles stand for "thingness" or any object; they
    neither represent circularity, nor roundness. The concepts of
    containing figure-ground relation may be formed at this stage.
(c) Combinations of circles and randomly directed "straight" lines
    follow, such as the "sunburst patterns". Shape of objects is to
    a degree differentiated.
(d) Vertical-horizontal relationships (figure D1): All parts are
    related to one another by horizontal-vertical order, i.e. by the
    greatest contrast of direction. One reverts to circles or scribble
    if unable to draw the parts or the object. To quote:
    "Not one line can be changed without disturbing the structural
     organization of form. If a change is undertaken in one part,
     it demands also a change in the others in order to maintain
     the unity of form.
     Only through their relation to the whole do the parts obtain
     structural meaning.
     Furthermore, each single part is clearly discriminated from
     every other part. The relationship of the greatest contrast
     of direction of lines and the relationship of figure and ground
     constitute together an inseparable totality of form."
(e) Diagonal relationships (figure D2): These allow the representa-
    tion of movement.
(f) More complex angular relationships.
(g) Fusion of object parts together.
(h) More complex drawings, representation of depth, relation of all
    objects to the scene asa whole, etc.

References

1. T. Kasvand, Some Observations and Experiments on the Elements for a Picture Language, NRC report. (Under preparation).

2. T. Kasvand, Some Observations on Linguistics for Scene Analysis, Computer Graphics, Pattern Recognition and Data Structures, UCLA Conference, May 14-16, 1975. IEEE Cat. N. 75CH0981-1C.

3. Methodologies of Pattern Recognition, edited by S. Watanabe, Academic Press, 1969, Pattern Recognition Applied to the Counting of Nerve Fiber Cross-Sections and Water Droplets, pp. 333-343.

4. T. Kasvand, M. Milner, Pattern Recognition Applied to Measurement of Human Limb Positions During Movement, Journal of Cybernetics, 1972, 2,1, pp. 66-78.

5. Graphic Languages, Edited by F. Nake and A. Rosenfeld, North Holland Publ. Co. 1972. Some Thoughts on Picture Languages, pp. 163-184.

6. K.S. Fu, Syntactic Methods in Pattern Recognition, Academic Press, 1974.

7. P.A. Kolers, Some Psychological Aspects of Pattern Recognition, Recognizing Patterns, The MIT Press, 1968, Editors P.A. Kolers and M. Eden.

8. W. Ellis, ed., A Sourcebook of Gestalt Psychology, Humanities Press Inc., 1967.

   a) The Unity of Senses (pp. 210-216)
   b) Numbers and Numerical Concepts in Primitive Peoples (pp. 265-273)
   c) Gestalt Theory (pp. 1-11)
   d) Laws of Organization in Perceptual Forms (pp.71-88)
   e) Analysis of a Case of Figural Blindness (pp. 315-325)

9. J.J. Gibson, The Senses Considered as Perceptual Systems, Houghton Mifflin Co., 1966.

10. P.C. Dodwell, Visual Pattern Recognition, Holt, Rinehart and Winston Inc., 1970.

11. D.H. Hubel, T.N. Wiesel, Perceptive Fields, Binocular Interaction and Functional Architecture in the Cat's Visual Cortex, J. Physiology, Vol. 160, 1962.

194

12. M.D. Levine et al., Computer Determination of Depth Maps, Computer Graphics and Image Processing 1973, pp. 131-150.

13. T. Kasvand, Iterative Edge Detection, Computer Graphics and Image Processing, 1975, 4, pp. 279-286.

14. A.L. Zobrist, W.B. Thompson, Building a Distance Function for Gestalt Grouping, IEEE C-24, No. 7, July 75, pp. 718-728.

15. M.D. Kelly, Edge Detection in Pictures by Computer Using Planning, In Machine Intelligence 6, edited by B. Meltzer and D. Michie, Am. Elsevier Publishing Co., 1971, pp. 397-409.

16. S.L. Tanimoto, T. Pavlidis, A Hierarchical Data Structure for Picture Processing, Princeton University, Department of Electrical Engineering, TR151, August, 1974.

17. T. Kasvand, Segmentation of Single Gray-Level Pictures of General 3D Scenes, Second International Joint Conference on Pattern Recognition, August 1974, pp. 372-373.

18. N.H. Mackworth, A.J. Morandi, The Gaze Selects Informative Details Within Pictures, Perception and Psychophysics, 1967, Vol. 2(11), pp. 547-552.

19. K. Price, A comparison of Human and Computer Vision Systems. Sigart Newsletter, No. 50, February 75, 5-10.

20. Discussions on "Vision", Sigart Newsletter, No. 52, June 1975.

21. J.J. Gibson, The Perception of the Visual World, Houghton Mifflin Co., 1950.

22. K. Koffka, Principles of Gestalt Psychology, Harcourt, Brace and World Inc., 1963.

23. C.E. Osgood, Methods and Theory in Experimental Psychology, Oxford University Press, 1953.

24. M. Wertheimer, Untersuchungen zur Lehre von der Gestalt. Psychologische Forschung, 1923, 4, pp. 301-350. (See ref. 8d for a similar article in English).

25. G.T. Buswell, How People Look at Pictures, University of Chicago Press, 1935.

26. A.L. Yarbus, Eye Movements and Vision, Plenum Press, 1967.

27. P.A. Kolers, Reading Picture Bandwidth Compression, Editors, T.S. Huang and O.J. Tretiak, Gordon and Beach, 1972.

28. M.V. Srinivasan et al., A Probabilistic Hypothesis for the Prediction of Visual Fixations, IEEE, SMC, Vol. 5, No. 4, July 75, pp. 431-437.

29. A.R. Luria, Higher Cortical Functions in Man, Basic Books Inc., 1966.

30. M. von Senden, Space and Sight, Methuen and Co. Ltd., 1960.

31. R. Lewin, The Brain: New Light on Seeing and Perceiving, No. 118/1974/Spectrum/8, British Science News.

32. C. Blakemore, G.F. Cooper, Development of the Brain Depends on the Visual Environment, Nature, Vol. 228, October 31, 1970.

33. O.D. Creutzfeld, P. Heggelund, Neural Plasticity in Visual Cortex of Adult Cats After Exposure to Visual Patterns, Science, Vol. 188, 6 June 1975, pp. 1025-1027.

34. R. Arnheim, Art and Visual Perception, University of California Press, 1954.

35. H. Schaefer-Simmern, The Unfolding of Artistic Activity, Its Basic Processes and Implications, University of California Press, 1950.

A RELATIONAL APPROACH TO THE RECOGNITION OF DISTORTED PATTERNS

J. R. Ullmann

Division of Computer Science
National Physical Laboratory
Teddington, Middlesex, ENGLAND

Department of Applied Mathematics and Computing Science
University of Sheffield, Sheffield, Sioztn, U.K.

Abstract: Practical machines for recognizing speech and handprint are designed to tolerate various distortions of patterns that are to be recognized. A new method of recognizing distorted patterns is based on determining whether spatial relationships are preserved. within a specified tolerance. This paper is intended to serve as a simple introduction to this new method which is presented elsewhere.

I. Introduction

Figure 1 is a classic basic diagram in communication theory. A receiver is required to determine which of a set $\{y_1,\ldots,y_\omega\}$ of possible signals has been transmitted over a noisy channel. Well known theory [1] tells us how to make an optimal decision as to which of $\{y_1,\ldots,y_\omega\}$ has been transmitted, using statistics obtained from noisy signals that have previously been received.

Figure 2 differs from Figure 1 only in that each of the possible transmitted signals belongs to one of a set of classes $\{\Omega_1,\ldots,\Omega_r,\ldots\Omega_\omega\}$ of signals, where $\Omega_r = \{y_{r1}, y_{r2},\ldots,y_{rj},\ldots y_{r_{\sigma_r}}\}$.

Suppose now that the receiver is not required to decide precisely
which of the possible signals $\{y_{rj}\}$ has been transmitted, but
instead to decide which of the classes $\Omega_1, \ldots \Omega_\omega$ a transmitted signal belongs to. Well known techniques of pattern recognition,
such as nearest neighbour methods and methods of potentials, provide solutions to this figure 2 problem that use training sets of
previously received noisy signals. This is particularly true when,
for each r, at least some of the members of Ω_r constitute some
sort of cluster or set of clusters, and $y_{r1}, \ldots y_{r\sigma_r}$ are not known
a priori to the receiver.

Figure 3 differs from figure 2 in that transmitted signals
are subjected not only to noise but also to distortion. Each
transmitted signal, regardless of its class, is subjected to a
distortion selected from a fixed set, A, of distortions. In the
case where signals or patterns are two-dimensional, the set A might
be for instance include dilation, shift, tilt, some general perspective distortions, and a large number of complicated distortions
such as those that stretch different parts of a pattern by different amounts. In general, a distortion alters the position of at
least part of a pattern to which it is applied, but noise does not
have this effect, and here we have a distinction between noise and
distortion.

Let us say that the figure 3 problem is to assign a received
signal to one of $\Omega_1, \ldots, \Omega_\omega$, using training sets of previously received signals that have been in some way labelled to indicate
which of $\Omega_1, \ldots, \Omega_\omega$, they should be assigned to. Let us say also
that in the figure 2 case, the training set signals or patterns
are in some way labelled to indicate their recognition class, so
that for the limited purposes of the present we shall be concerned
only with "supervised" learning.

To follow our introductory line of thought one step further,
consider two pattern recognition machines that are respectively
solutions to the figure 2 problem and the figure 3 problem. We

suggest that if the figure 3 recognition machine were used for recognizing digitized handprinted characters, speech, or vectocardiograms, then it would yield lower recognition error rates than would be obtained from the figure 2 recognition machine in the same application. This suggestion is <u>not</u> based on mathematical analytical theory, but instead on experimental knowledge that, for instance, it is often possible to distort a specimen of the character '5' written by one person so as to make it identical to a specimen of '5' written by someone else. Similarly it may be possible to distort the speech spectrogram of the word 'five' spoken by one person so as to make it identical to the spectrogram of 'five' spoken by someone else. Practical speech and character recognitions are designed to tolerate many such distortions, and these systems are therefore more like solutions to the figure 3 problem than to solutions to the figure 2 problem. We suggest that for applications such as handprint and speech recognition, figure 3 is a better model than figure 2.

However, much of the theoretical literature on pattern recognition is concerned with problems which are much more like that of figure 2 than figure 3. For instance, distortion is scarcely mentioned in any of the pattern recognition textbooks reviewed by Cover [2], though [3] does deal with perspective distortion. Instead of tackling the figure 3 problem as radically as the figure 2 problem has been tackled, it has been usual to try to eliminate the effects of distortion by ad hoc intuitively designed techniques that more or less transform the figure 3 problem into the figure 2 problem, e.g. [4,5]. If the results of this approach were always entirely satisfactory in practice, then there would be less motivation to tackle the figure 3 problem from first principles. Perhaps the scarcity of basic theoretical solutions to the figure 3 problem is one of the many reasons for the gap between theory and practice that Blackwell [6] has lamented.

II.   Conservation of Positional Relationships within Tolerance

To discuss the problem of distortion in more detail, let us return to Figure 3 and by way of a simplified example suppose that y_{rj} is the black and white character '5' shown in figure 4(a). Suppose that the set A of distortions in figure 3 is such that each member of A changes figure 4(a) into one of the 5's shown in figure 5; and conversely each '5' in figure 5 is related to figure 4(a) by one distortion in A. Let us now arbitrarily choose some pairs of black elements of figure 4(a) and join the two elements in each pair by a line as shown in figure 4(b). The black elements in figure 4(b) are numbered 1,...,12 for reference.

We hope that it is intuitively obvious which black element in figure 4(a) corresponds to which black element in any '5' in figure 5. An examination of fig. 5 reveals that the relative positions of the pair of elements (1,2) in figure 4(b) is either unchanged by distortions in A or is changed to the configuration shown on T in figure 6(b). The same is true for (2,3), (3,4), (6,7) and (11,12) in figure 4(b). The pair (4,5) is either unchanged by distortions in A or is changed to the configuration shown in figure 6(a), and the same is true for (5,6). The pair (1,9) is either unchanged or is changed to one of the configurations shown in figures 6(i), (j), (k). By comparing figure 5 with figure 4(b) it can be seen that figure 6 is in fact a complete list and specification of the configurations to which distortions in A can take the selected pairs in figure 4(b); except that figure 6 does not show the trivial cases where the relative positions of a pair of elements are unchanged. We shall refer to the set that comprises these trivial cases together with the configurations shown in figure 6 as the tolerance set for figure 4(b).

A machine could easily recognize all the 5's in figure 5 by storing them explicitly and comparing an unknown pattern with these 47 stored patterns separately. However, in a more realistic example there would not just be 47 different versions of a character,

as shown in figure 5, but many millions, and it would not be practical to store them all explicitly. So let us abandon the idea of
explicitly storing all the distorted versions of a character and,
for introductory purposes, seek alternative methods of recognizing
the 5's in figure 5.

Figure 6 contains less information (i.e. can be specified by
fewer bits than figure 5, and in a more realistic example the
analogous disparity would be very much greater. Let us therefore
consider storing in a recognition machine a specification of the
tolerance set (i.e. figure 6 plus cases where the relative positions of elements are unaltered by distortion) instead of figure 5,
and using this data to achieve automatic recognition of every '5'
in figure 5.

The simplest recognition rule would be: -

Rule 1: Recognize an unknown pattern X as '5' if corresponding to every one of the chosen pairs of elements in figure
4(b), X contains a pair that is within tolerance.

What we mean by "within tolerance" can be very easily understood
by means of examples: X contains a pair within tolerance of (1,2)
is X contains a pair of black elements in either of the configurations shown in figure 6(b). X contains a pair within tolerance of
(3,7) if X contains either of the configurations shown in figure
6(c). From these examples it can be seen how the tolerance set is
used in the application of rule 1.

It is important that, by construction, rule 1 necessarily
recognized every '5' in figure 5 as '5'. However, rule 1 also
erroneously recognizes many non-fives as '5', e.g. the '2' in
figure 7(a). The pairs in figure 7(a) that correspond to pairs
in figure 4(b) are indicated in figure 7(b).

Suppose that rule 1 is tested by applying it to randomly
generated patterns. We hope it is obvious that the number of
non-fives misrecognized as '5' would generally decrease if the
number of selected pairs in figure 4(b) were increased (and if

202

the tolerance set were updated accordingly). Another way of reducing the misrecognition rate would be to use n-tuples of black
elements instead of the pairs indicated in figure 4(b), the tolerance set being amended accordingly. Rule 1 would of course have
to be amended to say "chosen n-tuples" instead of "chosen pairs".

An n-tuple of elements of figure 4(b) can be regarded as a
geometrical feature. Conversely, a feature such as the top left-
bend of '5' is an n-tuple of elements of this '5'. We might now
re-word rule 1:

Rule 1(a): Recognize an unknown pattern X as '5' if corresponding to every one of a chosen set of features of
figure 4(b), X contains a feature that is within tolerance.

In practical character recognition it is common to normalize
the height, width, and position of a character so that it fits
snugly into a standard rectangle [8]. The rectangle is divided
into zones, and regions within the rectangle can be conveniently
specified by specifying combinations of zones, e.g. [9,10]. Rule
1(a) can then be improved requiring that each feature occurs in X
within a positional tolerance specified in terms of zones. The
idea is that distortions in A (figure 3) only shift features within limited regions within the standard rectangle, and lower misrecognition rates are attainable by using this positional restriction instead of ignoring it.

Another practical development is to insist not only that X
must contain various prescribed features within tolerance but also
that X must not contain various other prescribed features within
tolerance. This idea is used for instance in [9,10,11].

Despite these developments, the literature (see [8]) suggests
that it is necessary to use quite large features (i.e. n-tuples of
elements where n is quite large) in order to make misrecognition
error rates tolerably small. With large features (large n) it is
not practical to store the tolerance set explicitly as in figure 6
because the storage cost would be too high. Instead, in order to

determine whether X contains a feature that is within tolerance, it is usual (e.g. [10,11]) to employ a Boolean function that is designed to be true if and only if X contains this feature within tolerance. For instance, it can easily be seen that the Boolean function in [11] for the top left corner of '5' is designed to tolerate limited variations in shape (and also noisy raggedness) of this feature.

We have loosely and perhaps too briefly indicated how practical developments of rule 1 lead to complicated Boolean recognition structures. Microprogramming [18] may mitigate the implementational difficulties, but thousands of man-hours are still required to arrive at fairly successful logical designs. We suggest that the main trouble with this approach is that it leads to an overwhelmingly complicated logical design problem. Sheer unmanageable complexity appears to be the limiting factor in this approach to the recognition of distorted characters or other distorted shapes or patterns.

In the hope of avoiding this limiting complexity, let us return to first principles and again use the figure 5 example to illustrate basic ideas. Let us again consider the set of pairs indicated in figure 4(b).

This example is unrealistic in that each of the 47 distortions in A takes figure 4(a) to a '5' that is a configuration of exactly 12 black elements. There is a 1:1 correspondence between the black elements of figure 4(a) and the black elements of each of the 5's in figure 5. In every case the 1:1 correspondence maps each of the pairs in figure 4(b) into a corresponding pair within tolerance, because of the definition of the tolerance set. So we can formulate: -

Rule 2: Recognize an unknown pattern X as '5' if there is a 1:1 correspondence between the black elements of figure 4(b) and X maps each of the pairs in figure 4(b) into a corresponding pair within tolerance.

By construction, rule 2 necessarily recognizes all the 5's in figure 5 as '5'. Rule 2 does not erroneously recognize figure 7(a) as '5', but rule 1 does make this mistake, as we have remarked previously. To see why rule 2 does not recognize figure 7(a) as '5', consider for example element 9 in figure 4(b). There is no black element in figure 7(a) that has a black element above it within tolerance of the (1,9) pair, and a black element to the left of it within tolerance of the (8,9) pair, and a black element to the left of it within tolerance of the (10,9) pair. Therefore, there is no 1:1 correspondence between figure 4(b) and figure 7(a) that maps every one of the pairs in figure 4(b) into a corresponding pair in figure 7(a) within tolerance.

Figure 7(a) is just one example of a non-five misrecognized by rule 1 but not by rule 2, and it would be possible to provide many further examples. Rule 2 misrecognizes fewer patterns than rule 1, and it achieves this by insisting that corresponding pairs intersect at corresponding elements in the unknown pattern. Rule 1 merely insists that corresponding pairs occur in the unknown pattern but does not insist that they intersect at corresponding elements.

Distortions that conserve spatial relationships within tolerance have been fundamental to previous work, e.g. [12,13,14], and rule 2 is merely a simple means of insisting that spatial relationships are conserved within tolerance, (hence the title of this paper). We remarked previously that the misrecognition error rate of rule 1 can be reduced by using n-tuples, where n is quite large, instead of 2-tuples, but this leads in practice to complexity problems. The use of rule 2 instead of rule 1 may provide a means of reducing the misrecognition error rate without increasing the value of n and so without being eventually defeated by complexity. This is why we are interested in practical developments of rule 2. Besides, we feel that the literature shows rule 1, though seldom explicitly formulated, to have received already almost as much attention as it deserves.

To use rule 2 we require a technique for finding a 1:1 correspondence that preserves tolerance, and this problem is closely similar to the problem of determining graph isomorphism. The pairs in figure 4(b) can be regarded as lines or edges of a graph. Fortunately we have found a procedure for graph isomorphism [15] that can be readily adapted for use in rule 2; which means that this approach to the recognition of distorted shapes may not now be combinatorially hopeless, though five years ago it might well have been so judged.

In figure 4(b) we chose to consider pairs rather than n-tuples of black elements because pairs present the simplest case and make figure 6 easy to draw. If we had chosen all possible pairs rather than those indicated in figure 4(b), then the misrecognition error rates of rules 1 and 2 would have been lower, but their implementational cost would have been higher. The arbitrarily chosen set of pairs shown in Figure 4(b) is sufficient for the introductory purposes of the present paper. For instance, this set is sufficient for illustrating the important difference between rules 1 and 2 in terms of figure 7.

To determine whether there is a 1:1 correspondence in conformity with rule 2, we could use enumeration together with a procedure like the refinement procedure in [15] to reduce the total amount of computation to a tolerable level. Alternatively, at the cost of increased misrecognition error rates, we could omit the tree-search enumeration part of [15] and just use the refinement procedure. The deterioration in error rates could be rectified by increasing the value of n, and/or by using more pairs of n-tuples. We suggest that it would be more economical to do this than to use the tree-search enumeration part of [15]. This suggestion is the reason for our abandonment of the tree-search in the recognition procedure [16] that the present paper is intended to introduce. This procedure [16] has two important advantages. First, it can be implemented in remarkably simple highly parallel

asynchronous digital hardware, as in [14,15]. Secondly, it can
readily be extended to the real-life case where we are looking
for a many: many correspondence, instead of a 1:1 correspondence,
in rule 2. This is the real-life case because when a pattern is
digitized and subsequently the original pattern is distorted and
then digitized again, there is generally not a 1:1 correspondence
but a many: many correspondence between the elements of the two
digitized patterns, as illustrated in figure 3 in [16]. The
figure 5 example has been artificially contrived to exhibit only
1:1 correspondence because this is more easily understood than
the realistic many: many case that is dealt with in [16].

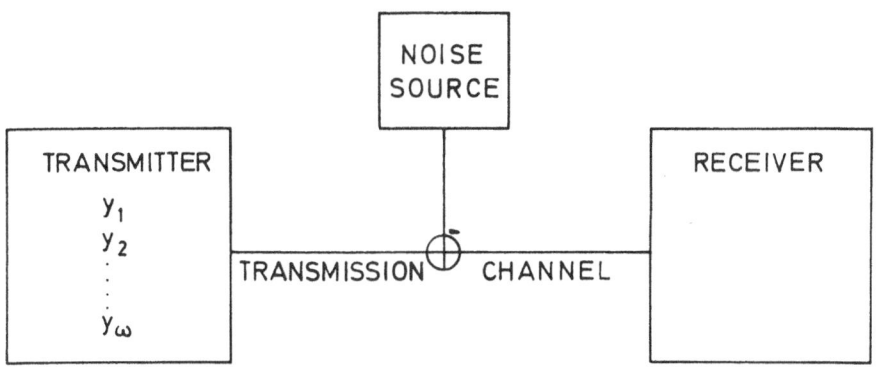

Figure 1.   Classic representation of transmission over a noisy
              communication channel.

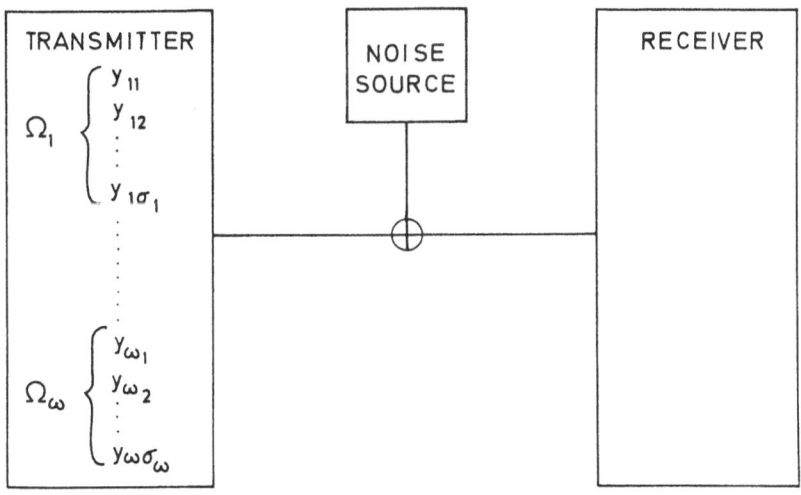

Figure 2.   An elaboration of Figure 1.

208

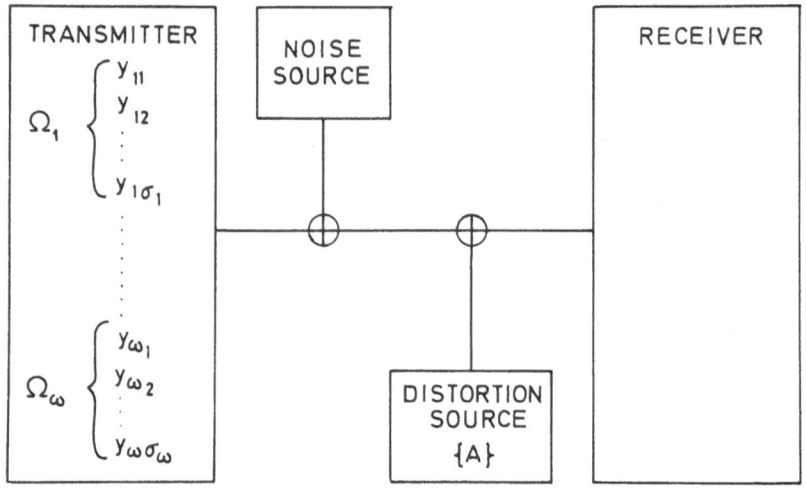

Figure 3.   Representation of a channel that introduces geometrical distortion as well as noise.

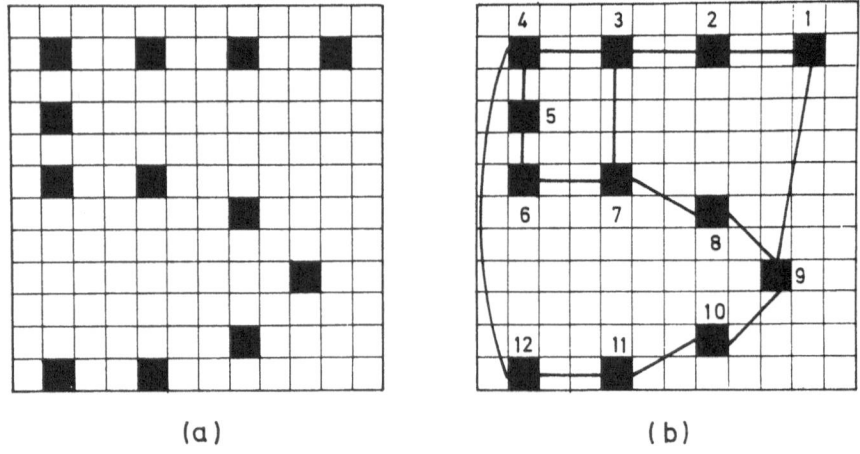

(a)   (b)

Figure 4(a).   A reference '5'.   (From [7], with permission).
Figure 4(b).   Selected pairs in Figure 4(a).   (From [7], with
permission).

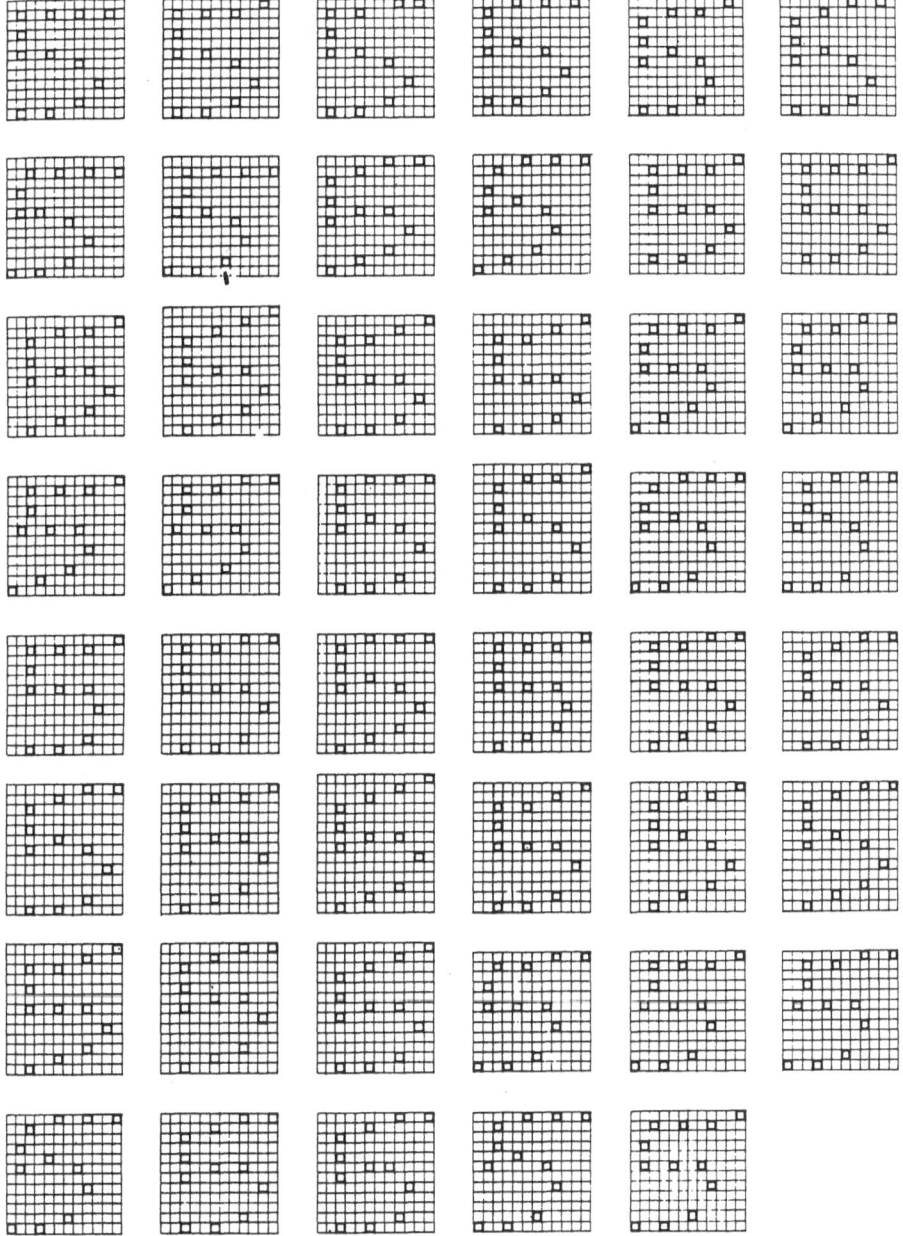

Figure 5.   Distorted versions of Figure 4(a). (From [7], with permission).

210

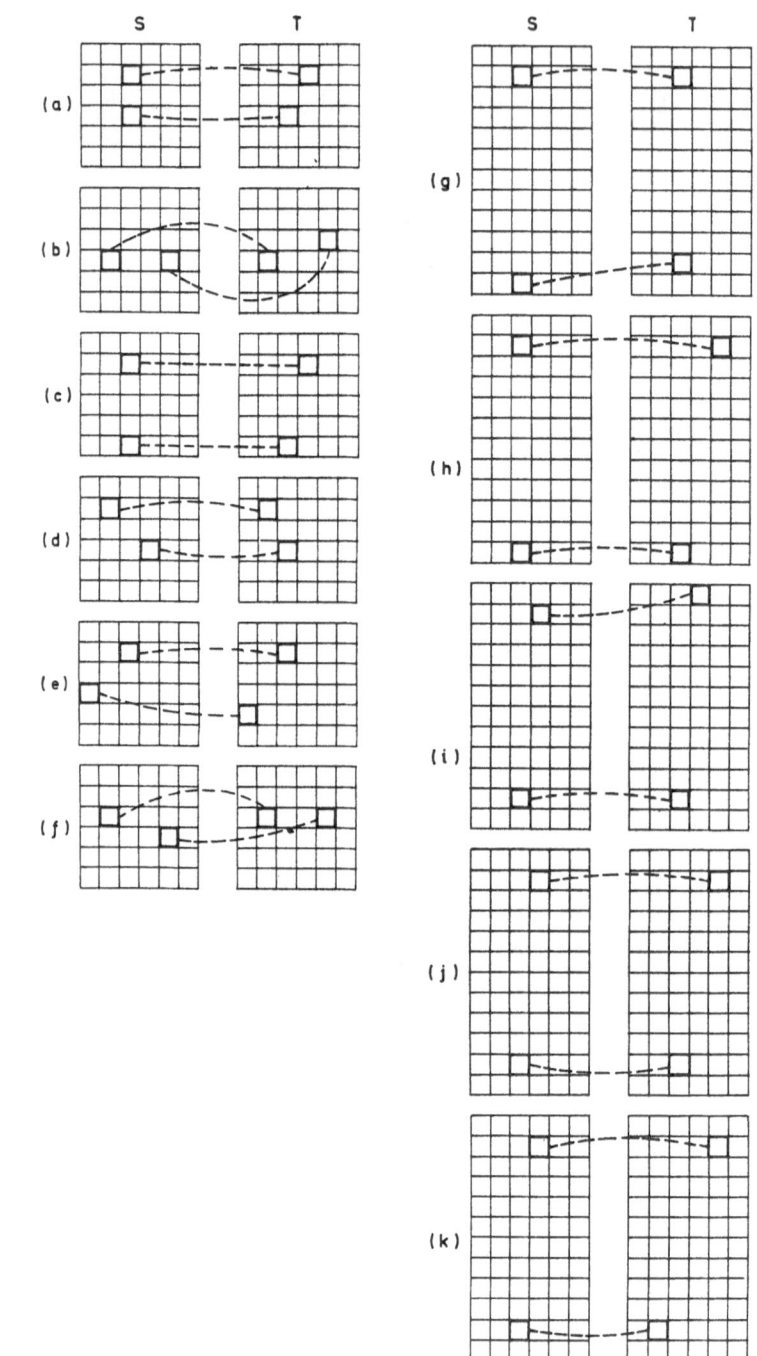

Figure 6.   Non-trivial members of the tolerance set for Figure
             5.   (From [7], with permission).

211

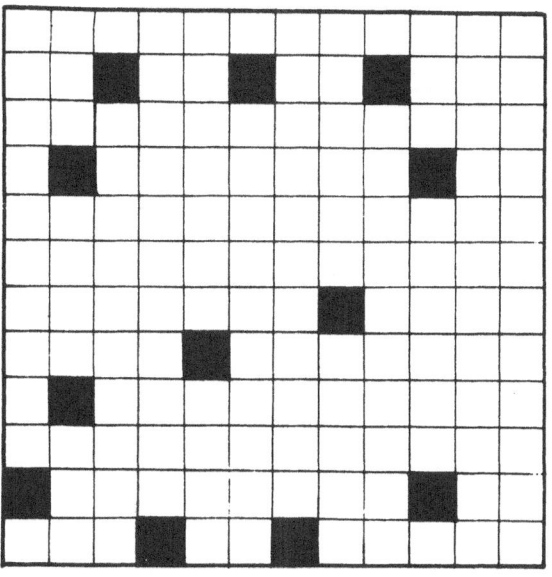

(a)

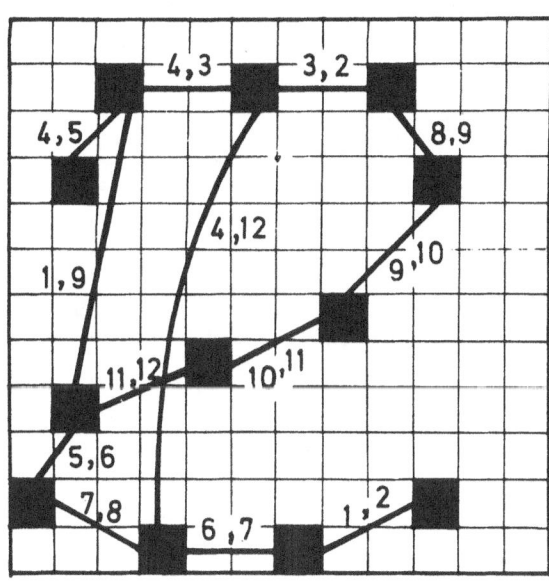

(b)

Figure 7(a). A specimen of '2'.

Figure 7(b), Pairs in Figure 7(a) that are common to Figure 4(b).

References

1. Davenport, W. B. and Root, W. L., _Introduction to the Theory of Random Signals and Noise_, New York, McGraw-Hill, 1958.

2. Cover, T. M., Recent Books on Pattern Recognition, _IEEE Trans. on Information Theory_, Vol. IT-6, No. 6, Nov. 1973, pp. 827-833.

3. Duda, R. O. and Hart, P. E., _Pattern Classification and Scene Analysis_, Wiley Interscience, 1973.

4. Munson, J. H., Experiments in the Recognition of Handprinted Text: Part I, Character Recognition, _1968 Fall Joint Computer Conference_, pp. 1125-1138.

5. Sammon, J. and Sanders, J., Method for Recognizing Characters, _U.S. Pat._ 3, 755-780, Aug. 1973.

6. Blackwell, F.W.. Combining Mathematical and Structural Pattern Recognition. _Second International Joint Conference on Pattern Recognition_, Copenhagen, August, 1974, pp. 78-80.

7. Ullmann, J. R. _Pattern Recognition Techniques_. London: Butterworths, and New York: Crane Russak, 1973.

8. Ullmann, J. R. Picture Analysis in Character Recognition. In _Digital Picture Analysis_, Edited by A. Rosenfeld. Springer Verlag, forthcoming.

9. Rohland, W. S., Traglia P. J., and Hurley, P. J. The design of an OCR system for reading Handwritten Numerals. _1968 Fall Joint Computer Conference_, pp. 1151-1162.

10. Hunt, D. J. Improvements in or Relating to Optical Character Recognition System. _U.K. Pat._ 1 345 032, January 1974.

11. SCAN-DATA. Improvements in or Relating to Character Recognition Systems. _U.K. Pat_ 1 271 705, April 1972, _U.S. Pat_ 3 613 080, October 1971.

12. Simon, J. C., Checroun A., and Roche, C. A Method of Comparing two Patterns Independent of Possible Transformations and Small Distortions, _Pattern Recognition_, Vol. 4, No. 1, January 1972, pp. 73-81.

13. Fischler, M. A. and Elschlager, R. A., The Representation and Matching of Pictorial Structures, _IEEE Transactions on Computers_, Vol. C-22, No. 1, January 1973, pp. 67-92.

14. Ullmann, J. R., Correspondence in Character Recognition, _Machine Perception of Patterns and Pictures_, Conference Series No. 13, Institute of Physics, London, 1972, pp. 34-44.

15. Ullmann, J. R., An algorithm for Subgraph Isomorphism, Accepted in JACM and Scheduled to appear in January 1976 issue.

16. Ullmann, J. R., Subset Methods for Recognizing Distorted Patterns, Not yet published.

17. Andrews, D. R. and Atrubin, A. J., Character Recognition Apparatus, _U.K. Pat._ 1, 293 381, October 1972.

PICTURE PROCESSING

Azriel Rosenfeld and Joan S. Weszka

Computer Science Center
University of Maryland
College Park, Maryland 20742

Abstract: This paper reviews the fundamentals of automatic
picture processing and scene analysis. It discusses computer-
based methods of segmenting pictures into meaningful parts; determining properties of the parts and relationships among the parts;
and using this information to construct descriptions of the pictures. The material is organized by principal areas of application,
including document reading, high-energy physics, cytology, radiology, and remote sensing of the environment.

I. Introduction

Work in various areas of pictorial pattern recognition began
over 20 years ago. An extensive literature has accumulated during
that period, much of it concentrated in a number of specific areas
of application. These areas include document processing, high-
energy physics, cytology, radiology, and remote sensing, among
others.

This paper surveys some of the basic picture analysis techniques that have been developed for use in pictorial pattern recognition systems. For each of the five major application areas
listed above, techniques that are especially relevant to that area
are discussed. Thus the presentation here is only superficially

application-oriented; it deals primarily with techniques, but these are arranged according to some of their principal applications.

There are many general collections of papers and journal special issues on pictorial pattern recognition, which will not be cited here. A series of bibliographical reviews of the general field of picture processing may be found in [1-5], while some textbooks are [6-9]; texts dealing with pattern classification in general are not cited here (but see [8]). Mention should also be made of a recent collection of review papers [10] covering the five application areas that are treated in this paper, each written by an expert in the area. A few additional references on the individual application areas are given in their respective sections.

Since the techniques reviewed in this paper are generally basic and standard, references on individual techniques have not been given, nor have illustrations of how these techniques work on real data been provided in all cases. The reader is referred to textbooks and surveys such as [6-10], and to the references on the application areas given in the sections below, where an abundance of citations and examples can be found, and where many techniques of a more specialized nature are described.

II. Document Reading

The earliest collection of papers on automatic character recognition appeared in 1962 [11]. Both before and since then, many meetings have devoted sessions to character recognition, and several books on the subject have also appeared [12-14], as well as numerous review papers. Since the character recognition field is a highly commercial one, the patent literature is an unusually rich source of information on practical systems; see, e.g., [14], and its author's paper in [10]. The subject is often called "optical character recognition" (OCR), not because it is usually implemented optically (though it sometimes is), but to distinquish it from magnetic ink character recognition (MICR), which is an even more widespread commercial character reading technique.

Recognition problems in document reading range from mark sensing, to recognition of fixed-font printed characters (sometimes using special fonts designed to facilitate recognition), to reading handprinted and handwritten material. The classes of characters that must be recognized may include simple marks, numerics, alphanumerics, or exotic character sets (map symbols, mathematics, Chinese, etc.). Thus document reading presents a broad range of technical problems. In this section we treat only a few of the basic techniques that are common to many character recognition problems: thresholding (for mark sensing, or for discrimination between characters and paper); template matching (for detection of characters having known shapes); and geometrical normalization (for recognition of known shapes or patterns that have unknown positions or orientations). Many of the techniques discussed in later sections may also be applicable to character recognition, particularly the shape analysis techniques of Section 4; but in this section we deal primarily with known shapes, with the understanding that for recognition of handprinted and handwritten material, or of printed material coming from an unknown font, the more general methods of Section 4 would usually be necessary.

2.1 Thresholding

One often needs to detect the presence of an object in a picture, or to segment the picture into objects and background, where the objects are consistently darker (or lighter) than the background. For example, in document reading one may want to detect the presence of a mark on a paper, or to determine which parts of the paper contain printed characters and which are blank; in these cases, the mark and characters are usually darker than the paper. Examples can also be found in other areas of picture analysis. In a bubble chamber picture, the bubble tracks are darker than the background; in a photomicrograph of a mitotic cell,

the chromosomes are darker than the background; in satellite imagery of cloud cover, the clouds are brighter than most terrain
types; whicle in imagery of the earth's surface, bodies of water,
as seen in certain spectral bands, are darker than most terrain
types.

In any of the situations just described, the picture can in
principle of segmented, or the objects detected, by simple pointwise <u>thresholding</u> of the picture's gray level, where the threshold
is chosen so that object points (usually) have above-threshold gray
levels, and background points have below-threshold levels. In
mathematical terms, let $f(x,y)$ be the gray level of the given picture at the point (x,y). Then thresholding the picture at threshold t gives rise to the two-valued picture $f_t(x,y)$ defined by

$f_t(x,y) = 1$ if $f(x,y) \geq t$; $= 0$ otherwise

A useful variation is to suppress the gray levels of background
points by setting them to zero, but to preserve the gray levels of
object points; this gives rise to the "semi-thresholded" picture
$f_s(x,y)$ defined by

$f_{st}(x,y) = f(x,y)$ if $f(x,y) \geq t$; $= 0$ otherwise

The results of thresholding a handwritten signature, using various
threshold levels, are shown in Figure 1.

One way of choosing a threshold to extract a given class of
objects is to examine the frequencies with which the various gray
levels occur in the picture. Let $p_f(z)$ be the number of times
that gray level z occurs in the picture f (we assume here that z
can take on only a discrete set of values); $p_f(z)$ is called the
gray level <u>histogram</u> of f. When a picture contains objects that
have a characteristic range of gray levels, the presence of these
objects often gives rise to a peak on the picture's histogram,
while the background will generally give rise to another, larger
peak. In other words, if a picture contains two populations of
points, object points and background points, whose gray levels
generally lie in different ranges, when we can expect the picture's

histogram to be bimodal, i.e., to contain two peaks, one corresponding to each population. Evidently, a reasonable way to choose
a threshold t in order to distinguish between object and background
points is to let t be the gray level corresponding to the bottom
of the valley between the two peaks. The histogram of the original
picture in Figure 1a is shown in Figure 2; note that when we use
a threshold corresponding to the valley bottom, as in Figure 1c,
we obtain a reasonable segmentation of Figure 1a into characters
and paper.

Another approach to threshold selection is to start with an
arbitrary threshold t_0, examine the results of thresholding at t_0,
and raise or lower the threshold accordingly. For example, if we
examine Figures 1b and 1d, we see that the characters extracted
using that threshold are too thick and too thin, respectively.
Given some method of measuring character thickness (see Section 4
on shape analysis), we can apply it to the threshold picture and
decide whether the threshold should be raised or lowered. This
process can be repeated until the results are satisfactory. Many
other techniques exist for refining the accuracy of threshold
selection, and for removing the pictorial noise that results from
imperfect thresholding, but space does not permit their discussion
here.

In many cases, the proper threshold will not be the same
everywhere in the picture. In character recognition, for example,
the characters may not be equally dark in all parts of a page, or
the page may not have been evenly illuminated by the scanning system. The most straightforward way to deal with this situation is
to divide the picture into relatively small windows (e.g., a few
character sizes in diameter), and threshold each window independently. Windows whose histograms are not markedly bimodal may not have
to be thresholded at all (since they may contain no characters),
or we can pick thresholds for them by interpolating from nearby
windows which were bimodal.

2.2 Template Matching

One can detect the presence of a known shape or pattern in a picture by matching the picture against a template of the given pattern. For example, this problem arises when one has to recognize printed characters, coming from a specific type font.

The most commonly used measures of the mismatch between a template g and a picture f are of the form

$$\iint |f(x,y)-g(x,y)|^k dxdy \qquad \text{(or more concisely: } \iint|f-g|^k),$$

where k is usually taken to be 1 or 2. A popular measure of match is the correlation coefficient

$$\iint fg/\sqrt{\iint f^2 \iint g^2}$$

which has value 1 when f = cg for some constant c, and < 1 otherwise. To find a copy of g in f, one must compute some such match (or mismatch) measure for every displacement of g relative to f (i.e., g(x-a,y-b) rather than g(x,y)), and look for "match peaks", or threshold the match values.

Matching g with f in every relative position is a computationally costly process -- and even more so if the orientation or size, as well as position, of g in f is unknown. Shortcuts exist, involving use of the Fourier transforms of f and g to compute the correlation, or using the results of partial matching to determine whether it seems worthwhile to complete the match computation; but the details cannot be given here.

Figure 3 shows the results of matching a triangle with a set of shapes, using both the $\iint|f-g|$ and correlation measures. It is seen that the (mis)match peaks are not sharp, and that there are many near misses, due to partial matches. Better results are obtained if we match outlines, rather than solid objects, as in Figure 4.

For two-valued patterns, say having values 0 and 1 only, another way to define a match measure is as follows: Let $\bar{g}$ be the "negative" of g that has 0's where g has 1's and vice versa. Then $\iint(fg-f\bar{g})$ has its maximum possible value when (1) f has 1's wherever g has 1's, and (2) f has 0's wherever $\bar{g}$ has 1's (i.e., wherever g has 0's); this integral is thus a measure of the match between f and g. More generally, if the pattern to be detected consists of two parts, one part having high gray levels and the other part low gray levels, we can also use a two-valued pattern template of the form $g-\bar{g}$, where g has 1's at the high-valued pattern points, and 0's at the low-valued points; indeed, here too, $\iint f(g-\bar{g})$ has its maximum possible value when (1) f has high values where g has 1's, and (2) f has low values where g has 0's, so that $\iint f(g-\bar{g})$ is a measure of the match between f and the desired pattern.

2.3 Geometrical Normalization

As just seen, template matching is effective in detecting a pattern only when the pattern and template have the same position, orientation, and size. One can avoid the need to search through all possible positions, orientations, and sizes by devising methods of geometrically normalizing the given picture (which we shall assume here to contain only a single pattern), so that the pattern has a standard position, etc.; or by devising geometrically invariant properties, whose values do not depend on the position, etc., of the pattern, and using the values of these properties to identify the pattern.

One way of normalizing with respect to position is to compute the autocorrelation or Fourier power spectrum of the given picture f; these are, respectively, defined by

$$C_{ff} = \iint f(x,y) \ f(x+a,y+b) da db$$

$$|F|^2 = \left| \iint e^{-2\pi j(ux+uy)} f(x,y) dx dy \right|^2$$

It can be shown that C_{ff} and $|F|^2$ are invariant under translation of f, i.e., they are the same for any $f(x+\alpha,y+\beta)$ as they are for $f(x,y)$. Analogous transforms can be defined which yield normalization with respect to orientation and size.

Another approach to position normalization is to shift the centroid of f to some standard position; we recall that the coordinates of the centroid are

$$\overline{x} = \iint x f(x,y) dx dy / \iint f(x,y) dx dy$$

$$\overline{y} = \iint y f(x,y) dx dy / \iint f(x,y) dx dy$$

Similarly, we can normalize with respect to orientation by rotating f so that its principal exis of inertia (i.e., the line through $(\overline{x}, \overline{y})$ about which f's moment of inertia is least) has some standard orientation. In general, we can define combinations of moments of f that are invariant under various types of transformations; recall that the (i,j)th moment of f is defined by

$$m_{ij} = \iint x^i y^j f(x,y) dx dy$$

(so that $\overline{x} = m_{10}/m_{00}$, $\overline{y} = m_{01}/m_{00}$).

If an object 0 has already been extracted from f, we can normalize 0 by shifting it, rotating it, etc., so as to standardize the position, orientation, etc. of some unique feature of 0 (e.g., its longest projection or cross-section). Conversely, once 0 is normalized, we can use projections or cross-sections of 0, is given directions and positions, to extract useful information from 0 for recognition purposes. This method of normalization, as well as the principal axis method, are illustrated in Figure 5.

III. High-Energy Physics

Nuclear particle trace detectors, such as bubble and spark chambers, are used extensively in high-energy physics. Millions of photographs obtained from these devices are analyzed and measured every year. From the measurements, information about particle kinematics can be derived. Many systems have been developed for scanning and analyzing bubble and spark chamber photographs. A series of international conferences on data processing in high-energy physics have been devoted, to a significant extent, to discussions of these systems; see the relevant paper in [10] for a guide to this literature.

The tracks in a bubble chamber picture are thin, dark, noisy curves on a lighter background, shaped essentially like arcs of circles (where the radii are not exactly known). To analyze such a picture, we need techniques for detecting and tracking curves,

and for describing and recognizing their shapes; this section describes such techniques. It should be pointed out that there are
other classes of pictures which also consist of dark curves --
fingerprints, for example -- and to which the same types of techniques are generally applicable.

3.1 Curve Detection

In a digital picture, a smooth curve looks locally like a
straight line segment; thus it should be possible to detect curves
by some sort of template matching technique, using line segments
as templates. For dark curves on a light background, the template
$g-\overline{g}$ of Section 2.2 for a vertical line segment would have the form

$$
\begin{array}{ccc}
-1 & 1 & -1 \\
-1 & 1 & -1 \\
-1 & 1 & -1
\end{array}
$$

and similarly for other orientations. As seen in Figure 6, however,
if we apply the template just described to a picture containing a
vertical line in noise, we obtain a very noisy output. This is
because the template yields high match values at high-valued noise
points, not just at points that lie on vertical lines; indeed, a
strong noise point can yield a higher match value than a weak
vertical line. Similarly, the template responds to vertical edges,
and a high-contrast edge can yield a higher match value than a
weak line.

These observations suggest that it is not safe to use the
linear operation $\iint f(g-\overline{g})$ to detect lines or curves, unless one
can be certain that there are not edges or noise points present
that have higher contrast than the curves. If this cannot be
guaranteed, it becomes necessary to introduce some degree of non-
linearity into the line detection operation. To see how this can
be done, let the gray levels of the picture points in the neighborhood of a given point e be

$$
\begin{array}{ccc}
a & b & c \\
d & e & f \\
g & h & i
\end{array}
$$

Then we can discriminate against vertical edges by requiring that

thickness. An example of the results that can be obtained in this way is shown in Figure 7.

Techniques analogous to those just described can be used to detect sharp angles, branch points, crossing points, and endpoints of curves.

3.2 Curve Tracking

The local processes of curve detection just described are not able to cope with curves that have large gaps. Even for unbroken curves, they do not give us any information as to how many curves are present, nor do they tell us anything about the overall shapes of the curves. To obtain such information, one can <u>track</u> each curve, starting from one of its ends; the sequence of moves made in the course of this tracking process constitute a description of the curve's shape (see Section 3.3), and the number of times that tracking has to be carried out is the number of curves that are present. We shall see below that tracking also allows us to bridge gaps in a curve.

Given that we have detected a point p that may be the end of a curve, we can examine its neighbors and decide which of them (e.g., the darkest one, call it q) is the next point on the curve. Now we pick a dark neighbor r of q, other than p, as the next point; and so on. If we wish, we can bias the procedure against sharp turns by choosing r on the basis, not only of its darkness, but also of how well it continues the direction pq. At succeeding steps, we can use a smoother approximation to the direction of the curve based on more predecessor points, to predict the direction of the next point; or we can make a higher-order prediction involving both the slope and curvature of the curve as thus far tracked. (On approximations to the slope and curvature of a curve see Section 3.3.)

If we are tracking a curve and it comes to an end, we can search further out in (or near) the predicted direction to see whether the curve continues on the other side of the gap.

$$b+e+h > a+d+g \text{ and } > c+f+i$$

which will be satisfied if b, e, h lie on a line (or if one of them
is a noise point), but not if they lie on an edge. Similarly, we
can discriminate against noise points by requiring

$$b > \frac{a+c}{2} \text{ and } e > \frac{d+f}{2} \text{ and } h > \frac{g+i}{2}$$

which will be satisfied if b, e, h lie on an edge or line, but not
if one or two of them are noise points. Finally, we can discriminate against both noise points and edges by requiring that

$$b > a, \; b > c, \; e > d, \; e > f, \; h > g, \text{ and } h > i$$

In all of these cases, the match value can still be defined as,
say,

$$b+e+h - (a+c+d+f+g+c)/2$$

which is the same as the value for a linear operator, designed to
yield match value zero for constant input (a=b=···=h=i).

The results of applying the linear and nonlinear operations
just described to a vertical line in noise are shown in Figure 6.
Note that the nonlinear operator does discriminate against noise,
but introduces breaks in the line at places where a high-valued
noise point occurs adjacent to the line (so that one of the noise
discrimination conditions is invalid). The nonlinear operators
will also not tolerate gaps in the curves; but this can be circumvented by using operators based on larger neighborhoods, and re-
laxing the logical conditions by requiring that most, but not
necessarily all, of the inequalities must hold.

To detect arbitrary curves, we can apply line segment detection
operators in all possible directions

```
x   x   x    x
x   x   x    x
x , x , x ,   x , etc.
```

and take the maximum of the results as the match value. To generalize the process to thick curves, we can use analogous operators
in which a, b, c,... are not single points, but rather averages
over neighborhoods whose diameter is equal to the desired curve

In general, the farther away one has to search, the less precise
should be the prediction of where the continuation ought to be
found. A procedure of this sort can be designed to bridge gaps
of any desired size. Examples are not shown here, since there
are so many possible varieties of tracking schemes.

If it is known that the curves to be tracked have slopes that
always lie in a certain range, say 45° to 135°, then we can use a
simpler tracking procedure in which we examine the picture row by
row. If we have tracked a curve down to point p on the kth row,
then the next point q should be one of the neighbors of p on the
k+lst row, since the curve cannot be crossing a row at an angle
more oblique than 45°. We can track all the curves in the picture
simultaneously in the course of such a row by row scan. This type
of assumption is valid for many of the curves in a bubble chamber
picture, since the tracks of the beam particles all have roughly
the same direction.

3.3 Curve Analysis

When we track a curve from point to neighboring point, the
sequence of directions of the moves that we make from neighbor to
neighbor constitutes a complete description from which the curve
can be reconstructed (given a starting point). Since a point in
a digital picture array has only four neighbors (or eight, if we
count diagonal neighbors), the directions can be encoded as two-
(or three-) bit numbers, e.g., 0 = 0°, 1 = 90°, 2 = 180°, 3 = 270°.
The sequence of these numbers is called the chain code of the
curve. The chain code of a simple curve is shown in Figure 8.

If we use a curve's chain code to define the slope or curvature (= rate of change of slope) of the curve at a point, we find
that they are always multiples of 90° (or 45°, if we allow diagonal
moves), so that they are not very useful in predicting the behavior of the curve. It is usually more appropriate to define a
smoothed slope by averaging the directions of several unit steps,
and a smoothed curvature as the rate of change of the smoothed

slope. "Angles" on the curve can now be defined as points where
the smoothed slopes on the two sides of the point differ significantly.

The chain code provides a position-invariant description of
a curve, since the starting point is arbitrary; and if we use a
difference chain code (i.e., we encode the differences between the
slope of successive unit steps), we get a description that is also
rotation-invariant, since the starting direction is now also arbitrary. For a closed curve, we can derive invariant descriptions
by using parametric equations for the curve -- e.g., $x = f(t)$, $y =$
$y = g(t)$, where $0 \leq t \leq 1$, and f and g are periodic with period 1;
by adding constants to $\hat{f}$ and g, we can make $f(0) = g(0) = 0$, say,
which gives us position invariance. If we now expand f and g in
Fourier series, and take the power spectrum, we can obtain rotation
invariance as well. There are many variations on the idea of using
transforms to define curve descriptions.

Curves of known shape can be detected by matchine their chain
codes against "template" codes. Specific shapes such as straight
lines or circular arcs can be detected by using special coordinate
transformations. For example, if we choose the origin at a point
p of the arc, and the x-axis as the tangent to the arc at that
point (assuming that we can compute a good approximation to the
tangent), then the equation of a circle of radius r in this coor-
dinate system becomes $\frac{x^2+y^2}{2y} = r$; thus if we compute $\frac{x^2+y^2}{2y}$ for all
curve points near p, those that lie on a circle of radius r will
all yield $\frac{x^2+y^2}{2y}$ values near r. In other words, if we find a large
number of points near p that all give approximately the same value
(say r) of $\frac{x^2+y^2}{2y}$, the given curve must be a circular arc and must
have radius r. Other coordinate transformation techniques exist
for detecting straight line segments in a picture.

IV. Cytology

There have been major applications of pictorial pattern recognition techniques in three areas of cytology: hematology,

exfoliative cytology, and cytogenetics. Typical problems in the
first two areas include automation of the differential white blood
cell count, and automatic dection of abnormal Pap smears. In the
third area, the standard problem is that of identifying and measuring the individual chromosomes that appear in an image of a mitotic
cell. This last problem involves the separation of the chromosome
spread into connected components, as well as identifying and separating touching or overlapping chromosomes; and making size and shape
measurements on the individual chromosomes. This section will
deal with topological and shape analysis techniques. Problems in
automated blood cell counting and Pap smear analysis typically
involve measures of both shape and texture of the cells and cell
nuclei; texture measures will be discussed in Section 5.

The literature on biomedical pattern recognition dates back
several decades, and a series of meeting has been devoted, in
particular, to cytology automation. The proceedings of the last
such meeting can be found in [15]. Two earlier meetings are
[16-17]; for a detailed history of the subject, see the survey
paper on it in [10].

4.1 Connected Component Analysis

Suppose that a picture has been segmented, say by thresholding
(see Section 2.1) into objects (e.g., chromosomes) and background.
A row-by-row tracking scheme can be used to separate the objects
into distinct connected components, and to give the points of each
component a unique label. The scheme is as follows: On the first
row of the picture, each run of object points is assigned a distinct label (A, B, C, D in Figure 9). Suppose now that we have
completed labelling the nth row, and are ready to process the
$(n \pm 1)$st row. For each run ρ of object points on the latter row,
if ρ is not adjacent to any such run on the nth row, we give the
points of ρ a new label, not previously used (e.g., label E in
Figure 9). If ρ is adjacent to exactly one run σ of object points
on the nth row, we give ρ's points the same label that σ's points

have. Finally, if ρ is adjacent to two or more runs of object points on the nth row, we give it (say) the lowest of their labels (this happens to the C's and D's in Figure 9 on the 5th row, and to two runs of B's on the 6th row); if these labels were different, we record the fact that they have now been found to be the same (here: D=C). When the entire picture has been processed in this way, we can go back through it and replace redundant labels by, say, their lowest equivalent labels (here: replace all D's by C's). Note that the number of inequivalent labels used is the same as the number of objects; thus our scheme can be used to count (connected) objects.

The tracking procedure just described can also be used to analyze the shapes of the connected objects; in particular, the objects can be segmented into pieces at points where runs merge, split, or change drastically in length. However, this method has the disadvantage that its results depend strongly on the orientation of the object.

4.2 Border Analysis

A connected object has one or more borders along which it is adjacent to its background (there is more than one border if the object has holes; see object B in Figure 9). Each of these borders can be regarded as a closed curve (though it may pass through some points twice, when the object is thin). A border following algorithm, similar to the curve following algorithm of Section 3.2, can be devised which visits the border points in sequence and returns to its starting point. As in Section 3.3, the border can thus be represented by a chain code; and if we know, for at least one border point, one of its neighbors that is not an object point, then there are straightforward procedures for reconstructing the object by tracing its border and then "coloring in" its interior. Border chain codes can be used in shape matching, Fourier description, etc., just as in Section 3.3.

The perimeter of an object can be defined as the number of

steps required to traverse its border(s). The relative magnitudes of perimeter and area (commonly expressed by the ratio P^2/A) can be used as a measure of shape complexity. (The area of an object in a digital picture is, of course, just the number of points in the object.) A border can be segmented, e.g., at points where it makes sharp turns (see Section 3.3), and the lengths of the parts -- chromosome arms, for example -- can be measured.

An object is called <u>convex</u> if, for every pair of points p,q in the object, the straight line segment pq lies entirely within the object. Evidently, it is sufficient that this be true when p and q are border points. If the chord pq lies outside the object, the part of the background surrounded by $\overline{pq}$ and by the object is a concavity of the object; we can construct the "convex hull" of the object by adjoining to it all its concavities. The definitions of these concepts for digital pictures are somewhat more compli- cated, since straight lines of arbitrary slopes must be used, and since we want to ignore concavities that are due to the digitiza- tion process itself (e.g., the two-point object ^{x}x should not be concave); the details will not be given here.

4.3 Skeletonization

If an object is elongated, it is often convenient to repre- sent the object by specifying its "skeleton", which consists of lines down the middle of the object's "limbs". These concepts are not as rigorously well-defined as the concept of a border curve, but in practice one can define algorithms for "thinning" or "skele- tonizing" elongated objects which give acceptable results.

Operationally, elongated parts of an object can be defined as follows: Suppose that we shrink the object by simultaneously changing all its border points to background points, and that we repeat this process t times. Let us now re-expand the object by changing all the border points of its background to object points, and repeat this too t times. It can be shown that when we are finished, all the object points must have belonged to the object originally; but some object points may have been lost, since some parts of the object may have disappeared completely during the shrinking process. Let C be a connected component of lost object points. Since C disappeared during the shrinking, every point of C is at most t steps away from the background; thus C has "width" at most 2t. Hence if C has area greater than (say) $10t^2$, we can call C elongated, since its "length" (= area/width $\geq 10t^2/2t = 5t$) is at least 2 1/2 times its "width".

One way to define the "skeleton" of an object is as consisting, for t = 1, 2, 3,..., of those points which remain after t steps of shrinking, but which disappear after t+1 steps of shrinking and one step of expansion. This approach is illustrated in Figure 10a-b. Unfortunately, the skeleton obtained in this way is generally not connected. To obtain a connected skeleton, we can proceed by shrinking the object from one direction at a time, e.g., first remove all north border points (= points whose upper neighbor is in the background), then all east border points, then all south, then all west, and repeat; but never removing a point whose removal would disconnect the object points in its neighborhood, or which is isolated. We also never remove a point that has only one object point in its neighborhood, since this would cause even a thin curve to shrink at its endpoints. It can be shown that if we let this process continue until no further points are removable, what remains is a connected "skeleton" of the original (connected) object; this is illustrated in Figure 10c.

V. Radiology

There are many applications of pictorial pattern recognition in radiology, as indicated in the survey paper on that topic in [10]. Typical problems include locating the heart boundary on a chest x-ray, in order to measure heart volume; and analyzing the texture of the lung tissue, in order to detect pneumoconiosis (black lung disease). In Sections 5.1-2 we review some edge detection and texture analysis techniques.

232

A chest x-ray is composed of several types of regions -- heart, lungs, ribs, etc. -- that have known relationships to one another. To analyze such a picture, it is usually necessary to determine which regions on the picture are of each type; for example; we want to detect the heart boundary, not the lung boundary; and we want to measure lung texture, not rib texture. We can use the known facts about the regions, represented in the form of a relational structure, to guide the analysis of the picture. Our choice of analysis operations and criteria can be made to depend on this knowledge. Relational structures for picture description are discussed in Section 5.3. A similar approach can be used to analyze other types of pictures in which where are regions or objects of known types that satisfy known relationships -- e.g., pictures of human faces.

5.1 Edge Detection

An edge in a picture is a place where there is an abrupt change in gray level. (Edges defined by abrupt changes in texture, rather than gray level, will be discussed in Section 6.1.) Thus edges can be detected by applying derivative operations of various sorts to the picture; at a place where there is an abrupt change, the derivative (in the direction of change) will have a high value. It is usually desirable to use derivative operators which are isotropic, i.e., which respond to edges in any direction. The simplest such operator is the magnitude of the gradient, defined for the picture $f(x,y)$ by

$$\sqrt{(\frac{\partial f}{\partial x})^2 + (\frac{\partial f}{\partial y})^2}$$

For a digital picture, we must use differences rather than derivatives; thus, we use $\Delta_x f \equiv f(x+1,y) - f(x,y)$ instead of $\frac{\partial f}{\partial x}$, and $\Delta_y f \equiv f(x,y+1) - f(x,y)$ instead of $\frac{\partial f}{\partial y}$. We can also, if we wish, approximate the square root of the sum of the squares by the sum, or the maximum, of the absolute values. The result of applying such a digital gradient operation to a picture is shown in

Figure 11. Many other edge detection operators can be defined;
the details are beyond the scope of this paper. In particular,
local thresholding (Section 2.1, end) can be used to detect edges,
in windows of the picture that have strongly bimodal histograms.

When the edge detection operator is applied at every point of
a picture, as in Figure 11, the results are often noisy; the points
where the operator's output has high values do not necessarily form
a set of closed curves constituting object boundaries. The boundaries may have gaps, and there may be spurious "edge points" that
do not lie on boundaries. To handle these problems, one can apply
curve detection and tracking operations to the edge output; these
operations can be used to detect and reject edge points that do
not lie on curves, and to bridge gaps in the curves.

5.2 Texture Analysis

A region in a picture can be characterized by various textural properties, such as coarseness and directionality. A coarse
texture is composed of relatively large "elements", while a fine
texture is composed of smaller "grains", and a directional texture
contains elongated "streaks" (which may or may not be lined up in
the same direction). No attempt will be made here to define the
term "texture" rigorously; but it is generally agreed that textures contain repetitive elements or subpatterns. The texture of
a region can be uniform, or it can vary systematically across the
region (e.g., coarseness decreases with distance from the observer,
when a textured surface is seen in perspective).

A classical method of analyzing the texture of a window in a
picture is to compute the window's Fourier power spectrum $|F|^2$
(see Section 2.3). For a coarse texture, $|F|^2$ will drop off rela-
tively slowly with distance from the origin, while for a fine-
grained texture it will drop off rapidly. Thus coarseness can be
analyzed by computing $\psi(r) \equiv \int |F|^2 d\theta$, which is the average of $|F|^2$
on a circle of radius r about the origin, and seeing how fast $\psi(r)$
decreases as r increases. Similarly, to detect (global) direction-
ality in a texture, we can compute $\Psi(\theta) = \int |F|^2 dr$, which shows how

$|F|^2$ varies with direction; for an isotropic texture, this will be relatively constant, but for a directional texture, it will have significant peaks and valleys. The power spectra of two texture samples are shown in Figure 12.

Another approach to texture analysis is as follows: For any vector $\delta = (\Delta x, \Delta y)$, let $M_\delta(i,j)$ denote the number of times that a point having gray level j lies at displacement δ from a point having gray level i, in the given region. For a directional texture, $M_\delta(i,j)$ will depend on the direction of δ; thus the variation in M with direction can be used to measure directionality. For a coarse texture, $M_\delta(i,j)$ will be small if δ has small magnitude and i is very different from j, since within the texture elements, points should have similar gray levels; while for a fine texture, even for small δ and i,j different, $M_\delta(i,j)$ can be relatively large, since (i,j) no longer lie in the same texture element. Thus a comparison of M_δ's, for various magnitudes of δ, can be used to estimate texture coarseness. As an alternative to this approach, let $D_\delta(k)$ denote the number of pairs of points, having relative displacement δ, whose absolute gray level differnece is k. The variation in $D_\delta(k)$ with the direction of δ can be used to measure directionality; while for k large (equivalent to i and j very different, above), the variation in $D_\delta(k)$ with the magnitude of δ can be used to measure coarseness.

Textures can differ not only in coarseness, directionality, etc., but also in (average) gray level; a texture can be generally dark or generally light, while still having the same coarseness. Most of the standard texture measures are sensitive to gray level differences; when comparing textures to one another, it is desirable to cancel out the effects of such differences. This can be done by normalizing the pictures' gray scales, so as to force them all to have a standard gray level histogram (e.g., all gray levels occurring equally often). Suppose there are m possible gray levels $0,\ldots,m-1$; then if we change the lowest mth of the picture points' gray levels to 0, the next lowest mth to 1,..., the highest mth to m-1, we obtain a transformed picture in which all gray levels occur the same number of times. This grayscale transformation is useful not only in texture analysis, but in picture matching as well, to compensate for overall grayscale differences between the pictures being matched. It has already been performed on the original pictures in Figures 11-12; an example of its effects on a picture similar to Figure 11a is shown in Figure 13.

5.3 Relational Structure

A picture composed of objects or regions can be described by a relational structure, such as a graph, in which the nodes represent the objects, and related objects are joined by arcs. Each node is labeled with a list of properties, or property values, of the corresponding object or region (e.g., area, elongatedness, convexity, texture coarseness, etc.); and each arc is labeled with a list of relationships, or relationship values, that hold for the corresponding pair of objects (e.g., adjacency, relative distance and direction, etc.).

If we construct such a relational structure for a given picture, we can determine whether the picture is a well-formed in stance of a particular class of pictures by comparing the resulting structure with a model or set of models (i.e., prototype structures) that describe typical instances of pictures belonging to the given class. This matching process often needs to be done hierarchically -- i.e., substructures are matched against substructures in the model; then the configuration of the substructures is matched against the corresponding configuration in the model; and so on -- because the structures are often very complex. Such a hierarchical matching process is analogous to the parsing process in linguistics. In fact, formal grammars can be defined for classes of relational structures ("graph languages" or "web languages"), and the recognition of a picture f as belonging to a given class can be implemented by "parsing" f's relational structure with respect to a grammar for the given class. A detailed

discussion of these concepts is beyond the scope of this paper; for
an extensive treatment of syntactic methods in pattern recognition
see [18].

VI.   Remote Sensing

Pictures of the earth's surface, or of cloud cover, obtained
by aircraft or satellites are among the hardest types of pictures
can contain curves (e.g., roads or rivers), objects, and textured
regions; the regions may be quite variegated, and there may be
gradual transitions from one region to another, as the type or
usage of the terrain, or the type of cloud cover, changes. Many of
the techniques described above can be applied to remotely sensed
imagery. In addition, this section describes techniques for segmenting a picture by "texture thresholding" and "texture edge detection", and techniques of region growing and picture partitioning,
which can be useful for analyzing such imagery (see Sections 6.1-2).

When we analyze terrain or cloud cover pictures we usually
have no map or relational structure to guide us (as we did in such
cases as chest x-rays or human faces), unless we are dealing with
a region of the earth's surface that is known in advance and that
has already been mapped at an appropriate scale. Nevertheless, we
do have general knowledge about the types of properties or relations
that are legal; for example, we know that field boundaries are
usually straight, except possibly when the field borders on a lake
or river. It is generally impractical to embed all of this knowledge into a relational structure, since such a structure would be
unmanageably complex; moreover, our knowledge involves extensive
use of conditional statements, inference, etc., and is not always
easy to express explicitly. Rather, the knowledge must be implicitly built into the procedures that we devise to analyze the pictures.

There have been many meetings devoted to automatic imagery
interpretation and machine processing of remotely sensed data;
for a more detailed review of the subject, see the survey paper
on it in [10]. Much remote sensor imagery is multispectral, i.e.,

brightness is measured in a number of different spectral bands (including the infrared), so that color and temperature information is available at each point, rather than just gray level. Many of the standard image analysis techniques, such as thresholding, template matching, edge and curve detection, and texture analysis, can be generalized to handle such vector-valued images directly; research in this area should lead to the development of new classes of image analysis algorithms for processing multispectral remote sensor data.

6.1 Texture Thresholding and Edge Detection

Suppose that we are given a picture containing textured objects on a differently textured background, or two adjacent, differently textured regions. We cannot extract the objects from the background by ordinary thresholding, as in Section 2.1, since the gray level ranges of object and background will usually overlap; and we cannot detect the objects' edges, or the edge between the two regions, by applying an ordinary difference operator, as in Section 5.1, since such an operator will respond to all the edges of the individual texture elements. However, we can devise generalized methods of thresholding and edge detection that will work in these cases.

Let us first assume that the two textures differ in average gray level, which will often be true. Then if we blur the picture sufficiently, the gray level ranges of the two regions will eventually become disjoint. (This is because when we average a large number of identically distributed random variables, the mean remains the same, but the standard deviation becomes small.) It will thus become possible to select a threshold that separates the regions. This approach is used in Figure 14 to separate "solid" from broken cloud cover on a meteorological satellite picture.

A similar approach will work for edge detection. Let us take differences of gray levels of pairs of points in the blurred picture, where the points are twice the blur radius apart, so that the difference represents, on the original picture, a difference of adjacent, nonoverlapping average gray levels. This difference will be high in the vicinity of the edge between the two regions, as seen in Figure 15a; and it will be highest when the midpoint between the two points lies just on the edge, so that we can localize the edge sharply by suppressing local nonmaxima of the differences of averages, as illustrated in Figure 15b.

We can handle cases where the textures do not differ in average gray level, but do differ in coarseness or directionality, by modifying the approach as follows: Suppose that we first apply an isotropic difference operator to the picture, say the magnitude of the gradient. In a finely textured region, there will be more high-gradient points per unit area than in a coarsely textured region; thus the two regions will now differ in average gray level, and they can be separated by blurring and thresholding, or the edge between them detected by blurring and differencing, as in the preceding two paragraphs. Differences in directionality can be handled similarly, by using directionality sensitive difference operators such as Δ_x and Δ_y, rather than the isotropic gradient operator.

6.2 Region Growing and Partitioning

In this section, we discuss some general methods of dividing pictures into regions each of which is uniform, and differs from the adjacent regions, in some sense (e.g., in texture). We assume below that we are given a measure of nonuniformity $\psi(R)$ that we can compute for any given region R, and/or a measure of difference $\Psi(R_1,R_2)$ that we can compute for any given pair of regions R_1,R_2.

One approach to partitioning a picture is to start by subdividing it into small "cells", just large enough so that the nonuniformity measure is well-defined for them. We can now start with any cell R, and examine one of its neighboring cells, S. If $\Psi(R,S)$ is below some threshold (or, alternatively, if $\psi(R \cup S)$ is below some threshold), we merge R and S to obtain a region R_1. We now examine a cell S_1 adjacent to R_1, and if the threshold criterion is met, we merge R_1 and S_1 to obtain R_2; and so on. When the region can no longer grow, we can start again with a cell outside it, and so on until no further growth is possible anywhere in the picture. Of course, the results will depend, in general, on the order in which the candidate cells are examined.

The above approach considers only (textural) uniformity or difference, and pays no attention to the shapes of the growing regions. If desired, we can also take shape into account; for example, we might want to allow a merge only if it decreases the complexity of the region's shape (as measured, say, by P^2/A; see Section 4.2), or we can at least give some weight to complexity change in making the merge decision. We can also take into account the strength of the border between the two regions (i.e., the average value of some edge detection operator along their common border), to avoid making merges that ignore major edges.

At the other extreme, we can start by subdividing the entire picture into a small number of regions, e.g., quadrants, and compute ψ for each part. If the result is below some threshold, that region need not be subdivided further; if it is above the threshold, we do subdivide it. At any stage, we can also compute Ψ for any adjacent pair of regions (or ψ for their union), and if the result is below some threshold, we can merge them. This process can be continued until no further splits are necessary, and no further merges are possible. Here too, the results depend on the order in which the tests are applied; and here too, shape and border strength can be taken into account, if desired, in making split and merge decisions. One can also use a compromise approach in which one starts with an intermediate-scale partition (rather than with small cells, or with the entire picture), and performs splitting and merging as indicated by the ψ and Ψ tests. There are many possible variations on this approach, and examples will not be given here.

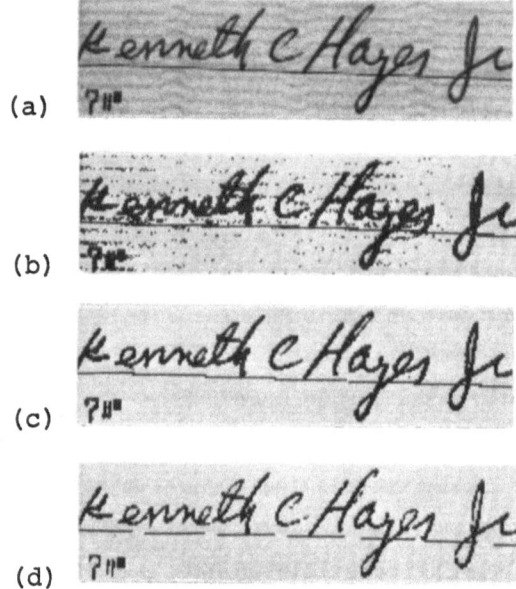

Figure 1. Thresholding a handwritten
signature.
a) Original
b-d) Results of thresholding
(a) at 22, 30, and 41, respectively, on a gray scale
of 0 to 63.

Figure 2. Histogram of the gray levels
in Figure 1a.

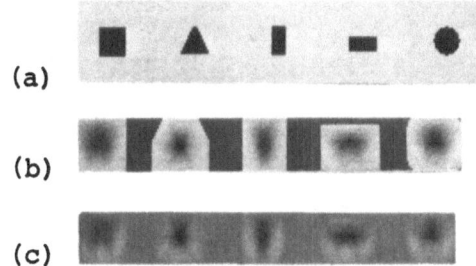

(a)

(b)

(c)

Figure 3. Results of matching a triangle with a
set of shapes.
a) Original shapes
b) Correlation of triangle with (a)
c) $\iint |f-g|$ for triangle and (a)

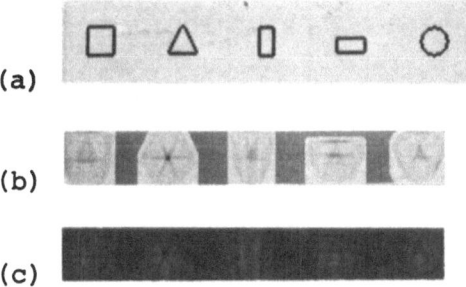

(a)

(b)

(c)

Figure 4. Results of matching outline, rather
than solid, shapes.
a) Original shapes
b) Correlation of outline triangle
with (a)
c) $\iint |f-g|$ for outline triangle
and (a)

242

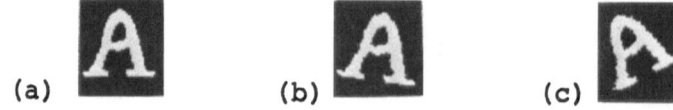

(a)　　　　　　(b)　　　　　　(c)

Figure 5.　Two methods of geometrically normalizing
an object.
a)　Original
b)　Result of making principal axis of
(a) vertical
c)　Result of circumscribing a minimum-
area rectangle around (a), and making
its long side vertical

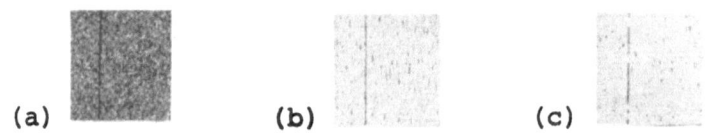

(a)　　　　　　(b)　　　　　　(c)

Figure 6.　Linear and nonlinear line detectors.
a)　Vertical line in noise
b)　Result of applying the linear line
detection operation $\iint f(g-\overline{g})$ to (a)
c)　Result of applying the nonlinear
operation, using all nine comparison
conditions, to (a)

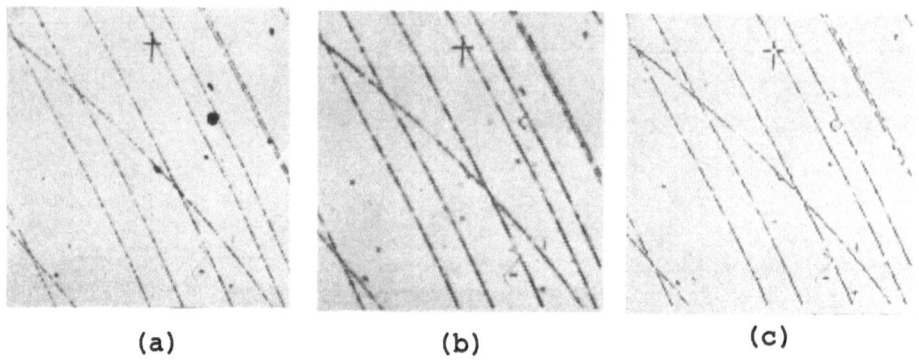

(a)　　　　　　(b)　　　　　　(c)

Figure 7.　Linear and nonlinear curve detection.
a)　Portion of bubble chamber picture
b-c)　Results of applying linear and nonlinear line detection operations, in
all possible directions, to (a).
Pictures (b-c) have been multiplied
by 2 to improve their visibility.

```
70000 07000 00770 77070 77070 00100 10010 10007
07070 01010 10100 00000 07707 07070 67777 77777
76565 65656 56565 65656 55666 66756 66663 66565
65555 45554 54444 54545 47556 56563 75565 65656
56563 44444 43433 33333 33444 34437 44444 44444
11111 12222 23333 32333 32333 33233 33323 33327
22121 22121 22121
```

(a)   (b)

Figure 8. A simple curve and its chain code.
           a) Curve (starting point is the uppermost point
               direction is clockwise)
           b) 3-bit chain code of (a), broken into blocks
               of five for greater readability


```
111    111   1111   1          AAA    BBB    CCCC   D
11     111   11111  11         AA     BBB    CCCCC  DD
        1 1  1111   11                B B    CCCC   DD
11     11 1   111 11           EE     BB B    CCC DD
 1     11 1   1111             E      BB B    CCCC
 1     111     11              E      BBB      CC
```

        (a)   (b)

Figure 9. Connected component labeling by tracking.
           a) Input picture (1's=object points,
               blanks=background points)
           b) Results of labeling (a) row by row; see text

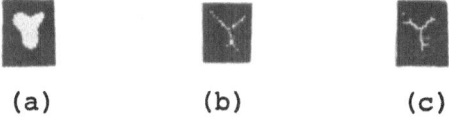

        (a)   (b)   (c)

Figure 10. Skeletonization.
            a) Chromosome
            b) Skeleton of (a) obtained by in-
                crementally shrinking and re-
                expanding
            c) Skeleton of (a) obtained by re-
                peatedly removing border points
                whose removal does not disconnect their
                neighborhoods.

244

(a)   (b)

Figure 11.   Digital gradient operation.
          a) Original picture (portion of a dental
             x-ray, with flattened gray level histo-
             gram; see text)
          b) Magnitude of the gradient of (a), with
             each picture point multiplied by 2

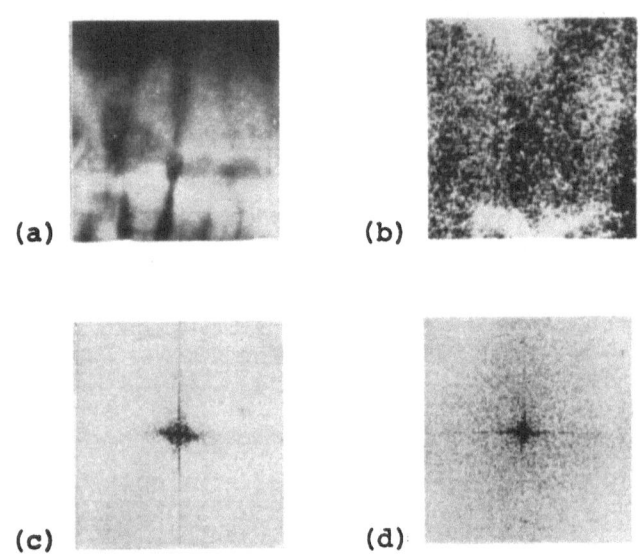

(a)   (b)

(c)   (d)

Figure 12.   Fourier power spectra.
          a-b) Originals
          c-d) Power spectra

(a)   (b)

Figure 13.   Gray level histogram standardization.
          a) Original picture (portion of a
             dental x-ray)
          b) Result of forcing the gray levels
             in (a) to occur equally often

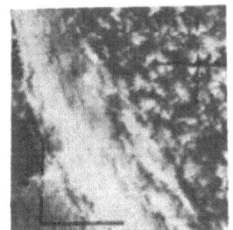

(a)

(b)

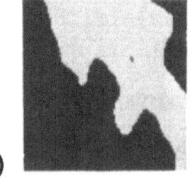

(c)

Figure 14. Texture separation by blurring and
thresholding.
a) Original picture (taken by a meteorological satellite)
b) Result of blurring (a) (averaging over
a 16 by 16 neighborhood at each point)
c) Result of thresholding (b) at 22

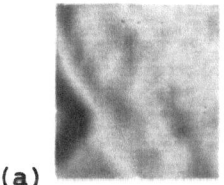

(a)

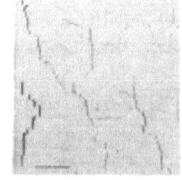

(b)

Figure 15. Texture edge detection,
a) Result of taking the max of horizontal
and vertical absolute differences
between averages over adjacent, nonoverlapping 16 by 16 neighborhoods in
Fig. 14a
b) Result of suppressing nonmaxima in
(a)

Note: These pictures have been multiplied
by 2 to improve their visibility.

References

1. A Rosenfeld, Computing Surveys 1, 1969, 147-176.

2. A. Rosenfeld, Progress in picture processing: 1969-71, ibid. 5, 1973, 81-108.

3. A. Rosenfeld, Picture processing: 1972, Computer Graphics and Image Processing 1, 1972, 394-416.

4. A. Rosenfeld, Picture processing: 1973, ibid. 3, 1974, 178-194.

5. A. Rosenfeld, Picture processing: 1974, ibid. 4, 1975, in press.

6. A. Rosenfeld, Picture Processing by Computer, Academic Press, New York, 1969.

7. H. C. Andrews, Computer Techniques in Image Processing, Academic Press, New York, 1970.

8. R. O. Duda and P. E. Hart, Pattern Classification and Scene Analysis, Wiley, New York, 1973.

9. A. Rosenfeld and A. C. Kak, Digital Picture Processing, Academic Press, New York, 1976 (in press).

10. A. Rosenfeld, ed., Digital Image Analysis, Springer, Berlin, 1976 (in press).

11. G. L. Fischer, Jr. et al., eds., Optical Character Recognition, Spartan, Baltimore, 1962.

12. R. A. Wilson, Optical Page Reading Devices, Reinhold, New York, 1966.

13. V. A. Kovalevsky, ed., Character Readers and Pattern Recognition, Spartan, New York, 1968.

14. J. R. Ullmann, Pattern Recognition Techniques, Crane, Russak, N. Y., 1973.

15. B. H. Mayall, guest ed., Journal of Histochemistry and Cytochemistry 22, 1974, 451-765.

16. W. H. Tolles, ed., Data Extraction and Processing of Optical Images in the Medical and Biological Sciences, Annals N. Y. Acad. Sci. 157, 1969, 1-530.

17. D. M. Ramsey, ed., Image Processing in Biological Science, U. of Calif. Press, Berkeley and Los Angeles, 1968.

18. K. S. Fu, Syntactic Methods in Pattern Recognition, Academic Press, New York, 1974.

SEQUENTIAL AND PARALLEL THRESHOLDING OF IMAGES

L. Cordella[+], M. J. B. Duff[^] and S. Levialdi[+]

[+]Laboratorio di Cibernetica, CNR, Gruppo Elaborazione Forme
[^]University College London, Image Processing Group

I. Introduction

Various approaches to parallel computation can be found in the literature (see for example[1,2,3,4,5]). In this paper we will discuss how an existing parallel machine, the CLIP processor[6], implements a program that performs a specific image processing task.

After summarizing how a sequential computer may implement the task we will illustrate the successive phases of its execution by means of the parallel machine, timing them in terms of clock cycles and showing the influence of the array architecture on the structure of the program.

We will assume to use an array having the same characteristics of the currently working CLIP $3^{(7)}$ but of larger area (i.e. number of array cells). This array is assumed to be constructed using TTL medium scale integrated circuits and will be called CLIP 5.

The behaviour of a CLIP 5 parallel processor can be summarized in the following four points:
1)   The computer is able to extract as 0- or 1- elements from a
   binary digital image the 0- or 1- elements having a defined

neighbourhood. The neighbourhood can be restricted to any subset of the set of elements eight connected with the cells under consideration.

2) Any boolean operation between corresponding elements of two binary matrices can be performed.

3) A process referred to as propagation can be effected in which a signal from a cell is transmitted to its neighbours and from those to their neighbours and so on, resulting in the propagation of this signal through the whole array.

4) A branch instruction can be implemented which, according to the contents of a memory matrix (empty or not), allows the selection of alternative pathways in the program.

The times in clock cycles (cc) required to perform each of the quoted operations, including input and output of data, are: 2 cc for operations mentioned in 1) and 2), $(2 + 0.1n)$ cc for operations of the type 3) assuming propagation through n cells and 1 cc for operation 4).

A grey level image can be handled by the machine if suitably represented on a set of binary matrices whose number is equal to the number of bits necessary to represent the maximum grey level value in the image (see section 3).

II. The Task

The preprocessing of images often consists in extracting a subset of the given images so that only the significant part of information contained in them is retained. A particularly useful subset is that obtained by "thresholding" the image at a given grey level value. This may be achieved automatically by performing measurements on the grey level histogram of the image. We decided to test the performance of the parallel machine in implementing this task since it involves many arithmetical operations.

When using both a sequential computer and the parallel processor, we will consider the implementation of the "mode method" as reported in[8]. In other words we will start from the hypothesis that the subset of the input image to be extracted, has a range of grey levels different from those of the rest of the image, in such a way that the grey level histogram shows a peak in that range. The threshold values (one in some cases) coincide with the values corresponding to the minima of the valleys bordering that peak.

The basic procedure for automatically selecting the threshold value, can be subdivided into three parts: the first is devoted to the histogram construction, the second to valley detection in the histogram, so obtaining the threshold value, and the third to the relabelling of all elements as 1-elements if above threshold and as 0-elements if equal or under threshold. (Refer to figure 1).

III. Sequential and Parallel Execution

The implementation of the thresholding process is described briefly in the following, assuming the use of a conventional mini-computer. We assume the input image to be digitized into 32 grey levels and stored in a memory of n^2 words. Since we are interested in finding the dependency of processing times on the characteristics of the input image, we will not discuss the consequences of using sophisticated programming techniques because we estimate that they do not significantly influence this dependency. The first part of the program can be implemented by generating a raster scanner which reads the grey value L of each element and increments a counter $C(L)$. Each loop of the process requires approximately 20 clock cycles. Since n^2 elements are scanned, the complete process will require about $20n^2$ clock cycles. The second part of the program locates the minimum (only one in the case we consider) in the histogram and requires a time which can be ignored in comparison with n^2 for n greater than 10. Finally for the third part of the program, since every single element has to be relabelled a time again proportional to n^2 is required. The total execution time required is not less than $t_s = 30 \, n^2$ cc. We will now explain the execution of the same task by means of a CLIP 5 machine. To store a grey level image, a "bit-plane" stack organization is used where, in each column of the stack, a grey level value is encoded in binary form. The extraction of all elements having the same grey level L is performed by a combination of boolean operations between the planes of the stack. Such elements are stored as 1-elements on a binary matrix $A_1(L)$. An example is shown in figure 2. In general this process can be performed with 3 array operations each requiring two clock cycles; for 32 grey levels 6x32 = 192 cc. are therefore required. At this point we must count the 1-elements belonging to each of the $A_1(L)$ matrices to obtain the values of the ordinates of the grey level histogram.

Firstly the content of each column is computed obtaining a binary number which represents the total number of 1-elements present in that column. The program which implements such counting can be summarized as follows:

1) $A_1(L) \cdot A_2 \rightarrow B$

2) A (+) $B \rightarrow A$

3) Shift $A_1(L)$ down by one row $\rightarrow A_1(L)$

4) $A_1(L) = \emptyset$? If YES, STOP; if NO go to 1)

Program 1

In the first step an AND is performed between the input matrix $A_1(L)$ and matrix A_2 whose bottom row is filled with 1-elements.

The second step provides a particular operation, "column incrementation", indicated by (+) in the program (see below). The contents of A_1 are shifted down by one row. If A_1 is not empty after shifting, a new AND is performed between A_1 and A_2 (whose contents remain invariant during the whole process) and so on until after shifting, A_1 becomes empty. Column incrementation implies the addition of a 1 to the binary contents of a column of A whenever a 1-element is present on the corresponding column of B. Of course, this applies simultaneously to all the columns.

Every element receives information from its bottom neighbour; furthermore every i-th cell (i = 1,...,n) performs the following boolean operations between its inputs a_i and b_i

$$s_i = a_i \oplus (b_i + r_{i-1})$$
$$r_{i-1} = a_{i-1} \cdot (b_{i-1} + r_{i-2}).$$

We will illustrate a numerical example where only the number of 1-elements present in a specific column of A is counted (refer to Table I). The second and third columns of Table I contain the binary numbers belonging to a pair of corresponding columns of matrices A and B respectively; the following three columns are computed from the top to the bottom by applying the given expressions of s_i and r_{i-1}. The last Table column contains the result of the operation, that is the number of elements present in the considered column of $A_1(L)$. Note that the boundary conditions of the array are such that for i=1, $a_{i-1} = b_{i-1} = 0$.

The whole process above described takes $32 \cdot n \cdot (7 + 0.1 \log_2 n)$ clock cycles. The first number indicates the number of grey levels and the second one the maximum number of elements present in a column (corresponding to the number of iterations of the process). The term in brackets is the time required by one iteration of program 1. The first and third instructions of program 1 require 2 clock cycles each to be implemented, the fourth instruction (branch) requires one clock cycle whilst the second one, since it involves propagation, employs $(2 + 0.1 \log_2 n)$ clock cycles, where $\log_2 n$ is the length of the longest propagation path. In the next step all the numbers in the columns are added together so as to obtain the total number of 1-elements in $A_1(L)$, displayed in the first column of a new matrix. This is achieved by left-shifting the contents of A by n/2 columns and placing the result in A_3, then by adding A and A_3 and placing the result in A, then by shifting A by n/4 columns, storing the new result in A_3, adding A_3 to A and placing the result in A and so on, until in the first column of A the total sum of elements present in $A_1(L)$, that is those elements having the same grey level, is obtained. Note that all the remaining columns are left empty. The time taken to perform every shift is two clock cycles and consequently the total time involved is 32·2·n clock cycles. The factor n results from the sum of the geometrical series of ratio 1/2 and of terms n/2, n/4 and so on. The way in which the contents of every column of A can be added to the contents of the corresponding columns of A_3 is explained in detail in [10] using some results described in [9]. The time required to perform this binary column addition for all grey levels, so as to obtain one binary number in the first column of 32 matrices, is given by the following expression:

$$32 \cdot \log_2 n \cdot (8 + 0.1 \; \log_2 n^2)$$

where 32 is the number of grey levels and $\log_2 n$ the number of times the sums are performed, since such is the number of terms of the geometrical series previously mentioned. The term in brackets has a meaning analogous to the one given for column incrementation.

The second part of the process detects the valley of the histogram so as to automatically select the threshold value. The histogram matrix is shifted one place to the left and subtracted from the original histogram matrix; the sign bit of the differences (column by column) appears in the top row of a difference matrix. We will conventionally assign to the valley, the position of the first negative incremental difference following a positive difference. This position corresponds to a well defined grey value.

The binary subtraction between columns, due to the CLIP architecture, is formally analogous to the one used for column addition, therefore for further details refer again to [10]. The time required for obtaining a matrix where the sign bits occupy the top row, is (8 + 0.1 n) + 2 where the part inside brackets of the first term stands for the time needed to implement the

subtraction program. The second term represents the time taken to
extract the information from the top row of the matrix.

To determine the valley position we must shift the sign bit
row one place to the left and perform a new subtraction. The
time involved in this last operation is only 4 clock cycles, two
for shifting the row and the remaining two for the subtraction
between corresponding bits of the two rows. The bit 1 in the row
of the matrix H where the result of the subtraction is stored,
locates the minimum of the histogram and therefore the required
threshold value.

The location of this position is performed together with the
relabelling process, as is explained in the following. The complete parallel execution can be followed both in terms of its
subtasks and of the corresponding times by referring to figure 1.

A memory matrix Z is loaded with a 1-element in the left
corner of the top row. An AND is performed between Z and the
matrix H. If the resulting array is empty the contents of Z are
shifted one place to the right and, at the same time, the contents of the 6-bit-plane stack (which originally contained the
grey level image) are decremented by one.

This procedure is iterated until the results of the AND
operation between H and Z produces a non-empty array; at this
point the 6th plane containing the sign bit will have 1-elements
whenever the corresponding column originally had a grey level v
value smaller than that of the valley. By simply inverting the
contents of such an array the required thresholded image is obtained. The total time involved is smaller than 500 cc.

The full expression for the total amount of time, in clock
cycles, that a CLIP 5 machine requires to perform thresholding of
an n x n image with 32 grey levels, is:

$$t_p \stackrel{\sim}{=} 6\cdot 32 + (7 + 0.1\ \log_2 n)\cdot 32\cdot n + 32\cdot 2n + 32\cdot \log_2 n\cdot$$
$$(8 + 0.1\ \log_2 n^2) + 31\cdot 4 + 2 + (8 + 0.1n) + 2 + 4 + 500$$

Assuming $\log_2 n \cong 7$, the previous expression simplifies as follows

$$t_p \cong 300n + 2700$$

Although the expression of t_p appears essentially as linearly dependent on n whilst the expression of t_s is quadratically dependent on n, the presence of large constant factors in t_p, makes the parallel machine particularly advantageous for n > 50 (practical applications require n $\geq$ 100).

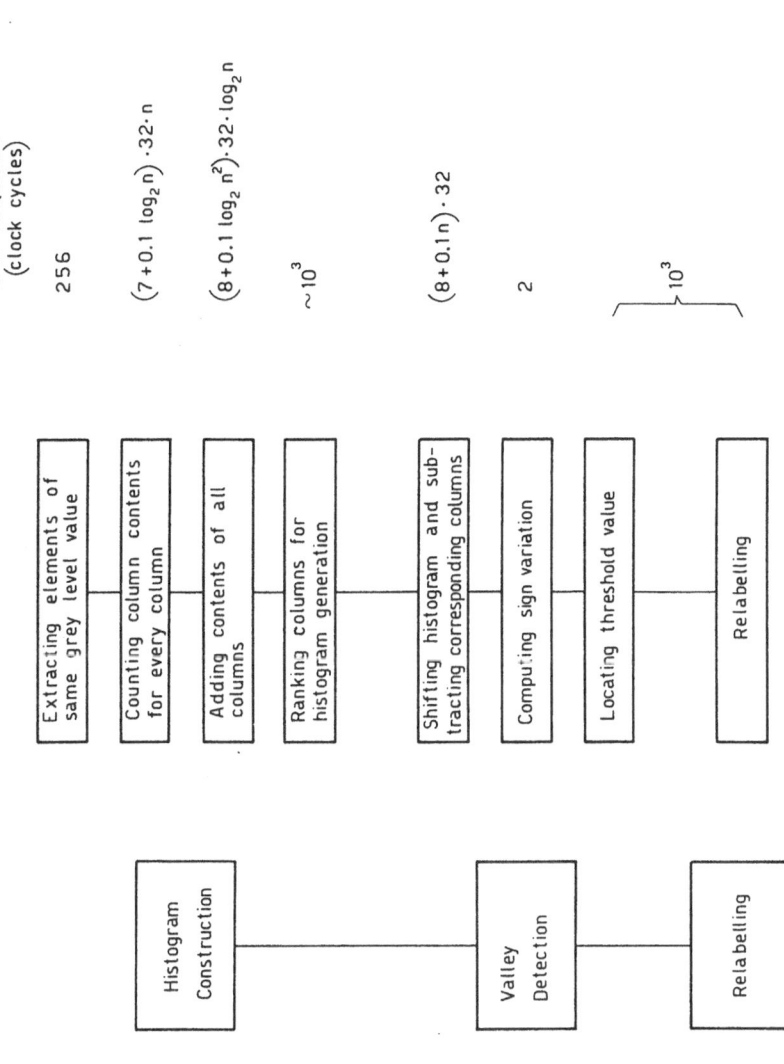

257

TIME REQUIRED
(clock cycles)

256

$(7 + 0.1 \log_2 n) \cdot 32 \cdot n$

$(8 + 0.1 \log_2 n^2) \cdot 32 \cdot \log_2 n$

$\sim 10^3$

$(8 + 0.1 n) \cdot 32$

2

10^3

Extracting elements of same grey level value

Counting column contents for every column

Adding contents of all columns

Ranking columns for histogram generation

Shifting histogram and subtracting corresponding columns

Computing sign variation

Locating threshold value

Relabelling

Histogram Construction

Valley Detection

Relabelling

Figure 1
On the left: a block diagram showing the three main steps of the process, both in the sequential and parallel cases. In the middle: a more detailed block diagram of the parallel implementation. On the right: the times required by the parts of the parallel program shown on the left.

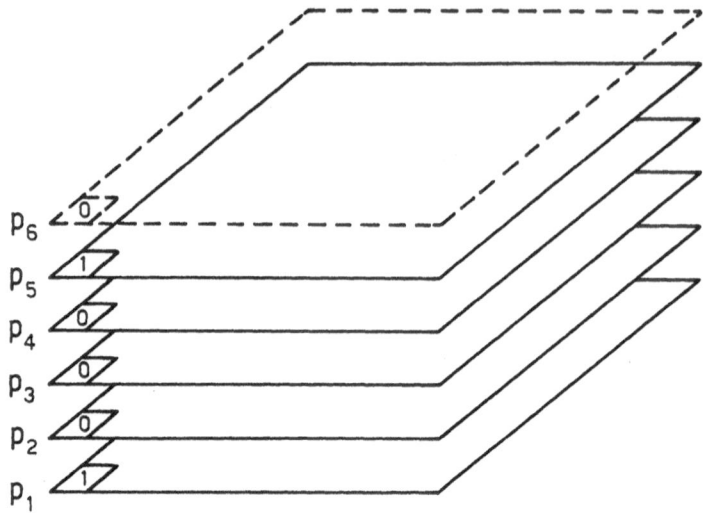

Figure 2
Bit-plane stack organization. To obtain all the elements with grey level 17, $(p_1 \cdot p_5) \cdot (\bar{p}_2 \cdot \bar{p}_3 \cdot \bar{p}_4)$ has to be performed. The plane p_6 is left for the sign bit when needed.

	i	a_i	b_i	r_{i-1}	$b_i + r_{i-1}$	s_i
lsb	1	1	1	0	1	0
	2	1	0	1	1	0
	3	1	0	1	1	0
	4	0	0	1	1	1
msb	5	0	0	0	0	0

Table I
Example of column incrementation showing the carry bit propagation.

References

1. Miller, R. E. "A comparison of some theoretical models of parallel computations", IEEE Trans. on Comp., C-22, 710, Aut. 1973.

2. Winograd, S. "Parallel Iterative Methods", in Complexity of Computer Computations, Plenum Press, 1972.

3. Beyer, T. W. "Recognition of Topological Invariants by Iterative Arrays", Ph.D. Thesis, M.I.T., 1969.

4. Arcelli, C. and Cordella, L. "Concavity Point Detection by Iterative Arrays", Computer Graphics and Image Processing 3, 1974, 34-37.

5. Orcutt, S. E. "A novel parallel computer architecture and some applications", Technical Report 71, 1974, Digital Systems Laboratory, Stanford Electronics Laboratories, Stanford, Calif.

6. Duff, M. J. B., Watson, D. M., Fountain, T. J. and Shaw, G. K. "A cellular logic array for image processing", Pattern Recognition 5, 1973, 229-247.

7. Duff, M. J. B., Watson, D. M., -CLIP 3 Operating Manual, Internal Report 73/4 - Image Processing Group, University College London.

8. Rosenfeld, A. "Picture processing by computer", Academic Press, 1969, p. 132.

9. Duff, M. J. B. - Arithmetic operations in CLIP 3, Internal Report 75/5; Image Processing Group, University College London.

10. Cordella, L., Duff, M. J. B. and Levialdi, S. - In preparation.

X-RAY IMAGE PROCESSING

M. Tasto

Philips Forschungslaboratorium Hamburg GmbH
2 Hamburg 54, Germany

I. The Problem

The automatic evaluation of medical X-ray images with the
goal to relieve medical doctors of some of their routine work is
of increasing interest. Careful investigation of the ways doctors use X-ray images shows that the main areas where machines can
be useful and economically feasible are automatic measurements and
automatic screening. It does not appear reasonable, at present,
to consider the general daily X-ray inspection work as a subject
for automatization.

The goal of our work is to determine system concepts and
algorithms for specific evaluation problems which can be implemented using existing hardware at reasonable cost and which require acceptable computation time.

II. Automatic Measurements in X-Ray Images

Examples of measurement problems and their medical relevance
are given in [1], [2], [3], and [4], namely heart width, volume
and shape from chest X-ray images, left ventricular volume and
boundary motion from cineangiograms, blood flow measurements,
bone measurements for skeletal age determination, etc.

The important properties of the class of pictures used for measurements are:

a) The object to be measured is always in the picture.

b) It may be partially covered by other objects.

c) The orientation is roughly known (say to within 10 degrees).

d) Size and shape are roughly known to within 20 or 30% variation, if the patient age is known.

e) Location of the object to be measured relative to certain other objects is roughly known.

These properties allow us to use top-down methods. First, a coarse survey of the major object of the entire scene is obtained at low resolution, i.e., using only a small number of pixels. Thus, data rate and number of computations are kept small. Next, the information obtained is used [5], [6] to determine a subarea of the picture which is then scanned at a higher resolution for a more refined analysis. This method helps to reduce the large amount of data associated with X-ray images such that it can be handled with existing technology and acceptable computation times.

Coarse object location: Four examples of coarse object location are discussed. A well known procedure is the signature method [7], where two projections of a picture are used to approximately locate dominating objects in a picture. In our medical examples the number of data words obtained from scanning could be kept at a few hundred.

Motion extraction methods [8] can be used for coarse object location in cases where the object of interest is the only one in the picture exhibiting size or brightness variations with respect to time. Cineangiographic recordings of left ventricles filled with contrast medium have this property. The brightness variance or similar measure with respect to time is determined for all pixels of a low resolution (say 32 x 32 pixels) picture, and an automatically found threshold is applied to discriminate motion areas from no-motion areas (Figure 1).

A somewhat more general method is template matching [9], where the machine finds an object in an X-ray image when a line drawing of a typical example of that object is given. Limited shape deviations are tolerated by the method. It uses a spatial distance measure (Figure 2) which allows to restrict the computation to additions and memory accesses, thus it is considerably faster than the common correlation method.

The simplest method for coarse object location is the prediction method applicable for the detection of slowly moving objects recorded on TV or cinefilms: The object boundary found in one frame is used to detect that in the next frame [10], [6].

A practical machine should also have a facility to bypass the automatic coarse object search by lightpen or similar device.

Refined detection of object boundaries: Using the coarse object boundary found by one of the methods above, a more precise boundary is determined within an uncertainty range. The maximum-gradient criterion can be used [10], where the directions in which the gradient is determined are perpendicular to the guiding boundary as shown in Figure 3.

Performance: In most cases the exact size of an object measured in an X-ray image cannot be determined. Hence, the performance of an automatic measurement system can only be found by comparison with measurements taken manually from X-ray images, which are, of course, subject to errors themselves. In order to determine typical accuracies obtained, the following comparisons were made for the example of left ventricular volume measurement:

1. Doctor against himself with 3 months delay between measurements.

2. Doctor A against Dr. B.

3. Doctor against engineer experienced in measuring ventricle volume.

4. Doctor against machine.

5. Engineer against machine.

Results for three patients with a total of about 120 frames are shown in Figure 4. Apparently the consistency of doctor A is very good, yet the agreement between different doctors and between doctors and engineers is worse. Agreement between the machine and doctors or engineers is comparable or slightly worse.

Experience shows that in cases of very poor picture quality the machine fails completely, whereas humans always find "something" to measure.

<u>Technical realization</u>: The measurement system for left ventricular volume determination is under development. A 32 k - 16 bit computer does the processing of the data and the control of a lightpen unit and a scanner (Figure 6). Standard TV signals are scanned with variable resolution and scan area as shown in Figure 5. A variable low-pass filter is realized by combined hardware (linewise) and software (columnwise) integration.

III. Automatic Screening

With respect to the scene analysis problem, X-ray images subject to automatic screening have the following properties:

1. There are various objects visible that are not of interest.

2. The objects of interest (tumors, mocrocalcifications, etc.) may or may not be in the picture, or there may be more than one object of interest.

3. Orientation, size, and shape are not known except for some general shape properties.

4. There is no a priori knowledge about the location of objects of interest.

These properties do not allow us to use top-down methods. The entire picture must be searched, and the amount of data to be processed becomes extremely large especially when the objects to be detected are small. In the following we discuss the detection of microcalcifications in female breast X-ray images as a typical example. Microcalcifications are irregularly shaped bright spots

with sharp edges and size between 0.1 and 1 mm. The smaller ones
may be confused with noise, artifacts and sometimes with blood
vessels and breast structure, the larger ones are usually well
visible [11], [12], [13], [14]. Since they are so small, approximately 10 million pixels per picture must be scanned and processed,
with commonly 4 pictures taken per patient. This cannot be handled
by a conventional computer in reasonable processing time.

A possible solution [15] is to design the recognition process
using a tree structure as shown in Figure 7, where the features
are determined from a window moved over the entire picture (Figure
8). The first move is realized by a special purpose hardware,
which rapidly determines simple features and decides on whether
pixels are candidates for microcalcifications or not. Such features may be local brightness maxima and the amount of brightness
with respect to the environment. This preselection reduces the
number of candidates to approximately $0.5 \cdot 10^{-3}$ of the total
(Figure 9). So far, experiments have been made with 3 features:
Local maximum, brightness difference relative to environment, and
number of zero-one transitions within a thresholded window contents as shown in Figure 10. Scatter plots of the latter two
features for different examples of pictures are shown in Figure 11.

So far, a correct recognition rate of 95% or better appears
possible. Yet, the false alarm rate is too high, partly as a result of artifacts. Therefore, present investigation centers on
the problem of comparing two projections of each breast for the
purpose of verification. A major difficulty is the deformation of
the breast during the processing of taking X-ray pictures, which
usually differs for two projections. We are attempting to solve
the problem by a combination of "rubber-stretching" and correlation
algorithms.

IV. Conclusions

Automatic measurements of organ sizes in medical X-ray pictures can be realized with existing serial computers at reasonable

cost and computation time, if top-down methods are used, and if the data rates and number of computations are kept low by using "intelligent" scanners, whose parameters are controlled by a computer.

Detection of tumors, microcalcifications, etc. does not allow the use of a priori information, hence the entire picture must be scanned and processed. In order to achieve acceptable computation times, this may require combination of special purpose hardware processors with conventional computers.

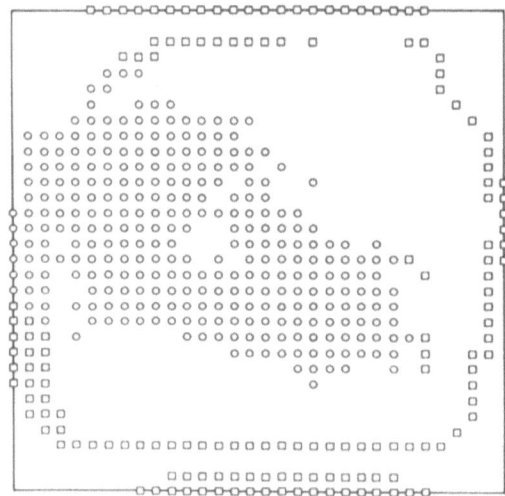

Figure 1
Binary picture before and after
noise cleaning (□ points removed
by noise cleaning procedure).

Figure 2
Template superimposed in
boundary points of given
scene. The template is close
to the object of interest.

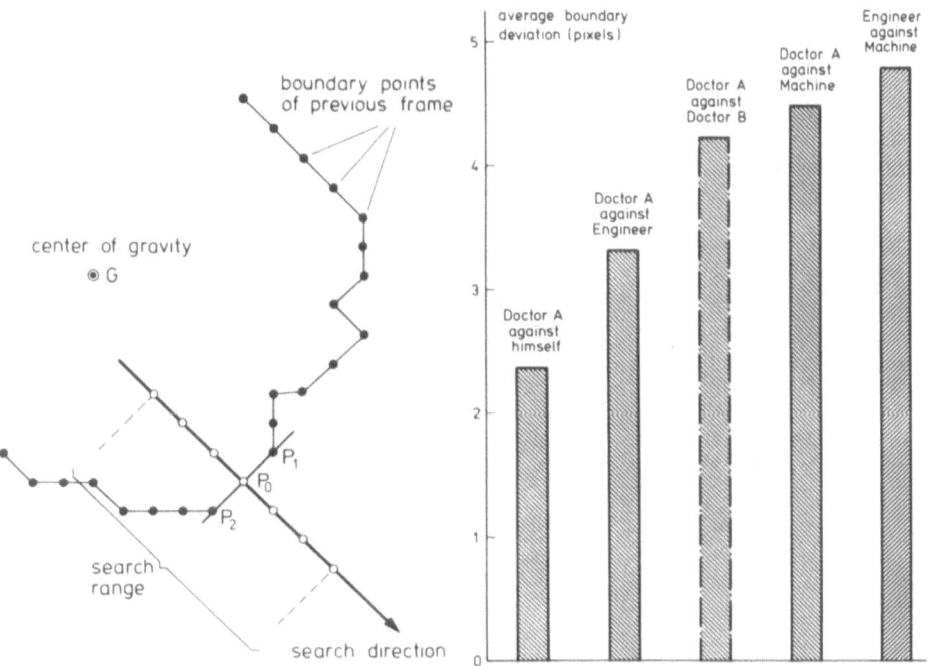

Figure 3
Principle of guided
boundary detection.

Figure 4
Human vs. human and machine vs.
human measurement comparison.

268

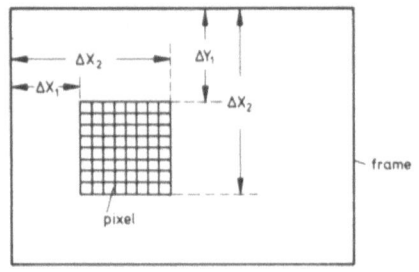

a) small subarea, high resolution

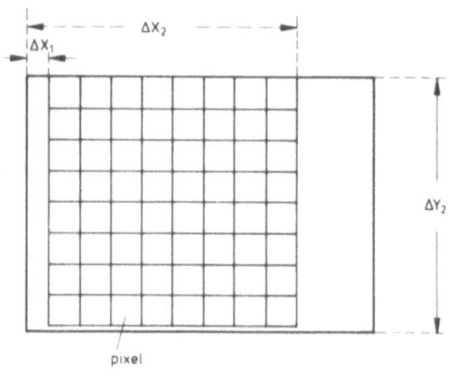

b) large subarea, low resolution

Figure 5
Computer controlled scanning.

Figure 6
The grafomed system for
automatic or computer assisted
measurements in X-ray images.

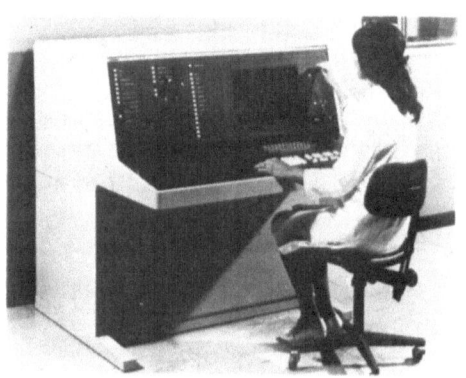

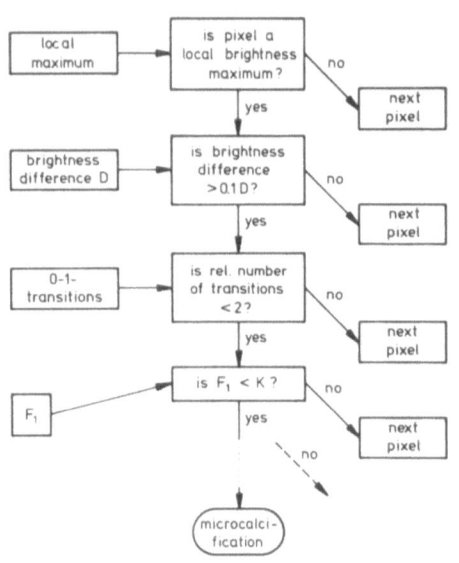

Figure 7
Decision tree for the detection of microcalcifications.

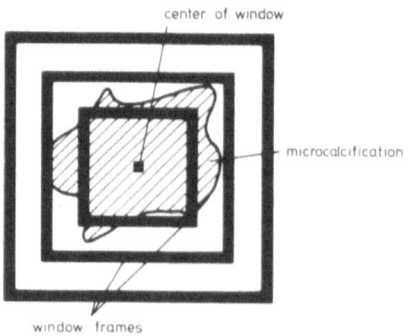

Figure 8
Window operator covering up
to 40 x 40 pixels.

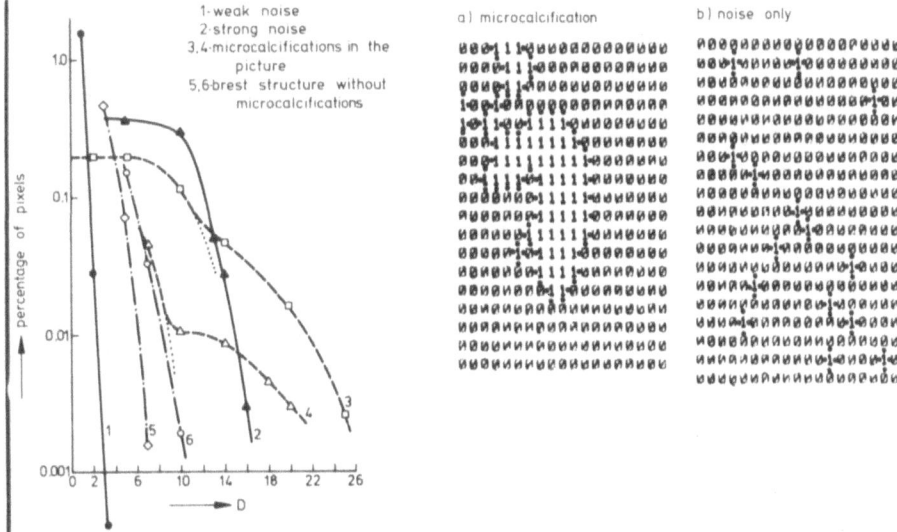

Figure 9
Percentage of pixels whose
brightness is below D.

Figure 10
Thresholded content of 19 x 19
window.

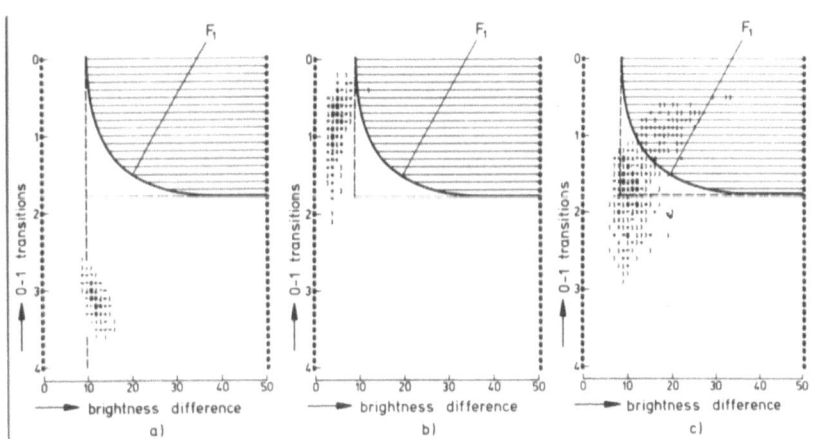

Figure 11
Scatter plots in two dimensional feature space: (a) noise only;
(b) breast structure without microcalcifications; (c) breast
structure with microcalcifications.

270

References

1. Lusted, Keats: <u>Atlas of Roentgenographic Measurements</u>, Yearbook, Medical Publishers, Inc., 1967.

2. Reindell, et al.: <u>Funktionsdiagnostik de gesunden und kranken Herzens</u>, Thieme Verlag, 1967.

3. Heintzen, P. H., ed.: <u>Roentgen-, Cine- and Videodensitometry</u>, Thieme Verlag, 1971.

4. Grenlych, W. W., Pyles, S. I.: "Radiographic Atlas of Skeletal Development of the Hand and Wrist,"Stanford, 1959.

5. Griffith, A. K.: "Edge Detection in Simple Scenes Using A Priori Information", <u>IEEE Trans. Comp.</u>, Vol. C-22, No. 4, April 1973.

6. Spiesberger, W., Tasto, M.: "Machinaal meten aan röntgenop-namen"(Dutch), Philips techn. T., 35, 179-182, 1975, n.o.6.

7. Kruger, R. P., Townes, J. R., Hall, D. L., Dwyer, S. J. III and Sodnick, G. S.: "Automated Radiographic Diagnosis via Feature Extraction and Classification of Cardiac Size and Shape Descriptors", <u>IEEE Trans.</u>, Vol. BME-19, No. 3, May 1972, pp. 174-186.

8. Tasto, M.: "Motion Extraction for Left Ventricular Volume Measurement", <u>IEEE Transactions on Biomed. Eng.</u>, Vol. BME-21, May 1974, pp. 207-213.

9. Tasto, M., Block, U.: Locating Objects in Complex Scenes Using a Spatial Distance Measure, Proceedings 2nd Intern. Conf. on Pattern Recognition, Copenhagen, August 1974.

10. Tasto, M.: Guided Boundary Detection for Left Ventricular Volume Measurement, Proceedings First Intern. Joint Conf. on Pattern Recognition, Washington, D. C., October 1973.

11. Hoeffken, W., Lanyi, M.: Röntgenuntersuchung der Brust, Stuttgart, 1973.

12. Gershon-Cohen: <u>Atlas of Mammography</u>, Berlin, 1970.

13. Winsberg, F., Elkin, M., Maey, J.: "Detection of Radiographic Abnormalities in Mammograms by Means of Optical Scanning and Computer Analysis", <u>Radiology</u> 89 (1967) 211.

14. Ackerman, L. V., Gose, E. E.: "Breast Lesion Classification by Computer and Xeroradiography", <u>Cancer,</u> Vol. 30, October 1972, p. 1025-1035.

15. Tasto, M.: Automatische Mammographie-Auswertung: Erkennung von Mikroverkalkungen, Tagungsband Medizin-Technik, Stuttgart, Mai 1975.

RECOGNIZING BINARY PICTURES BY THEIR CONTOUR SLOPE SEQUENCE

Stein Grinaker

Norwegian Defense Research Establishment
N - 2007 Kjeller, Norway

Abstract: Two principles for classifying binary pictures
by contour analysis are compared. The methods are two variants
based on the slope sequence, allowing a one-to-one mapping from
contour to contour function, and the contour slope density introduced in (3).

Fourier analysis of the contour functions have been considered.
A few very simple geometric-shaped objects are used in testing the
methods.

Idealized contour data have been applied to obtain an indication of the quality of the methods on optimal input data. Digital,
binary pictures, some very noisy, have been applied in order to
investigate a practical case.

Some of the results are presented.

I. Introduction

Classification of a 3-dimensional object is usually done by
classifying the object's projection onto a picture plane. A
method of classifying binary, 2-dimensional figures is presented,
assuming a black and white picture available by pre-processing
the original picture.

The feature extraction is based on contour analysis. As in the papers of Zahn and Roskies (1) and Freeman (2) the slope sequence is considered. This is done in such a way that a one-to-one mapping from the contour to the contour function is obtained. Two variants are considered and compared with the method of contour slope density, introduced by Sklansky and Davison (3).

We want a real-time classification system, analyzing every second half-picture from a TV-camera, i.e., 25 scene analysis per second. In addition the system has to be low cost and small size hardware implemented, and invariance with respect to rotations and translations of the object in the picture plane is required.

By using the Fourier transform of the contour-functions, these requirements will be satisfied using the slope sequence in about the same manner as by using the slope density. The former, however, will tend to be slightly more expensive. Bearing this in mind, this presentation will concentrate on a comparison of the classifying ability of the two methods.

A few very simple geometric-shaped figures are used in testing the methods. Both noiseless and noisy contour data have been applied, and some typical results are presented.

II. The Contour Functions

In the presentation of the contour functions, polygonals whose lines are commensurable with respect to a predefined δ-vector are used. Let the contour consist of a sequence of such vectors, orientated in such a manner that a convex figure always will be on the right side of the vectors, and let the subscript increase by following the contour counter-clockwise.

A. The Contour Slope Density (CSD)

The CSD is defined by

$$f(\Theta) = \lim_{\substack{\Delta\Theta \to 0 \\ \delta \to 0}} \frac{n\delta}{\Delta\Theta}$$

δ is the length of the vectors, and n is the number of elements contained in $\{\Theta_i | \Theta \leq \Theta_i < \Theta + \Delta\Theta\}$ where Θ_i is the angle of the i th vector

with respect to the horizontal axis. Graphically this will be
equivalent to marking the number of vectors in the angular interval {$\Theta,\Theta+\Delta\Theta$>, normalized by the ratio $\delta/\Delta\Theta$.

As an example, consider the rectangle in Figure 1. 20% of
the contour has a slope of $\pi/2$ (a_1), 20% a slope of $3\pi/2$ (a_2),
while the angles π and 2π each make 30% of the contour (b_1 and
b_2).

Note that, if considering only convex contours, the drawing
of the contour will be possible when the CSD is known. This will
be feasible because the angle, Θ, will be a monotone function
of the distance around the contour, and in this way the CSD will
contain the information of the slope sequence. However, if the
contours also have concavities, the reconstruction will be impossible, and there will be an infinite number of contours giving
the same CSD.

We may immediately note some fundamental properties of the
CSD: It is periodic ($T=2\pi$), it is independent of translations of
the object, and rotation of the object implies translation of $f(\Theta)$.

By normalizing the CSD, i.e., normalizing the polygonal's
perimeter, $f(\Theta)$ will exclusively depend on the shape of the contour.

B. The Contour Slope Sequence (CSS)

We found the CSD insufficient to represent concave figures,
because the independent variable did not contain information of
the sequence around the contour. The CSS is based exclusively on
the dependence between the angle of the slope, Θ, and the distance
around the contour, l. This function should then ensure a one-to-
one transformation from contour to contour function.

Consider the rectangle used when illustrating the CSD method.
We now (Figure 2) draw a line at an angle $\pi/2$, of length proportional to a_1, continue with a line proportional to b_1, at an angle
π, and so on. When the contour has been completed, the angle has
increased to 2π. The proportionality coefficient has been chosen
as 1.

Note, however, that this function does not contain the important property of the CSD of being periodic, i.e., by following the contour once more, another function appears, differing from the first by the constant 2π. This defect is, however, easily overcome by a simple modification of the slope diagram. We find the angular difference between the contour and the circle of the same perimeter, i.e. the difference between the initial diagram and the straight line $1 \cdot 2\pi/T$. This new function will then be periodic. The initial step-function will now be replaced by a sawtooth-function, having a falling slope of $-2\pi/T$. T denotes the perimeter of the contour and should usually be normalized.

The sawtooth-coded CSS is then defined by

$$g_1(1) = \Theta(1) - 1 \cdot 2\pi/T$$

Another variant of the CSS is pulse-coded. The amplitudes of the pulses are given by the angular differences between connected δ-vectors. The widths of the pulses are proportional to the number of consecutive δ-vectors at the same angle with respect to the horizontal axis. The separation between two following pulses is identical to the width of the first one. Figure 3 illustrates the method used on our rectangle.

Also the CSS is periodic (T = the perimeter) and independent of translations of the object. Rotating the object will result in a horizontal translation of the contour functions depending on the movement of the contour starting-point. In addition $g_1(1)$ will be vertically translated depending on the angle of rotation.

III. Fourier Analysis

When using these contour functions to identify objects in a multicategory case, the decision will be based on the likelihood between the contour function of the object and the predefined pattern functions of the categories. Several classification algorithms, basing the decision on the contour function itself, are available. By introducing Fourier analysis of the contour functions we will, however, obtain several simplifications.

Let $f(x)$ be a bounded, periodic function, having a finite
number of discontinuities. $f(x)$ may then be represented by its
Fourier series, defined by

$$f(x) = c_o + \sum_{n=1}^{\infty} c_n \cos \left(\frac{2n\pi}{T} x - \psi_n\right)$$

To obtain a feature vector dependent only upon the shape of
the contour function, we may use a truncated set of the coefficients, c_n, as features. The optimal dimension of the feature
vector, i.e. the dimension resulting in the minimum error rate,
will depend on the decision of the contour function, the objects
to be classified and the signal-to-noise ratio. A sophisticated
solution of this problem, has, however, not been enforced. The
number of harmonics used in the following test, 7-10 depending
on the contour function under consideration, will, however, maximize the minimum vector distance between the patterns in the
testing set.

The most important advantages obtained by Fourier analysis
should then be:

a) Data reduction
    The continuous contour function is replaced by a low-
    dimensional feature vector
b) The feature vector will exclusively depend on the shape
    of the contour
c) Noise filtering
    By using the truncated Fourier spectrum, the higher
    frequencies generated by the quantization will be ig-
    nored.

An interesting detail should also be mentioned:

Based on the CSD or the sawtooth-coded CSS, an object and
its reflection will have identical Fourier spectra. In fact, by
reflecting the contour, the two contour functions will be flipped
about one or both of the axes, and their Fourier spectra will
remain unchanged (Figure 4). This implies still more data

reduction, but also lost information. The two functions can not discriminate between objects seen from opposite directions.

The very most important advantage gained by using the Fourier analysis is, however, the possibility of getting a quick and inexpensive classification, feasible by reading the picture and computing the feature vector in parallel.

Consider the feature extractor based on the CSD. When a δ-vector is found, its contribution to the Fourier coefficients depends exclusively on the slope angle, θ. By prestoring all possible additions, these parts may be read using θ as the input signal, and then be added to the parts of the coefficients computed from the earlier detected contour path.

Based on the CSS, the additions to the Fourier coefficients will depend on the angular difference between one δ-vector and the next one, which is easily computed, and the vectors distance from the contour starting-point, i.e. the abscissa of the contour function. Considering a binary scene, Figure 5 shows 4 states of a TV-scan. It is easily seen that when the δ-vector is detected, its distance from the contour starting-point may very well be unknown. Furthermore, we are not sure whether two contour paths really are parts of the same contour.

These difficulties are easily overcome by computing a separate feature vector for each contour part. This can be done by degrees as the δ-vectors are detected. Afterwards one has to compensate for the distance between the origin of one contour function and the origin of the text, and the vectors obtained from the same object are added. The CSS-period has to be computed in the preceeding TV-frame.

IV. Experimental Results

A few very simple geometric-shaped objects are used to test the methods. Five pictures of each object, varying the distance and the orientation, are used. Some representative results are presented in Figure 6. For comparison, the results using noisless contour data are marked. These data were also used to compute the patterns. The results are presented as vector distances between the N-dimensional feature vector of the object and each of the pattern vectors, normalized with respect to the mean of the two vectors.

Using the nearest-neighbour classification algorithm, the shortest vector distance indicates the pattern of the object. The mean and the spread of the distances between the pattern and the feature vectors of the objects of the same category are marked.

These classifications indicate that the CSD as well as the sawtooth-coded CSS discriminate satisfactorily. The pulse-coded CSS, however, seems to be too sensitive with respect to noise, indicated by the misclassifications. Working on nearly noiseless contour data, this method will, however, discriminate even better than the other methods under consideration, especially when classifying contours of only slightly different shapes. An indication of this is the discrimination of the right-angled pentagon and the right-angled triangles. This set of objects is, however, unsuitable as a basis for this statement. However, other testing sets, more suitable, have been considered.

V. Conclusions

The unsatisfactory way of classifying concave objects by the CSD seems to be a serious disadvantage in several classification problems. However, when parts of the objects are hidden, which may very well happen in several applications, it should be practical to split the contour into only convex parts, taking, however, the sequence of the contour parts into account. Under such conditions the CSD feature extractor is preferable because of the simple hardware implementation. However, the decomposition of the contour makes it necessary to have a great number of patterns and increased processing time. When the whole contour is available, one classification per object is preferable. In most cases, one will be confronted with the concavity classification problem, and the CSS is assumed to be the most satisfactory feature extractor considered in this presentation, especially when arbitrary objects may appear.

When classifying easily discriminated objects, the sawtooth-coded CSS should be preferable, since this method does not require the same accurate data as the pulse-coded CSS, and the hardware implementation should not be much more expensive than for the CSD.

When discriminating nearly identical objects, however, the necessary disintegration in the detector and the accurate treatment of the signals should prior the pulse-coded variant because of its discriminating ability.

In some cases this method may also be preferable because of the possibility of discriminating reflected objects.

We have found that all three methods have some advantages. The sawtooth-coded CSS will in most applications of contour analysis work satisfactorily, and be the most general basis for the feature extractor, though in special cases the others may be preferable.

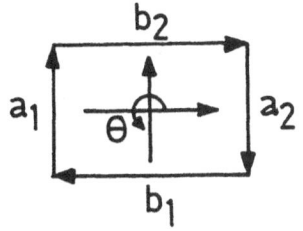

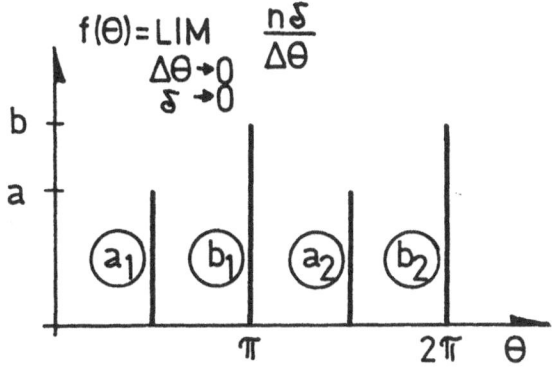

Figure 1
The contour slope density of a rectangle.

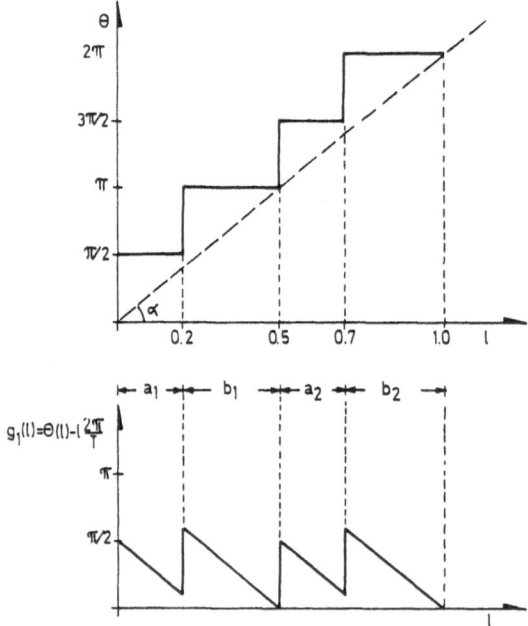

Figure 2
The sawtooth-coded CSS of a rectangle.

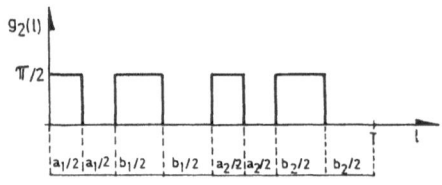

Figure 3
The pulsecoded CSS of a rectangle.

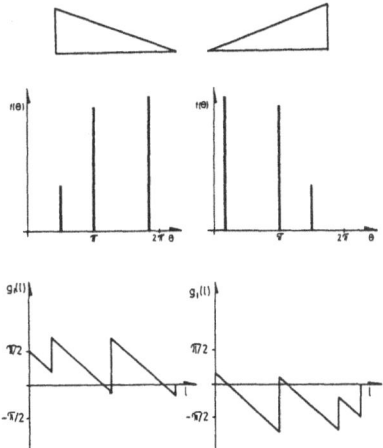

Figure 4
Due to reflection of an object, the CSD and the sawtooth-coded
CSS will be flipped about one or two axes.

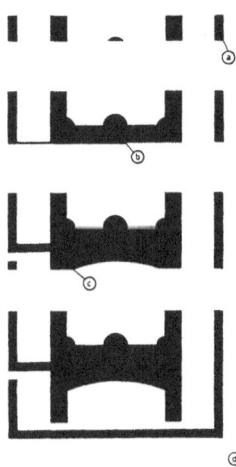

Figure 5
Four states of a TV scan, indicating the difficulties of a real-
time sequential contour analysis.

284

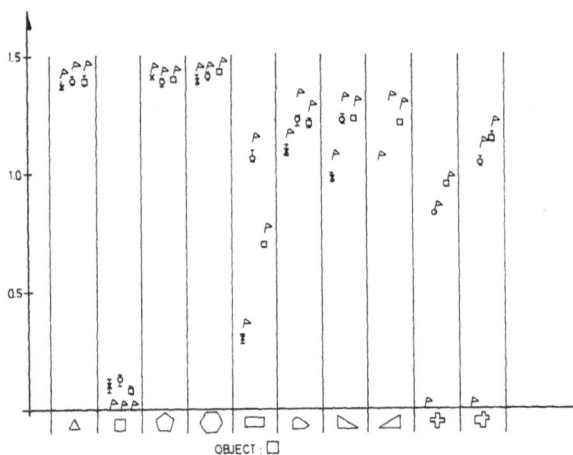

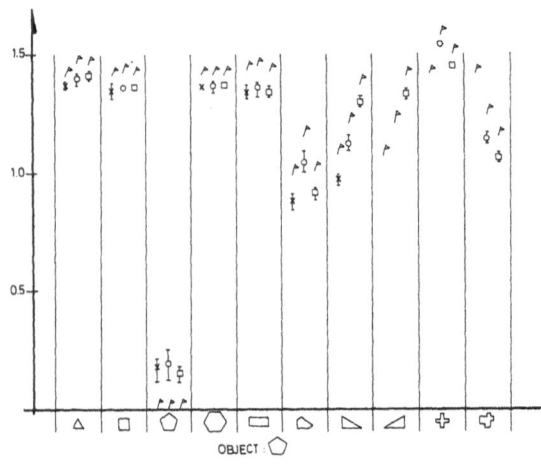

Figure 6 (cont.)
The classification results explained by vector distances in
feature space. Each column shows, from left to right, the results
using the CSD (=✗), the sawtooth-coded CSS (=○), and the pulse-
coded CSS (=◻) on the noiseless contour data and the experimental
data (=⊬) respectively.

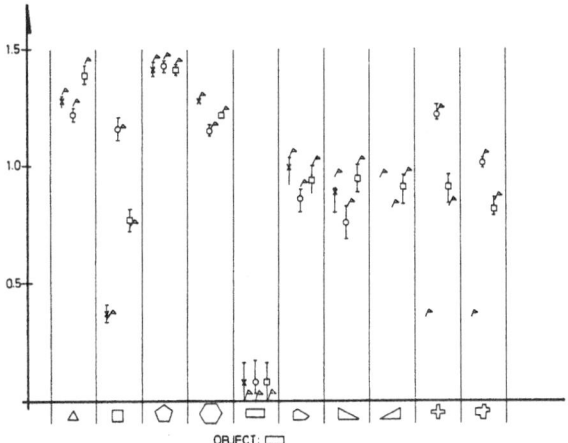

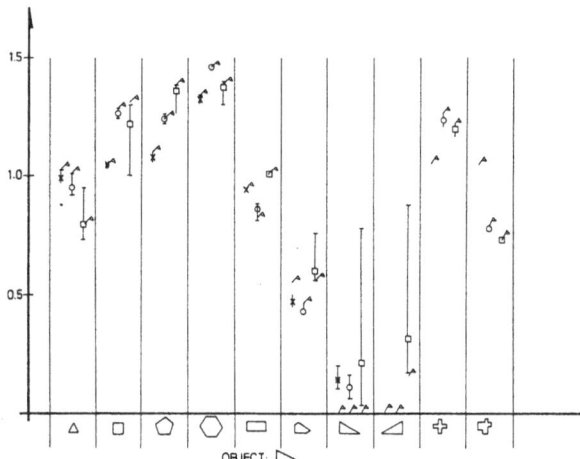

Figure 6 (cont.)

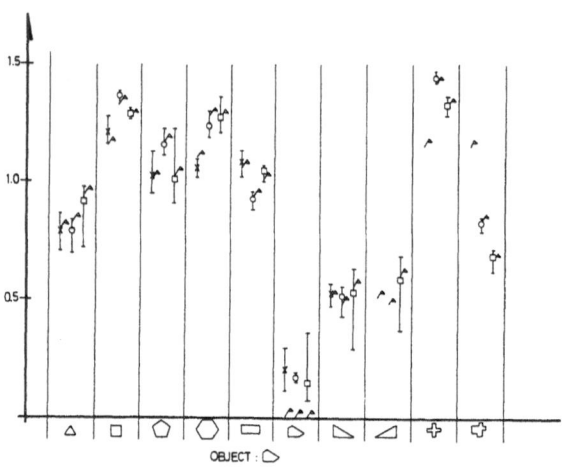

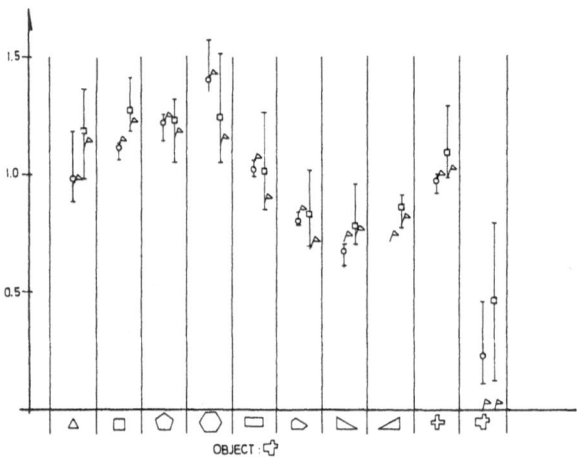

Figure 6

References

1. Zahn, C. T. and Roskies, R. Z., "Fourier Descriptors of Plane Closed Curves", IEEE Trans. Computers, C-21, No. 3, March 1972.

2. Freeman, H., "On the Encoding of Arbitrary Geometric Configurations", IRE Trans. Elec. Comp., EC-10, pp. 260-268, June 1961.

3. Sklansky, J. and Davison, G. A., Recognizing three-dimensional objects by their silhouettes, AGARD Conference Proceedings 94 on Artificial Intelligence, 1971.

ON SPEECH RECOGNITION AND SPEECH UNDERSTANDING SYSTEMS

Renato De Mori

Politecnico di Torino
Corso Duca degli Abruzzi 24
10129 - Torino, ITALY

I.   Introduction

Speech recognition researches begun probably in 1950 with the design of an automatic recognizer of the ten spoken digits [1].

Several projects using special purpose machines or general purpose computers were developed in the following twenty years and the set of words recognized became larger up to contain 200 words [2]. The results obtained were encouraging in some cases (recognition rates from 80 to 98%), but they were always restricted to a limited number of well trained speakers. The systems used in such projects will be reviewed briefly in the following, nevertheless the main point they made evident is that the possible applications of such methods did not go beyond the voice command of a desk calculator and that, for this purpose, they were too much expensive.

Some observers think that, far from approaching the end of the task, we are only just getting an idea of the size of the problem.

The reasons of the limited results obtained so far are probably in the fact that speech recognition is not merely a pattern matching problem, but a complex procedure of language understanding. It is important to mention Pierce [11] at this point who believes that a general purpose speech recognizer will not be successful until it can match some of the highest levels of human ability. This new view for the problem implies new methodologies and requires new research to be done but it opens new areas of possible applications.

Speech understanding is the recognition of spoken sentences instead of isolated words, with particular emphasis to the meaning of the sentence even if all the words are not correctly recognized.

Accomplishing this task requires the conception of a model for speech perception where all the sources of knowledge such as phonetic and phonological rules, lexicon, syntax, semantics and pragmatics employed by humans are properly represented in the recognition system and a strategy is defined to establish how to use them in order to interpret a spoken waveform.

An extended field of useful applications would become realizable once automatic speech understanding will be possible; some of them are listed in recent report [3] and are recalled here. The advantages of such applications come from the ease and convenience of using speech in carring informations.

The data rate of speech is substantially faster (about 10 times) than writing; furthermore speech can be conveniently conveyed practically everywhere through the telephone network. Some of the envisaged applications are: querying a data management system, data acquisition of formatted information, querying the operational status of a computer, consulting on the operation of a computer, automatic reservation and travel information systems, air traffic controller, medical history taking, automatic protocol analysis, robot management.

A large amount of researches are implied for defining the contents and the structure of the knowledge sources the speech understanding systems has to consult when trying to attempt the learning of a sentence. They go from the signal processing techniques to the semantic model of the speaker's world.

It is impossible to review the details of the work done for all the levels of speech understanding. The attention will be limited in this report to the problem of extracting patterns from the speech data and to establish a connection between these patterns and the phonological structure of a spoken language. This aspect seems to involve remarkably pattern recognition theories.

Some generalities on speech production and perception can be found in [5]. They show with Chistovich [20], Klatt [4], Fant [22], Gumetsky et al. [14] [15] how speech recognition researches may have a lot in common with the studies of spoken natural languages, their production and their perception.

II. Techniques For Speech Analysis

Frequency-domain representation of speech information appears advantageous mainly for two reasons.

The mechanism of speech production can be described for many sounds in terms of resonant frequencies. Furthermore, evidence exists that the ear makes e crude frequency analysis in processing speech [5].

Moreover, a Fourier transform cannot be performed on a long interval of the speech waveform. In such case, the obtained spectrum would exibit an average of the characteristics of the sounds contained in the interval. In order to analyze portions of the speech waveform corresponding to a single sound, it is necessary to introduce a running window that selects only small intervals of the waveform for the analysis.

The window introduces errors in the computed spectra and care has to be taken in order to avoid that such errors mask the acoustic properties that have to be extracted from the spectra.

Assuming $x(t)$ be a periodic signal to be analyzed and $w(t)$ be the windowing signal, the resulting signal $s(t)$ is given by:

$$s(t) = x(t) \cdot w(t) \qquad (1)$$

Taking the Fourier transform $S(f)$ of (1) one gets:

$$S(f) = W(f) \oplus X(f) = \int_{-\infty}^{\infty} W(f - \lambda) \ X(\lambda) \ d\lambda \qquad (2);$$

where $W(f)$ is the Fourier transform of $w(t)$ and $X(\lambda)$ is the Fourier transform of the periodic signal $x(t)$; $X(\lambda)$ can be expressed as follows:

$$X(\lambda) = \sum_{n=-\infty}^{\infty} Z(f) \ W_o(f - n \ F_o) \qquad (3).$$

F_o is the fundamental frequency of the speech signal, u_o is the Kronecker delta that is one for $f = n \ F_o$ and zero elsewhere; $Z(f)$ is a continuous function of f having values equal to the harmonics of $x(t)$ at multiples of F_o. The (2) can be rewritten in a form that makes evident the errors introduced by the window in the computed spectra at the multiples of F_o:

$$S(x \ F_o) = \sum_{m=-\infty}^{\infty} W(n \ F_o - m \ F_o) \ Z(m \ F_o) \qquad (4).$$

Some types of windows and their spectra are shown in fig. 1. The frequency scale is normalized with respect to $f_o = \frac{1}{T}$ where T is the duration of the window. A comparison of the three spectra shows that the Hamming window introduces small errors (less than 40 dB) if $2 \ f_o < F_o$; this condition corresponds to a window interval at least twice the fundamental period.

Larger window intervals are required to obtain the same results with the parzen window or the rectangular window.

If the windowed signal $s(t)$ is sampled, it is represented by a series of numbers:

$$s(0), \ s(\tau), \ s(2\tau), \ s(3\tau), \ \ldots, \ s(n\tau), \ \ldots$$

where τ is the sampling period. The sampling frequency $f_s = \frac{1}{\tau}$ has to be at least twice the highest frequency that gives a contribution different from zero to the spectrum; f_s may vary depending on the filtering applied to the original signal.

Spectra of $s(t)$ can be computed from its samples using the DFT (Discrete Fourier Transform) algorithm as follows:

$$S(k\Omega) = \sum_{n=0}^{N-1} s(n\tau) \, e^{-jnk\Omega\tau} \tag{5}.$$

$\Omega = \dfrac{2\pi}{N\tau}$ is the spectral resolution and $N\tau$ is the duration of the window. Better spectral estimates are obtained if $N\tau$ is a multiple of $\dfrac{1}{F_o}$.

In this case the spectral analysis is said to be "pitch-synchronous".

A fast algorithm, for obtaining short time spectra, named Fast Fourier Transform (FFT), can be found in [6].

A lot of experiments, carried out in the last 25 years, show that the most important features that exibit a correspondence between the linguistic structure of the language and its spectral realizations are the time evolutions of the energy concentrations.

The frequencies corresponding to the centers of gravity of such zones are the formant measurements.

The ripple introduced on the spectra by the window can make erroneous or impossible the detection of some formants. For this reason appropriate methods have been introduced for spectral smoothing. One of such methods, named "cepstral analysis", consists in computing the logarithm of the magnitude of the spectrum and to perform a FFT on this logarithm. The spectrum obtained is called "cepstrum" and its frequencies are called "quefrencies". The effects of the window gives contributions mainly at high quefrencies. These contributions can be eliminated by low-pass filtering the cepstrum. The FFT of the filtered cepstrum is a smoothed version of the logarithmic spectral magnitude of the original signal. The method, described in details in [8], is very time expensive even if it allows one to obtain from the cepstrum also the pitch by high-pass filtering the cepstrum itself. The peaks of the ripple in the original spectra have, in fact, a distance proportional to the fundamental frequency.

As other method for obtaining smoothed spectra consists in modelling the vocal tract by al all-pole transversal filter. The

parameters of the model are obtained by an algorithm that tries
to predict a sample $x(n\tau)$ of the speech signal, given p previous
samples:

$$x(n\tau-\tau), \; x(n\tau-2\tau), \; \ldots, \; x(n\tau-k\tau), \; \ldots, \; x(n\tau-p\tau).$$

The predicted sample $x'(n\tau)$ is given by:

$$x'(n\tau) = \sum_{k=1}^{p} a_k \, x(n\tau - k\tau) \tag{6}$$

For each sample, a prediction error is defined as follows:

$$e(n\tau) = x(n\tau) - x'(n\tau) \tag{7}$$

The prediction coefficients $\{a_k\}$ are computed by minimizing
the mean square prediction error. If the signal is windowed, the
minimization of the error can be extended only to the duration of
the window.

Three basic methods have been proposed for computing the coefficients of the model; they are named the direct, the autocorrelation and the covariance method and are described and discussed
in [9].

Given a series of samples $\{x(n\tau)\}$, $-\infty \le n \le +\infty$, its z-transform $X(z)$ is defined as follows;

$$X(z) = \sum_{k=-\infty}^{+\infty} x(k\tau) \, z^{-k} \tag{8}$$

Taking the z-transforms of the signal $x(n\tau)$ and the error
$e(n\tau)$ one gets:

$$E(z) = X(z) \left(1 - \sum_{k=1}^{p} a_k \, z^{-k}\right) = X(z) \, H(z) \tag{9}$$

with:

$$H(z) = 1 - \sum_{k=1}^{p} a_k \, z^{-k} \quad \cdot$$

$H(z)$ is the transfer function of a filter that receives at
its input the speech samples and gives at the output the samples
of the prediction error.

The (9) can be rewritten as follows:

$$X(z) = \frac{E(z)}{H(z)} \qquad (10).$$

The prediction error can now be seen as the excitation of a filter having transfer function $\frac{1}{H(z)}$ that gives, at the output, the speech signal; this filter is a transversal filter and is considered a possible model of the vocal tract.

Many experiences showed that the prediction error is, in many cases, very similar to the excitation signal of the vocal tract and can be approximated, for the voiced sounds, by a Kronecker delta.

This suggests to consider an approximation $\hat{X}(z)$ of $X(z)$ given by:

$$\hat{X}(z) = \frac{A}{1 - \sum_{k=1}^{p} a_k z^{-k}} \qquad (11),$$

where A is the z-transform of a single input pulse (the digital version of the Kronecker delta).

An estimate of the smoothed spectrum can be computed from (11) putting $z = e^{j\omega\tau}$ as follows:

$$\hat{X}(\omega) = \frac{A^2}{\left| 1 - \sum_{k=1}^{p} a_k e^{-jk\omega\tau} \right|^2} \qquad (12).$$

Fig. 2 shows a spectrum obtained by FFT; fig. 3 shows a smoothed version obtained by linear prediction.

For nasals and nasalized sounds, a model with poles and zeros has been proposed [10]; the z-transform of its transfer function can be expressed as follows:

$$H(z) = \frac{1 + \sum_{i=1}^{q} b_i z^{-i}}{1 + \sum_{i=1}^{p} a_i z^{-i}} \qquad (13).$$

The coefficients b_i and a_i can be computed using a recursive algorithm based on Kalman filtering.

Using the methods presented in this paragraph it is possible to visualize a spoken sentence by a spectrogram.

A spectrogram is a three-dimensional representation that has time, frequency and energy density as dimensions. In practice spectrograms are plotted on two dimensions with the energies represented with gray levels. Fig. 4 shows the spectrogram of the sample sentence "vorrei cancellare una prenotazione" (I would like to cancel a reservation). Spectra are obtained by pitch-synchronous Fast Fourier Transform.

III. Sources of Knowledge for Speech Recognition

It is a common opinion that speech perception and understanding is performed through several levels of processing where different sources of knowledge are involved [3]. For example, the knowledge of the lexicon and the syntax of a language are certainly used for compensating an imperfect comprehension of the elemental sounds or phonemes contained in the verbal message. Moreover semantic and pragmatic constraints are also used in understanding "what was said". The spoken sentence, in other words, must have a conceptual coherence in itself and with what was previously said in a talk.

A strategy of speech understanding that uses the sources of knowledge at different levels is necessary because no methods are actually known for extracting acoustic patterns from which a completely correct transcription of the spoken message can be obtained. Experiments of perception of sentences belonging to a language that is unknown to the listener showed that even humans correctly recognize a small percentage of phonemes in a sentence [12].

Speech understanding is probably carried out with a process of emission and verification of hypotheses. A preliminary set of hypotheses is emitted on the basis of some patterns, extracted from the speech parameters (typically the speech spectra).

These hypotheses are ambiguous in the sense that many of them can refer to the same time interval of the speech signal. The consistency of the hypotheses and the possible concatenations with them is evaluated at the higher levels where syntactic and semantic models are principally used. At these levels hypotheses about the entire sentence are emitted. Some of these hypotheses may require the verification of the presence of some element at the lower levels. For example, an hypothesis about a word may require the verification of the presence of a syllable that was not previously hypothesized in analyzing the acoustic patterns.

A very interesting experience was developed by Klatt and Stevens [18] to support such approach. They hand-simulated the function of the various components of a speech understanding system with an experiment in which a set of unknown spoken sentences were identified by visual examination of broadband spectrograms and machine-aided scanning of a 200-word lexicon. In that experiment, a phonetic transcription was first made from the information contained on a broadband spectrogram of each utterance. The trancription performance of the investigators was rather poor: 10 percent of the segments went undetected, an additional 17 percent of the segments were mislabeled and 40 percent of the remainder were only partially transcribed in terms of phonetic features.

The lexicon was then scanned by providing a partial feature string to the computer. The computer responded with all lexical items consistent with that feature specification. As might be expected with an crrorful input, the words suggested by the computer were rarely the correct ones. There was a median of 5 words in the computer response to each lexical search question, and in only one trial in four was the correct wrod among those suggested by the computer.

This made the going very tough in the stages because there were few syntactic and semantic constraints to fall back on. Sentences did not form a connected discourse so global semantic predictions were meaningless. It was authors' impression that syntactic and semantic consistency constraints could not be applied with confidence until a nearly complete sentence hypothesis had been worked out.

The factor that allowed to identify 97 percent of the words correctly was an ability to return to the spectrographic evidence to accept or reject a word hypothesis. Post-mortem analysis revealed that everytime a correct word appeared as one of the lexical hypotheses generated by the computer, it was verified correctly at that time by the experimenter.

Numbers like the probability that a syllable corresponds to a given portion of the spectrogram can be associated with an hypothesis. Such numbers can be used for ordering the competing hypotheses and for driving the strategy in the directions where meaningful sentences have good probabilities to correspond to the parameters extracted.

The design of such strategies as well as the construction of efficient models of knowledge sources cover a wide field of Artificial Intelligence and will not be treated here. A good framework of the state of the art can be found in [13]; other contributions are reported in [14], [17].

The need for involving many sources of knowledge in speech understanding is also supported by the experts in speech perception for which the language is composed of segments arranged in hierarchically ordered layers [19], [22].

IV. Feature Extraction From the Acoustic Parameters

Short-time spectrograms, obtained with the techniques described in a previous paragraph are the basic measurements used for speech analysis.

These parameters are combined with the signal R.M.S. amplitude and with the time evolutions of the fundamental frequency (pitch).

There are several algorithms and methods for extracting the fundamental frequency; a good description of them can be found in Flanagan [5]. These methods, as well as the methods for obtaining

the spectrograms can be analog or digital. Analog methods generally use filters and operate in real-time while the digital ones
are often slower but more accurate and reliable.

The phonetic properties of a spoken language have been expressed since long-time by means of a set of "distinctive features".

The basic principle of distinctive features implies that all
members within a group of phonemes (e.g. all stop sounds or all
nasal sounds) have a feature in common in terms of the human production process and in terms of corresponding speech wave characteristics and auditory sensations. One and the same processing
stage would suffice in an automatic recognition process for each of
the distinctive features requiring a number of processors equal to
the number of features of the classificatory system. There are
different possible choices for the set of phonemes of a given
language and for their distinctive features.

Evidence available today appears to indicate that there is no
simple transformation from the cues directly obtainable by signal
processing techniques to the phonetic features. Rather, a complex
encoding takes place where information regarding a particular feature of a segment may in fact be carried by neighboring segments
[24].

On the basis of such considerations, it seems more appropriate
[16] to consider a syllabic segment as a unit even if some further
subdivisions of such units into phonemic and subphonemic segment
may be possible.

For this purpose a syntax-controlled procedure for segmenting
the Italian language into syllabic segments [16] is reported in the
following. A similar procedure was proposed at about the same
time by Mermelstein [24] for the English.

A block diagram of the segmentation procedure is shown in
fig. 5.

The secondary characteristics and some global spectral features, are used for performing a preliminary classification of

speech tracts into elemental fragments (EF) to be used in the segmentation process. The segmentation process which is syntax-controlled by a grammar subdivides the continuous speech into pseudo-
syllable segments (PSSO in whibh coarticulation effects are expected to be more evident.

Amplitude A, pitch P, and two parameters LV and R_v, related
to the high frequency energy and the ratio between high and low
frequency energies are encoded by linguistic descriptors into
phrases of two languages L_1 and L_2; then the linguistic descriptions LD1 and LD2 are recognized by an acceptor controlled by a
grammar G1. The elemental fragments (EF) corresponding to Vowels
(V), Unvoiced Tracts (UT), Silences (SL) and Voiced non-vocalic
tracts (VC) are so generated and used by another acceptor, controlled by a grammar G2, that recognizes PSS within which coarticulation effects are more likely to appear. The grammar G2 is defined as follows:

$\quad$ G2: $(V_t, V_n, P1 \quad P2, (PSS))$: $V_t = ((SL), (V), (UT), (VC))$
$V_n = ((PSS), (VLK), (UN))$
$\quad$ P1. $(VLK) \rightarrow (V) / (VC) (V)$
$\qquad$ $(UN) \rightarrow (SL) / (UT) / (SL) (UT) (SL)$
$\quad$ P2. $(PSS) (VIK) \rightarrow (V) (VLK) (VLK) / (UN) (VLK) (VLK)$
$\qquad$ $(PSS (UN) \rightarrow (V) (VLK) (UN) / (UN) (VLK) (UN) / (V)$
$\qquad\qquad$ $(VLK) (VC) (UN) / (UN) (VLK) (VC) (UN)$.

The first four production of P2 are expected to isolate speech
portions where the effects for coarticulations in the Vowel-Conso-
nant-Vowel utterance are most evident, while the last two productions should isolate tracts where there may be the effect of "vowel
reduction". Two successive PSS may overlap when, for example, there
are more consecutive Consonant-Vowel utterance with voiced consonants. In this case an internal vowel is contemporaneously included at the end of a PSS and at the beginning of the successive one;
this is accordance with the fact that the shapes of voiced-consonant
spectra depend on the vowels both before and after the consonant.

The following example will clarify how does the segmentation procedure work. It belongs to a protocol for an automated reservation and travel information system. The sentence is:

Vorrei cancellare una prenotazione

(I would like to cancel a reservation).

It spectrogram is shown in fig. 4 and is segmented as follows:

giving 12 pseudo-syllable-segments.

For each syllabic segment, the following language, reported in [17], can be used for describing the patterns of the parameters that are perceptually significant.

Amplitude Description (ADES)

The amplitude description has the primitive forms represented by the following non-terminal alphabet:

V_1: {BLT, C1, C2, C3, C4};

These forms are related to a terminal alphabet containing there symbols representing a linear approximation of the amplitude curve; the terminal alphabet is:

V_2 = {h: horizontal tracts, a: ascendent tracts,
        d: descendent tracts};

and the composition rules are:

$$(BLT) = (C3)* (C1) (C4)*$$

$$C1 = ad + ahd$$

$$dC2a = dha$$

$$C3a = aha$$

$$dC4 = dhd$$

The compositions are performed by a simple finite-state automaton, operating in a time close to the real-time.

Each primitive symbol is followed by four attributes: the duration, the amplitude of the first point, the abscissa and the amplitude of the maximum. These parameters allow one to reconstruct the amplitude waveforms with a polynomial approximation.

Pitch Description (PDES)

Pitch description is very similar to the amplitude description, except that a new symbol is provided for the silences or the unvoiced tracts.

Description of Spectral Features

The description SDES for a voiced PSS is characterized by the following rules:

SDES → ββ *

β = F1T + F2T + F3T + F4T + F5T ,

where FiT is a tract where i formant linears have been detected.

The descriptions of such tracts are:

F1T = (F1D) (A1D) (b)

F2T = (F1F2D) (A1A2D)

F3T = (F1F2D) (A1A2D) (F3D) (A3D)

F4T = (F1F2D) (A1A2D) (F3F4D) (A3A4D)

F5T = (F1F2D) (A1A2D) (F3D) (A3D) (F4F5D) (A4A4D).

Where FhD is the description of the time evolution of the h-th formant frequency;

Ah+D is the description of the time evolutions of the h-th formant amplitude

(b) is the description of the frication parameters for fricative sounds;

FiFjD is the description of the evolution of F_i and F_j in the F_i F_j plane;

AiAjD is the description of the evolutions of the amplitudes A_i and A_j in the A_i A_j plane.

The descriptions have two types of primitive forms, namely lines and stable zones.

The primitives are detected using an algorithm presented in [29]. A stable zone corresponds to a quasi-stationary portion of the speech waveform and is represented by a symbol S with the following attributes: the duration and the gravity center coordinates of the points belonging to the stable zone.

The lines are represented by one of eight slope symbols, k, l, m, n, o, p, q, r, corresponding to angular sectors of 45°, followed by two numerical attributes: the duration, the line length.

The choice of the maximum allowable error in linear approximation is a compromise between compression and fidelity. This value certainly need not fall below the limens of the perception of formants, that is 3% of the formant values.

The maximum error has been selected in order to obtain the detection of a single stable zone for all the non reduced vowels in a corpus of 50 sentences. Values of 70 Hz for the first formant, 150 for the second and 300 for the third, have been found.

Assuming a gaussian distribution of the errors over the stable zone, a total average value of the errors over the three formant regions of 5% is obtained. Similar results are obtained for the lines.

Fig. 6a shows the three formants detected for the PSS " reu".

For each formant point, the corresponding energy is recorded and plotted in fig. 6b. These values will be referred to as formant amplitudes.

In order to have a time-independent representation of formant evolutions, some parametric graphs are derived from formants and formant amplitude patterns.

The graphs shown in fig. 7a are obtained representing the first two formants in fig. 6a by a planar graph in the F_1-F_2 plane, where each point corresponds to a time sample and having F_1 and F_2 as coordinates. Analogous graphs are plotted in the A_1 - A_2 plane and along the F_3 and A_3 lines, as seen in fig. 7b.

Fig. 7a contains also the slope-code for lines.

The description of the sample syllable "Λreu" is the following:

F_1-F_2 D: p(7, 200) m(3, 250) S(24, 500, 1700) q(3, 800)
S(8, 400, 730)

A_1-A_2 D: p(9, 1.8) l(2, 0.8) S(16, 1.3, 1.5) r(8, 1.0)

F_3 D   : l(10, 100) S(7, 2350, 0) o(4, 200) S(10, 2200) l(4, 100)
A_3 D   : o(8, 0.8) l(4, 0.4) S(16, 1.5, 0) o(7, 1.5).

The possible concatenations at the boundaries between sub-segments having a different number of formants are expressed by the predicates defined considering the following equations:

F2T   = LF1 ⊕ LF2 + LF1 . LF2
F3T   = CCF3 + CF2 . LF3 + LF1 . CF3 + LF1 . LF2 . LF3
CF(i) = LF (i - 1) ⊕ LF(i) i = 2, 3 .
CCF3 = CF2 ⊕ LF3 + FL1   CF3.

LF(i) represents the i-th formant.

The symbols used and the operator ⊕ need to be defined with some comments. For the tracts where two or three formants are detected, it is necessary to specify whether or not they exhibit nodes. In the latter case the primitives of the description are separated by a dot (for example LF1 . LF2). In the former case an operator defines how two formant lines are connected in a single picture (case of CF(i)) or how a picture is connected with a formant in a more complex picture (case of CCF3). The possible connections between two pictures, Φ and Ψ, are synthetically represented as Φ ⊕ Ψ and are defined in accordance with the following rule:

Φ⊕ Ψ = (Φ - Ψ) + (Φ ⊥ Ψ) + (Φ x Ψ)

Each picture is assumed to have a head (H) and a tail (T). For a formant line the head is the point with highest value of n (the time reference) and the tail is the point with lowest value of n. The three operators to the right of the above rule are defined as follows:

Φ-Ψ : H(Φ) ≡ H(Ψ)
Φ⊥Ψ :   T(Φ) ≡ T(Ψ)
ΦxΨ :   (T(Φ) ≡ T(Ψ)) Λ (H(Φ) ≡ H(Ψ));

where H(Φ) and T(Ψ) correspond respectively to head of Φ and tail of Ψ and ≡ means coincident.

Non-sonorant Tract Description

The tracts having a single formant are the consonants that are both voiced and non-sonorants. The distinctive feature "non-sonorant" can be detected by analyzing the energy of the spectrum in the 4 ÷ 10 kHz band [23].

This feature can be proficously used to choose a broad frequency range (0.1 ÷ 10 kHz) for spectral analysis that is required for the non-sonorants while an analysis in a 0.1 ÷ 5 kHz band with higher accuracy is more suitable for the sonorants.

The non-sonorants can be described by subdividing their average spectrum into the 11 zones reported in Table 1 [25].

Table 1

Frequency bounds (kHz)	Symbol
1 ÷ 2	FA
2 ÷ 2,5	FB
2,5 ÷ 3	FC
3 ÷ 3,5	FD
3,5 ÷ 4	FE
4 ÷ 4,5	FG
4,5 ÷ 5	FH
5 ÷ 6	FK
6 ÷ 7	FL
7 ÷ 8	FM
8 ÷ 10	FN

The description is obtained by computing the gravity center of the spectrum energy in the frequency interval from 1 to 10 kHz and issuing a symbol of Tab. 1 according to its frequency. The two other symbols are obtained, corresponding to the initial and final frequency of the spectral interval where the energy is concentrated.

The three other symbols are issued, according to the positions of the first three relative maxima belonging to three different classes.

Fig. 8 shows the spectrum of the fricative sound /s/ and its description.

For the voiced fricatives only one formant below 1 kHz is

detected and a special single formant tract is considered; it is
described by a single line description followed by the 1 ÷ 10 kHz
description of the type of the unvoiced fricatives.

A more sophisticated method of feature extraction consisting
in having several weighted choices for each syllable is presented
in [17].

V. Pattern Classification Problems in Speech Recognition

Although the previous paragraphs have shown that speech understanding is not simply a problem of pattern classification, it
is seasonable to review briefly the classification techniques that
have been employed. These techniques have been applied for classifying phonemes, syllables or entire words and are useful in
studing the mechanism of hypotheses emission and verification of a
speech understanding system.

It is interesting to quote Hyde [26] for this purpose: "At
first sight the different methods used to classify the patterns
appearing at the output of the signal analyser cover a wide range
of techniques, but for the purposes of comparison it is useful to
make something of an oversimplification and regard each one as a
combination or an elaboration of three basic forms of recognizer.
We shall refer to these as the pattern matching classifier, the
trainable classifier, and the feature detecting classifier."

A pattern matching classifier was used in one of the first
recognizers of isolated words proposed by David, Biddulph and
Balashek [1]. The machine derives a pattern in the F1-F2 plane for
each spoken digit.

The F1-F2 plane is divided into 30 rectangles and the energy
in the frequency bands corresponding to 28 of the 30 rectangles is
considered as the information of a channel.

As the speech trace travels about the frequency area, an output is obtained from a given channel as long as the trace dwells
within the particular area associated with that channel.

In order to explore each digit pattern for recognition criteria a relay is associated with each square arranged to charge a

condenser through a resistance when the contacts of the relay are closed. Matching in performed by looking for the highest relative correlation coefficient between a set of the new incoming data and each member of a set of reference patterns.

The correlation coefficient is given by:

$$r = \frac{\sum\limits_{i=1}^{n} \frac{x_i \, y_i}{n} - \bar{x}\,\bar{y}}{\sigma_x \; \sigma_y} \qquad (14)$$

$$\bar{x} = \frac{\sum\limits_{i=1}^{n} x_i}{n} \qquad (15)$$

$$\sigma_x = \sqrt{\sum\limits_{i=1}^{n} \frac{x_i^2}{n} - \bar{x}^2} \qquad (16)$$

where x_i represents sequential channel contributions of an unknown signal and y_i the corresponding series of contributions due to the prototypes learned or established previously. Definitions of $\bar{y}$ and σ_y are sinilar to (15) and (16); n is the number of channels.

An other interesting application of recognition of isolated words is due to Pols [27]. In this approach a word is described by a sequence of points in a multidimensional space. The 17 coordinate values of the points represent the levels in the 17 bandfilters, sampled every 15 msec, after logarithmic amplification and envelope peak detection. Using a principal c omponent analysis [28], a three-dimensional subspace was derived which explained most of the variance (78%). The unknown word is thus represented as sequence of points in three dimensions and is compared with reference traces using a probability score.

Time normalization is performed linearly in this application. In a similar approach [2] a time normalization using dynamic programming was performed.

A linguistic approach for pattern matching was proposed by

De Mori [29]. In this approach a spoken word is represented by a
time-normalized graph in a plane. The graph is described in terms
of stable zones, silences and lines. Such local aspect description
is composed by finite-state automata into more complex form descriptions called "global aspect descriptions" that are sent to a
set of finite-state acceptors. Each acceptor corresponds to a word
and reaches its final state when the word is recognized.

All these methods give high reocgnition scores for a limited
vocabulary and for a limited group of speakers.

Among the trainable classifiers, it is worth mentioning the
system proposed by Dammann [30].

It uses a sumuration element fed by a binary pattern whose
bits can be differently weighted by adjustable gains. The output
of the summation element is sent to a threshold element whose output is compared with a desired output.

During training, a coded representation of the sample (for
example, digitized outputs of a bank of detected filters) is presented on the first input of the comparator. On the second input,
the code representing the desired output class is presented. The
adaptive threshold element describes an hyperplane that bisects a
hypercube to form a binary distinction. By varying the weights
according to an algorithm, the training phase positions the hyperplane to divide the vertices of the hypercube into two classes.
All vertices falling on one side of the plane give an output +1 and
all vertices on the other side give an output -1. A number of such
elements in parallel can be used to form a binary code that will
designate one class out of a larger number of classes. A similar
application using threshold gates to recognize a subset of phonemes
to be further processed by a sequential unit that takes into account for the phoneme durations is presented in [31].

More sophisticated statistical decision techniques are proposed for speech recognition in [32].

A recognition system based on the detection of distinctive
features, detected where they appear as context-independent, was

proposed by Wiren and Stubbs [33]; more sophisticated algorithm
for extracting distinctive features from the speech parameters
where proposed by Hughes and Hemdal [23] and others among which
it is worth to mention the MIT acoustic classifier described in
[34].

A system for the recognition of spoken words using distinctive features and phonological rules recently proposed by Itahashi,
Makino and Kido [39] will briefly described in the following.

A set of nine parameters are extracted every 10 ms by band-
pass filtering the speech waveform. Let $Y_i^k = Y_{ir}^k$ ($r = 1, 2, \ldots, 9$)
denote such parameters which should be categorized as the feature
plus ($k = +$) or minus ($k = -$), where i indicates the material number ($i = 1, 2, \ldots, n$) and r represents each of the nine parameters.
The distinctive features of phonemes are represented by the linear
combinations of these parameters, such as:

$$F(Y_i^k) = \sum_{r=1}^{9} C_r Y_{ir}^k \; ; \quad i = 1, 2, \ldots, n \; ; \quad k = +, - \qquad (17).$$

The coefficients $\{C_r\}$ are determined so that the ratio of the
variance between two classes $\{F(Y_i^+)\}$ and $\{F(Y_i^-)\}$ to the sum of
variances within each class becomes maximum. That is, it is desired to maximize G given by the following equations:

$$G = G(C_1, C_2, \ldots, C_9) = \frac{D^2}{S} = \frac{\left(\sum\limits_{r=1}^{9} C_r d_r \right)^2}{\left(\sum\limits_{p,q=1}^{9} C_p C_q S_{pq} \right)}$$

$$d_r = \bar{Y}_r^+ - \bar{Y}_r^- \; ; \quad \bar{Y}_r^k = \frac{1}{n} \sum_{i=1}^{n} Y_{ri}^k, \quad k = +, -$$

$$S_{pq} = \sum_{i=1}^{n} \{ (Y_{pi}^+ - \bar{Y}_p^+)(Y_{qi}^+ - \bar{Y}_q^+) + (Y_{pi}^- - \bar{Y}_p^-)(Y_{qi}^- - \bar{Y}_q^-) \}$$

$$p, q, r = 1, 2, \ldots, 9 \qquad (18)$$

The set of coefficients that maximizes G will be given by making
the partial differentiation of G by C_r zero. The coefficients are

determined of the distinctive features.

An unknown input is segmented according with the strong variations of the distance between two feature frames (each frame is a set of feature values corresponding to a 10 msec. interval) defined as follows:

$$d_t = \left\{ \sum_{i=1}^{9} (f_{ti} - f_{t-1,i})^2 \right\}^{\frac{1}{2}} \tag{19};$$

f_{ti} is the i-th feature value at time t.

For each input word a matrix is obtained; each column corresponds to segment and each row to a feature.

For each word of the lexicon a standard feature matrix is obtained using some typical feature values for phonemes modified by the phonetic context according with the phonological rules.

Finally the distance between the input and the standard feature matrix is calculated for each item of the dictionary and the item of minimum distance is taken as a recognized output. The distance is defined as the sum of absolute values of differences of corresponding entries of two features matrices.

A table of probability data for sequences of phonemes could be also used for reducing the number of trials in apphoneme by phoneme recognition system, following a method used by Denes and Fry [35]. Other interesting applications are reported in [36], [37], [38], [40].

An example of syntactic recognition of auditory patterns using stochastic automata is reported in [17] for a process of emission and evaluation of hypotheses and is briefly recalled here.

At the beginning of the understanding, the segmenter represents the spoken sentence as a continuous sequence of PSSs. This sequence is the first segmentation hypothesis. Then for the voiced portions of each PSS, the most likely formants are extracted and a description is generated.

Then the descriptions are processed under the control of a grammar of speech and are translated into possible phonetic transcriptions, with associated the probability $P(S_j/\Omega_l)$ that the syllable S_j corresponds to Ω_l, the l-th segment of the spectrogram of the spoken sentence.

The grammar of speech is a stochastic grammar representing the possible patterns for each coarticulation instance, corresponding to the concatenations of elemental fragments generated by the segmentation grammar.

The starting symbol of the grammar of speech is PSS; the terminal alphabet contains all the symbols with which the descriptions are made; the non-terminal alphabet contains all the possible concatenations of phonemes for which coarticulation affects the formant patterns even after the description approximations. The non-terminal alphabet contains also the symbols emitted by the auxiliary units preceding each SFSA, and acting as translators of the descriptions made of symbols, attributes and probabilities to symbols and probabilities, provided that some relations hold between the attributes. Finally, the productions of the grammar of speech are right-linear stochastic rewriting rules, derivable from the SFSA inferred by the procedure that is described in [25].

Hypothesis evaluation is performed with a procedure whose block diagram is shown in fig. 9.

When a syllable or a coarticulation segment is hypothesized on a certain portion of the spectrogram, the SFSA of that segment and the corresponding description translator are built up from the grammar of speech.

This operation is simple and fast due to the straightforward relations between the productions and the automata. The syllable description is processed by the description translator (DT).

The DT translates a primitive form, with its attributes to describe correctly some formant evolutions, into a symbol and its associated probability. The symbol is emitted only if some conditions on the attributes are verified.

These conditions are stored for a talker and a typical lexical position of the segment and can be modified by some speaken

dependent modifiers, acting mainly on the formant loci for the
stable-zones constraints.

In addition, some lexical dependent modifiers, acting mainly
on the durations, change the constraints in accordance with the
stress of the segment.

The design of such modifiers that also involves the knowledge
of probability distributions is actually limited to spectral loci
and the influence of the stress on the durations, pitch and amplitudes. A lot of investigations are still to be done for characterizing the individual influence on formant evolutions and loci
for syllables embedded in continuous speech and the approach followed here should be considered a first approximation.

The input to the DT is the description d_{i1}.

The output of the DT is a string g_{i1} of symbols without attributes obtained from d_{i1} which is a string of symbols with attributes; together with g_{i1}, the probability $P(d_{i1}/g_{i1})$ is obtained.
Finally, the g_{i1} is processed by the SFSA and, if the g_{i1} is recognized, the probability $P(g_{i1}/S_j)$ is given. All the obtained
probabilities are processed by an algorithm that gives $P(S_j/\Omega_1)$.
The details of such algorithm can be found in [17].

An example of the translator for the syllable shown in fig.
16 is reported in Table 2 while the corresponding SFSA is reported
in fig. 10 where le is for length, d for duration, b_1 and b_2 are
respectively the first and second gravity center coordinates for
the stable zone, the probabilities are assumed to be 1 for sake
of simplicity.

The formants have been extracted with linear prediction and
have probability 1 (non alternative paths were possible).

The description coming out from the translator is:

g_1^j = ABFCGOLINDPNDQOQ

that is recognized with probability:

$P(g_1^j / S_j)$ = 0,23.

Fig. 11 shows the acoustic patterns of the voiced portions of the PSSs belonging to the sample sentence considered before as a segmentation example.

When the automaton corresponding to a given pseudo-syllable has been learned an algorithm described in [25] is applied to check if the considered pseudo-syllable can be further subdivided into acoustically independent units.

Furthermore many automata corresponding to syllables whose phonemes differ for few distinctive features have considerable portions in common (e.g. the formant amplitude pattern). These automata can be reduced to a single one where some translations or transitions are valid only for same syllables.

The structure of the source of knowledge at the phonetic level is characterized by stochastic rules that may be refined during learning when more insight in the properties of the auditory patterns will be gained.

Finally, the stochastic rules partially refer to different possibilities of articulation and partially to the noise introduced by the algorithims that transforms the speech waveform into auditory patterns. The noise effects are probably independent from the particular syllable compositions and could be characterized by a single grammar induced by error transformation using an algorithm proposed by Fung and Fu [41].

Conclusions

Speech recognition researches have now evidenciated that several sources of knowledge have to be involved when designing a speech understanding system. These sources of knowledge, like the relations between syllables and acoustic patterns, the models for syntax, semantics and pragmatics, the ways for representing inter-speakers and intra-speaker variabilities are still to be defined completely. A strategy about the emission and verification of hypotheses at different levels is not definitely established. The efforts in the definition of the above points should not be only devoted to the creation of structures and algorithims, they should also attempt to learn much more about speech than we actually know.

314

With this perspective the results obtained will have their own utility even if the final goal of having a voice-controlled information system has not yet been achieved.

Table 2

Symbol of the DT output	Symbol of the DT input description	Constraints
A	p	$(5 \leq d \leq 15)$ $(100 \leq le \leq 300)$
B	m	$(2 \leq d \leq 7)$ $(100 \leq le \leq 300)$
C	q	$(2 \leq d \leq 7)$ $(600 \leq le \leq 1200)$
D	l	$(d \leq 16)$ $(50 \leq le \leq 150)$
E	s	$(0.5 \leq b_1 \leq 1.6)$ $(b_2 = 0)$
F	s	$(10 \leq d \leq 30)$ $(400 \leq b_1 \leq 700)$ $(1500 \leq b_2 \leq 1900)$
G	s	$(d \leq 12)$ $(300 \leq b_1 \leq 500)$ $(600 \leq b_2 \leq 800)$
H	p	$(le \leq 1)$
I	r	$(le \leq 1.2)$
L	s	$(0.6 \leq b_1 \leq 1.6)$ $(0.5 \leq b_2 \leq 1.6)$
M	s	$(0.2 \leq b_1 \leq 0.8)$ $(0.1 \leq b_2 \leq 0.4)$
N	s	$(2000 \leq b_1 \leq 2500)$ $(b_2 = 0)$
O	l	$(le \leq 1.5)$
P	o	$(50 \leq le \leq 300)$
Q	o	$(le \leq 0.5)$
R	n	$(6 \leq d \leq 15)$ $(200 \leq le \leq 400)$

Acknowledgements

This work was performed at the Centro di Elaborazione Numerale dei Segnali, Turin, Italy and was supported by the Consiglio Nazionale delle Ricerche of Italy.
The authors are grateful to Professor R. Sartori and to Professor A.R. Meo for their many useful suggestions and encouragement.
They feel also indebted to Professor K.S. Fu for his valuable suggestions and criticism offered during their visits to Purdue University (USA) undertaken through NATO travel grant no. 822.

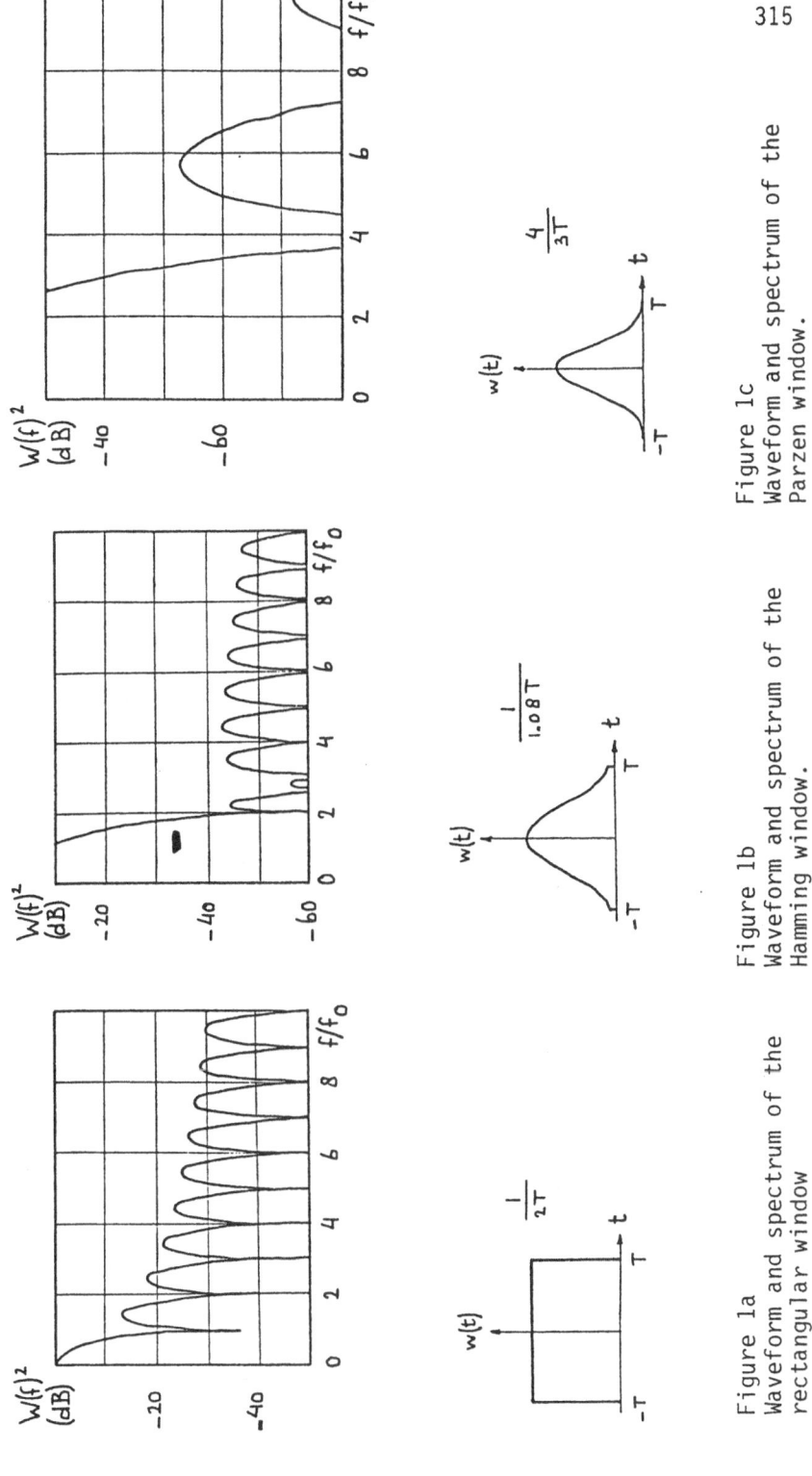

315

Figure 1a
Waveform and spectrum of the
rectangular window

Figure 1b
Waveform and spectrum of the
Hamming window.

Figure 1c
Waveform and spectrum of the
Parzen window.

316

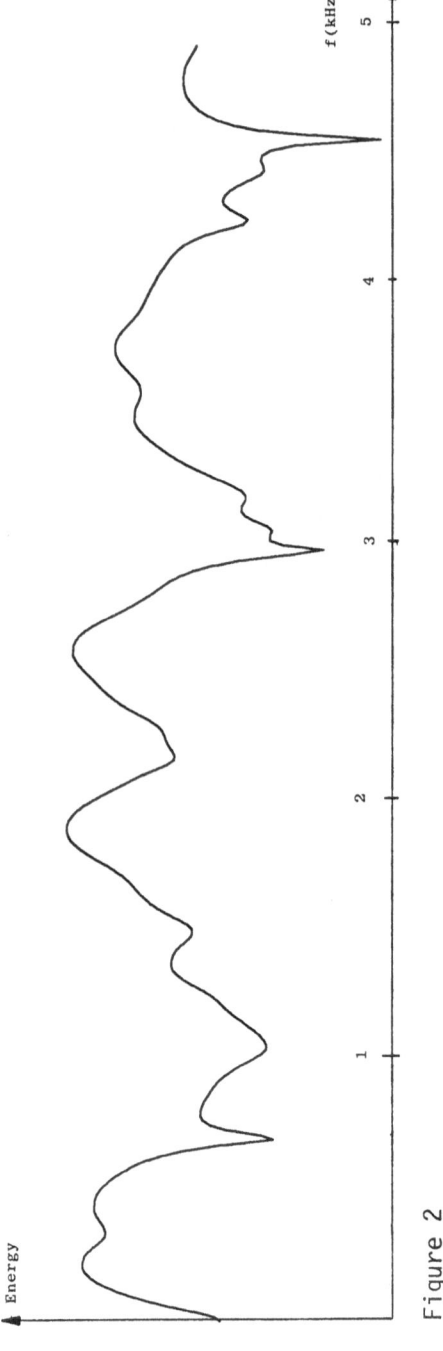

Figure 2
Spectrum of the Italian vowel /e/ obtained with pitch-synchronous F.F.T.

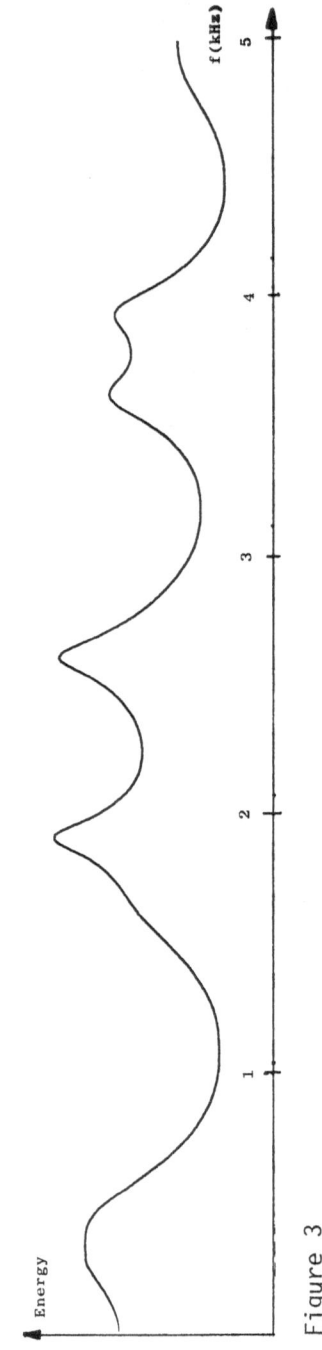

Figure 3
Spectrum of the same vowel as in Figure 8 obtained with linear prediction (p=14).

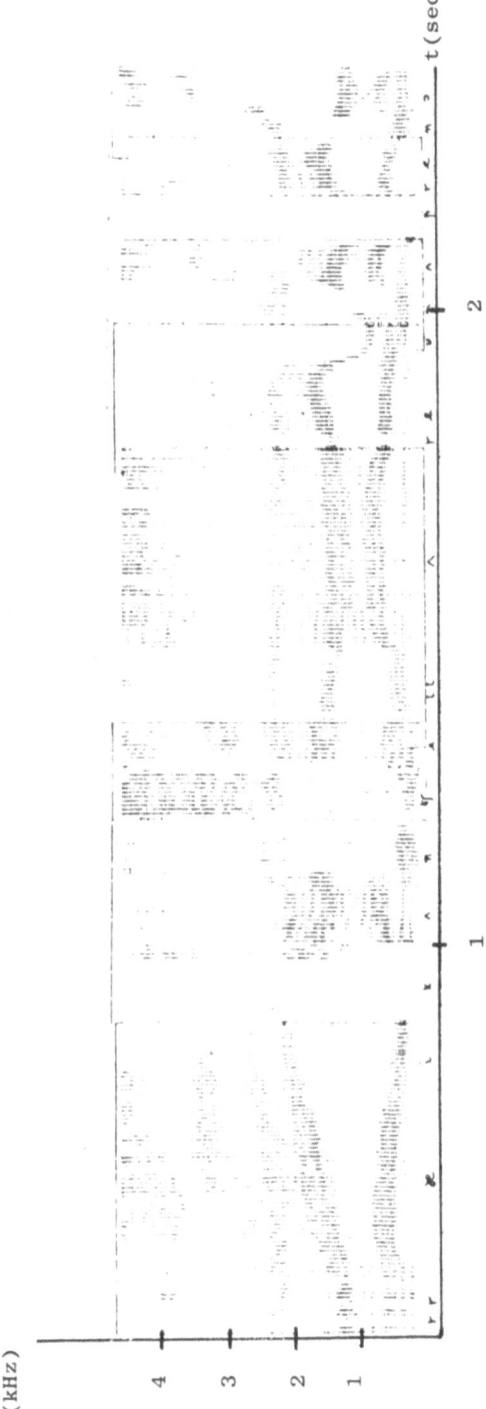

Figure 4
Digital spectrogram of the sentence: "(vo)rrei cancellare una preno(tazione)".

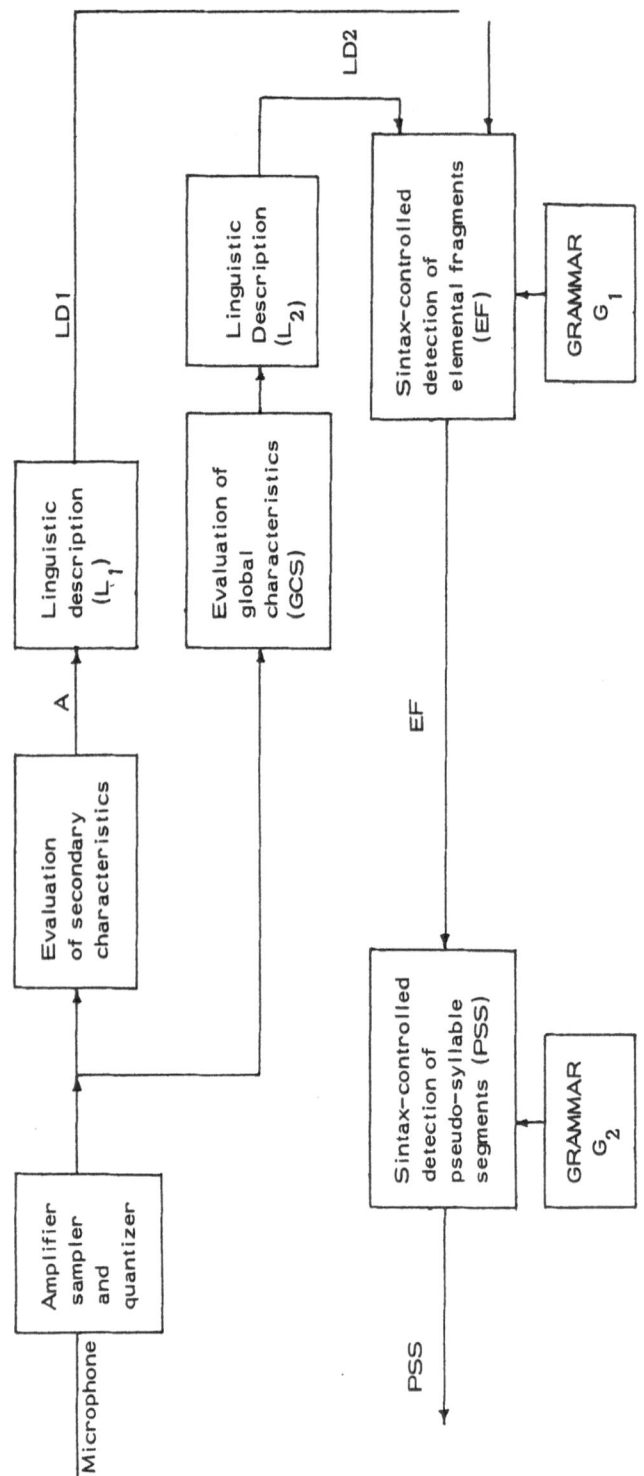

Figure 5
Block diagram for syntax-controlled segmentation.

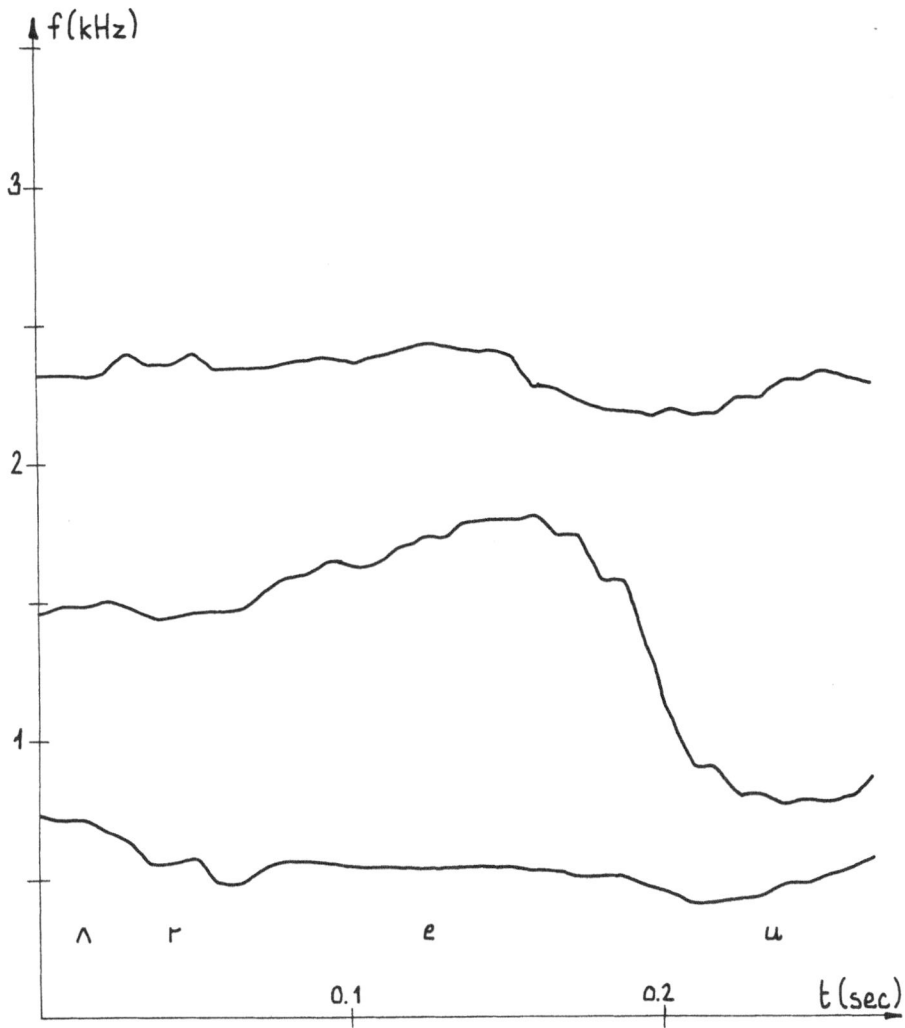

Figure 6a
Formants of the syllable ʌreu.

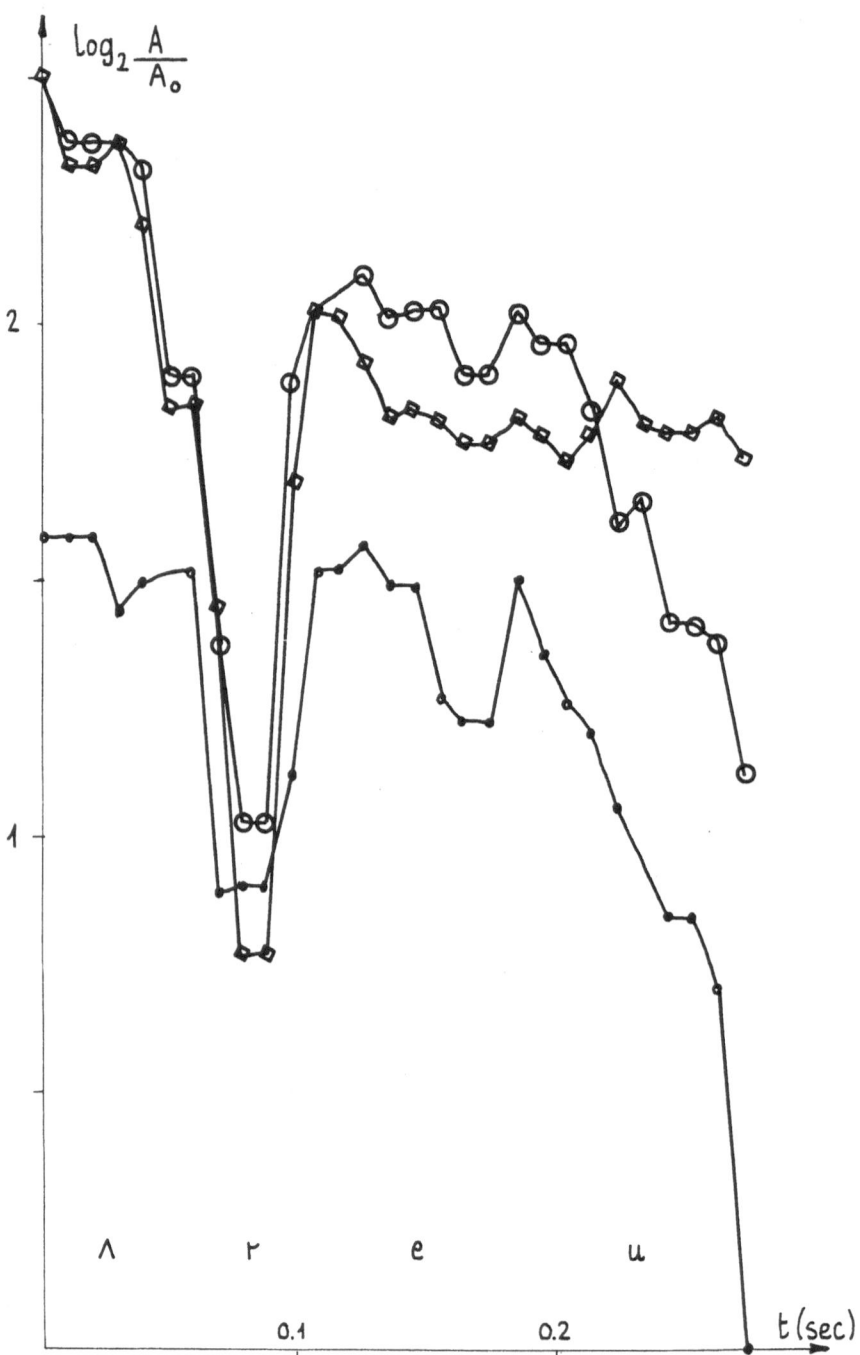

Figure 6b
Formant amplitudes of the syllable ʌreu.

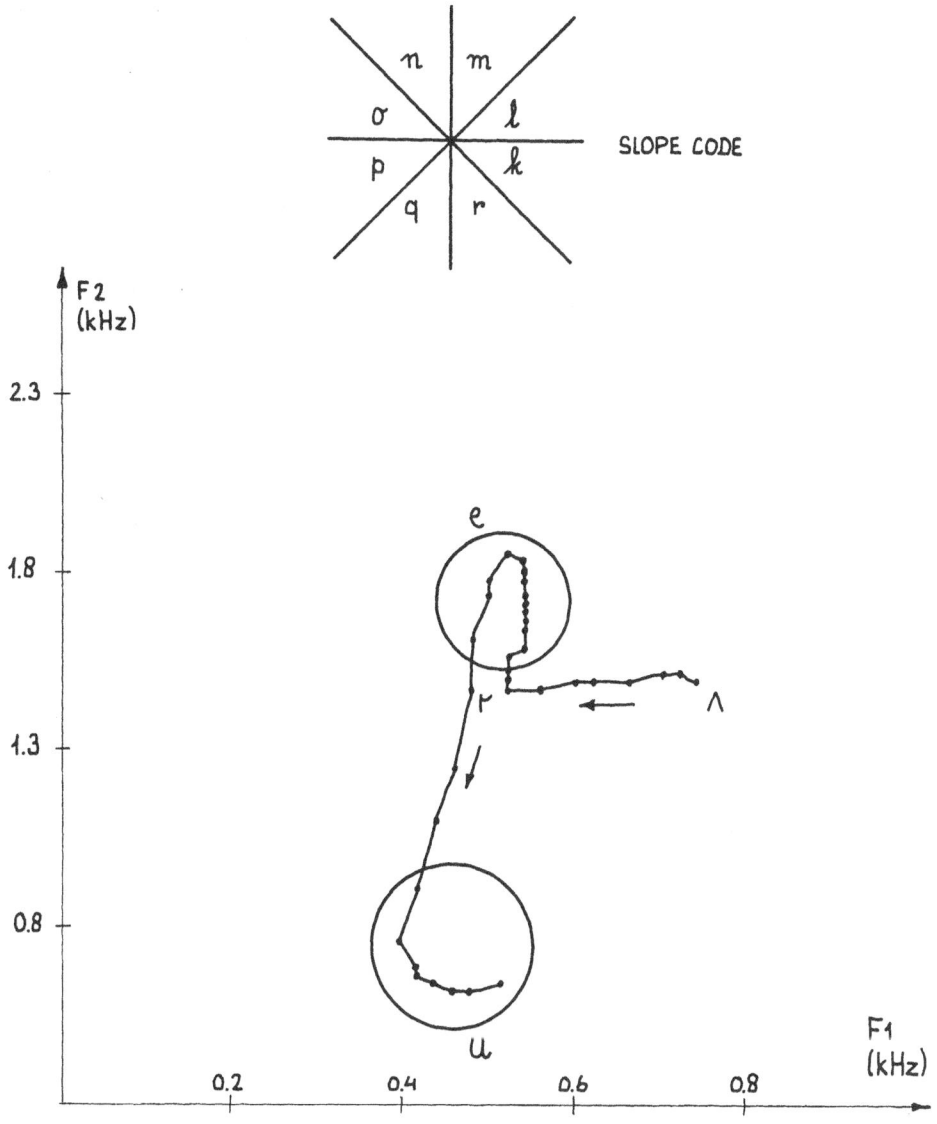

Figure 7a
Parametric graph in the F1-F2 plane for the formants of Figure 6.

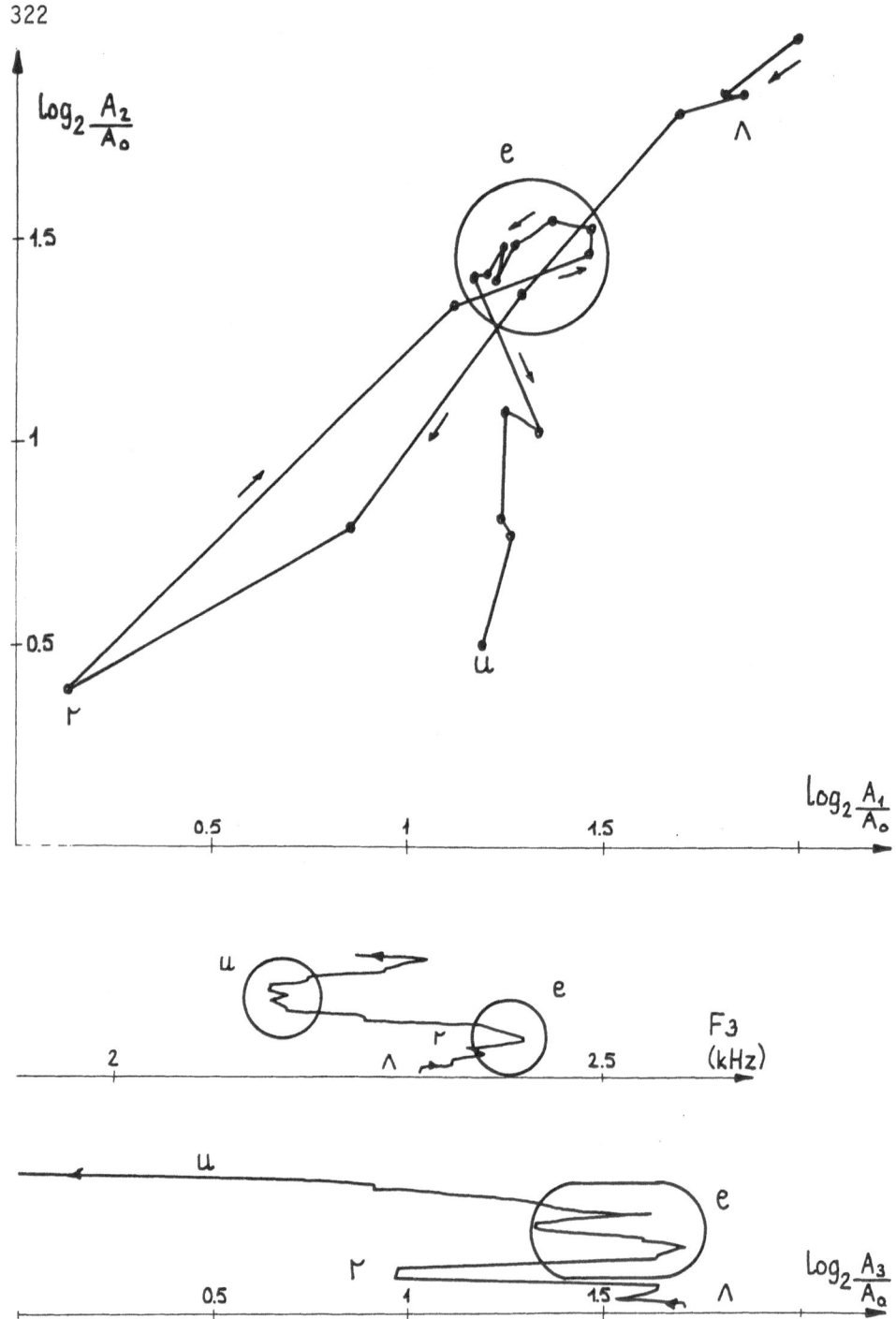

Figure 7b
Other parametric graphs of the sample syllable ʌreu.

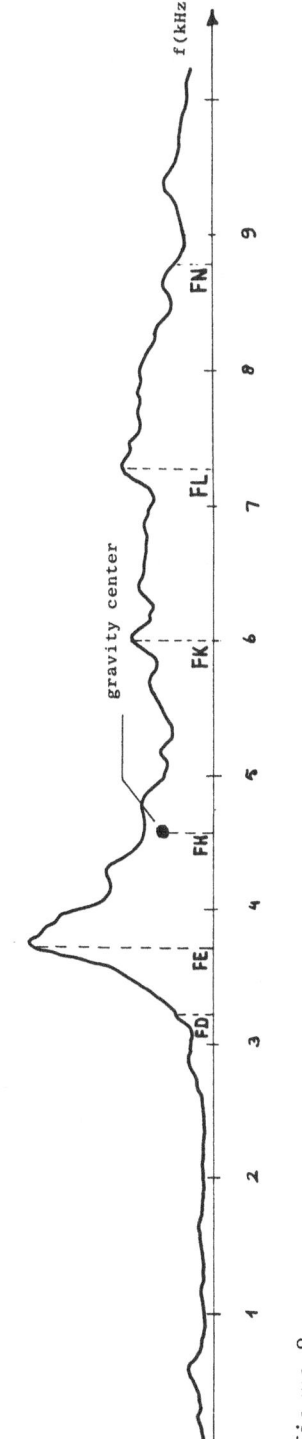

Figure 8
The spectrum of the fricative /s/ and its description.
Description: FH FD FN FE FL FK.

324

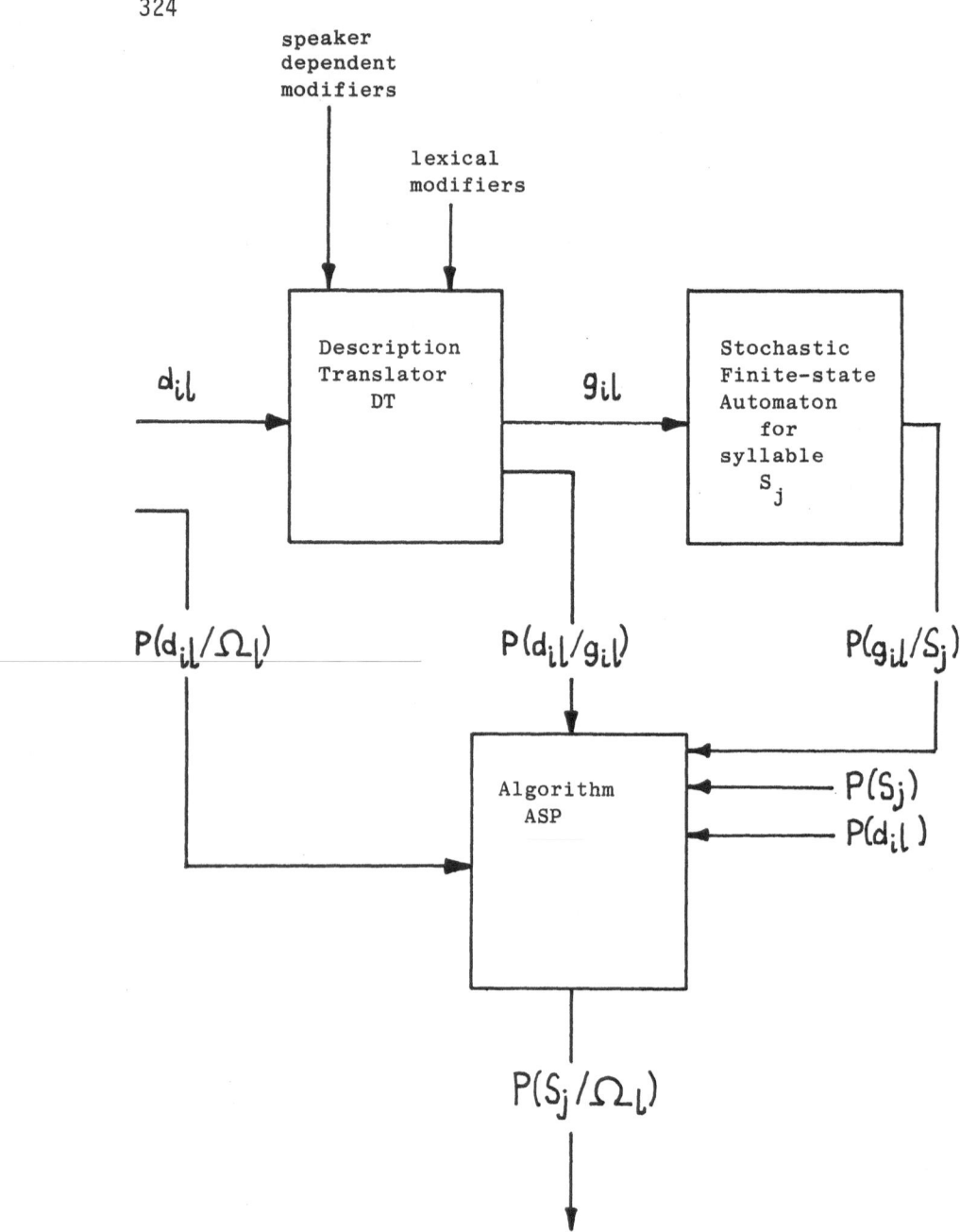

Figure 9
Algorithm for hypothesis evaluation.

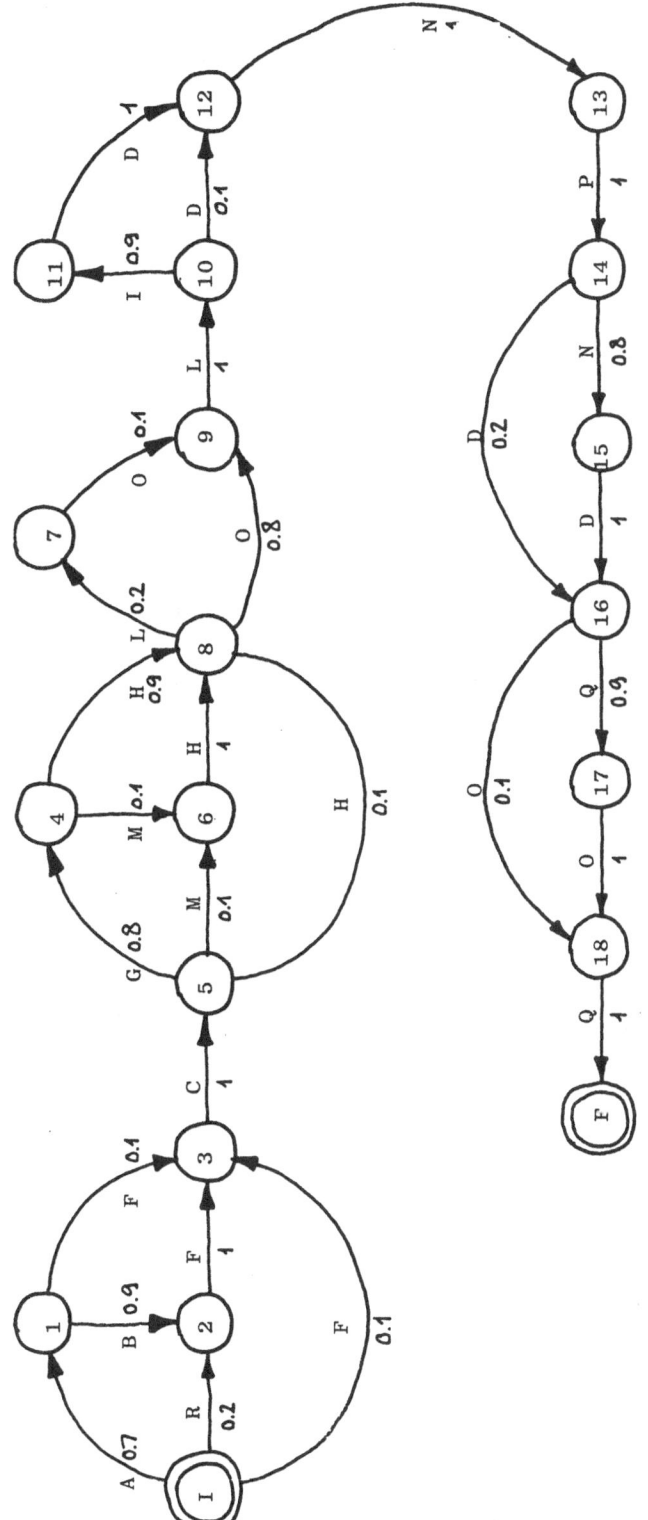

Figure 10
SFSA for the syllable Areu.

326

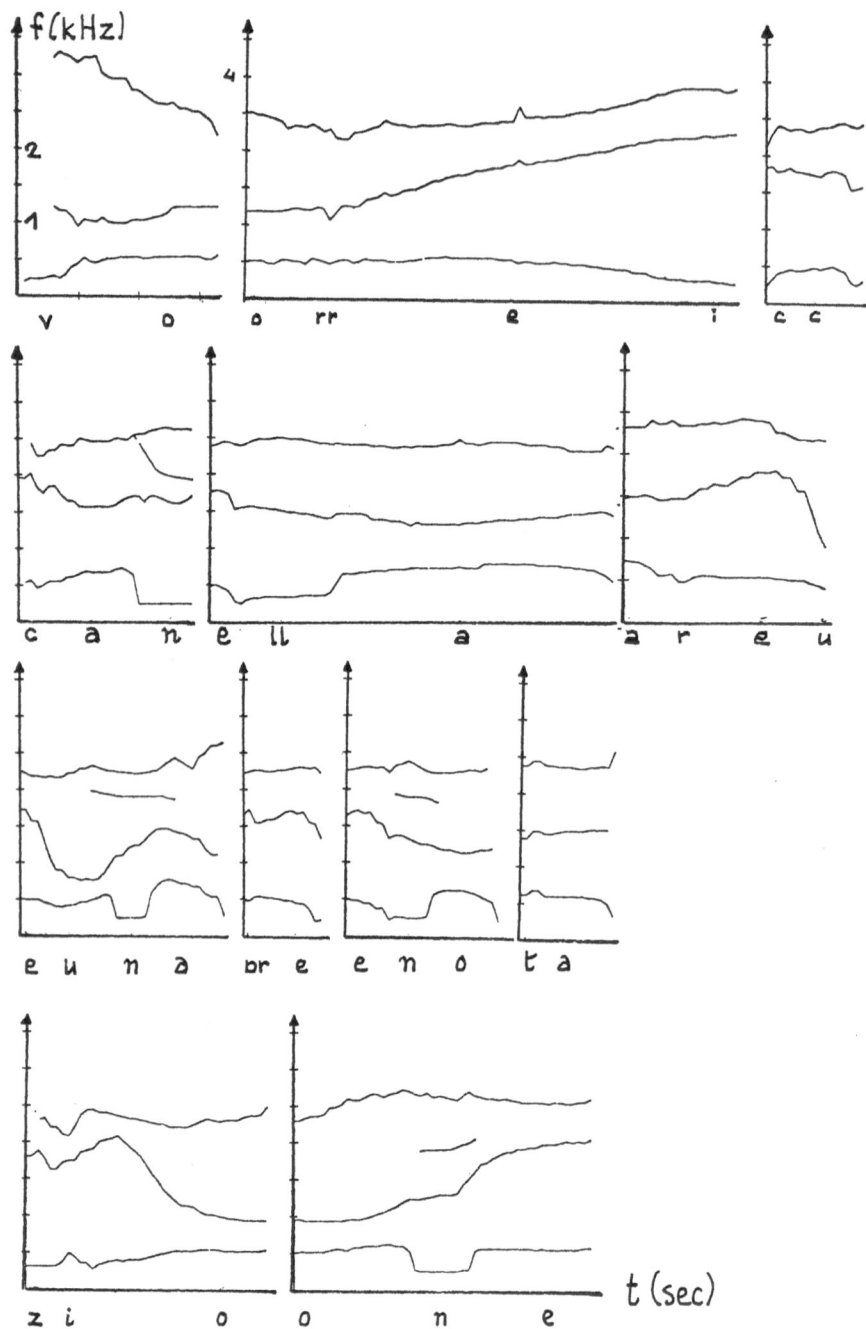

Figure 11
Formants for the syllables extracted from the
spectrogram of figure 4.

References

1. H. K. Davis, R. Biddulph, and S. Balashek, "Automatic Recognition of Spoken Digits", J. Acoust. Soc. Amer. 24, 637-642 (1952).

2. V. M. Velichiko, N. G. Zagoruiko, "Automatic Recognition of 200 Words", International Journal On Man-Machine Studies, 2, pp. 223-234 (1970).

3. A. Newell, J. Barnett, C. Green, D. Klatt, J.C.R. Licklider, J. Munson, R. Reddy, W. Woods, "Speech Understanding Systems: Final Report of a Study Group", North-Holland (1973).

4. D. H. Klatt, "On the Design of Speech Understanding Systems", Proceedings of SCS-74, pp. 277-289, Stockholm 1974, to be published by Addison-Wesley.

5. J. L. Flanagan, "Speech Analysis, Synthesis and Perception", Springer-Verlag, Berlin 1972 (II ed.).

6. B. Gold, C. M. Rader, "Digital Processing of Signals", McGraw Hill, ed. 1969.

7. A. M. Liberman, "The Grammars of Speech and Language", Cognitive psychology, Vol. 1, No. 4, October 1970, 301-323.

8. R. W. Schafer, L. R. Rabiner, "System for Automatic Formant Analysis of Voiced Speech", J.A.S.A., 47, pt. 2, pp. 634-648 (1970).

9. J. Makhoul, J. Wolf, "Linear Prediction and the Spectral Analysis of Speech", Bolt Beranek and Newman, Cambridge, Mass, Tech. Rep. 2304, Aug. 1972.

10. B. Gardini, A. Serra, "Identification of Speech Parameters Using a Recursive Method", Proc. SCS 74, Preprint Sess. 1.

11. J. R. Pierce, "Whither Speech Recognition", J. Acous. Soc. Amer. 46, 1049 - 1051 (1969).

12. L. Shockey, R. Reddy, "Quantitative Analysis of Speech Perception: Results from Transcription of Connected Speech from Unfamiliar Languages", Paper of SCS-74 to be published by Addison-Wesley.

13. L. Erman ed: "IEEE Symposium on Speech Recognition", Carnegie-Mellon University, Apr. 1974, (IEEE Cat. No. 74CH0878-9 E).

14. R. Gumetsky, B. M. Gura, M. F. Derkach, D. S. Marchuk, L. N. Mishin, M. E. Chaban, "A Model of Words and Simple Phrases Recognition", Proceedings of Lvov University, Series of Biology, n. 8, 1974.

15. M. Derkach, R. Gumetsky, B. Gura, L. Mushin, "Automatic Recognition of Simplified Sentences Constructed of the Limited Lexicon", Paper of SCS-74. To be published by Addison-Wesley.

16. T. De Mori, "Design for a Syntax-Controlled Acoustic Classifier", Proc. IFIP Congress 74, Vol. 4, pp. 753-757, North-Holland (Aug. 1974).

17. R. De Mori, S. Rivoira, A. Serra, "A Speech Understanding System with Learning Capability", Proc. Fourth International Joint Conference on Artificial Intelligence (Tbilisi - URSS - Sept. 75), pp. 468-475.

18. D. H. Klatt, K. N. Stevens, "On the Automatic Recognition of Continuous Speech: Implications of a Spectrogram-Reading Experiment", IEEE Transaction on Audio and Electroacoustic, Vol. AU21, pp. 210-216 (June 1973).

19. A. M. Liberman, F. S. Cooper, K. S. Harris, P. F. Mac Neilage, M. Studdert-Kennedy, "Some Observations on a Model for Speech Perception", Models for the Perception of Speech and Visual Form. Ed. by W. W. Dunn, MIT press, 1967, pp. 68-77.

20. V. A. Kozhevnikov and L. A. Chistovich, "Speech: Articulation and Perception", transl. by Joint Publications Res. Service, JPRS 30, 543 (1965).

21. M. Halle and K. N. Stevens, "Speech Recognition, a Model and a Program for Research", IRE Trans. Inform. Theory, Vol. IT-8, pp. 155-159, Feb. 1962.

22. G. Fant, "Automatic Recognition and Speech Research", STL/QPSR 1/1970, pp. 16-31, Jan.-Mar. 1970.

23. G. W. Hughes and J. F. Hemdal, "Speech Analysis", Rep. AFCRL-65-681 (P13552), Purdue University (1965).

24. P. Mermelstein, "A Phonetic-Context Controlled Strategy for Segmentation and Phonetic Labelling of Speech", Proc. IEEE - CMU - Symposium on Speech Recognition - pp. 144-148, Apr. 1974.

25. R. De Mori, S. Rivoira, A. Serra, "Automatic Learning of Spectral Features Extracted from Continuous Speech", Proc. Third International Congress on Cybernetics and Systems, Bucharest (Romania), Aug. 1975, (in press).

26. S. R. Hyde, "Automatic Speech Recognition-State of the Art in 1972", in Machine Perception of Patterns and Pictures. The Institute of Physics, London, Bristol, Ap. 1972, pp. 109-116.

27. L. C. W. Pols, "Real-Time Recognition of Spoken Words", IEEE Trans. Comp. C-20, 1972-1978 (1971).

28. L. C. W. Pols, "Dimensionsl Representation of Speech Spectra", 7th Int. Congr. Acoustics, Budapest, Paper 25C7 (1971).

29. R. De Mori, "A Descriptive Technique for Automatic Speech Recognition", IEEE Transactions, on Audio and Electroacoustics, Vol. AU21, pp. 89-100 (Apr. 73).

30. J. A. Dammann, "Application of Adaptive Threshold Elements to the Recognition of Acoustic-Phometic State", J. Acoust. Soc. Amer. 38, 213-223 (1965).

31. R. De Mori, L. Gilli, A. R. Meo, "A Flexible Real-Time Recognizer of Spoken Words for Man-Machine Communication", International Journal of Man-Machine Studies, Vol. 2, No. 4, December 1970, pp. 317-326.

32. P. D. Welch, R. S. Wimpress, "Two Multivariate Statistical Computer Programs and Their Application to the Vowel Recognition Problem", J. Acoust. Soc. Am., Vol. 33, No. 4, Apr. 1971.

33. J. Wirew, H. L. Stubbs, "Electronic Binary Section for Phoneme Classification", J. Acoust, Soc. Amer., Vol. 26, No. 6, Nov. 1956.

34. C. J. Weinstein, S. S. McCandless, L. F. Mondshein, V. Zue, "A System for Acoustic-Phonetic Analysis of Continuous Speech", IEEE Symposium on Speech Recognition, Carnegie-Mellon University (Apr. 1974), pp. 89-100.

35. D. B. Fry, "Theoretical Aspects of Mechanical Speech Recognition", J. British Inst. Radio Eng. 19, 211-219 (1959). Also, P. Denes, "The Design and Operation of the Mechanical Speech Recognizer at University College London", J. Acoust. Soc. Amer 33, pp. 219-229.

36. B. Gold, "Word-Recognition Computer Program", Res. Lab. Electron, MIT Rep. No. 452, June (1966).

37. D. R. Reddy, "Computer Recognition of Connected Speech", J. Acoust. Soc. Amer., Vol. 42, pp. 329-437, Aug. 1967.

38. J. Makhoul, "Speaker-Machine Interaction in Automatic Speech Recognition", MIT RLE Technical report No. 480, 1970.

39. S. Itahashi, S. Makino, K. Kido, "Discrete-Word Recognition Utilizing a Word Dictionary and Phonological Rules", IEEE Transactions on Audio and Electroacoustics, Vol. AU-21, No. 3, June 1973, pp. 239-249.

40. R. Vives, J. Y. Gresser, "A Similarity Index Between Strings of Symbols - Application to Automatic Word and Language Recognition", Proc. first IJCPR - Washington '73 CHO 821-9C.

41. L. W. Fung, K. S. Fu, "Syntactic Decoding for Computer Communication and Pattern Recognition", Rep. TR-EE 74-47. School of Electrical Engineering, Purdue University, West Lafayette, Indiana, USA, Dec. 1974.

THE UCLM4 PROGRAMMABLE SPEECH RECOGNITION MACHINE

W. K. Taylor

University of London

I. Introduction

The final objective of the research and development to be described is the fabrication of LSI microcircuits that will perform all the functions of a general purpose pattern recognition system including preprocessing of input patterns, electrical programming and reading of a non-volatile parallel memory and real time classification or rejection of unknown input patterns. Progress towards this objective is at present only limited by the high cost of small scale LSI production but the feasibility has been established by the fabrication and testing of the only new component required, a resistor programmable read only memory or R-PROM. This device[1], in conjunction with well established drive and read circuits, automatically forms hard wired connections required for synthesizing the linear discriminant functions of the Taylor-Steinbuck linear separator[2] which were used successfully in the UCLM3 pattern recognition machine[3] to read OCRB font.

The present paper shows how the same R-PROM system can be applied to speech recognition if the microphone output is suitably preprocessed in real time and the results stored in shift registers to form pattern vectors $\underline{X}$. At any instant of time the

pattern vector is similar to that produced by a printed alpha-
numeric character as it passes the optical window of the UCLM3 OCR
machine.

Similar problems are encountered in the recognition of spoken
words and printed words since in both cases it is necessary to
emply a window or field that will accommodate the largest pattern
contained in the training set of sample patterns. The microphone
input resembles the input from a linear array of photodiodes in
that a temporary store is required to build up the complete pattern as the information arrives serially in time and it is convenient to use analogue or digital shift registers for this purpose. Their content, after the complete input word has been
heard or seen by the input transducers, is the input pattern vector $\underline{X}$. Complications arise due to the variability of spoken
word, pitch and duration (and to different sizes of print in OCR)
since a window that will just accommodate the largest pattern
may also hold several small patterns. One system for dealing with
this problem uses a size invariant parallel preprocessor, but in
the present application the speakers were supplied with feedback
in the form of a "speak now" light that indicated readiness for
the next word. This limitation should be overcome by employing
a more sophisticated preprocessor but without changing the organization of the memory and classification circuits. By increasing
the size of the memory it should then be possible to handle continuous speech.

II. The Speech Preprocessor

In selecting the parameters of a pattern recognition preprocessor there is usually a conflict between resolution and generalization which tend to be inversely proportional. For a large vocabulary that is not specifcally selected to give large differences between all words the speech spectrograms must have a frequency and time resolution that will separate the closest words.
The ability of the system to tolerate different versions of the

same word, however, tends to improve if the resolution is reduced. In the UCLM4 the resolution is relatively poor since only five bandpass filters are used, as compared with 19 in the Threshold Technology VIP 100, for example. This gives wide tolerances with the small vocabulary of ten spoken digits for which a group of four arbitrarily selected speakers produced 95% correct recognition without feedback and 100% with feedback and error correction. These results were obtained with a single sample pattern vector per word, representing an average for the four speakers. If the sample pattern vectors for only one of the speakers were stored then that speaker was recognized at the 99% level without feedback but the performance of the other three was slightly reduced.

Any new speaker who is not sufficiently well recognized can have sample vectors stored in the R-PROM until his performance is satisfactory without causing interference with previously stored vectors. It is thus possible to combine a multiplicity of memories by piecewise-linear techniques so that the closest sample vector for each speaker is automatically selected and made to indicate the word classification and also the identity of the most probable speaker if required.

Selection of the centre frequencies gains and bandwidth of the five filters was based on observation of speech spectrograms. The lowest filter was centered on 225 Hz, the next three spaced by one octave at 450, 900 and 1800 Hz and the fifth at 7000 Hz to detect fricatives. Each filter has a Q of 3 and a gain adjusted to give approximately equal RMS filter outputs for the ten spoken digits. The five filter outputs are rectified and passed through low-pass active filters cutting off at 25 Hz to produce five analogue signals a_1-a_5. Each signal is compared with the mean $\bar{a}$ plus a threshold a_t. Binary signals x_1-x_5 are producdd such that x_i="1" if $a_i > \bar{a} + a_t$ and x_i="0" if $a_i < \bar{a} \; a_t$. The threshold a_t is adjusted to give very infrequent "i"s due to background noise. Considerable amplitude information is thus discarded by this coarse

quantization but computer simulations preserving the analogue
signals have shown little improvement over the binary digitiza-
tion. In hardware there is significant simplification since a
short term memory consisting of five inexpensive digital shift
registers is used to store the incoming word pattern vector $\underline{X}$.
Each register stores 40 samples from one of the five filter units
spaced in time by sampling pulses from a 40 Hz clock to give a
0.8 seconds time window. At normal speaking rates each of the
ten digits fits inside this window to produce a pattern vector $\underline{X}$
with N=200 components, selected from the possible set of 2^{200}
binary vectors in 200 space. A typical set of $\underline{X}$ vectors obtained
experimentally for the spoken digits zero-nine is shown in Figure
1 arranged as column vectors corresponding to the contents of the
five 40 bit shift registers placed end to end.

The large size of the vectors will not permit indication of
"1" and "0"'s by printed symbols and the positions of "1" are
indicated by dots. Arrows indicate the points of entry to the
five shift registers from the bandpass filters.

The variability of speech from a given speaker who is trying
to repeat the same digit in the same way is so large that in 200
samples it was found that all the pattern vectors were different.
They do, however, form a cluster in 200 space and the ten clusters corresponding to the ten digits are linearly separable. The
simplest measure of mismatch between an input vector $\underline{X}$ and a
stored vector $\underline{X}_m$ is the Hamming Distance (H) which could be
found by counting the "1"'s at the outputs of 200 exclusive or
gates, each with one input connected to the ith component of $\underline{X}$
vector and the second input connected to the corresponding component of the stored vector $\underline{X}_m$ as illustrated in Figure 2. In
general we store M sample vectors $\underline{X}_1 \ldots \underline{X}_m \ldots X_M$ to represent M
classes and for the spoken digits M is at least 10 but could be
several hundred if the system is required to handle a wide range
of speakers, accents or languages. When the classes are no longer

linearly seaprable correct classification can always be achieved by piecewise linear separation which only requires a slight modification of the hardware.

Summation of the M columns of N exclusive or gate outputs yields M Hamming distances H_1 ....H_M, the smallest of which indicates the correct nearest neighbour (NN) classification of the input vector $\underline{X}$, except that a reject class can be included if the smallest H is larger than a threshold value H_t.

The hardware realization of the scheme in Figure 2 is expensive and complex in terms of wiring for large NM values but a far simpler realization exists in the R-PROM which replaces the MN storage locations, the MN exclusive or gates and the M summing devices in one extremely simple, low cost, reliable, high speed parallel device.

III. The R-PROM Solution

All the operations performed by the system of Figure 2 in synthesizing the Hamming distances are effectively realized by the R-PROM network shown in Figure 3. It is convenient to choose power supply levels for the shift registers so that the logic high level for "1" is represented by zero voltage and the logic low level for "0" is represented by -1 unit of voltage, this unit being typically 5V. The Q and Q outputs of each shift register position supply the 2N horizontal conductors of the R-PROM matrix which has M vertical conductors.

Each R-PROM is fabricated in the same standard way and has a resistor at each of the 2NM crossover points before programming takes place. The resistors are produced by a carefully controlled process that gives them closely controlled fusing characteristics when the voltage across them is twice the normal operating voltage. Programming sample vectors into the memory is achieved by speaking into the microphone so that the sample vector enters the shift register and comes to rest automatically in a standard central position. Assuming that this sample belongs to class m it

is only necessary to apply unit voltage to the mith vertical conductor. This has the effect of applying two units of voltage to
the resistors supplied by the $\underline{X}$ vector negative unit voltages on
the horizontal conductors, thereby causing them to fuse and become
open circuit. The remaining horizontal conductors supply zero
volts to the resistors that only experience one unit of voltage
and therefore remain intact. When the programming voltage is removed from the vertical conductor to leave an open circuit the
voltage on this mth conductor is zero since all the resistors that
were supplied by unit negative voltages have been eliminated. The
mth column of the memory matrix thus stores the sample vector $\underline{X}_m$
and the open circuit voltage on the mth column conductor is $-H_m$,
the Hamming distance between any input vector $\underline{X}$ and the sample
vector $\underline{X}_m$ preceeded by a negative sign. The negative sign is
selected so that the maximum voltage produced after all M columns
have been programmed corresponds to the minimum Hamming distance
between any input vector $\underline{X}$ and the M sample vectors. Unambiguous
digital indication of this nearest neighbour classification i (0,
1, ...M) is produced by the M+1 parallel comparators, the zero
class indicating a reject or "don't know" condition for which the
nearest neighbour $\underline{X}$ is at a Hamming distance greater than a
threshold H from the input vector $\underline{X}$.

The same R-PROM system can be used with other forms of preprocessing, distance measurement and feature selection. With
binary vectors, for example, the Euclidean distance measure is
obtained by introducing M square root modules before the comparators. This would have no significant effect on the classification
except that **for** the same dynamic signal range small Euclidean
distances would be given more relative weight than large distances.
Assuming that the maximum Hamming distance of H=N=200 produces
unit voltage then unit H.D. produces 1/200 unit voltage. For the
corresponding maximum Euclidean distance E= $\sqrt{H}$ to produce the same
unit voltage the gain of the square root system is required to be

$1/\sqrt{200} = 1/14.1$. Unit Hamming distance thus produces a change of $1/14.1$ units of voltage and the initial sensitivity is 14 times greater. This, however, is at the expense of one half the sensitivity to unit distance changes near H= 200, the sensitivities being equal at H = 50 = 200/4. It would seem therefore that the considerable expense and complexity incurred by taking the Euclidean distance in place of the Hamming distance would make the system inferior by over emphasizing the small changes in $\underline{X}$ that occur from one utterance to the next of the same word by the same speaker.

No attempt has been made to identify significant features in the spectral analysis but if features were extracted by a preprocessor the same R-PROM could still be used on the new $\underline{X}$ vectors which hopefully would be in more widely separated clusters for different words but more closely packed for the same word class. One preprocessor that is relatively simple to implement gives the City Block Distance by representing distance in each dimension by the number of "1"s in each $\underline{X}$ vector component. The Hamming distance may thus be regarded as the simplest case of City Block Distance for which the maximum distance is one unit. With this form of coding the general case of q-level quantized N dimensional space can also be handled by the system of Figure 3 if q threshold comparators are introduced at each input, increasing the dimensionality of $\underline{X}$ to qN. In practice it may be possible to reduce N as q increases.

IV.   <u>Experimental Results</u>

An economy in the number of sample pattern vectors was made by taking a form of average vector for each word over 25 samples per word from 4 speakers. The maximum possible score obtainable for each component of the vector obtained by summing the 100 sample vectors for each word is 100. The word sample vector components were made "1" or "0" depending on whether the summation vector component was above or below 50. An average score of 95%

over the ten spoken digits was obtained for the four speakers as
compared with 99% for one speaker when only his own averaged sample
vectors were stored. As a practical test of the machine the recognition outputs were coded to control the motion of an X-Y plotter
pen which was magnetically coupled to a toy car on the track shown
in Figure 4. Each of the four speakers found little difficulty
in using his voice to guide the car round the track without enter-
ing the shaded area. At a subsequent open day demonstration a
high proportion of visitors could perform this task using the same
ten sample vectors.

References

1. United States Patent 3863231, January 1975.

2. Sandoval, V. H., "On the Hyperplanes of the Taylor-Steinbuch
   Linear Separator", IEEE Transactions on Computers, EC 15-6,
   p. 935, 1966.

3. Al-Kibasi, K. T. and Taylor, W. K., "The UCLM3 Programmable
   Pattern Recognition Machine", 2nd International Joint Con-
   ference on Pattern Recognition, Copenhagen, 1974, IEEE Cat.
   No. 74CHO885-4C.

Figure 1.

Typical 200 dimension pattern vectors $\underline{X}$ produced by the spoken digits Zero, one, ...nine.

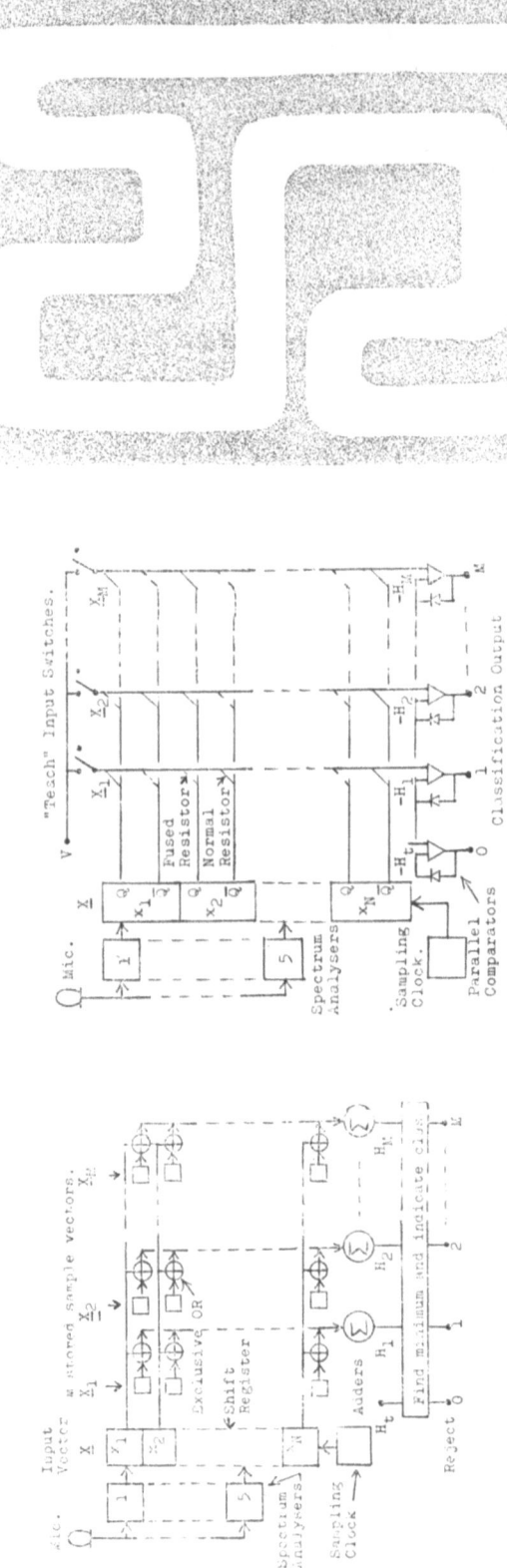

Figure 2. Digital Speech
Recognition System.

Figure 3. Speech Recognition
System Using Resistor-PROM.

Figure 4. "Road Network" Nego-
tiated by voice controlled "car".

PEAK ANALYSIS OF ELECTROPHORETIC STRIPS

M. Badiali[+], D. H. Ballard[+], A. Bertuzzi[++], M. Matteucci[+]

[+]Laboratorio Tecnologie Biomediche, C.N.R., Rome, Italy
[++]Centro di Studio dei Sistemi di Controllo e Calcolo Automatici,
C.N.R., Rome, Italy

I. Introduction

Electrophoresis of seroproteins is a method for the examination of the protein composition of the human blood. In view of the different charge/weight ratio of the various proteins, it a certain quantity of serum placed on an adsorbent support strip (e.g. cellulose acetate) is subjected to the action of an electric field, the proteins contained in the serum migrate at different speeds. By interrupting the migration at a suitable moment, a series of parallel bands of increased optical density corresponding to the different protein fractions is obtained on the strip. The electrophoretic waveform (electropherogram), which is interpreted by the laboratory analyst, is then obtained from the strip by means of optic scanning.

Waveform 1 in fig. 1 is a normal electropherogram: the basic protein fractions (albumin and α, β and γ globulins) and the corresponding zones are indicated. The presence or absence of given fractions, the measurement of their different percentages (areas bounded by the corresponding peaks) and more generally the pattern of the waveform give diagnostic indications for a wide variety of pathologies [1].

The automatic or semiautomatic devices used by the analysts, however, merely compute the percentages of the various fractions. They do not take into account other characteristics of the wave-forms which are fundamental for correct diagnosis, namely the shape and position of the peaks.

The present work proposes a method for the automatic analysis of electrophoretic waveforms which utilizes as much as possible of the information the analyst obtains a visual examination of the strip [2,3]. This analysis, resulting in a qualitative and quantitative description of the waveforms, makes it possible to assign them to one of a given number of classes.

II. Description of the Data Base

Fig. 1 shows six electropherograms, the first normal and the others pathological. The waveforms have all been standardized, as described further on. They show clearly the differences in pattern between pathological cases and the normal case: the additional monoclonal band, which can be anywhere in the zone of the γ-globulins in 2, the diminution of the γ-globulins in 3, the increase of the α_2 globulins in 5 and of the γ-globulins in 6, the increase of the γ-globulins with β-γ binding in 4. These differences may, of course, be so slight as to be imperceptible even to the experienced human observer.

The sample set used for the design and for the testing of the entire recognition system was supplied by the Analysis Laboratory of Civil Hospital at Sondrio, Italy. It consists of 140 labeled cases subdivided as follows: 20 cases belonging to class 1, 25 to 2, 20 to 3, 26 to 4, 28 to 5 and 21 to 6. The cases were considered to be representative of the true variability in the data and had been identified at the Hospital also on the basis of the patients' case sheets; the a priori classification of the samples was therefore considered known without uncertainty.

III. Description of the System

Fig. 2 shows a block diagram of the system for the acquisition and processing of data. An electro-optical device scans the strip.

The voltage amplifier makes it possible to utilize the whole dynamics of the A/D converter and the filter to eliminate the mains noise from the signal. The wave pattern is visualized on a CRT. The analog signal is sent to a ch nnel of the A/D converter of a system with central unit type HP 2100. The signal is digitized and processed as described in fig. 3.

This figure shows a diagram of the programs for waveform analysis. By means of subprogram ACQ, the teletype controls the acquisition of the signal. The preprocessing includes the programs that delimit the part of interest (DELE), eliminate the drift and normalize the length and the total area bounded by the waveform (STAND). Then the peaks are identified with MIMAX and the features chosen are measured by PARAM. Finally the feature values are normalized with SMV and passed to the classifier CLAS which supplies the class membership probabilities.

IV. Data Preprocessing

Fig. 4 shows the action of the preprocessing programs. The digitized waveform is stored in a vector of 512 elements, the last 12 of which are used for an identification label. In a) the curve indicates the acquired waveform of length L_a. The part of this curve which is of interest has a length L, which depends on the type and the preparation of the strip and is therefore variable.

The first phase of the preprocessing is the determination of the beginning and ending points of this part by comparing the values of the ordinates with the values of the extreme zones (indicated in the figure with 1 and 2) corresponding to the transparency of the cellulose acetate. It is more difficult to find the final point because the ratio between the signal and the noise, caused by imperfections of the support material or the preparation, is lower. In this way the double hatched zones are eliminated.

The second phase is the compensation of any drift on the amplitudes (due to slow variations in the transparency of the acetate support), which would lead to errors in the computation

of the fraction percentages. So a linear correction is carried
out by eliminating the triangle which is shaded in the figure.
The constant value indicated by the dotted area is also eliminated.

In the last phase length L, which does not have a diagnostic
value, is normalized to L_s by linear transformation of the abscis-
sae. The normalized waveform is stored in a vector with 256 elements: the graph is shown in b). Also the total area bounded is
normalized because it does not have a diagnostic value.

V. Feature Measurement

Fig. 5 shows the features. Different combinations of them
have been used for the classification, as will be indicated in
the next section.

For the measurement of some of these features, it is necessary first to identify the peaks, that is, to associate each of
them with the corresponding type of protein (see fig. 1). This
identification, which can be considered a classification problem,
is complicated by the following three factors: a) for a series of
reasons a peak may be absent, b) the peaks may be in different
locations translated from the "normal" one, c) monoclonal gamma-
pathies (class 2) produce an additional peak which may appear anywhere in zone γ and more rarely in zones α and β. The MIMAX subprogram finds in the first place the maxima and minima of the
standardized waveform. The maxima are then labelled, according
to the particular protein fraction they represent, taking into
account both the normal peak sequence and the distance of each
peak from the albumin one. Once the peaks have been identified,
the percentages of the corresponding proteins are obtained by
measuring the bounded areas (indicated in the figure with F_1, F_2,
F_3, F_4, F_5, F_6). A measure of the so-called "β-γ binding" (important for the identification of hepatic cirrhosis) is obtained from
the part of the waveform in the β-γ transition zone by means of
the parameter

$$F_{11} = \sum_{i=M}^{N} f_i \, sen^3 \left(\frac{\pi}{N-M} (i-M) \right)$$

where f_i indicate the ordinates lying between the Mth and the Nth. Other parameters can be obtained to characterize the shape of given peaks.

To measure the features indicated further on, it is not necessary, on the other hand, to identify the peaks. The feature F_7 equal to

$$F_7 = F_1 / \sum_{i=2}^{6} F_i$$

gives the albumin/globulin ratio which is of considerable diagnostic value. On the peak at the extreme right, which is always a -globulin or a monoclonal band, the following features are measured: F_8 is the value of the ordinate, F_9 and F_{10} are respectively measures of its peakedness and symmetry and are given

$$F_9 = m_4 / (m_2)^2$$
$$F_{10} = m_3 / (m_2)^{3/2}$$

where m_2, m_3, m_4 are the moments of order 2, 3 and 4 of the part of the waveform comprised in a suitable window centered on the maximum. On the most elevated peak of the central zone of the waveform are measured the features F_{12}, F_{13}, F_{14}, respectively the ordinate, the distance from the albumin and the peakedness. Measures of β-γ binding and of the peakedness and symmetry different from the ones indicated were used and evaluated.

The features chosen are of empirical type, that is, they are oriented to the detection of the peculiarities, indicated by the experience of the analysts, which characterize the patterns corresponding to the classes. The relevant information is distributed in a very non-uniform way in the waveform and concerns very particular aspects of it. For this reason these features have been preferred for the time being to the ones obtained with representation methods which take into account the whole pattern. It has been found that both the coefficients of the Fourier expansion and the moments of the waveform are very sensitive to differences irrelevant to the classification.

VI. Classification Procedures

As regards the classification methods, two different ways were taken.

As the first attempt a classification method was chosen based on potential functions for the estimation of the probability density functions for the six classes considered and on Bayes' decision rule for the assignment to the class [4,5]. It is pointed out that no a priori indication was available about the distributions. The essential data of the classifier are indicated in fig. 6. The latter shows, for each class, the number of samples available for the construction of the discriminant functions g_i and the functional form chosen for them. As is known, these functions g_i may be viewed as estimates of the conditional probability density functions $p(\underline{x}/S_i)$, where S_i indicates the i-th class. From them are obtained, assuming equal a priori probabilities $P(S_i)$, the estimates of the a posteriori probabilities $P(S_i/\underline{x})$, that is the values P_i. The figure shows also a part of the computer output obtained by applying the potential function method to a group of samples of class 1 and a group of samples of class 4. In this case the individual sample classified was not included for the construction of the respective discriminant function (the leaving-one-out method, see next section).

Various classification attempts were carried out with different subsets of the set of features indicated in the preceding section. Dimension N of the feature space varied in the different tests and consequently the smoothing parameter σ of the potential function. A search for the optimal subset of features by statistical methods was not carried out; the selection was made by means of classification tests and direct clustering observation on two-dimensional subspaces defined by various pairs of features.

A second classification method was subsequently attempted. It consists of a multi-stage decision process in which the features are measured and used sequentially. Fig. 7, which now substitutes

the right part of the diagram in fig. 3, shows the structure of the decisional tree: it indicates the features measured
at each stage and the respective decision. The choice of this
structure is described and justified by what follows. Only the F_9
feature turned out to be sufficient to separate without overlapping in the available sample set the cases in which a monoclonal
band appears in the γ-globulins zone. Features F_{12}, F_{14} were used
in stage 2. to distinguish the cases in which the monoclonal band
appears in the central zone. It should be noted that in the first
two stages it is not necessary to identify the peaks. The identification is carried out in stage 3. in which two features are
used to discriminate class 4. The discriminant functions for
stages 2. and 3. are both piecewise linear; since the feature
space is reduced to a plane they were chosen by observing the
clustering of available samples on it. At stage 4. the separation
between the four remaining classes is carried out by measuring
features F_3, F_6, F_7; the four discriminant functions are 2nd order
polynomials found by a minimum square error procedure (pseudoinverse method) [6]. Since it was recognized, however, that in this
stage there is a considerable overlapping between the classes due
a) to the transvariance between the normal class and each of the
pathological classes and b) to cases with more than one pathological characteristic, the class membership probabilities were also
computed by the potential function method.

VII. Results and System Evaluation

An estimate of the probability of misclassification of the
recognition system when the potential function classifier is used
was obtained by means of the leaving-one-out method applied to the
140 samples [7]. Fig. 8 shows the confusion matrix for a test in
which N=6; it is quite representative of the best results obtained,
and gives an estimate of the error probability equal to 8.6%.
This should be a good estimate in view of the ratio of feature
size to sample size [8]. For comparative purposes, the figure

shows also the confusion matrix obtained by the so-called resubstitution method for the same samples and features. This method gives a very optimistic estimate of the classification error: it should be noted that 100% accuracy on the design set could always be achieved by potential functions [9].

Fig. 9 shows the results obtained using the tree method. The design set consisted of the 140 samples. For the test 60 labelled samples subsequently available, mainly normal ones, were used. The two matrices concern the case in which, at stage 4, the discriminant functions - the features remaining the same - are constructed by means of the pseudoinverse method and the potential functions method. The percent of misclassification is comparable with the one obtained using the other method. It is considered necessary, however, to have a larger test set to improve and validate the procedure.

VIII. Conclusions

This work shows the feasibility of a completely automatic system for the analysis of electrophoretic strips. Its principal limitation, according to the authors, lies in the limited sample set that was available. With a larger set it would probably be possible to reduce the error rate and consider new classes. The set should contain strips from various analysis laboratories; since, unfortunately, the preparation methods are not yet standardized, the strips produced are different; this is important for the acquisition and preprocessing of the data.

The results obtained with the tree classifier are considered to be of a certain interest. It is easily implementable, fast and does not require the storage of a high number of samples if the decision rules are all of the polynomial type. Finally, the use of this type of classifier could make it possible to construct a specialized device that would carry out all the operations.

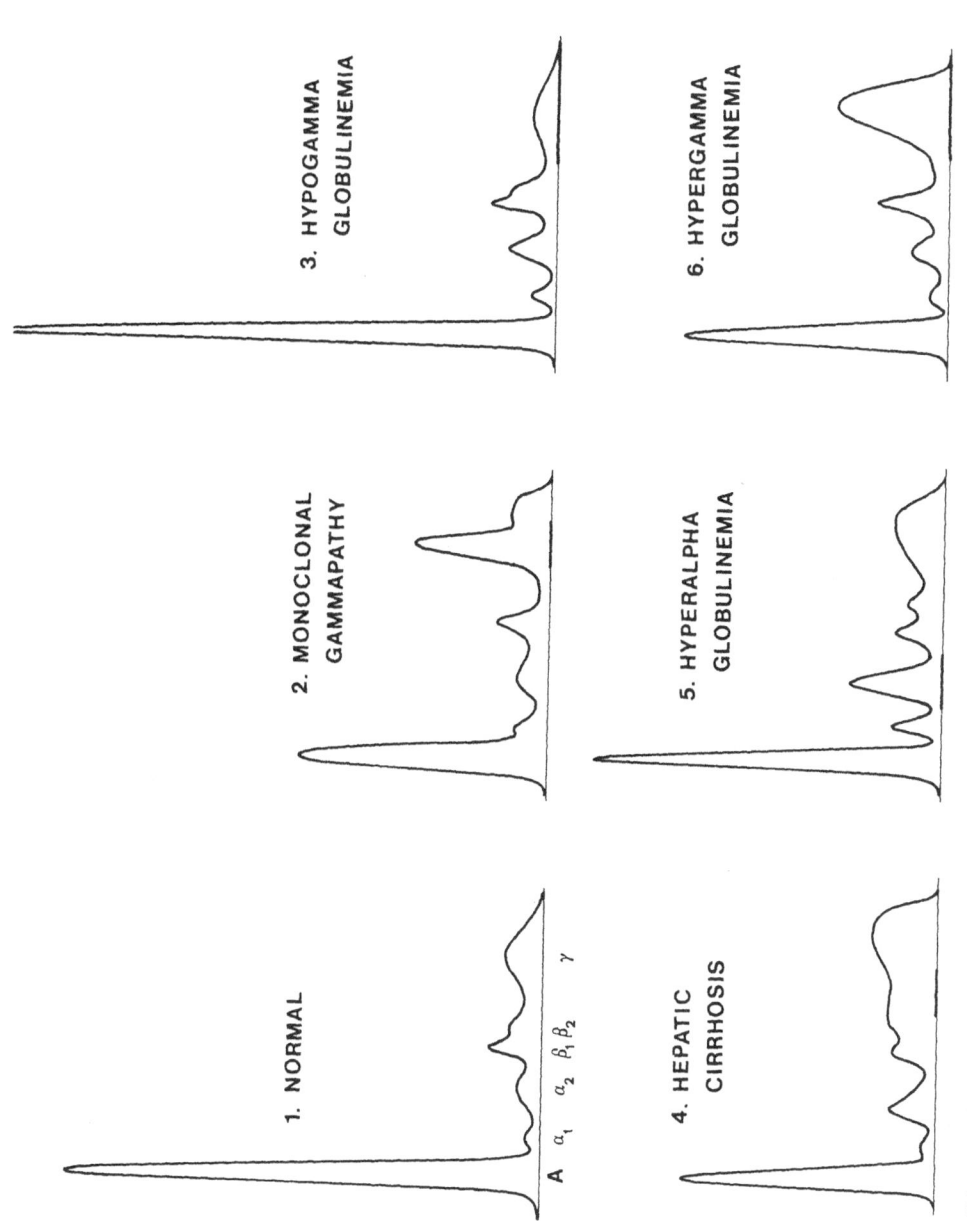

Figure 1

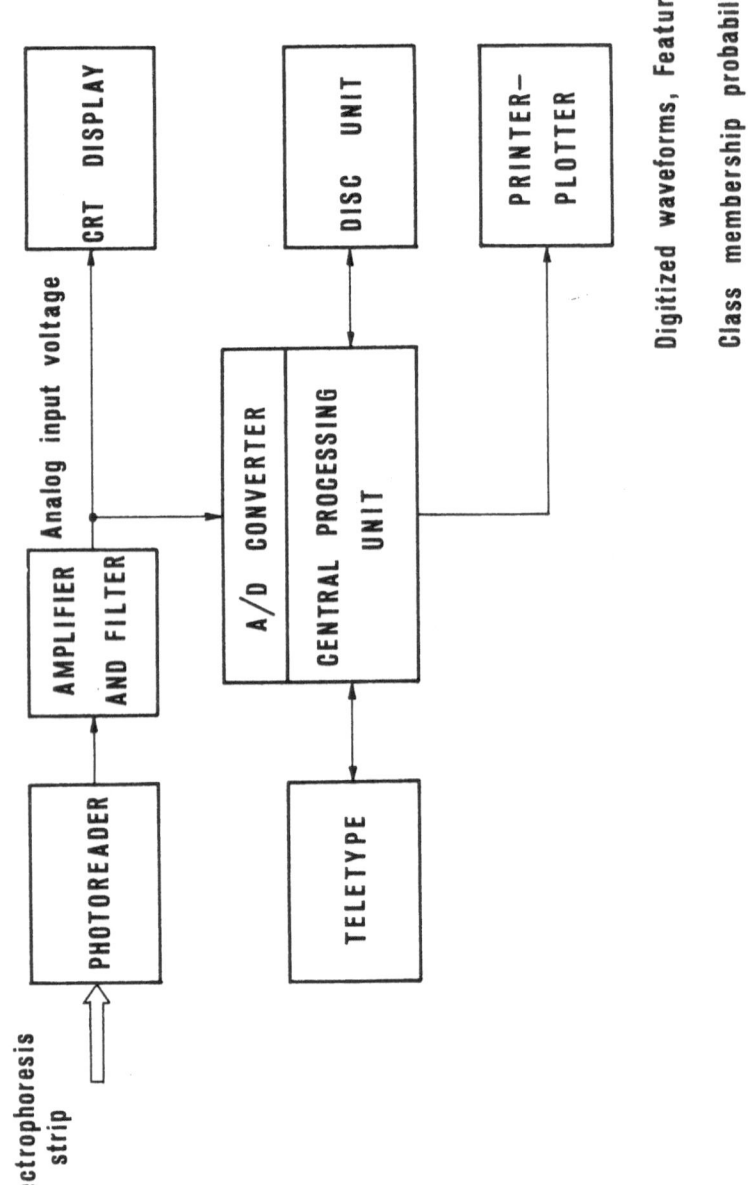

Figure 2

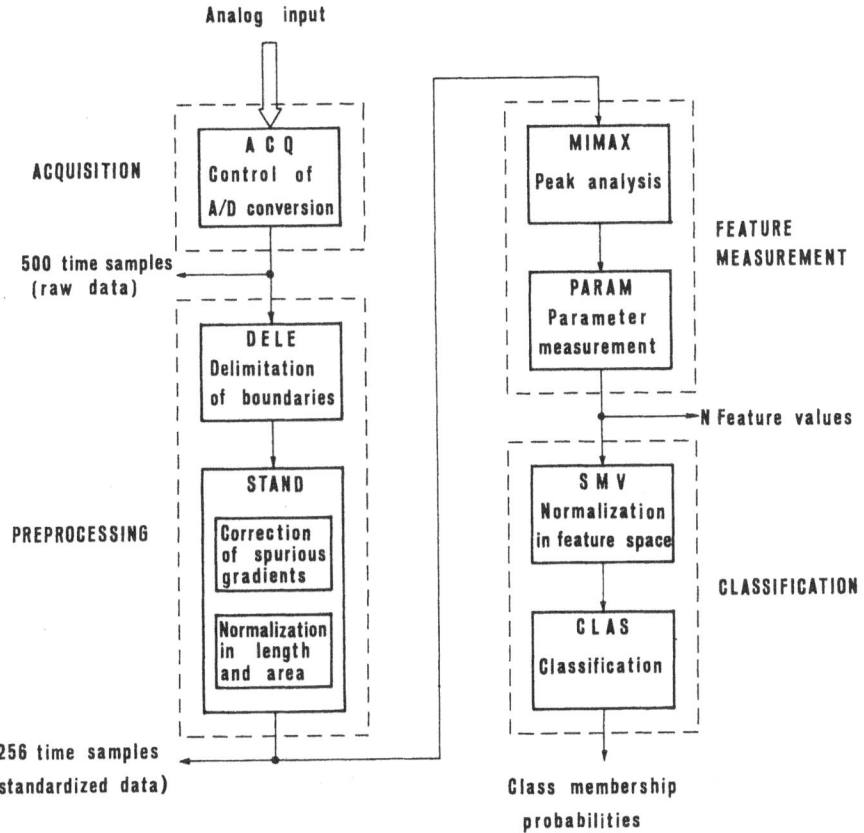

Figure 3

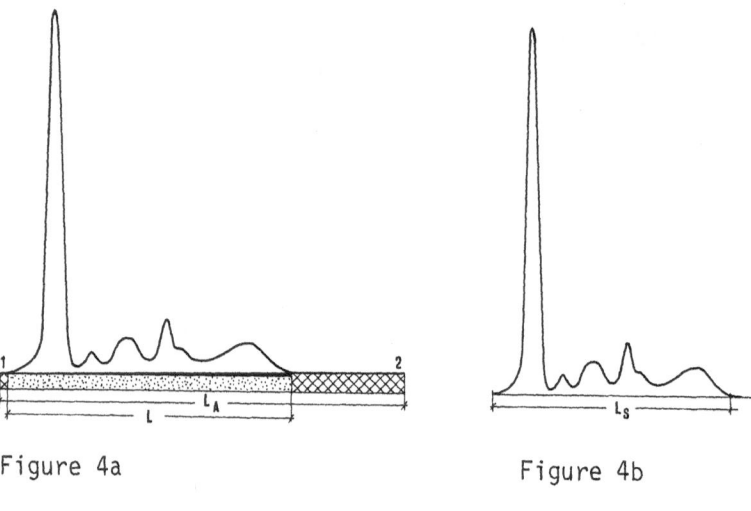

Figure 4a

Figure 4b

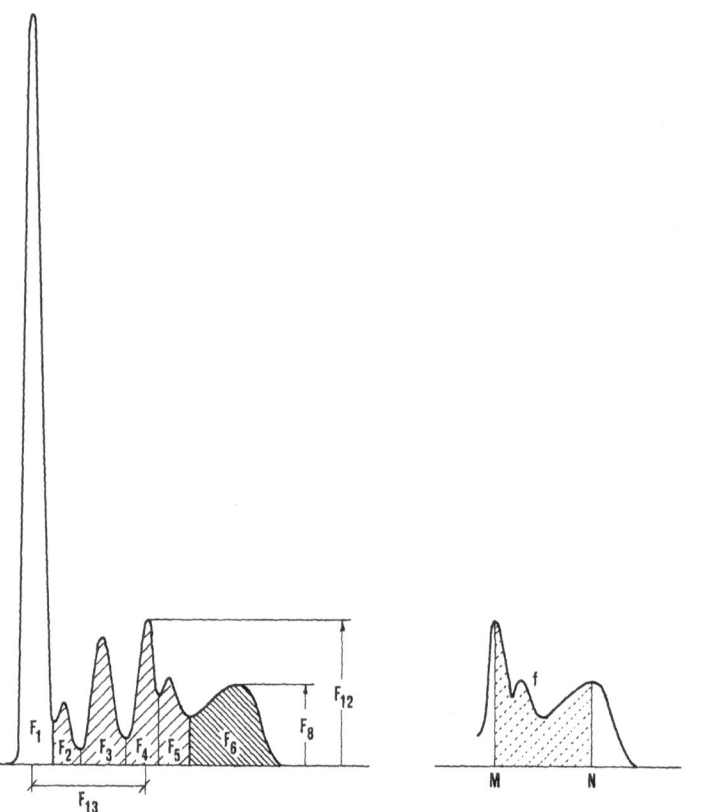

Figure 5

CLASS	SAMPLES
1	20
2	25
3	20
4	26
5	28
6	21

$$g_i(\underline{x}) = \frac{\sum\limits_{m=1}^{M_i} \phi(\underline{x},\underline{y}_m^{(i)})}{M_i} \qquad i=1,2,\ldots,6$$

$$\phi(\underline{x},\underline{y}_m^{(i)}) = \frac{1}{(2\pi\sigma^2)^{N/2}}\; e^{-\frac{(\underline{x}-\underline{y}_m^{(i)})^T(\underline{x}-\underline{y}_m^{(i)})}{2\sigma^2}} \qquad i=1,2,\ldots,6$$

$$P_i = g_i(\underline{x})\Big/\sum\limits_{k=1}^{6} g_k(\underline{x}) \qquad i=1,2,\ldots,6$$

SAMPLE	g_1	g_2	g_3	g_4	g_5	g_6	P_1	P_2	P_3	P_4	P_5	P_6	CLASS
1	.217E+00	.263E-03	.104E+00	.420E-02	.869E-01	.463E-01	47.4	.1	22.6	.9	18.9	10.1	1
2	.285E+00	.356E+00	.363E-01	.150E-01	.468E+00	.122E+00	57.8	.0	7.4	.4	9.5	24.9	1
3	.355E+00	.182E-04	.978E-01	.810E-04	.429E-02	.111E-01	75.8	.0	20.9	.0	.9	2.4	1
4	.302E+00	.643E-05	.119E+00	.208E-03	.659E-02	.229E-01	66.9	.0	26.5	.0	1.5	5.1	1
5	.161E+00	.829E-04	.423E-01	.500E-04	.526E-02	.252E-01	68.8	.0	18.1	.0	2.2	10.8	1
6	.266E+00	.142E-04	.368E-01	.159E-02	.406E-01	.880E-01	61.5	.0	8.5	.4	9.4	20.3	1
7	.346E+00	.366E-04	.148E+00	.597E-04	.165E-02	.382E-02	69.2	.0	29.7	.0	.3	.8	1
8	.317E+00	.295E-04	.128E+00	.895E-05	.588E-03	.310E-02	70.7	.0	28.5	.0	.1	.7	1
9	.342E+00	.327E-04	.874E-01	.352E-03	.148E-01	.457E-01	69.7	.0	17.8	.1	3.0	9.3	1
10	.226E+00	.223E-04	.441E-01	.526E-02	.692E-01	.105E+00	50.3	.0	9.8	1.2	15.4	23.4	1
11	.406E+00	.207E-04	.146E+00	.175E-03	.583E-02	.193E-01	70.3	.0	25.3	.0	1.0	3.3	1
12	.312E+00	.189E-04	.185E+00	.567E-04	.130E-02	.314E-02	62.2	.0	36.9	.0	.3	.6	1
13	.185E+00	.483E-04	.263E-01	.906E-02	.107E+00	.114E+00	41.9	.0	6.0	2.1	24.3	25.8	1
14	.341E+00	.150E-04	.133E+00	.406E-04	.232E-02	.113E-01	69.9	.0	27.3	.0	.5	2.3	1
15	.216E+00	.141E-03	.163E+00	.861E-04	.167E-02	.340E-02	56.3	.0	42.3	.0	.4	.9	1
16	.127E+00	.444E-05	.856E-01	.193E-06	.323E-04	.517E-03	59.5	.0	40.2	.0	.0	.2	1
17	.232E+00	.135E-04	.833E-01	.148E-02	.213E-01	.209E-01	64.7	.0	23.2	.4	5.9	5.8	1
18	.235E+00	.202E-04	.762E-01	.410E-04	.163E-02	.278E-02	74.5	.0	24.1	.0	.5	.9	1
91	.141E-07	.152E-09	.112E-12	.742E-01	.992E-07	.291E-02	.0	.0	.0	96.2	.0	3.8	4
92	.221E-06	.207E-08	.464E-11	.729E-01	.149E-05	.667E-02	.0	.0	.0	91.6	.0	8.4	4
93	.310E-08	.451E-08	.173E-12	.175E-01	.552E-06	.808E-02	.0	.2	.0	68.4	.0	31.5	4
94	.179E-02	.504E-05	.279E-05	.124E-01	.773E-02	.504E-01	2.5	.0	.0	17.2	10.7	69.7	6
95	.829E-04	.678E-05	.279E-07	.112E-01	.175E-02	.260E-01	.2	.0	.0	28.7	4.5	66.6	6
96	.361E-06	.148E-08	.208E-10	.158E+00	.138E-05	.334E-02	.0	.0	.0	97.9	.0	2.1	4
97	.401E-06	.827E-08	.212E-10	.182E+00	.341E-05	.545E-02	.0	.0	.0	97.1	.0	2.9	4

Figure 6

354

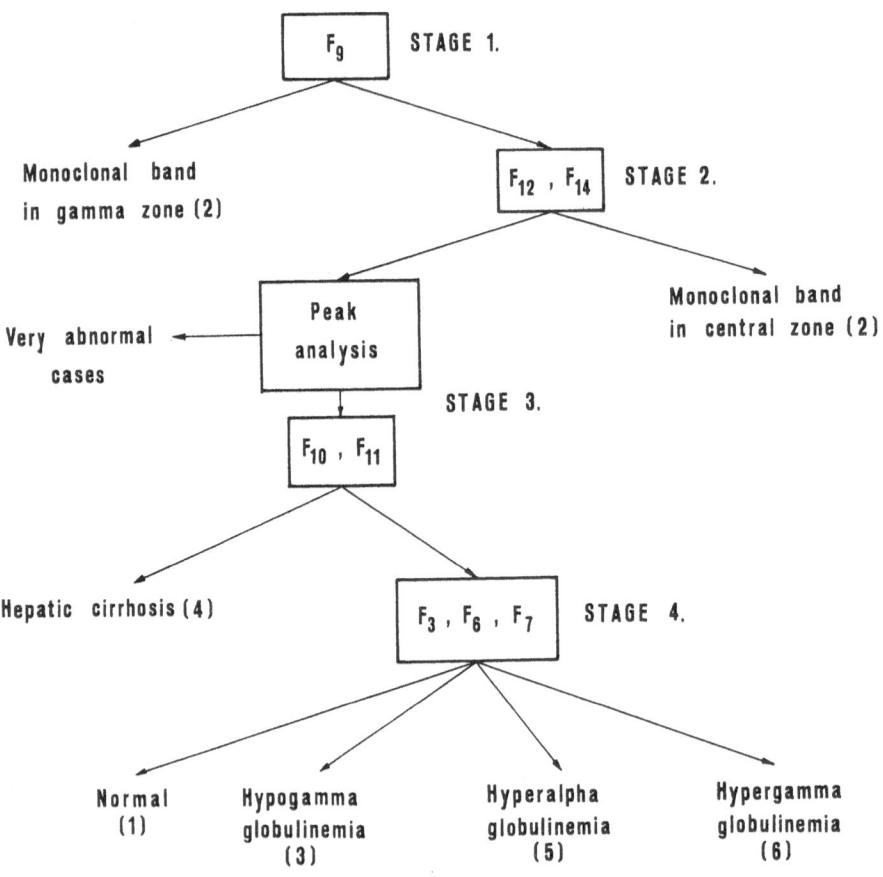

Figure 7
F_9 degree of peakedness of peak in Gamma zone
F_{12} elevation of highest peak in central zone
F_{14} degree of peakedness of highest peak in central zone
F_{10} degree of asymmetry of peak in Gamma zone
F_{11} measure of Beta-Gamma binding
F_3 percent of Alpha 2
F_6 percent of Gamma
F_7 Alpha-Gamma ratio

POTENTIAL FUNCTIONS CLASSIFIER

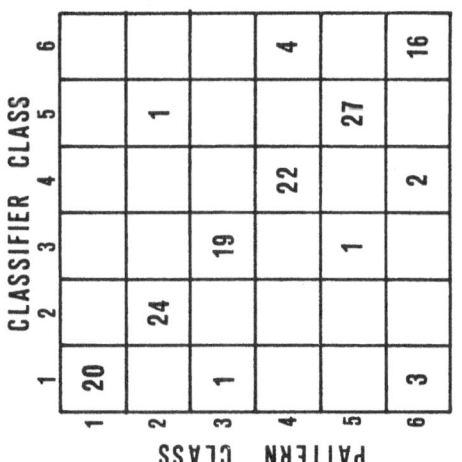

LEAVING-ONE-OUT METHOD
140 SAMPLES
6 FEATURES

RESUBSTITUTION METHOD
140 SAMPLES
6 FEATURES

Number of misclassifications: 4
Percent of misclassification: 2.9
Pathological samples assigned
to normal class: 2

Number of misclassifications: 12
Percent of misclassification: 8.6
Pathological samples assigned
to normal class: 4

Figure 8

DECISION TREE CLASSIFIER

MSE CLASSIFIER
60 NEW SAMPLES
3 FEATURES

PF CLASSIFIER
60 NEW SAMPLES
3 FEATURES

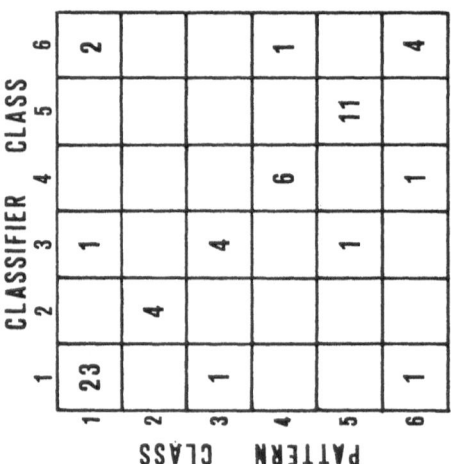

Number of misclassifications: 8
Percent of misclassification: 13
Pathological samples assigned
to normal class: 2

Number of misclassifications: 6
Percent of misclassification: 10
Pathological samples assigned
to normal class: 1

Figure 9

References

Sunderman, F. W., "Studies of the Serum Proteins VI. Advances in Clinical Interpretation of Electrophoretic Fractionations", Amer. J. Clin. Path., 42, no. 1, 1964.

Porta, F., "Program definition for the automatic analysis of electrophoretic data", Technical Note, Civil Hospital at Sondrio, March 1974.

Vettori, P. G. Paleani, Badiali, M., Bertuzzi, A., Lori, A., Matteucci, M., Palomba, R., Toriontano, G., "The Automatic Classification of Clinical Laboratory Data", IEEE International CISMEL Symposium, September 1974.

Duda, R. O., Hart, P. E., "Pattern Classification and Scene Analysis", J. Wiley & Sons, New York, 1973.

Braverman, E. M., "On the Method of Potential Functions", Automat. Remote Contr., 26, 2130-8, 1965.

Wee, W. G., "Generalized Inverse Approach to Adaptive Multiclass Pattern Classification", IEEE Trans. Comp., C-17, 1157-64, 1968.

Toussaint, G. T., "Recent Progress in Statistical Methods Applied to Pattern Recognition", Proc. 2nd IJCPR, August 1974.

Foley, D. H., "Considerations of Sample and Feature Size", IEEE Trans. Inform. Theory, IT-18, 618-26, 1972.

Meisel, W. S., "Potential Functions in Mathematical Pattern Recognition", IEEE Trans. Comp., C-18, 911-8, 1969.

PATTERN RECOGNITION IN THE SOCIAL SCIENCES

J. M. Blin*
A. B. Whinston†

I. Introduction

The primary purpose of this paper is to illustrate the usefull-
ness of pattern recognition concepts and methods in the social
sciences in general and, more specifically, in Economics. The
need for classification methods in various areas of economic research has been understood by a number of authors. For instance
to evaluate and explain the performance of certain sets of stocks,
a number of authors have proposed to use discriminant analysis to
partition such a set and isolate the particular characteristics of
the companies which could explain differential performances among
such stocks [38]. More recently it has been proposed to use certain pattern recognition methods to improve business forecasting
performance [27]. Other authors have also outlined the possible
role of classification methods in sociological research [40]. All
these attempts, however, view pattern recognition methods as convenient tools of classification of certain data to enable the de-
cision-maker to infer from the characteristics of such classes a

*Northwestern University, School of Management, Evanston, Illinois.
†Krannert School, Purdue University, West Lafayette, Indiana 47907.

set of rules to guide him in his choices. Whether he is interested
in forecasting business conditions three or six months from now,
or whether he seeks to explain the difference in stock performance
by a number of objective factors characterizing the firm which has
issued this stock, his need for classification is motivated by
decision-making considerations. But there is also a deeper use
to be made of pattern recognition theory: it concepts can be used
as models to resolve certain basic theoretical issues. This view
of pattern recognition methods in economics was first explored by
Blin in [8]. This work has dealt with the theory of aggregation
and group decision making from a pattern recognition viewpoint.

First he has shown that the question of deciding collectively
on a number of group issues, say, various levels of spending on
alternative public goods, e.g. on environmental protection vs.
energy generation or defense spending, or massive subsidization
programs for mass transit, can be adequately modelled as a classical pattern recognition problem. The features of the individual p
preference patterns are simply the collective issues and the preferred decision on each issue for any individual is the value which
this preference pattern takes on this dimension. The interesting
question, of course, is the policy issue: given a certain set
of individual preferences, revealed directly or indirectly via
electoral contests, surveys or interviews, what group preference
pattern should we pick to maximize satisfaction among all concerned
citizens? Or, put more directly, what budgetary choices should we
make to achieve maximal agreement among conflicting view points?
Using various discriminant functions to classify individual preferences into typical pattern classes we can derive decision procedures to arrive at collective decision on such issues.

In some further work Blin and Whinston [14] have introduced
the notion of an order of priorities ("saliency") among the issues
(the features) considered by the group. The existence of such
priorities leads to the consideration of explicit trade-offs

between issues among individuals. The kinds of decentralized
decision rules which can be used to effect those trade-offs have
been examined. Also the investigators have proposed to use the
notion of fuzzy (social) preferences to model group decision
making procedures [15]. In this context, they have been able to
show that social choice theory provides a natural completely
non-stochastic framework of interpretation for fuzzy set theory.

In this paper, we shall survey some of these contributions
from the standpoint of pattern recognition theory to show the
kinds of economic problems which can be structured in that framework and demonstrate the usefulness of such models. Our discussion will be organized as follows: First we will outline how an
n-dimensional continuous feature space can serve as a model to
represent certain economic entities. Then we will deal with the
more restricted but, also, more realistic case of a discrete
feature space. In this space we will show how the use of certain
non-linear discriminant functions affords a solution to one of
the central problems of group decision-making theory.

2.1 <u>The notion of feature space in economics</u>

Economic theory has often used the concept of feature space
under a variety of names. In onsumer theory, for instance, one
of the basic issues is to model and explain the particular bundle
of commodities purchased by a given individual faced with a certain
income and certain prices. Usually the explanation is based on
some view of individual rationality as a maximizing (or minimizing)
proposition: the consumer is assumed to be maximizing his utility
which is simply some real-valued function of the consumer's preference ordering over the set of all available commodity bundles,
the commodity space. This set is often modelled as the n-dimensional real, or euclidean space, where each dimension corresponds
to a commodity. The possibility of having certain "lumpy" or
indivisible commodities sometimes leads to certain restrictions
on this space e.g. only the integer points can be allowed. In any

case, the basic theory of consumer choice first makes a certain
number of assumptions regarding consumer rationality, and then proceeds to investigate their logical consequences. The result is a
well-developed set of propositions about certain properties of
consumer choices. Some of these propositions are purely static in
nature, as when we specify the conditions characterizing an equilibrium point - i.e. a point in the commodity space, a given bundle
of commodities, which is such that the consumer has no incentive
to move away from it unless his tastes, his income, or the prices
change. One such condition states that, at equilibrium, the consumer derives an equal marginal utility per dollar spent for any
two commodities. Other propositions are more dynamic as when we
state the reaction of a consumer to a certain price change. In
all these cases, however, the validity of such propositions is
premised on the validity of our basic assumptions about consumer
behavior. Besides the maximizing hypothesis which can hardly be
questioned, but only refined, it is most often assumed that the
consumer has a complete preference preordering R over the commodity
space. This means, in particular, that (1.) given any give two commodity bundles x^i, x^j available to the consumer, one of three cases
hold:

> (i) x^i R x^j (R = "... at least as preferred as...")
> (ii) x^j R x^i
> (iii)   or both

(2.) R is a reflexive relation: x^i R x^i, (3.) and R is transitive relation, i.e. given any three bundles x^i, x^j, x^k we have
x^i R x^j and x^j R $x^k \rightarrow x^i$ R x^k. This last property cannot
be rejected if we wish to avoid reaching indeterminate solutions,
as will be the case in problems of group decision making (see
below). A number of objections can be raised against this transitivity property in the context of individual choice but they can
usually be overcome by extending the notion of a consumer utility
function. At any rate once it is accepted, this property raises a

more practical problem: in actual individual choice experiments,
it has often been noted that certain cyclical preferences can be
observed; for instance a consumer in a paired comparison experiment is asked to state his preference (or indifference) for one
of the two items in any two pairs. If we then try to infer from
his answers a complete preference ordering, we may find that he
prefers x^i to x^j and x^j to x^k but he also prefers x^k to x^i. Many
explanations can be found for such behavior: we may choose to
blame the experimental design, or the consumer faulty memory; we
may also point out the inherent "incomparability" of the alternatives; or we may stress the multi-dimensional character of the
alternatives as when we look at the various characteristics of a
product (price, external appearance, other physical characteristics,
etc). This last route actually leads to some rather interesting
insights as will be illustrated below. At this point, however, we
should note that the question of deciding how to classify actual
preference orderings obtained from choice experiments, into transitive vs. intransitive ones, provides a rather simple illustration
of the use of "fuzzy" discriminators. (Blin et. al. [12]). We
now examine some of these results.

2.1.1 Classifying Individual Preference Orderings

Consider a finite set of objects S (commodity bundles for
instance). A binary relation R on S is simply a subset of the
product space of S ($R \subset S \times S$). Let R be the set of all such
binary relations on S. We can think of each $R_i \varepsilon R$ as a preference pattern characterized by a certain number of features. Let
$|S| = n$. In general any R_h consists of n^2 features viz. all the
elementary pairs (i, j) for i,j = 1,2,...,n. For preference relations, however, we can discard some of these features, given the
properties of R. Specifically if we consider the binary relations
on R which are irreflexive and asymmetric [1]) we only need to know
$C_n^2 = \frac{n(n-1)}{2}$ features, one for each pair (i,j). Among the C_n^2 binary
patterns R_i, only n! are strictly transitive. The problem is to

devise a classifier which will consider any input preference R_i and decide whether it belongs to the transitive or intransitive class. Let C_t and C_i denote these two classes (C_t, $C_i \subset R$). Strictly speaking, of course, C_t has sharp boundaries since we can always say unambiguously whether an input pattern R_i violates transitivity or not. This view, however, will be of little help in assessing the results of paired comparison experiments since a certain amount of intransitivity is almost always found, especially when n is large. Thus, the real problem is to devise a way of tracing the fuzzy boundaries of the classes C_t and C_i. A membership function can be defined for the sets C_t and C_i. First write the input pattern R_h as a binary (n x n) matrix M where $m_{ij} = 1$ if i R_h j and 0 otherwise. Thus $m_{ij} + m_{ji} = 1$ (i,j = 1,2, ...,n; i $\neq$ j). Let s be the score vector of M: $s_i = \sum_{j=1}^{n} m_{ij}$.

(Intuitively s_i is the number of alternatives which are ranked below i in R_i). It can be shown that the following function t(n,s) expresses the number of intransitive triples [2] in R_i:

$$t = \frac{n}{24} (n^2 - 1) - \frac{1}{2} \Sigma \left(s_i - \frac{n-1}{2}\right)^2 \qquad (1)$$

By taking the ratio of the actual number of 3-cycles (t) to the maximum number of 3-cycles (t max $= \frac{1}{24} (n^3 - n)$) and subtracting this ratio from one we obtain the following membership function:

$$\xi = 1 - \frac{24t}{2} \qquad \text{(n odd [3])} \qquad (2)$$

With this membership function ξ, the set C_t of transitive preference pattern is delineated as a fuzzy set. In a similar fashion a membership function δ can be defined for the set C_i. Both sets are shown to be fuzzy convex sets. Hence so is their intersection. This allows us to determine the optimal separating hyperplane between C_t and C_i, which is such as to achieve the maximal degree of separation between C_t and C_i. Furthermore, a number of immediate extensions are possible: if we feel that the loss resulting from misclassification is not even for the two classes C_t and C_i, we can weigh the membership functions so as to shift the pattern classifier toward the core of C_t or C_i. We postpone our discussion of the use of loss functions in economic pattern classification to the next section.

2.1.2 <u>Consumer preferences in a continuous feature space</u>

The previous example was meant to illustrate how the notions of classifiers acting over an appropriate feature space are useful in the study of consumer preferences. A number of other models can also be used in consumer theory. First of all, as we said earlier, the assumption of a one-dimensional real-valued utility function is not necessary. In fact when observing intransitive individual preferences, it can be viewed as an oblique reminder of the multi-dimensional nature of individual preferences. Conflicting preferences may lead to circularities in revealed preferences. 4) Mod Modelling commodities as multi-attribute entities was first suggested by Lancaster [29], [30]. This trend has also been noticeable among statisticians dealing with the construction of consumer price indices. They have proposed the notion of an "hedonic price index" taking account of the multiplicity of attributes which consumers expect to find in the goods they purchase. The theoretical foundation for this approach can be found in the attitude theories of social psychology. These models have been used extensively by marketing researchers to try (a) to isolate the basic dimension (features) perceived by consumers and (b) to use the consumers' attitude towards such attributes to predict their actual purchase of a specific commodity brand of good among a set of closely competing brands (See, for instance, [3], [4], [5], [6], and [7].

In all these models, the feature space is formed by crossing the various attributes which are perceived as relevant in defining a product and distinguishing between competing brands. The patterns in this space are simply the various brands of a given product, or class of products. The goals of the investigator are:

(1.) to assess the relative importance of these features in explaining a given choice (this is known as the problems of feature selection and feature weighting in pattern recognition theory); (2.) to derive certain natural product clusters, that is to group various brands into classes on the basis of their relative proximity on one or several dimensions; and (3.) to use these results obtained from sample patterns to predict future choices and compare various alternatives in new products design. As we can see those three lines of research are quite parallel to what has been observed in pattern recognition theory. The connection however has not been perceived by these authors. For purposes of illustration, we will focus on the case of public goods.

Let us suppose that the dimensions of consumer preferences refer to the various public issues which are actively debated in a society. For instance, these could be such questions as the level of spending on defense, or the issue of spending on mass transit vs. highway systems, or any other issue which is deemed important by a large number of citizens in a society. All these questions are normally referred to as "public goods" issues on the economics literature. In recent years, attention has shifted from private to public goods allocation in economic theory. The basic problem in public goods decisions is the fact that these are necessarily joint decisions in the sense that they are going to affect most citizens, (usually all of the, but to various degrees) and thus require some form of group agreement - at least in a democracy. The conflict of individual interests is at the heart of the public goods issue. When a near unanimity of citizens agree on a course of public action little debate occurs. But, more usually, there are strong antagonistic interests which favor different policies on such issues. The question then becomes: (1.) what sorts of compromises can (should?) be reached and (2.) how can they be reached; the former is a descriptive question since it involves the proper partitioning of the society into different classes of opinions to yield some sort of notion of mutual distances between these classes; the latter is more normative, at least potentially, inasmuch as it raises the question of what kinds of group decision rules can be relied on and how they operate. This has been extensively studied by economists in the past two decades, under the name of "social choice theory". We hope to be able to show in the next two sections what has been contributed by the introduction of pattern recognition concepts.

2.2 Individual preferences over public goods

2.2.1 The continuous case ([8] [7])

In this section, we examine the following model. Let $(F_1, F_2,...,F_N)$ be the N features characterizing consumer preferences. Each feature corresponds to a public issue on a broad sense. For the time being we assume each F_i to be real-valued [5]. The feature space F_N is then:

$$F_N = \prod_{i=1}^{N} F_i \tag{3}$$

First each consumer is mapped into F_N; and then we seek to determine natural pattern classes $(C_1, C_2,...)$ in F_N where a set of points $(x^1, x^2,...)$ is grouped in one class whenever their overall pairwise similarity is larger than their dissimilarity with points lying outside of this class. At this point no similarity index has yet been developed. A natural way to measure similarity is to adopt some metric over F_N. Once this is done we can cluster the points in F_N to delineate the various prototypes of citizens' preferences. In a sense, this is the role of political parties and a number of authors have, in fact, investigated the consequences of certain distributions of preferences in F_N for the candidates' electoral strategies. (See [23], [24], [25], [26] for instance). For our purpose the following points should be noted. First of all a number of pattern classifiers can be devised to cluster the individual preferences x^h. As we know discriminant functions $g_i(x)$ (i, j = 1,2,...,) can be used as classifiers by using the following classification rule:

Map x^h into C_i $<=>$ $g_i(x^h) > g_j(x^h)$ $\forall j \neq i$ $\qquad$ (4)

The decision boundary between classes C_i and C_j is then defined by the equation:

$$g_i(x^h) - g_j(x^h) = 0 \qquad (5)$$

Consider first the general linear classifier where $g(x) = g_1(x^h) - g_2(x^h)$

$$g(x) = -(x-\bar{x}_1)'(x-\bar{x}_1) + (x-\bar{x}_2)'(x-\bar{x}_2) = 0 \qquad (6)$$

or

$$g(x) = w \cdot x - k \quad \text{(k is a constant)} \qquad (7)$$

where

$$W = (\bar{x}^1 - \bar{x}^2) \qquad (8)$$

$$K = -\frac{1}{2}|\bar{x}^2|^2 + \frac{1}{2}|\bar{x}^1|^2 \qquad (9)$$

and $\bar{x}^1$ and $\bar{x}^2$ are the centroids of the two clusters C^1 and C^2 respectively. The knowledge of this weight vector W leads to a number of interesting policy observations since it describes both the magnitude of the differences of opinion on each issue and also the kind of direction in which we would be likely to move if one group were to attract citizens from the other group.

A special case of linear classifier is afforded by the <u>minimum distance</u> classifier whereby we use m reference patterns[6] $P_1, P_2, \ldots, P_m$ representing the m classes of opinions in a given society. We then map each consumer in one (and only one) of these m classes so that the Euclidean distance $d(x, P_i)$ between that consumer's preference (x) and point P_i is minimum. Specifically the distance function is:

$$d(x, P_i) = |x - P_i|^2 = x.x - 2xP_i + P_i \cdot P_i \qquad (10)$$

To minimize d is equivalent to maximizing the new discriminant function

$$d_i^*(x) = xP_i - \frac{1}{2}P_i \cdot P_i \qquad (11)$$

Our decision rule can then be stated:

$$x \in C_i \quad <=> \quad d_i^*(x) > d_j^*(x) \quad \forall i, j = 1,2,\ldots,m \qquad (12)$$
$$i \neq j$$

or

$$\text{Maximize} \quad d_i^*(x) \tag{13}$$
$$P_i \varepsilon \{P_1, \ldots, P_m\}$$

Such classification techniques have natural economic interpretation: they correspond to the gathering of individual votes on the public issues at stake - where the vote would actually be a rating and not only a Yes - or - No type of answer. In fact, this interpretation can be further formalized. It can be shown that social decision rules are simply classifiers acting over an appropriately defined feature space. This generalization is interesting for several reasons. First it provides a novel view of group decision processes. But, more importantly, it allows us to draw upon the known properties of various classifiers to devise new group decision processes. Our interest in such processes stems from the fact that existing methods of group decision-making often lead to basic inconsistencies in social decisions. Such inconsistencies can be traced back to the lack of discriminatory power of the classification procedure we use. Alternative procedures will then be devised to resolve this problem. Before examining this, we will conclude by stating an interesting result for the models discussed in this section.

This result is a characterization of a certain class of preference patterns $X \varepsilon F_N$ known as Pareto-optimal in the economic literature. The notion of Pareto optimality has been used by welfare economists for many years. It is one of the least value-restricted tool that can be used to rate various economic states $X \varepsilon F_N$. A state x^i is said to be (weakly) Pareto-superior to x^j if and only if

$$x^i R_h x^j \qquad h = 1, 2, \ldots, \ell \tag{14}$$

where R_h is the preference pre-ordering of the hth consumer. In other words each consumer finds x^i at least as good (R) as x^j on his own preference scale. If there exists at least one consumer h* who strictly prefers x^i to x^j then we say that x^i is strongly Pareto superior to x^j. In effect the Pareto criterion is a unanimity criterion since a point x^i is declared Pareto-superior to x^j if no consumer objects (and at least one prefers it in the strong case). It is easily verified that the Pareto criterion provides a partial ordering relation over the points in F_N. A point $x^i \in F_N$ is said to be Pareto-optimal if and only if $\nexists x^j \in F_N$ such that x^j is Pareto-superior to x^i.

An important question can then be raised once we have mapped the various citizens' preferences into points of F_N and clustered them according to some of the classification techniques proposed earlier: can we characterize the sets of points $p \subset F_N$ consisting of the Pareto optimal points in F_N? Let $P_1, P_2, \ldots P_m$ be the centroids of the n clusters of opinion in F_N.[16] The following theorem can be proven ([8]).

Theorem: In the above model, the set of Pareto optimal points $p \subset F_N$ is the convex closure of the set $\{P_1, P_2, \ldots, P_m\}$. Thus, the set p is a convex polytope in N-space and its vertices are the centroids $P_1, P_2, \ldots, P_m$.

From a policy standpoint, this characterization enables us to determine whether or not some conceivable public policy measures are unanimously agreeable to all citizens. If the status quo is a point $x^s \in F_N - p$ then there exists a number of points $x^1, x^2, \ldots \in p$ which are preferred to x^s by everyone. This remark leads to a number of public policy recommendations for instance in the field of taxation. These points are further developed in [8].

2.2.2 The discrete case

In this section, we shall extend our study of the relationship between pattern classifiers and group decision rules. To simplify the discussion we will start from the following example which models the well-known majority voting rule as a threshold logic unit. In the sequel, we drop the assumption of continuity of each feature and replace it by a discreteness assumption. In the case of public goods, one of the notorious facts is that they are indivisible, and, as such, each issue can usually be resolved only in a finite number of ways. In other words, the alternative courses of public action form a finite set over which the consumers have different preferences orderings. The question is to devise a way of representing preference orderings over a finite set, say S, as patterns in a feature space analogous to the space of public issues which we have used so far. First we note that any individual preference ordering R^h is simply a subset of the product space of S [7]:

$$R^h \subset S \times S \qquad (15)$$

This means that the elements of R^h are simply pairs of alternatives $(a_i, a_j) \in S \times S$. As pointed out earlier, because of the properties of R^h only $\binom{m}{2} = \frac{m(m-1)}{2}$ pairs need to be examined. For a strict preference ordering, only two options are available for each pair $a_i \ R^h \ a_j$ or $a_j \ R^h \ a_i$. Each preference pattern R^h is simply a point in F_N where each dimension of F_N consists of two points, say, $0(a_i \ R^h \ a_j)$ and $1(a_j \ R^h \ a_i)$. Each dimension of preference is an elementary preference i.e. a preference on a pair of alternatives. Thus we have:

$$F_N = \{0,1\} \times \{0,1\} \times \ldots \times \{0,1\} \qquad (16)$$
$$\text{N times}$$

where $N = \frac{m(m-1)}{2}$

A pattern $R^h \subset F_N$ is simply an N-dimensional binary vector. For instance if m = 3, we can label the dimensions: dimension 1 = $(a_1 \text{ vs. } a_2)$, dimension 2 = $(a_3 \text{ vs. } a_1)$, dimension 3 = $(a_2 \text{ vs. } a_3)$. The following pattern classes are admissible.

$$
\begin{aligned}
(101) &= (a_1 \ R \ a_2 \ a_3) \\
(001) &= (a_2 \ R \ a_1 \ R \ a_3) \\
(011) &= (a_2 \ R \ a_3 \ R \ a_1) \\
(010) &= (a_3 \ R \ a_2 \ R \ a_1) \\
(110) &= (a_3 \ R \ a_1 \ R \ a_2) \\
(100) &= (a_1 \ R \ a_3 \ R \ a_2)
\end{aligned}
\qquad (17)
$$

In general because of the transitivity requirement on R only m! pattern classes are admissible among the 2^N conceivable binary vectors in F_N. Each pattern class is a vertex of the N-dimensional hypercube. In our example, the two excluded vertices are:

$$(000) = (a_1 \ R \ a_3 \ R \ a_2 \ R \ a_1)$$
$$(111) = (a_1 \ R \ a_2 \ R \ a_3 \ R \ a_1) \tag{18}$$

i.e. the origin and the point symmetric to it along the main diagonal of this cube. As we have said earlier, the rationality requirement for individual preferences amounts to rejecting such intransitive preference patterns as inadmissible. The necessity of such a requirement should be emphasized: without it, individual behavior cannot be rationalized; any choice we make can always be improved upon by picking the next alternative in the cycle [8]. In the sequel, we will discover that if we apply certain decision rules such as simple pairwise majority voting, we can easily find ourselves faced with a similar inconsistency in the group preference. This phenomenon, first discovered and studied by Condorcet, is known as the "voting paradox" or the "Condorcet effect". It is at the heart of modern social choice theory. Its importance can be seen from the following fact: if each defeated alternative is removed from further consideration by a committee or any other group debating the alternatives, an astute committee member can always maximize his chances of seeing his top alternative adopted by postponing the vote on this alternative. And any alternative adopted can always be defeated by another coalition. This situation spells paralysis or some sort of breakdown for the group which has to make a decision. Before analyzing the reasons for the occurrence of this paradox, it will be useful to show how the process of simple majority voting amounts to a sequence of threshold logic units.

Let $R^1, R^2, \ldots, R^\ell$ denote the ℓ preferences in a society of ℓ individuals, with each R^h written as a (column) binary vector. Form the $(N \times \ell)$ matrix $[X] = \frac{1}{\ell} [R^1, R^2, \ldots, R^\ell]$. We denote a a generic now vector of [X] by $x_{(ij)}$ to stress the fact that it contains the elementary preferences of each individual on the i vs. j issue.

Consider the N elementary discriminant functions

$$g_{(ij)}(x_{(ij)}) = \begin{cases} 1 & \text{iff} & x_{(ij)} \cdot \vec{1} > \frac{1}{2} \\ 0 & \text{iff} & x_{(ij)} \cdot \vec{1} < \frac{1}{2} \end{cases} \quad \text{what if} \quad \text{dot} \quad \text{prod.} = 1/2? \quad (19)$$

where $\vec{1}$ represents the 1-dimension unit vector.

The final step in reaching a group preference pattern is effected by using a global discriminant function g([X]) grouping the outputs of the elementary functions $g_{(ij)}(x_{ij})$.

$$g([X]) = [g_{(12)}(x_{12}), g_{(13)}(x_{13}); \dots ; g_{(m-1)m}(x_{(m-1)m})] \quad (20)$$

The output is simply an N-dimensional binary vector. Thus the process of aggregating individual preferences over S by pairwise simple majority voting can be viewed as a pattern recognition process where the classifiers are simply a sequence of threshold logic units. The following figure summarizes this process.

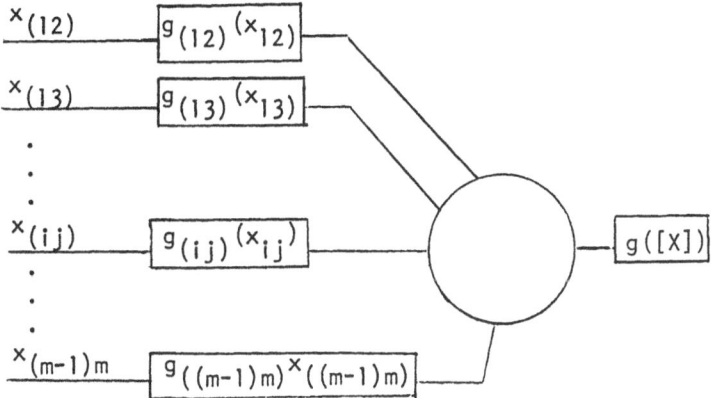

The geometric interpretation of the decision process is clear. Each elementary discriminant function $g_{(ij)}(x_{ij})$ is simply a hyperplane (intersecting the (ij) axis at the point $\frac{1}{2}$ and parallel to the other axes). It decides to enter a 1 (meaning that i is socially preferred to j) if and only if $x_{(ij)} \cdot \vec{1} > \frac{1}{2}$ and a 0 (meaning that the reverse social preference holds for j over i) if and only if $x_{(ij)} \cdot \vec{1} < \frac{1}{2}$. We can then readily see that there is no guarantee that the resulting output vector will depict a transitive (social) preference. Each threshold logic unit works <u>independently</u> of the others and cases will occur where the output vector $g([X])$ will be inadmissible as a preference pattern. The following example illustrates duch a case. Let $\ell = 11$ and $S = \{a,b,c,d\}$. Let the individual preference orderings be:

$$
\begin{array}{ccccccccccc}
R^1 & R^2 & R^3 & R^4 & R^5 & R^6 & R^7 & R^8 & R^9 & R^{10} & R^{11} \\[4pt]
a_1 & & a_1 & & a_2 & & a_2 & & a_3 & & a_4 \\
a_4 & & a_2 & & a_3 & & a_4 & & a_2 & & a_3 \\
a_3 & & a_4 & & a_1 & & a_3 & & a_4 & & a_2 \\
a_2 & & a_3 & & a_4 & & a_1 & & a_1 & & a_1
\end{array}
\qquad (21)
$$

Label the six dimensions of F_6 as follows:

$$
\left\{
\begin{array}{llll}
\#1 & a_1 \text{ vs } a_2 & \#4 & a_2 \text{ vs } a_3 \\
\#2 & a_1 \text{ vs } a_3 & \#5 & a_2 \text{ vs } a_4 \\
\#3 & a_1 \text{ vs } a_4 & \#6 & a_3 \text{ vs } a_4
\end{array}
\right.
\qquad (22)
$$

We can then write $R^1,\ldots,R^{11}$ in boolean vector form. The resulting matrix $[X]$ reads:

$$
\begin{array}{c}
[X] \\
(6 \times 11)
\end{array}
= \frac{1}{11}
\begin{bmatrix}
1 & 1 & 1 & 1 & 0 & 0 & 0 & 0 & 0 & 0 & 0 \\
1 & 1 & 1 & 1 & 0 & 0 & 0 & 0 & 0 & 0 & 0 \\
1 & 1 & 1 & 1 & 1 & 1 & 0 & 0 & 0 & 0 & 0 \\
0 & 0 & 1 & 1 & 1 & 1 & 1 & 0 & 0 & 0 & 0 \\
0 & 0 & 1 & 1 & 1 & 1 & 1 & 1 & 1 & 1 & 0 \\
0 & 0 & 0 & 0 & 1 & 1 & 0 & 1 & 1 & 1 & 0
\end{bmatrix}
\qquad (23)
$$

Applying simply majority voting yields:

$$
g([X]) =
\begin{bmatrix}
0 \\ 0 \\ 1 \\ 0 \\ 1 \\ 0
\end{bmatrix}
= a_1 \, R \, a_4 \, R \, a_3 \, R \, a_2 \, R \, a_1
$$

$$(24)$$

which is a cyclical preference. Presented in such terms the origin
of the paradox seems clear: the sequence of elementary decisions
is myopic: no account is taken of the compatibility or incompati-
bility of each decision with the previous ones. What is needed is
a global search method. In the next section, such a method, based
on a class of nonlinear discriminant functions, is presented.

 2.3 <u>A class of nonlinear discriminant functions for recognition of social preferences</u>

 2.3.1 <u>The basic shortcoming of a sequence of linear
classifiers</u> (as used in simple pairwise majority voting for instance) is their lack of discriminatory power to handle the kind
of indeterminate cases illustrated above. It is important to note
that such intransitive (group) preference patterns have indeterminate membership - at least with the classifiers used so far.
This can be seen by noticing that a cycle such as the one depicted
in equation (24) is obtained as the <u>union</u> of a finite number of
transitive patterns.

 In this example we have [9]:

$$(a_1 a_4 a_3 a_2 a_1) = (a_1 a_4 a_3 a_2) \cup (a_4 a_3 a_2 a_1) \cup (a_3 a_2 a_1 a_4) \cup$$
$$(a_2 a_1 a_4 a_3) \qquad (25)$$

In terms of pattern recognition and classifiers, this case corresponds to a <u>boundary pattern</u> where the pattern can be classified
equally well in any one of the four classes contained in the
union. The basic idea is then to devise a class of non-linear
classifiers whose higher discriminatory power will enable us to
obtain a unique solution in such indeterminate cases. To achieve
this, we should try and utilize <u>all</u> the information available from
individual patterns. First consider any row x_{ij} of the matrix
[X]. Define

$$Y_{(ij)} = x_{(ij)} \cdot \vec{1} \qquad (26)$$

Clearly (27)

$$0 \leq Y_{(ij)} \leq 1 \qquad (27)$$

$$Y_{(ji)} = 1 - Y_{(ij)} \tag{28}$$

Form the matrix $[Y]$ with the $m(m-1)$ $Y_{(ij)}$ entries. The (ij)th entry of $[Y]$ is simply $Y_{(ij)}$ i.e. the proportion of preference patterns where i comes ahead of j. From (28) it follows that the main diagonal of $[Y]$ consists of 0's:

$$Y + Y^{tr} = J - I \quad \text{where } J \text{ is an } (m \times m) \text{ matrix of}$$
$$\text{one's and } I \text{ is the } (m \times m) \text{ unit}$$
$$\text{matrix.} \tag{29}$$

Define the following class of discriminant functions:

$$g_1(Y) = \sum_{i<j} [\Pi_1 \cdot Y \cdot \Pi_1^{tr}]$$
$$\vdots$$
$$g_k(Y) = \sum_{i<j} [\Pi_k \cdot Y \cdot \Pi_k^{tr}]$$
$$\vdots$$
$$g_{m!}(Y) = \sum_{i<j} [\Pi_{m!} \cdot Y \cdot \Pi_{m!}^{tr}]$$

where Π_k is the kth permutation matrix of dimension $(m \times m)$. $\tag{30}$

As with any discriminant function the decision rule is simply: choose the kth class as the group preference pattern

$$\text{iff} \quad g_k(Y) > g_r(Y) \quad k,r = 1,2,\ldots,m!$$
$$\nabla\ k \neq r \tag{31}$$

The following figure illustrates our procedure:

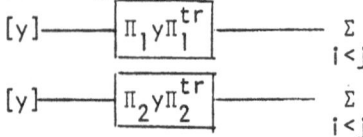

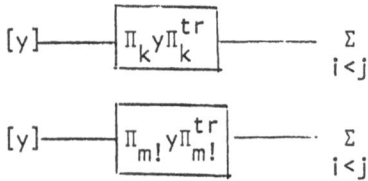

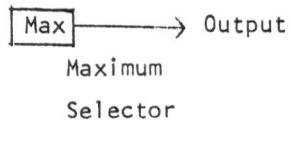

This procedure amounts to finding a simultaneous relabelling of both rows and columns of $[Y]$ so that the sum of the upper diagonal elements of the transformed matrix $[\Pi_k \cdot Y \cdot \Pi_k^{tr}]$ is maximal. Practically it amounts to finding that ordering which maximizes relative agreement; this is measured in a global (non-myopic) way by taking account of "nearest neighbor" preferences in the resulting order as well as the preferences over non-adjacent pairs. It can be easily verified, for instance, that the solution to our previous example is $(a_3a_2a_1a_4)$ - which is one of the patterns compatible with the initial cyclical pattern $(a_1a_4a_3a_2)$.[10] In this solution (or in any other of the feasible solutions) we have computed $g_k^i(Y)$ by taking account of the relative levels of agreement over (1.) the "nearest neighbor" pairs e.g. (a_3a_2), (a_2a_1), (a_1a_4) and (2.) all non-adjacent pairs (a_3a_1), (a_2a_4) and (a_3a_4). It can also be shown that the solution obtained by using such non-linear discriminant functions amounts to transforming the input data contained in [Y] to increase the distance between the solution pattern and the others ([11]). In this sense these classifiers have a higher discriminatory power than the simple threshold logic units normally used.

It is also worth pointing out that this method of reaching a determinate group preference pattern amounts to solving a quadratic assignment problem. Letting p denote the permutation mapping corresponding to a permutation matrix Π. The decision rule stated above (equations 30-31) can now be formulated as:

$$\underset{p\in\xi}{\text{Max}}\ \psi(p) = \underset{\substack{i,j \\ i\neq j}}{\Sigma}\ q_{ij}\ Y_{p(i)p(j)} \tag{32}$$

with ξ = set of permutation mappings, and

$$[g_{ij}] = \begin{bmatrix} 0 & 1 & 1 & . & . & 1 \\ . & 0 & 1 & . & . & . \\ . & . & . & . & . & . \\ . & . & . & . & . & 1 \\ 0 & . & . & . & . & 0 \end{bmatrix} \tag{33}$$

This alternative formulation presents a number of advantages; in particular, it is easily generalized and compared with existing methods of group decision. One of these methods is now discussed

and modelled within this framework to illustrate the flexibility
of our approach.

2.3.2 <u>One possible way of handling the kinds of indeter-
minacies</u> which we have discussed so far, is the Borda method. It
is named after its proponent J. C. Borda who devised it as an improvement over the simple plurality voting method whose limitations
are even more sever. In the plurality method, the alternative
which has the largest number of first place votes is picked as the
social choice. If we want we can also rank the remaining alternatives according to their respective number of votes. Borda pointed
out that this method is insensitive to the relative positions of
the various alternatives in a given individual order since the
only information which is used is the preferred alternative. In
effect it amounts to assuming that the other alternatives are all
indifferent to each other which is seldom the case. To remedy this
defect he proposes to let each citizen rank order the m alternatives
on a fixed integer-valued scale from 0 (the bottom ranked one) to
(m-1) (the top one). If we then sum the marks obtained by each
alternative across voters, we can use these numbers to rank the
alternatives: the alternative with the highest sum of marks is
"socially best" etc... This method can be represented in terms of
our previous model. It suffices to note that if we take the row
sum for each row of the [Y] matrix, this score is simply the
Borda score. Intuitively it represents the number of alternatives
which the ith item (for row i) has defeated in the individual preference orders. An equivalent representation for linear preference orders is to subtract from this score the sum of the corresponding (ith) column vector entities to take account of the number of items which have defeated i in the individual orders. We
can then use these entries (difference between row sum and column
sum score) as our ranking of the alternatives. This is simply the
Borda method. We can illustrate these calculations with our previous example (equation 21). The [Y] matrix reads:

$$[Y] = \frac{1}{11} \begin{bmatrix} 0 & 4 & 4 & 6 \\ 7 & 0 & 5 & 8 \\ 7 & 6 & 0 & 5 \\ 5 & 3 & 6 & 0 \end{bmatrix} \qquad (34)$$

The row-sum vector is:

$$r = \frac{1}{11} \begin{bmatrix} 14 \\ 20 \\ 18 \\ 14 \end{bmatrix} \qquad (35)$$

The column-sum vector is $c = \frac{1}{11} (19; 13; 15; 19)$. The Borda count is simply: $(\frac{-5}{11}; \frac{7}{11}; \frac{3}{11}; \frac{-5}{11})$ which yields the pre-ordering: $a_2 \ R \ a_3 \ R(a_1, a_4)$. To obtain the Borda winner in our formulation we only need to change the interaction matrix $[g_{ij}]$ to read:

$$[g_{ij}] = \begin{bmatrix} 0 & 1 & 1 & . & 1 \\ -1 & 0 & 0 & . & 0 \\ -1 & 0 & . & . & . \\ . & . & . & . & 0 \\ -1 & . & . & . & 0 \end{bmatrix} \qquad (36)$$

If we then solve:

$$\text{Max } (p) = \sum_{\substack{i,j \\ i \neq j}} g_{ij} \ y_{p(i) \ p(j)}$$

we get a_2 as our Borda winner. Also, if we look at the ordering of the sub-optimal solutions of (36) we obtain: $[a_3, (a_4 a_1)]$. The advantage of this presentation of the Borda solution is that it is easily extended and, as we will show, its natural generalization is simply our previous quadratic assignment solution. This can be seen quite readily if we re-write our interaction matrix as:

$$[g_{ij}] = \begin{bmatrix} 0 & 1 & . & . & 1 \\ -1 & 0 & 1 & . & 1 \\ -1 & . & . & . & . \\ . & . & . & . & 1 \\ -1 & . & . & -1 & 0 \end{bmatrix} \qquad (37)$$

In this matrix all the entries above the diagonal are +1 and all those below the diagonal are -1. Thus it takes account of the overall strength of one alternative and its weakness in a given order, and not as a top alternative irrespective of the other elements in the completion ordering as in the Borda count. Here again the argument in favor of this generalization is that it is not a myopic rule in the sense that it ranks an alternative as part of a whole ordering. Now it can be shown that the solution to (36) and (37) is the same as the solution to our original problem (33). This follows from the fact that maximizing the sum of the above diagonal elements in [Y] is equivalent to minimizing the sum of the entries below the diagonal. In fact the two sums always differ by a constant since we know (equation 28) that $Y_{ij} + Y_{ji} = 1$ ($i \neq j$; $i, j = 1,...,n$). Thus as [Y] has ($m^2 - m$) non zero entries (off the main diagonal):

$$\sum_{i,j} Y_{ij} = (m-1) + (m-2) + ... + 1 = \frac{m(m-1)}{2} \tag{38}$$

Let $\psi(p*) = \underset{p \varepsilon \xi}{Max} \; \psi(p)$. Clearly $0 < \psi(p*) \leq \frac{m(m-1)}{2}$

Then $\underset{p \varepsilon \xi}{Min} \; \psi(p) = \frac{m(m-1)}{2} - \psi(p*)$

We can, thus, see that the Borda method amounts to a very elementary view of the quadratic assignment method. Its natural generalization is simply the method we have proposed earlier (33). All these examples illustrate the usefulness of some basic pattern recognition concepts in Economics, and, in particular, in social choice theory. Various extensions have been provided and we now examine one of them to show how the same ideas can be used in some basic resource allocation problems. In [16], Blin and Whinston have proposed to introduce an order of priorities over the set of issues. This "saliency" hypothesis leads to the definition of preference patterns with an underlying order over the entries. We now consider such preference patterns.

2.4 Individuals preferences and ordered features

2.4.1 We now consider a finite set of social alternatives or, more briefly, a set of n bills:

$$B = \{b_1, b_2, \ldots, b_i, \ldots, b_n\} \tag{39}$$

Each individual (h) in the group G (society, assembly, etc.) is
assumed to have a certain hierarchical preference pattern over
these bills. Specifically an individual may choose any of m_i c
courses of action (levels of preference) for each bill b_i. (Note
that each m_i may differ from m_j for any $i \neq j$). Furthermore, each
individual is assumed to have a most salient alternative say b_k, a
second most salient alternative b_i, etc... In other words each
individual has a saliency (ordinal) scale for the various bills
which represents the order of priorities that he assigns to the
issues. This saliency scale is the basic preference structure for
any individual. Once it is determined, the individual then decides
on the outcome he prefers most for a given echelon on this scale,
i.e. which course of action m_i^* he sees as best from his standpoint
for the ith bill b_i. If there are three alternatives (n=3) and
two course of action on each bill (m_i = {Yes, No} or {Pass, Fail}
for all i = 1,2,3) an individual hierarchical preference structure
would then be written as:

$$(\sim 3; \; 2; \; \sim 1) \text{ where } \sim \equiv \text{not} \tag{40}$$

This means that: (i) for this individual the third bill is most
important, the second bill is next in importance and the first
bill of least importance, and (ii) the preferences on each bill are
of the (No; Yes; No) type. In regard to this saliency hypothesis,
we might note that it is one possible way of introducing some further information somewhat like an intensity of preference. In
effect we are making preference patterns into multidimensional
entities. There are n dimensions (n bills) which are ordered differently by each individual, according to his own saliency scale.
The preference patterns are simply represented by a subset of the
lattice points in an n-dimensional space and these lattice points

382

are linearly ordered by the saliency ordering of each individual.

The following example will serve as an illustration. Consider a set of three bills:

$$B = \{b_1, b_2, b_3\} \tag{41}$$

Assume each of these three dimensions of individual preferences is a discrete scale viz:

$$b_i; \sim b_i) \equiv (1; 0) \text{ for } i = 1,2,3 \tag{42}$$

To generate the 3-dimensional preference patterns, we need to consider only 2^3 lattice points in R^3. Moreover, the underlying saliency scale for an individual determines the ordering of these 3 dimensional patterns. For simplicity, suppose the saliency scale is simply the order $(\sim b_3 > b_2 > \sim b_1)$. Then the following tree enumerates all the preference patterns as the terminal nodes of the tree. For this individual the ordering of these patterns simply corresponds to the list of patterns read from top to bottom.

To characterize the (lexicographic) saliency condition, we need only note that upon scanning the set of 2^n patterns vertically -- i.e. one dimension at a time -- the most salient issue for that individual corresponds to the first entry which remains invariant in the first 2^{n-1} patterns. Sequentially, the second most salient issue will correspond to the entry that remains invariant in the first 2^{n-2} patterns etc...

This characterization can be used to test for the existence of an underlying saliency scale in any set of individual preference patterns. From an experimental design standpoint, two approaches could be used:

(i) On the one hand, we could directly ask the individual for his saliency scale on the issues then infer from it a theoretical ordering over his preference patterns, and finally compare it with his observed ordering. To simplify matters when a large number of issues are at stake, a good experimental procedure would consist in picking some pairs of patterns along the theoretical ordering a and ask him to order them. To devise "saliency tests" would involve

our allowing greater deviations from the theoretical ordering at
the bottom of the scale than at the top. For instance, in the
example below while we would insist on his ranking (010) > (110)
(the top pair of patterns) we might want to dismiss answers such
as (001) < (101) -- which is the reverse of the theoretical order
between the bottom two patterns in our example. Reasons for allowing variables degrees of freedom along this ordering will be
discussed separately.

   (ii) On the other hand, we could ask the individual to rank
order the set of 2^n n-dimensional patterns and look for evidence
of a saliency scale by just applying the characterization of the
saliency property which we have previously discussed. Here again,
a paired comparison experiment over some (or all) the patterns
could be used to derive a rank ordering (See [22], for instance).

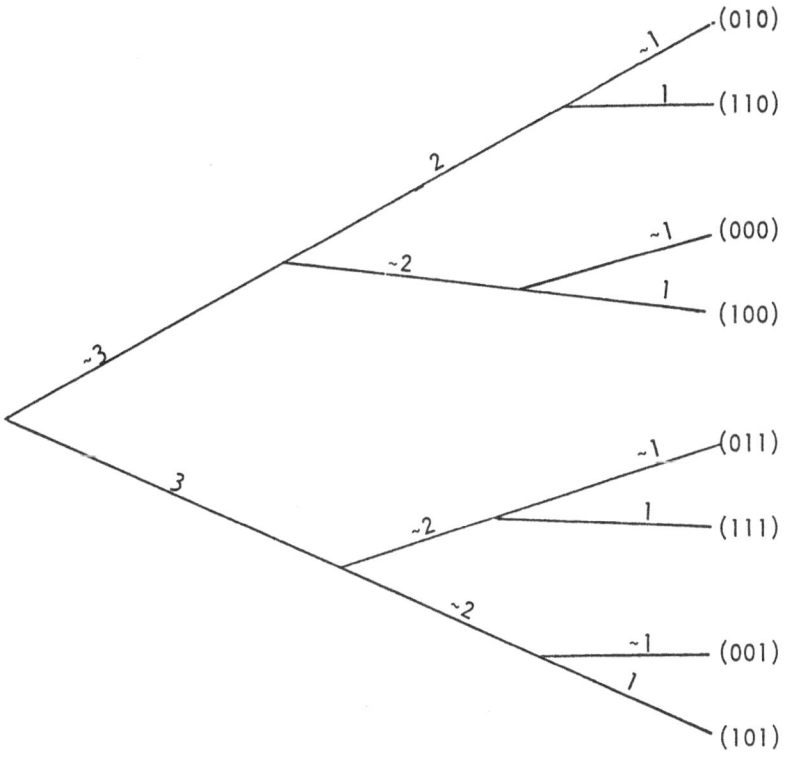

Turning back, now, to this notion of variable degrees of consistency which we may allow an individual as we move along a theoretical ordering of preference patterns, it should be noted that
there exists a simple justification for this apparent inconsistency.
Each individual may have a different degree of discrimination, a
different threshold which each issue must pass in order to become
effective in his preference structure. In other words, there may
exist two utility spaces that we must consider: the <u>theoretical
utility space</u> U_n of full dimension (n) i.e. including each and
every issue as a separate dimension; and the <u>perceived (or effective) utility space</u> U_k <u>for an individual</u> which is simply a subspace fo the full space U_n. The dimension (n) of the full space
is determined by considering each and every conceivable bill of
interest to any member of the society. Clearly the logic of the
saliency hypothesis requires that we also allow some individuals
to be concerned with only a few issues, say k of them. As the
concern threshold of an individual goes up k becomes smaller and
vice versa. This also means that if we set the preference patterns
P_t of an individual in an n-dimensional space, whereas his effective utility space U_k has dimension (k), we do not have a strict
ordering over the set $\{P_t\}$ but rather a pre-ordering with a set
of equivalence classes $\{C_1, C_2, ..., C_v\}$. An equivalence class C_v is
the set of all patterns $\{P_t\}$ which are similar up to the first k
entries. A simple projection mapping Π from U_n to U_k will col-
lapse each indifference class C_v into a k-dimensional point, and
the ordering will now be on these points. To illustrate these
concepts, suppose that in our above example k = 2, i.e. only ⌐3
and 2 are effective preference dimensions for a given individual
whereas he is really indifferent as to the first issue. Then the
set $\{C_v\}$ of equivalence classes reads

$$\begin{bmatrix} 010 \\ 110 \end{bmatrix} \quad > \quad \begin{bmatrix} 000 \\ 100 \end{bmatrix} \quad > \quad \begin{bmatrix} 011 \\ 111 \end{bmatrix} \quad > \quad \begin{bmatrix} 001 \\ 101 \end{bmatrix}$$
$$C_1 \qquad\qquad\quad C_2 \qquad\qquad\quad C_3 \qquad\qquad\quad C_4$$

This distinction between the effective choice space (U_k) and the full choice space (U_n) for an individual could be experimentally tested by replicating the ordering experiment for given pairs of vectors to test whether or not the ordering of certain pairs is stable over time. The fact that the dimension (k) of the effective choice space of an individual varies according to the individuals simply reflects the different degrees of concern among individuals. This will also allow for a natural direction of vote trading among individuals as we shall discuss below.

To stress the difference between this model and the previous model (Section 2.3) it should be noted that in the latter model the saliency scale is really degenerate as it consists of a single echelon; also there are m alternative courses of action. We now examine how such preference patterns with ordered features can be aggregated into a group pattern. It is clear that the kind of non-linear discriminant method we have used for the degenerate case may be used. But some modifications are necessary to make use of the saliency hypothesis. From an interpretation viewpoint, this assumption allows us to derive an actual method of arriving at group decisions in this context, based on the notion of vote trading among individuals.

2.4.2 Hierarchical vote trading and decentralized group decision-making

In this section we examine the logrolling hypothesis and its effect upon the group decision process, in the context of the individual choice model we have previously discussed. At the outset, we must clarify the vote trading rules that we will use. This is where the importance of the specific hierarchical choice model we have described, becomes apparent. In the absence of any hierarchy over the bills, the direction of vote trading between individuals remains ambiguous, since mere orderings do not carry any cardinaly information that would represent consumer's preference intensities. Furthermore it is also unclear what actual pattern of

386

vote trading would emerge -- if any -- since the incentive for vote trading exists only as long as a given majority has not yet been reached on a given issue -- assuming a majority voting decision rule.

In the present model, we first illustrate our discussion with the help of a simple example to clarify the trading rules that would prevail under the saliency hypothesis. Consider a society of three individuals: Mr. A., Mr. B., and Mr. C. The set of bills also consists of three issues (b_1, b_2, b_3) and each bill can be disposed of by adopting one of two alternative courses of action {Yes, No} $\equiv$ {1,0}. The complete preference structures of the three individuals are as follows:

$$\text{Mr. A:} \quad (\sim3 > 2 > \sim1) = (0; 1; 0)$$
$$\text{Mr. B:} \quad (\sim2 > \sim1 > 3) = (0; 0; 1) \tag{43}$$
$$\text{Mr. C:} \quad (\ 1 > 2 > \ 3) = (1; 1; 1)$$

Given the saliency condition for the individual preference structures, the corresponding complete orderings of the preference patterns of these three individuals would read:

Mr. A.	Mr. B.	Mr. C.	
(0 1 0)	(0 0 1)	(1 1 1)	
(1 1 0) ↓	(0 0 0) ↓	(1 0 1) ↓	
(0 0 0) ↓	(1 0 1) ↓	(1 1 0) ↓	
(1 0 0) ↓	(1 0 0) ↓	(1 0 0) ↓	(44)
(0 1 1) ↓	(0 1 1) ↓	(0 1 1) ↓	
(1 1 1) ↓	(0 1 0) ↓	(0 0 1) ↓	
(0 0 1) ↓	(1 1 1) ↓	(0 1 0) ↓	
(1 0 1) ↓	(1 1 0) ↓	(0 0 0) ↓	

(Note: For simplicity we have assumed that each individual effective choice space has full dimension i.e. $k = n = 3$)

Suppose the initial group decision rule is simple majority voting. The starting solution is then $(\ 1; 2; 3) = (0\ 1\ 1)$.

Upon examining the three most preferred patterns as given in (43) above, it appears that some vote trades are feasible. Specifically the behavioral rules for a vote trade to be "feasible" are the following: the logic of the saliency condition implies that each individual tries just to get his way on his own most salient issue and in order to effect this goal he will trade hierarchically by giving away his vote (reversing the order of his preference if necessary i.e. selling a yes vote on this issue for which he favors a no vote) on the lowest-ranking bill on his saliency scale, then the next to last bill etc., as long as he can find a trading partner to effect the trade.

In this case the following trades would be carried out:

Mr. A.	Mr. B.	one	no vote on 2
Mr. B.	Mr. A.	one	no vote on 3
Mr. A.	Mr. C.	one	yes vote on 1
Mr. C.	Mr. A.	one	no vote on 3
Mr. B.	Mr. C.	one	yes vote on 1
Mr. C.	Mr. B.	one	no vote on 2

$$(45)$$

The resulting group preference pattern then reads $(1; \llcorner 2; \llcorner 3)$ or $(1; 0; 0)$ which is different from the simple majority solution $(\llcorner 1; 2; 3)$ or $(0; 1; 1)$. Now from the standpoint of a decentralized vs. a centralized group decision process, the problem could be formalized as follows.

The individual decentralized decision process consists of n maximization problems of the type described by equations (33) - (35) above i.e.

$$\underset{p}{\text{Max}} \ \psi^1(p) = \underset{i \neq j}{\Sigma} \ q_{ij} y^1_{p(i)p(j)}$$

$$\underset{p}{\text{Max}} \ \psi^2(p) = \Sigma \ q_{ij} y^2_{p(i)p(j)}$$

$$\vdots$$

$$\underset{p}{\text{Max}} \ \psi^n(p) = \Sigma \ q_{ij} y^n_{p(i)p(j)}$$

$$(46)$$

In the case of $i, j = 1, 2$ i.e. only two courses of action are available as in our above example, the $[y]$ matrices for the subproblems would read:

$$[y^1] = \begin{bmatrix} 0 & 1 \\ 2 & 0 \end{bmatrix} \begin{matrix} 1 \\ {\sim}1 \end{matrix}; \quad [y^2] = \begin{bmatrix} 0 & 2 \\ 1 & 0 \end{bmatrix} \begin{matrix} 2 \\ {\sim}2 \end{matrix};$$

$$[y^3] = \begin{bmatrix} 0 & 2 \\ 1 & 0 \end{bmatrix} \begin{matrix} 3 \\ {\sim}3 \end{matrix} \tag{47}$$

and the solution would be the simple majority voting solution $(0; 1; 1)$.

Now from the standpoint of a centralized decision process to determine the same unique group pattern as obtained after vote trading, we could write a master problem of the same combinatorial optimization nature as the subproblems. To do this we must first note that the dimension of the $[y]$ matrix in the master problem would become equal to the number of points in the cartesian product of the row (and column) space of each individual subproblem.

For instance in our example let:

$$p = (0; 1) \times (0; 1) \times (0; 1) \tag{48}$$

Then p has 2^n points (patterns) each one of which corresponds to a row (and column) of $[y]$. More generally if (M_i) represents the set of courses of action on the ith alternative, then,

$$p = \prod_{i=1}^{n} (M_i) \tag{49}$$

The master problem which would lead to an equivalent (but cen-tralized) solution as the vote trading mechanism would simply be

$$\underset{p}{\text{Max}} \; \Phi(p) = \sum_{i \neq j} q_{ij} Y_{p(i)p(j)} \tag{50}$$

In our example for instance, Y would be:

	(100)	(111)	(110)	(101)	(011)	(010)	(001)	(000)	
	0	2	1	1	3	2	2	1	
	1	0							
	2		0						
	2			0					
Y =	0				0				(51)
	1					0			
	1						0		
	2							0	

(The other entries of Y can be readily computed from our example).

The optimal assignment for the first row is (100) which yields a score of 12 for the function. This solution is also the one obtained after vote trading. We conjecture that this similarity in the results obtained through a decentralized and then a centralized decision process is not a mere coincidence but is in fact true in general.

Proposition: Under the vote trading rules stated above the solution to the vote trading decision process is similar to the solution to problem (50) above.

To conclude we must emphasize the fact that this model provides a framework of analysis for hierarchical choice (which seems to be a common feature of actual citizens' preferences in actual group decision problems) and also integrates this hypothesis in the general context of a comparison between centralized vs. decentralized group decision processes.

2.4.3 Some other applications of preference patterns with ordered features

It may be useful to point out that the general problem of allocating a fixed amount of resources among individuals may be viewed in the framework we have presented. Traditionally, economists have studied resource allocation from the viewpoint of prices and markets. Prices are determined so that each decision maker chooses a rational selection with the total result being consistent in the sense of just allocating the available resources. However many allocation problems are determined outside the price market system in what may be called a bureaucratic environment. Here the social choice approach may give a useful basis for such decisions. To amplify our remarks we may present a simple example: Suppose that we have four managers and four secretaries. Assuming that each manager is to be assigned a secretary, the problem is to determine which assignment should be made. To formulate the problem let $s(i) = j$ represent the assignment of the ith secretary to the jth manager. A feasible allocation which we write as a 4-vector $(s(1), s(2), s(3), s(4))$ obviously requires that each secretary is assigned and each manager receives a secretary. We assume that each manager has a preference ordering over the feasible allocation. Our saliency condition can now be interpreted simply to mean that each manager is concerned about the secretary he receives and not about the allocation to other managers. Thus, for manager one, two allocations which assing him secretary 3 are equivalent in the preference ordering even though the other secretaries are assigned differently.

Actually, the saliency hypothesis allows us to handle both this extreme case of complete selfishness (no external effects as it is referred to in the economic literature) and other cases of partial externalities. In such cases the manager is ooncerned just, say, about which secretary he receives and then he is more concerned about whom Mr. j receives rather than Mr. k, etc... The ordering of the features of his preference pattern simply reflects his level of concern over the issues; and the issues, in this case, are resource allocation patterns.

Our model of vote trading can be applied to general resource allocation problems. Our allocation is a vector of integers with elements $(1, 2, 3, 4)$ where say the vector $(2, 3, 1, 4)$ indicates that manager 1 is assigned secretary 2, manager 2 is assigned

secretary 3, etc. Given each manager preference ordering we construct the quadratic assignment problem as before (equations 50-51)
In the context of the vote trading each manager can vote on each
of the allocations. As we have suggested, the centralized solution determined by the quadratic assignment problem, can be reached
by appropriate vote trades between the managers. Thus we can see
the very wide applicability of the saliency hypothesis since it
enables us to deal with resource allocation problems in non-market
environments, with and without externalities. And finally, it is
worth noticing how such familiar concepts of pattern recognition
theory as features, discriminant functions etc. can be used to
study the fundamental aggregation problem in Economics.

Acknowledgement

This work was supported in part by National Science Foundation Grant ENG 75-07845.

Notes

1) To simplify our discussion we only deal with linear orders instead of preorders. The case where indifference is also allowed can be studied along similar lines.

2) We only need to consider intransitive triples as opposed to cycles of length greater than 3 since it can easily be shown that: (a) the existence of a cycle of length greater than 3 implies the existence of a cycle of length 3, and (b) the lack of 3-cycles guarantees that a preference ordering is transitive (see [12]).

3) For n even these results are slightly modified.

4) This is quite analogous to the case of circular social preferences as it is discussed in section 2.2.2. Here the dimensions play the role of voters or viewpoints in the social choice context. For a discussion of some of the implications of this analogy, see [8] and [10].

5) In fact, public issues are usually characterized by a high degree of lumpiness, since the alternative courses of action are usually few and far apart. To take into account such "indivisibilities" we will also examine the case of a discrete feature in the sequel.

6) We use these points $P_1,\ldots,P_m$ as representative of the individual preferences in each class $C_1,\ldots,C_m$.

7) In this discussion --to avoid unnecessary developments-- we take R^n to be a strict ordering over S. Allowing for indifference between certain alternatives is a simple extension.

8) Some peolple have interpreted intransitivity as a case of indifference, in disguise, but it seems that this interpretation is seldom warranted. For each pair the consumer expresses a genuine preference in one direction, not indifference. Furthermore, in the context of social preferences this interpretation is quite erroneous.

9) In general, if S=m there are m transitive patterns in the union.

10) It is easily verified that this class of solutions will always display this feature.

References

[1]   Arrow, K. J., <u>Social Choice and Individual Values</u>, J. Wiley and Sons, New York, 1962, (2nd ed.).

[2]   Bass, Frank M., "The Theory of Stochastic Preference and Brand Switching", Institute Paper #415, Purdue University, June 1973.

[3]   _____, E. A. Pessemier and D. R. Lehmann, "An Experimental Study of Relationships Between Attitudes, Brand Preferences, and Choice", <u>Behavioral Science, 17</u>, November 1972, pp. 532-541.

[4]   _____, E. A. Pessemier, R. D. Teach and W. W. Talarzyk, "Preference Measurements in Marketing Research", <u>Proceedings of the American Marketing Association</u>, Fall Conference, 1969.

[5]   _____, and W. W. Talarzyk, "An Attitude Model for the Study of Brand Preference", <u>Journal of Marketing Research</u>, Volume IX, February 1972, pp. 93-96.

[6]   _____, D. J. Tigert and R. T. Lonsdele, "Market Segmentation: Group vs. Individual Behavior", <u>Journal of Marketing Research</u>, Volume V, August 1968, pp. 264-270.

[7]   Bernardo, J. J. and J. M. Blin, "A Mathematical Programming Model of Consumer Choice Between Multi-attributed Brands", Graduate School of Management - Northwestern University Working Paper #140-173, 1975.

[8]   Blin, J. M., <u>Patterns and Configurations in Economic Science</u>, D. Reidel Publishing Company, Dordrecht, Holland/Cambridge, Massachusetts, 1973.

[9]   _____, "Preference Aggregation and Statistical Estimation", <u>Theory and Decision</u>, Volume IV, No. 1, 1974.

[10]   _____, "The General Concept of Multidimensional Consistency: Some Algebraic Aspects of the Aggregation Problem", <u>Multiple Criteria Decision-Making</u>, J. Cochrane and M. Zeleny (Editors), University of South Carolina Press, 1973.

[11]   _____, K. S. Fu and A. B. Whinston, "Applications of Pattern Recognition to Some Problems in Economics", <u>Techniques of Optimization</u>, Balakrishnan (Editor), Academic Press, New York, 1972.

[12]   _____, K. S. Fu, K. B. Moberg, and A. B. Whinston, "Pattern Recognition and Micro-Economics", <u>Proceedings of the 1972 Conference on Cybernetics and Society</u>, 1972.

394

[13] _____, _____, "Pattern Recognition and
Quantitative Political Theory", IEEE Proceedings on Decision
and Control, 1972.

[14] _____, _____, "Optimization Theory and
Social Choice", Proceedings of the Sixth International Conference on Systems Sciences, 1973.

[15] _____, and A. B. Whinston, "Fuzzy Sets and Social
Choice Proceedings of the 1973 Princeton Conference on Information Sciences and Systems,

[16] _____, "Combinatorial Optimization and Preference
Pattern Aggregation", Lecture Notes in Computer Science, 4,
Springer-Verlag, Berlin, 1974.

[17] _____, The Use of Discriminant Functions in Group
Decision-Making", Proceedings of the Second International
Joint Conference on Pattern Recognition, 1974.

[18] _____, "A Note on Majority Voting Under Transitivity
Constraints", Management Science, Volume 20, July, 1974.

[19] _____, "Discriminant Functions and Majority Voting",
Management Science, January 1975.

[20] Buchanan J., and G. Tullock, The Calculus of Consent, University of Michigan Press, Ann Arbor, 1962.

[21] Coleman, J., "The Possibility of a Social Welfare Function",
American Economic Review, December 1966, pp. 1311-1317.

[22] David, H. A., The Method of Paired Comparisons, Ch. Griffin
and Company, London, 1969.

[23] Davis, O. and Hinich, M. J., "A Mathematical Model of Policy
Formation in a Democratic Society", Mathematical Applications
in Political Science, Volume II, Joseph Bernd (Editor), SMU
Press, Dallas, 1966.

[24] _____, "On the Power and Importance of the Mean Preference in a Mathematical Model of Democratic Choice", Public
Choice, Volume 5, 1968, pp. 59-72.

[25] _____, "Some Results Related to a Mathematical Model
of Policy Formation in a Democratic Society", Mathematical
Applications in Political Science, Volume III, SMU Press,
Dallas, 1967.

[26] _____, "An Expository Development of a Mathematical Model of the Electoral Process", The American Political Science Review, Volume 64, 1970, pp. 426-448.

[27] Fogler, H. R., "A Pattern Recognition Model for Forecasting", Management Science, Volume 20, No. 8, April 1974, pp. 1178-89.

[28] Fu, K. S., Sequential Methods in Pattern Recognition and Machine Learning, Academic Press, New York and London, 1968.

[29] Lancaster, K. J., "A New Approach to Consumer Theory", Journal of Political Economy, Volume 74, 1966, pp. 132-157.

[30] _____, Consumer's Demand: A New Approach, Columbia University Press, New York, 1971.

[31] Lehmann, D. R., "Television Show Preference: Application of a Choice Mode", Journal of Marketing Research, Volume 8, 1971, pp. 47-55.

[32] Mueller, D., Comment, American Economic Review, December 1967, Volume 57, pp. 1304-1311.

[33] Nillson, N. J., Learning Machines, McGraw Hill, New York, 1965.

[34] Pessemier, E. A., Burger, P. C., Teach, R. D. and Tigert, D. J., "Using Laboratory Brand Preference Scales to Predict Consumer Brand Purchases", Management Science, Volume 6, 1971, pp. 371-385.

[35] Park, R. E., Comment, American Economic Review, December 1967, Volume 57, pp. 1300-1304.

[36] Saaty, T. L., Optimization in Integers and Related Extremal Problems, McGraw-Hill, 1970.

[37] Sebestyen, G. S., Decision-Making Processes in Pattern Recognition, MacMillian Company, New York, 1962.

[38] Smith, K. V., "Classification of Investment Securities Using Multiple Discriminant Analysis", Krannert Research Institute, Purdue University, Working Paper No. 101, January 1969.

[39] Wilson, R., "An Axiomatic Model of Logrolling", American Economic Review, June 1969, Volume 59, pp. 331-341.

[40] Zagoruiko, N. G., and T. I. Zaslavska, "On the Possibility of Pattern Recognition Methods Utilization in Sociological Research", Quality and Quantity, Volume IV, No. 2, December 1970, pp. 365-374.

A SYSTEMS VIEW OF STRATEGY FORMULATION IN SOCIAL CHOICE VIA SYNTACTIC PATTERN RECOGNITION

Mary Louise Hatten

Boston University
School of Management
212 Bay State Road
Boston, Massachusetts 02215

I. Introduction

Since the allocation of limited resources among unlimited wants necessarily has far-reaching effects, economic systems are complex masses of relationships and interdependencies. Economic reality is not easy to model in its fullness. Mathematical models generally only address one small part of economic reality and must abstract away much of the economic system's richness and complexity. After this simplification, the mathematical model's relationship to the reality it was originally designed to represent may not be so clear.

The work here moves in an opposite direction from traditional, mathematical economic theory. This paper uses a modeling technique, syntactic pattern recognition, which, at first glance appears to have little application to economic reality. Through the use of grammars and automata, the staples of syntactic pattern recognition, however, an important subprocess in social choice, an individual's strategy formulation, is represented.

Social choice, or voting theory, is interesting to economists since voting results in public decisions on resource allocations. The individual's strategy formulation process is broken into 2 components, information gathering and strategy building, and both are modeled through language and automata theory. In this view, complex systems are broken into their component parts, and each modeled using techniques to explicitly represent their interdependencies and relationships, syntactic pattern recognition.

II. Pattern Recognition

Lest pattern recognition seem too esoteric a modeling technique to be applied to the social sciences, it should be noted that pattern recognition, in a very general sense, actually simulates human reasoning and decision making. Much human thought involves the classification of unknown objects to known groups, and it seems worthwhile to attack the problem of modeling the social sciences with logical thought processes, refined and generalized through pattern recognition. Pattern recognition may, in fact, be considered a system of rational decision making, where the possible decisions involve classifying objects as belonging to specific groups.

As a very immediate example of the universality of the pattern recognition process, consider your reading of this paper. As you process the image before you, your mind is comparing the type here with an idea of the form you believe certain letters should have, thus choosing the letters which the symbols represent. Further, you combine those characters to form words, phrases and thoughts which you compare, interpret and understand with your own known experiences and ideas. All in split seconds! The human brain is indeed a complex pattern recognition system, and the discipline of pattern recognition seeks to quantify and model the processes of the human classification system.

As part of an economic system, or any system, man reacts to his environment, processes information, and acts on his interpretation of that environment. Pattern recognition, specifically syntactic pattern recognition, can model these systems processes both in man and in his economic system. This paper examines these applications in social choice theory.

Pattern recognition infers structure on data, classifying unknown objects into known groups. The general pattern recognition process may be shown schematically as: The two basic types of pattern recognition are decision theoretic, or statistical, and syntactic. The first is the classical form of pattern recognition, the kind which has successfully applied statistical techniques to classify data on weather, aerial photographs, electrocardiograms, . . . into meaningful patterns. The second, to be used in this paper, has been more recently developed, and is based on a process rather than element view of the object to be classified. The most direct method of understanding syntactic pattern recognition is to compare it to statistical pattern recognition.

Statistical pattern recognition is a straightforward application of the general pattern recognition diagram. Features which give the most information on the object are selected by statistical methods, often factor analysis. Classification methods are then developed and tested to mathematically aggregate sets of features so that the objects are most accurately classified. Discriminant functions are common classifiers. With discriminant function classification, the object is said to belong to the class where the discriminant function score, based on the object's features, is highest. The feature selection and classification methods are both usually developed and refined using data on objects belonging to known groups, a training sample. Once an acceptable accuracy is obtained in classification of the training sample, the pattern recognition method is applied to objects whose membership in groups is not known. The hope is, of course, that the accuracy of the pattern recognition process on these objects with unknown group memberships will be of generally the same magnitude as it was in the training sample.

Syntactic pattern recognition takes a more relationship-oriented approach than decision theoretic pattern recognition.

Thus, syntactic pattern recognition is not such a direct interpretation of the general pattern recognition scheme. Rather, syntactic pattern recognition views data as sets of relationships
where a certain kind of relationship belongs to one pattern class.
In terms of the diagram of the pattern recognition process, the
box labelled "classifier" might be better termed "analysis of
relationships among features" to describe the syntactic form of
pattern recognition.

In contrast to decision theoretic pattern recognition which
looks at data as a series of features on the object to be classified, syntactic pattern recognition views objects of a class as
the product of a _process_ unique to that class. Syntactic pattern
recognition explicitly considers the system, the process which forms
the objects to be classified. Thus, in order to see if the object
could have been the result of a certain process, the process itself must be modeled and some method used to distinguish between
the results of one process and another. Syntactic pattern recognition uses language and automata theory to accomplish this. Formal languages model processes, and automata can be designed to
only "accept" or recognize the results of processes modeled by a
certain formal language. Definitions and a more detailed view
of formal language and automata theory, in the form in which they
will be used in this paper, are given in the Appendix.

In syntactic pattern recognition, grammars are used to model
the process of the class which results in objects belonging to
that class. Features of the object are represented by elements
of strings in the formal language formed by the class's grammar.
Powerful results in formal language theory exist to construct
machines, or, more precisely, automata, to recognize the strings
formed by certain classes of grammars. If the process can be
modelled by one of these types of grammars, the machine corresponding to the grammar is the pattern recognition system.

The logical foundations of syntactic pattern recognition may
be shown schematically. First, the process resulting in the object of a particular class may be seen at two levels: the direct
process-object relationship, and its representation by grammars
and languages. These two levels are shown as:

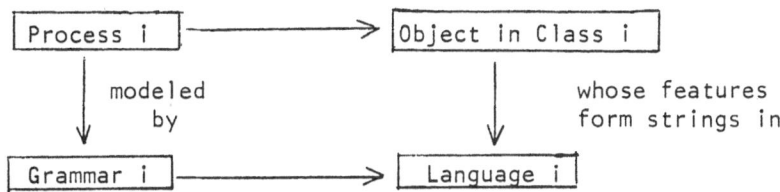

The process resulting in members of Class i is modeled by a
Grammar i. The features of the objects in class i make up elements
of strings in the Language i formed by the Grammar (process) i.

When the theoretical results on the existence of certain
machines to recognize strings in languages formed by special types
of grammars are added to the modeling system above, a syntactic
pattern recognition system to recognize objects from unknown
classes can be shown, as:

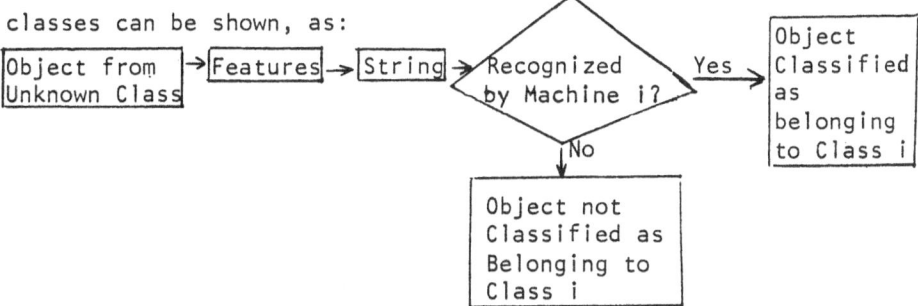

The features on the unknown object form a string. If Machine i,
which was designed to recognize strings in Language i (L_i), recognizes that string on the unknown object as belonging to L_i, the
unknown pattern is classified as belonging to Class i. This recognition may be interpreted as meaning that the object's features
are classified as resulting from Process i, so the object is said
to be a member of Class i. In this paper we will use both the
complete syntactic pattern recognition process, as well as formal
languages and automata, as modeling techniques.

While syntactic pattern recognition seems to be more complex and indirect than the more straightforward statistical approach, it seems possible that syntactic pattern recognition may be very useful in modeling economic phenomena. Economics is a <u>system</u> of relationships for the allocation of limited goods among unlimited wants. And syntactic pattern recognition, via language and automata theory, models relationships and interdependencies, rather than simply using data points with no view to the interdependencies which link them. And the interdependencies of an economic system are exactly what make it so rich. Thus syntactic pattern recognition should be able to model the most interesting aspects of economics.

In this paper syntactic pattern recognition will be used to model one element of social choice theory, an individual's formulation of his voting strategy. Voting theory, or social choice theory, represents public decisions on the allocation of resources. This modeling of social decision making should be useful to economists studying resource allocation.

III. <u>Social Choice</u>

Economics focuses on the problem of allocating limited resources among unlimited wants. The most commonly studied economic system to offer a solution to this problem is the private sector, characterized by the price system to allocate goods and services among rational consumers and freely competitive firms. Nevertheless, public decisions as well as private decisions determine the allocation of economic goods. And, while some may interpret social choice theory, or voting theory, as the domain of the political scientist, public decisions do affect resource allocations. Thus voting is a branch of economics, characterizing a public solution to the economic problem of allocating limited resources, and using the ballot box rather than the price system to make known the wishes of individuals.

Just as the private solution to the economic problem is

better known, so, too, a more elegant theory of private resource
allocation exists and less work on public allocation processes
has been done. Arrow's axioms to represent an ethical voting
system and his subsequent "impossibility theorem," on the existence
of such an ethical voting system to choose among more than three
alternatives is an important landmark in social choice theory.
His work certainly added formulism, since the ethics of the system
were precisely stated (Sen. pp. 37-38):

1) Condition of Unrestricted Domain - Voting rules works
(gives reflexive, transitive, complete, ordering among
alternatives) for every logically possible configuration
of individual preference orderings on individual orderings.

2) Weak Pareto Principle - if everyone prefers x to y, then
society must prefer x to y.

3) Independence of Irrelevant Alternatives - Social choice
over a set of alternatives depends only on those alternatives.

4) Nondictatiorship. There must be no individual that whenever he prefers x to y, society prefers x to y, regardless
of everyone else's preferences.

Arrow's impossibility theorem is an important negative result.
Nevertheless, even though Arrow showed public decisions cannot be
ethical by these standards, public decisions are made. Thus, the
methods by which these decisions are reached in real economic
systems should be of interest to the economist studying public
allocation of resources.

This paper applies syntactic pattern recognition to model
part of the social choice process, the formulation of the individual's strategy. This is actually only a subpart of the complete
social choice process, which will be defined here to consist of:
1) Socially acceptable voting procedures: 2) Legal procedures and
methods used in this particular situation: 3) Individual voting
strategies: 4) Actual voting. The formulation of the individual's
strategy will be used to illustrate an application of syntactic

methods to model economic systems. It will be shown that a formal
language and the automaton which accepts it can model the individual's information gathering stage, and another machine can model the
individual's strategy building process, where he produces his best
voting strategy, given the probable actions of others and the
voting method to be used in his society on this issue.

IV. Strategy Formulation

Strategy formulation is an important and crucial part of the
social choice process. Strategy formulation is not necessarily
a simple voting action taken to faithfully represent an individual's
preferences. Strategy is complex and many faceted. Preferences
at election time may be different than at the time the issues were
first presented. Voting may not reflect true preferences among
alternatives. The voting mechanism itself may, in fact, require
complicated planning and voting for unfavored alternatives in the
beginning to assure that a preferred choice is a viable alternative
in the later stages of the voting. For a further example of the
complexity of strategy, many of us have had experiences in voting,
whether at a national level or on university committees, where our
own most preferred alternative had a very small chance of being
selected. Sometimes, in fact, we may have voted for still another
possibility which had a reasonable chance of being selected, in
order to amoid the situation where the group chose the alternative
we considered least preferable.

Using social choice experience as background, we shall break
strategy formulation into two parts: a) information gathering, and
b) strategy building based on "usuable" information, the voting
methods, and the perceived strategies of other members of the
society. This division of strategy formulation into two parts represents common behavior in establishing preferences and strategy.
Our voting actions are influenced by those around us, and this
view of the strategy formulation process explicitly accounts for
the interaction of the individual with his environment, both social

and institutional. This representation is essentially a systems view of the strategy formation process.

V. Information Gathering

Just as you are recognizing patterns of letters on this page, it is reasonable that an individual recognizes patterns of preferences held by others on an issue, based on the signals, or information, he receives from them. Also note that you can only use patterns of letters to form words in the languages with which you are familiar. Patterns of letters forming words in other languages may have no affect on you. It is also possible in the strategy formulation process that an individual only accepts, or uses, information which is "reasonable" to him, information which does not contradict strongly held feelings he may have on the issue. Viewpoints strongly varying from his own and which he considers, "crackpot opinions," may have no effect. For example, the individual who considers himself a supporter of humane punishments would not take much stock of someone who makes a strong argument that bread thieves in a grocery store should be punished with the death penalty. Thus, in a pattern recognition sense, we may say that an individual will only be affected (meaning there exists a potential for changing his original opinion) by information leading to preferences somewhat similar to his own.

As a symbolic example, consider an individual receiving information on an issue among three alternatives, A, B, and C. We will differentiate between the individual's own feelings and the preference signals he receives from his environment by representing the individual by upper case preference expressions. The preference signals from his environment will be shown by lower case letters. The individual we are modeling has preferences A>B>C, where ">" is read "is preferred to," so "A>B>C" means A is preferred to B is preferred to C. Also assume that the individual considers any information "reasonable" in his view as long as he can infer from that information that A is preferred to C. If data that C is preferred to A comes to him, he rejects it as not useful since he believes A is preferred to C. In the symbolism used here, that means A must be to the left of C, so that a>b>c, a>c>b and b>a>c are acceptable preference signals from the environment. To stress the relationships, we show that the information which will affect the individual with whom we are concerned can be modeled by a formal language:

$$s \to Xc \qquad S \to Yb$$
$$X \to a>b> \qquad y \to a>c>$$
$$X \to b>a>$$

Where:

Start symbol = S
Nonterminals = {x,y}
Terminals   = {a,b,c,>}

Thus:

$$\{a>b>c, \; a>c>b, \; b>a>c\} = L(G_1) = L_1$$

While the grammar derivation is not so obvious, the individual's acceptable preference signals can also be generated by a Type 3 (regular) grammar[1], G_2, as:

$S \to aM$	$S \to aN$	$S \to bW$
$M \to >O$	$N \to >P$	$W \to >X$
$O \to bQ$	$P \to cR$	$X \to aQ$
$Q \to >T$	$U \to >V$	
$T \to c$	$V \to b$	

Where:

Start Symbol = S
Nonterminals = {S,M,N,O,P,Q,R,Q,T,U,V,W,X}
Terminals   = {a,b,c>}

Ther reader can verify that $L(G_2) = L(G_1) = L_1$.

In syntactic pattern recognition terms, the patterns which can be recognized by the finite state automaton which accepts the language above, L_1, formed by the regular grammar, are the

---

[1] A regular grammar has productions of the form:
    $X \to xY$
  or $X \to x$
      where X,Y represent nonterminals and
      x represents a terminal

preferences which are accepted as valid information by the individual. The machines simulate the individual sifting information
to accept that data which is "like" his own original feelings on
the issue. The information which is acceptable to him is held for
further use, as he will form his sincere (Farquharson's term)
preferences, based on both his original preferences and the information from his environment. For some cases, this will mean that
the information has not changed his original preferences, although
this is not necessarily the case.

To aggregate the data he has collected, the individual as-
sembles all the acceptable information he has gathered and, by some
judgmental process, evaluates the data which he felt could affect
him and decides if the information he has gathered should change
his original feelings. Thus the sincere preferences he feels by
the end of his information collection process could be different
than his original preferences.

As a simple model of the individual's judgment in reacting
to his data, suppose he counts all the data "bits" he has collected
and changes his preference to that inferred from the majority of
his information. This judgmental process can be modeled by a
machine, as:

$$\sigma(X{>}Y{>}Z,\ y{>}x{>}z) = Y{>}X{>}Z \qquad \sigma(X{>}Y{>}Z,\ \varepsilon) = X{>}Y{>}Z$$
$$y{>}x{>}z \ \varepsilon \ L_1$$

Where:

Upper case preference statements denote the preference state
of the individual.
Lower case preference statements denote information inputs,
which must belong to L_1, the set of acceptable information.
The initial state represents the individual's original
preferences.
The final state represents the individual's sincere preferences, the state which obtains when no further information
inputs exist.
ε = the string with no elements.

For example, the individual shown here whose original preference were A>B>C, on receiving input b>a>c, would change to

preference state B>A>C. Note that, although the individual in the above example chose his sincere preference to match the majority of his acceptable information bits where his own original preference was counted as one bit, this method did not imply his own original views were unimportant or even equal to others. Recall that he only accepted information on preferences not sharply different from his own, so his own views held much weight in the initial information gathering stage and thus heavily affect his selection of his sincere preference, when he aggregates and reacts to his information.

This information gathering step represents the individual educating himself and so forming sincere preferences based both on his original ideas and the ideas of others which he found acceptable. Although he started out with some set of original preferences, he uses the information he has gathered to "enlighten" himself and form sincere preferences to influence his strategy building.

VI. Strategy Building

In formulating his strategy, the individual collects and reacts to information in his environment. He reacts to information on two levels: the first to use his data on the issue to form his sincere preferences; and the second to use information on the preferences he believes others will display and the voting mechanism (order of presentation of alternative and the rule for selection among them) to be used. The first has been described in the previous section as information gathering to form sincere preferences. The second level is necessary so that he can tailor his voting behavior so the actual vote can most closely serve his interests. In this way, the strategic preferences which may be displayed by his voting behavior may be different from his true preferences. We shall term this second level of individual's reaction to the environment, strategy building.

Just as we can construct a language-automaton model of each

person's selection of a sincere preference, the basis of his sincere strategy, so, too, we can construct a machine simulating strategies of each individual, as he receives information on the probable actions of others and the voting method to be used on the issue. The individual states of this machine are strategic preferences and strategies, and the inputs are possible actions of others in the society and the voting method. The initial state is the individual's sincere preferences and his voting strategy to vote for his most sincerely preferred alternative; we shall call this his sincere strategy. The final strategy the individual will use in voting is the state reached when no further input messages occur. With no input at all from other members of the society, the strategy simulated by the machine will be the individual's sincere preferences and a vote for the most preferred alternative, the individual's sincere strategy.

To show what is meant by the individual strategy machines, suppose an Individual 1 with sincere preferences A>B>C ("on an issue of great importance to him") is in a society with Individuals 2 and 3 whose preference structures and voting strategies he perceives to be, respectively, b>a>c and c>b>a. Suppose also that the society is voting by the very common method of majority rule in which each member casts his vote for his most preferred alternative. Individual 1, knowing the others' preferences by communications from them or his own perception of their tastes, realizes that no alternative will win out, since each alternative will receive only one vote. He does not know which voter will have a deciding vote. If, however, he chooses to strategically represent his preferences as B>A>C and votes according to those preferences, he will be able to block the choice of his least preferred alternative, C.˙

Consider the strategy machine for Individual 1. It begins in the initial state "A>B>C, vote A" representing his sincere preference and strategy. The machine receives inputs of the perceived preferences of individual 2, b>a>c, and individual 3, c>b>a, and also input that he is choosing a strategy for voting by the method of majority rule. The next state of this strategy machine for individual 1 is "B>A>C, vote B" representing his strategic preference and strategy, given the information he has on the decision situation. If, as an alternate case, he had no information or perception of the preferences of others in the society, the machine would never change state from his sincere preference and vote for the most preferred alternative, "A>B>C, vote A". If, too, he revised his perceptions of the strategies of other individuals at any time before the actual voting, his strategy machine may move to a different strategy state in response to this changed input situation.

VII. <u>Summary</u>

This paper has explored the use of syntactic pattern recognition to model individual strategy formulation and voting in the social choice process. The information gathering step in strategy formulation was based on the representation of an individual sifting through information and preference signals in his environment, judging as usable those signals which did not strongly contradict his original beliefs on the issue. The individual was viewed as "recognizing" information bits which were in his language, those information pieces which were acceptable input for his preference formation. The information he accepted as relevant and the voting method to be used, as well as the voting behavior of other members of his society, will affect his actual voting strategy. For the second part of the strategy formation process, strategy building, the individual is modeled by an automaton which changes state as it processes environmental information; the states describe interim strategy selections. The state reached by this automaton when no more information is available describes the strategy which the individual will use.

The reader should not infer that syntactic representations of the information gathering and action selection processes are limited to social choice systems. Forthcoming work will show that such syntactic models are also useful to show person to person communication, influence, and their affect on individuals' actions. Such forays of syntactic pattern recognition into modeling organizational behavior and, more generally, man's basic interpretation of his environment and his reactions in it show that syntactic pattern recognition is far from being too abstract to be applied to cases of modeling in the social sciences. Economic, social, organizational systems - syntactic pattern recognition can be a useful foundation for modeling them all in their fullness, richness, and complexity, the qualities which make them most fascinating and exciting to the social scientist.

The use of syntactic pattern recognition, even in this limited example of strategy formulation, shows how relationships and processes of systems can be explicitly modeled. The system reacts to its environment, processes information and acts on its interpretation of the environment. This paper here has shown syntactic pattern recognition's applicability in one area, modeling part of a systems approach to economics. The future will hopefully bring successful extensions of this approach. Mathematical models are elegant; syntactic models of the economic system should provide a fuller and so better description of economic reality.

APPENDIX

Introduction

Using syntactic pattern recognition, objects in a particular class are viewed as the result of a process unique to that class. The classification itself is accomplished by a device which will only recognize the results of a particular process. In contrast to decision theoretic pattern recognition, syntactic pattern recognition explicitly considers the system which forms the objects to be classified. Generally, grammars are used to model the process and automata are the recognition devices. In this appendix, grammars and automata will be briefly described.

412

Grammars and Languages

In ordinary usage, a language must follow the rules of the grammar for that language. For example, the construction of an English sentence may be described as:

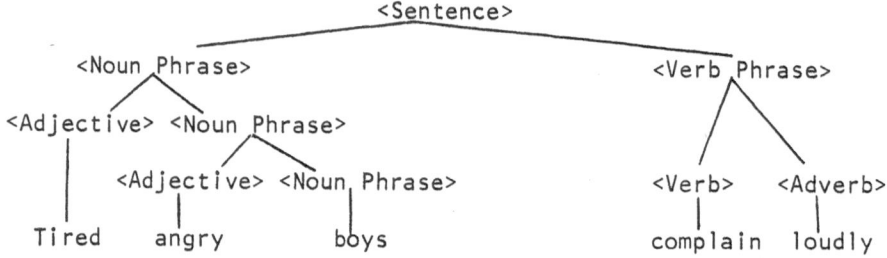

The bracketed expressions may be considered nonterminals and the nonbracketed words are terminals. The language is formed by the concatenation of terminals following the rules of the grammar, called the productions. One production here would be:

$$\text{<noun phrase>} \rightarrow \text{<adjective>} \quad \text{<noun phrase>}$$

Generalizing, the formal definition of a grammar, G, is a 4-tuple:

$$G = (V_N, V_T, P, S)$$

where V_N = nonterminal variables, usually upper case letters

V_T = terminal variables, usually lower case letters

P = set of productions

S = start symbol

We define the language generated by G, L(G), to be:

$$L(G) = \{w | w \ \varepsilon \ V_{T*} \text{ and } S \overset{*}{\underset{G}{\Rightarrow}} w\},$$ meaning that $w \ \varepsilon \ L(G)$ if and only if:

1) w, a string, consists solely of terminals, and

2) w can be derived from S by a series of productions in G.

J* is the notation referring to the set of all concatenations of $j_i \ \varepsilon \ J$.

For example, let $G = (V_N, V_T, P, S)$

where $V_N = \{S\}$, $V_T = \{0, 1\}$, $S = S$, P: $S \rightarrow 1S \qquad S \rightarrow 0$

If we use the notation j^n to refer to a string of n j's, $L(G) = \{1^n 0 | n > 0\}$.

Automata

Automata receive input, change internal state depending on
the input, and, in some applications, produce output in response
to input. While the transitions themselves describe processes,
automata are also useful because they can be designed to recognize input from certain types of grammars. A finite state automaton can recognize languages generated by regular[1] grammars. The
sense in which this recognition occurs will be described after the
automaton concept is formally defined.

A finite state automaton M over an alphabet Σ is a 5-tuple
$(K, \Sigma, \delta, q_o, F)$, where K is a finite, nonempty set of states, Σ
is a finite input alphabet, δ is a mapping of K x Σ into K, q_o in
K is the initial state, and F in K is the set of final states. If
$\delta(q,a)$ is a mapping of K x Σ into subsets of K, then the next
state from q upon receiving input string "a" may be one of a set
of possible states. This characteristic results in a nondeterministic finite automaton, since the next state is not necessarily
uniquely determined; this nondeterministic automaton is in contrast to δ being a mapping into individual members of K, which
results in a deterministic finite automaton. We note that δ-
mapping applied to a string operates sequentially from left to
right on the string. That is, $\delta(q_o, ax) = \delta(\delta(q_o, a), x)$.

By acceptance (recognition) we refer to a machine moving to
a final internal state when a member of a certain language is
used as input to the machine. Formally, a sentence x, a string,
is said to be accepted by M if $\delta(q_o, x) = p$, for some p in F. The
set of all x accepted by M is designated T(M). That is, T(M) =
$\{x \; \delta(q_o, x)$ is in F$\}$. And a string is accepted by a nondeterministic finite automaton if there exists some set of transitions
such that the machine moves to a final state on receiving that input. Thus if a finite automaton can be found which will recognize

---

[1]Productions of a regular grammar are limited to the form A $\rightarrow$ aB
and A $\rightarrow$ a, where A,B ε V_N and a ε V_T.

414

the acceptable procedures of a society, the machine in a sense
can simulate the society, by picking out its acceptable procedures
from a larger set.

Theorem. (Hopcroft and Ullmann, 1969). Let $G = (V_N, V_T, P, S)$ be
a type 3 (regular) grammar. Then there exists a finite automaton
$M = (K, V_T, \delta, S, F)$ with $T(M) = L(G)$.

Thus, regular grammars and finite automata are particularly
useful in pattern recognition, since finite automata may be designed which will only recognize the language of a regular grammar.

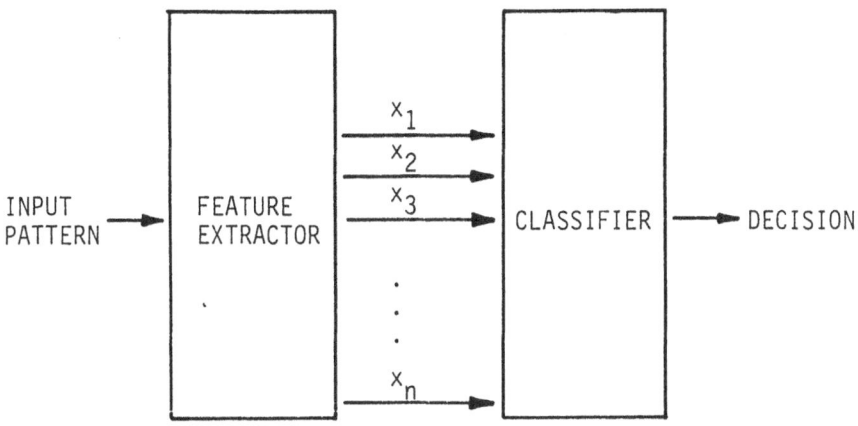

Figure 1
Source: Fu, 1968, p. 2.

References

1. Arrow, Kenneth J., <u>Social Choice and Individual Values</u>, 2nd Edition, Wiley, 1964.

2. Farquharson, Robin, <u>Theory of Voting</u>, Yale University Press, 1969.

3. Fu, K. S., <u>Sequential Methods in Pattern Recognition and Machine Learning</u>, Academic Press, 1968.

4. Hopcroft, John E. and Ullman, Jeffrey D., <u>Formal Languages and Their Relation to Automata</u>, Addison-Wesley Publishing Company, 1969.

5. Sen. Amartya Kurmar, <u>Collective Choice and Social Welfare</u>, Holden-Day, 1970.

OPTIMAL SELECTION AND SCHEDULING OF SORT PATTERNS

Frederick H. Murphy and Edward A. Stohr

Abstract: In this paper we describe an approach to the real-
time control of sorting operations in the presence of deadlines.
The problem arises in the postal service where mail has to be
sorted by zip codes and in the banking system where checks have
to be sorted according to the bank on which they are drawn. In
both applications losses are incurred if items miss their clearing
deadlines. For example, in check-sorting an extremely important
objective of the control system is to reduce the 'float' i.e.,
the total dollar value of the checks which miss their deadlines.
We show how the scheduling problem can be regarded as a problem
in pattern-recognition and propose a real-time control system
which utilizes a linear program for choosing between alternative
sort-patterns and assigning the various processing steps to the
time periods between deadlines.

I. Introduction

In this paper we are concerned with the design of optimal
control systems for the sorting of documents by computer-controlled sorting machines. The problem has great economic importance since it occurs both in the postal service where mail has
to be sorted by zip-code and in the banking system where checks

have to be sorted by the bank in which they are deposited for return to the banks on which they are drawn. A discussion of the mail-sorting problem is given by Horn [2], while a good description of an actual computer system for real-time control of check processing operations is given by Banham and McClelland [1].

In both the postal and banking applications computer-controlled reader-sorters are employed which read the documents using either optical character recognition techniques or magnetic ink character recognition techniques. The documents are then directed by the machine to a particular pocket or hopper based on their identification code. Since the number of final destinations for the documents far exceeds the number of pockets available on the sorter many items must be passed through the sorter more than once. Batches of documents arrive at random times through the day. The sorters group them according to their endpoint destinations. In the postal application the endpoints are associated with zip code regions; in the banking application the endpoints may be a collection of banks within a region, a Federal Reserve Bank, or a single bank which must be sent a large volume of checks. Batches of items to be sorted arrive at random times during the day. The sorting process is subject to a number of clearing deadlines and the performance of the system is closely related to the number and/or value of the documents which miss their deadlines on each day. For example, in check-sorting applications an important objective of the processing system is to minimize the total dollar value of checks which miss their deadlines since one day's interest will be lost on these checks.

II. Problem Statement

We now present some terminology and show how the scheduling problem can be regarded as a pattern recognition problem. For a given batch of checks containing n endpoints and a sorter with m pockets the sorting process, or 'sort-pattern', can be represented by a tree. For example if $m = 3$ and the number of endpoints,

n = 13, the tree may look like either of the trees in Figure 1.
All nodes connected to a single arc are called 'exterior nodes'
(Knuth [3]) and represent distinct endpoints for items. All other
nodes (the 'interior' nodes) represent 'rehandle' pockets i.e. a
pass of a subgroup of items through the sorter. Since we can always add endpoints of zero volume, we need only consider m-ary
trees, that is, trees where exactly m arcs emanate from each interior node.

Let v_i^b equal the expected number of items for endpoint i of
batch b and let w_i^b equal their expected value for i = 1,2,...,n.
Without loss of generality we order the endpoints so that
$v_i^b \geq v_{i+1}^b$ for i = 1,2,...,n. We say that a tree is an h-level
tree if the maximum number of arcs from the root to an endpoint
is h. A node is at level h if it is the hth node on the path from
the root to this node. Note that an endpoint at level h goes
through h-1 passes. For a given sort-tree define p_i as the number of passes for items of endpoint i. Let c_h be the cost of
sorting an item through h passes. We assume $c_h < c_{h+1}$. Non-
linearity of the costs allows for the probability that an item is
rejected by the sorter increasing more than proportionately with
the number of passes beyond the first. For a given batch the
processing procedure is completely specified by a sort-tree as
given above together with the sequence of passes or visits to
interior nodes.

In a previous paper [4], the authors have provided an algorithm which determines the class of sort-trees with minimum
total processing time, $\Sigma c_{p_i} v_i^b$, for a given batch, b. The algorithm allows for an optional constraint that certain 'special'
endpoints must be 'killed' or separated on the first pass. A
restriction on the allowable number of levels in the tree can
also be included if required. The output of the algorithm is a
tree of "Type 1" as shown in Figure 1(a) where the non-special
endpoints are ordered by volume from left to right and the special

endpoints (if any) are associated with the left-most exterior nodes at level one.

Sort-trees of the type shown in Figure 1a can be adjusted to allow for the presence of processing deadlines while still minimizing the average number of passes per item by shifting the interior nodes to different positions on the same level. In this way it is possible to construct a tree with minimal total processing time and in which the number of setups required to completely process all the endpoints associated with the most imminent deadline is minimized. Such a tree is shown in Figure 1(b) where the letters above each endpoint refer to the associated deadline with deadline 'a' being the most urgent and deadline 'b' the next most urgent and so on. A sort-tree of this form will be referred to as a 'Type 2' tree. Obviously, a number of different Type 2 sort-trees can be developed for a given batch - one for each deadline involving items in the batch. Type 2 sort-trees are obtained from Type 1 trees as follows. Order the endpoints at each level in the Type 1 tree from left to right by increasing time to deadline and within the group of endpoints for each deadline by decreasing value. Next associate each internal node with the highest priority deadline in the sub-tree for which it is a root and move it to the left until an endpoint with the same or higher priority deadline is encountered. Note that the endpoints associated with the different deadlines tend to be grouped together. Similarly, endpoints with high expected dollar value tend to be grouped together. Type 2 as well as other sort trees are used as data for the real time scheduling procedure described later.

The scheduling probelm can now be stated. A number of batches of items arrive throughout the day. The arrival times and composition of the batches can be predicted with reasonable accuracy. There are specified deadlines for each endpoint. Let T_t be the time interval between the $t-1^{st}$ and t^{th} deadline and let B_{it}^b be the value of endpoint i of batch b if it is processed during the t-1st interval. For example, in a check-sorting appli- cation this value is a function of the interest rate, of the ex- pected total value of checks for endpoint i within the batch, and of whether the processing for endpoint i is completed before or after its deadline. The batches are to be processed using one or more sorters. If there is more than one sorter, the definition of T_f is modified so that it equals the total available sorter time between deadlines t-1 and t. For expositional purposes the sorters are assumed to have m pockets, however the model can be generalized to allow for a multiplicity of sorter sizes. The time to process a batch of items through one pass is composed of a fixed setup time, c, plus a variable time, λ, per item.

A pass of a batch through a sorter creates a set of complete- ly separated endpoints and/or a new set of sub-batches to be sorted subsequently. At any time during the day there is a set of batches waiting for processing to begin and another collection of partially sorted batches. No distinction need be made between these two types of batches since the sorting pattern for a sub- batch can also be represented by an m-ary tree. We assume a real time processing situation. After each pass of a batch through a sorter a decision has to be made concerning the next batch to be processed and the sorting pattern to be used for the chosen batch.

In the language of pattern recognition theory the actual batch arrival times, the number of items in each batch and the value of each item constitute the 'pattern space'. To simplify, the problem we consider only a 'feature space' consisting of the expected batch arrival times, a^b, and the expected number, v_i^b, and total value w_i^b of the items for each endpoint i. The quantities can be obtained from past experience and updated continually by such techniques as exponential smoothing. The complete set of data, $\{a^b, v_i^b, w_i^b\}$, can be thought of as a 'template' which we are attempting to fit to the pattern space. We use this template to

help us make decisions with respect to the sort-pattern to be used
for each batch and the scheduling decisions associated with the
processing of the batches. If the pattern space as defined above
were known with certainty, then we could (at least in theory)
solve the problem once and for all by running the large mathematical program specified in [5]. The pattern recognition problem
is to detect the variations from the expected pattern as they
arise during the day and to alter the decision rules accordingly.
This is achieved by using a linear program which is run periodically throughout the day and which incorporates the latest information with respect to the set of actual feature values $\{a^b, v_i^b, w_i^b\}$.

III. Real-Time Scheduling Algorithm

To obtain a practical real-time scheduling system we decom-
pose the problem into two phases. In the first, a set of candidate sort-patterns is generated for each batch. Type 1 or Type 2
sort-trees as described earlier which have minimum total sorting
time are suitable candidates but the choice of sort-pattern is
not restricted. In the second phase these sort-patterns are incorporated in a linear program. The program chooses a sort-pattern for each batch from among those provided and assigns the
processing of each interior node in the selected pattern to a
time interval between deadlines. Ideally, the program should be
solved every time a sorter becomes available for another pass.
However, to reduce the computational burden a good compromise
would be to run the program periodically or at the time of arrival
of each new batch.

We define the following indices:

$r = r^{th}$ pattern for a given batch

$s = s^{th}$ interior node in a sort-pattern for a batch where
$s=1$ denotes the root of the m-ary tree and the other
interior nodes are enumerated from left to right on
successive levels in the tree.

The sort-patterns generated during the first phase provide the following information:

B_{rst}^b = the benefit obtained from isolating the endpoints associated with the sth interior node of the rth pattern for batch b in time interval between the $t-1^{st}$ and t^{th} deadline.

σ_{rs}^b = the total processing time assocated with the sth interior node of the rth pattern for batch b. (this includes the setup time, c, and variable time, λ, per item.)

We define the following variables:

$$v_{rst}^b = \begin{cases} 1 \text{ if interior node, s, of the } r^{th} \text{ pattern associated} \\ \quad \text{with batch b is processed in time period t} \\ 0 \text{ otherwise} \end{cases}$$

and the following index set:

$I_{(r,s)}^b$ = the set of interior nodes which are directly connected to the sth interior node in the rth pattern for batch b.

The objective is to maximize total benefits:

(1) $\max \sum_b \sum_r \sum_s \sum_t B_{rst}^b v_{rst}^b$

subject to the following constraints.

Time constraints:

(2) $\sum_b \sum_r \sum_s \sigma_{rs}^b v_{rst}^b \leq T_t$ for all t

Constraints arising from the precedence relations in the sort-patterns:

(3) $\sum_{u \leq t} v_{rsu}^b \geq \sum_{u < t} v_{r\hat{s}u}^b$, $\hat{s} \in I^b(r,s)$ for all r, s, t.

A requirement that all interior nodes be sorted and that a single pattern is chosen for each batch:

(4) $\sum_r \sum_t v_{rst}^b = 1$ for all s

For s = 1 the constraints (3) and (4) select a single pattern for each batch from among those provided. For each pattern selected we wish to ensure that every interior node is sorted. Let $\hat{r}$ be a selected pattern for batch, b. From (3), $v_{rst}^b = 0$ for

$r \neq \hat{r}$. This means that equations (4) are equivalent to:

(5) $$\sum_t v_{\hat{r}st}^b = 1 \qquad \text{for all } s$$

By the following Lemma these constraints guarantee that each end-point is isolated.

> Lemma: For a given number of endpoints, all sort-patterns contain the same number of interior nodes. This number is the largest integer less than $n/(m-1)$.

A proof of this Lemma is given in Knuth [3]. It implies that there is the same number of constraints of the form (5) for each sorting pattern. Therefore the constraints (4) guarantee the completion of the sort-pattern for each batch.

At the time the linear program is run a number of batches and partially processed sub-batches will exist in the system and it is necessary to include the relevant data for these batches. It is also possible to anticipate future batch arrivals by including data for artificial batches, b, with B_{rst}^b equal to zero if the batch is not expected to arrive during the current period, t. It would be economically infeasible to solve this integer program on a repetitive basis. We therefore solve it as a linear program and provide decision rules for dealing with any non-integer variables (see [5]). These decision rules also determine a tentative schedule for the processing of the interior nodes associated with each selected pattern. Processing continues according to this schedule until a new schedule is produced by another run of the linear program. Computational experience s shows that there are in fact relatively few non-integer variables in the final solution to the linear program. Also, Type 2 sort-trees tend to be selected by the linear program much more often than, for example, Type 1 sort-trees. However, the value of the optimal solution is relatively insensitive to the choice between alternative Type 2 sort-patterns for a given batch. This is because each Type 2 tree has its end-points grouped by time deadlines and because the total processing time is the same for each Type 2 tree.

In this paper we have described a straight forward and intuitively reasonable approach to the scheduling of sorting operations. Future work will involve experiments with the choice of a suitable data base of sorting patterns, with the times during the day at which the linear program is run and with the rules for making use of the linear programming solution.

(a)

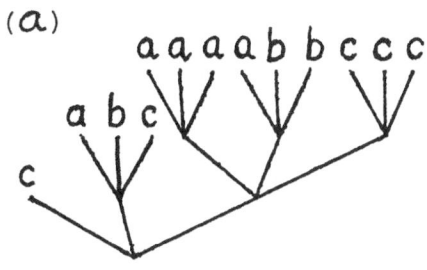

(b)

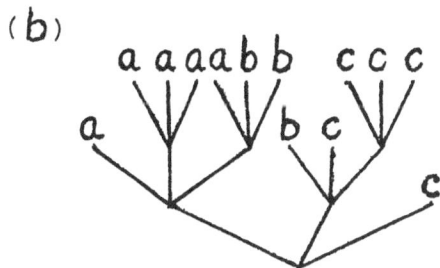

Figure 1a and 1b.

References

1. Banham, J. A. and McClelland, P., "Design Features of a Real-
   time Check Clearing System," IBM Systems Journal, No. 4,
   1972.

2. Horn, W. A., "Single-Machine Job Sequencing With Tree-like
   Precedence Ordering and Linear Delay Penalties," SIAM
   Journal of Applied Mathematics, Vol. 23, No. 2, September,
   1972.

3. Knuth, D. E., The Art of Computer Programming, Vol. 1,
   Addison-Wesley, Reading, Massachusetts, 1969.

4. Murphy, F. H. and Stohr, E. A., "A Dynamic Programming
   Algorithm for Check Processing," Discussion Paper No. 158,
   Center for Mathematical Studies in Economics and Management
   Schience, Northwestern University.

5. Murphy, F. H. and Stohr, E. A., "A Mathematical Programming
   Approach to the Scheduling of Sorting Operations," Dis-
   cussion Paper No. 164, Center for Mathematical Studies in
   Economics and Management Science, Northwestern University.

PATTERN RECOGNITION APPLICATIONS IN WORK WITH ANCIENT OBJECTS

Peter W. Becker

Electronics Laboratory
Technical University of Denmark
Lyngby, Denmark

I. Introduction

The purpose of this chapter is to direct the attention of the
pattern recognition community to an expanding area filled with more
or less unsolved problems where pattern recognition techniques may
be applicable. Our point of view will be that of a worker in the
field of pattern recognition reporting to fellow workers on a
number of representative and potential problems. It is hoped for
that this chapter may stimulate researchers in the field of pattern recognition to approach scientists working in departments of
history and in museums and thereby to initiate new interdisciplinary activities.

The chapter is organized as follows. In the Introduction we
present some necessary background information. To avoid too much
historical detail which may obscure the presentation we will time
and again, by means of an asterisk in the text, refer the interested reader to appropriate articles in Encyclopedia Britannica;
here the reader will find a scholarly, yet easy to follow, account
of the particular point in question. The next section has to do
with Numerical Taxonomy. The study of ancient objects, like the
study of botany and zoology has as a first requirement an adequate

and objective taxonomy. In this section cluster analysis in archaeology will be mentioned. Cluster Analysis has been dealt with in depth elsewhere in this book so our account will be rather cursory. We then turn to the pattern recognition aspects of the Seriation problem. Seriation methods are widely used to demonstrate the chronological development of languages, to study arrangements of developmental states of invertebrates, and to investigate evolutionary trends in fossil series and related anthropological questions (Hymes 1965). Seriation methods also find use in the chronological ordering of cultural assemblages of ancient objects. In the next section a particular technique - Nonmetric Multidimensional Scaling - is described in some detail. Then in the section on Miscellaneous Applications some problems are mentioned where pattern recognition techniques might be useful. Finally in the Epilogue we point to an exceedingly important and equally difficult pattern recognition problem.

II. Patterns in Prehistoric Developments

In the discussions of prehistoric artifacts, models of the past consciously or subconsciously tend to enter into the picture. Therefore a brief review of the most important schools may be in order (Daniel 1971).

(i) Until about 1820 the archaeological findings in Europe had not been conceptually ordered by any system. Mythological models where Trojans, Phoenicians, sons of Noah, and the Lost Tribes of Israel roamed the seas where in vogue. A hundred years ago the myths were supplemented by narratives of the allegedly sunken continents of Atlantis, the antediluvian world, and of Mu (for an account of these fables see Wauchope 1962). The theories are still with us, but at present they are believed in only by the lunatic fringe of prehistory.

(ii) In 1819 C. J. Thomsen from intuition arranged the collections in the Danish National Museum on the basis of three successive ages of Stone, Bronze and Iron, the model is motivated by

technological advances and it has later been elaborated upon. In
1843 Thomsen's pupil and successor, J. J. A. Worsaae (at the age
of 22) published "The Primeval Antiquities of Denmark"; he there
showed the correctness of the museum arrangement by observed
stratigraphy in the Danish peat bógs and funeral mounds. In this
book Worsaae - like any good pattern recognizer - asked: what is
revealed by the patterns? Especially Worsaae asked the fundamental
question: do cultural changes come about by diffusion or independent invention? The striking difference in style between stone
age and bronze age implements he ascribed to an invasion and take-
over by bronze age people (Glob 1974); the more gradual change in
style from bonze age to iron age he explained by lesser events
such as small immigrations from neighboring countries.

(iii) The patterns of prehistory may also be interpreted in
terms of ethnographical determinism as set forth 1877 by L. H.
Morgan in his book "Ancient Society". Here he distinguished seven
ethnic periods spanning from Savagery over Barbarism to Civilization. It is the assertion that parallels between the material culture patterns of prehistoric peoples and present day primitives
imply parallels in non-material culture; consequently certain
technological inventions and certain economic ways of life, determine and define the social and cultural life of the people concerned. (Morgan's ethnographical determinist model was virtually
canonized by Karl Marx who used it as basis for his book finished
by Friedrich Engels, on "The Origin of the Family, Private Property
and the State").

In closing it should be mentioned that behind any of the
theories lurk such questions as: what patterns do cultural changes
follow in time and in space? Is there a psychic unity of man
which produces similar elementary ideas everywhere and gave rise
to seven or eight independent first civilizations? The reader
interested in these matters is referred to "Analytical Archaeology"
by David L. Clarke (Clarke 1968) where these and related problems
are discussed in depth.

III. Numerical Taxonomy

In the middle of the eighteenth century at the time of
Linnaeus the learned world was being engulfed by an ever increasing mass of data released by the magnifying glass and the ex-
plorers' new discoveries. To keep track of the rapidly increasing
volume of information it became necessary to isolate and rank the
basic entities and populations of botany, zoology, chemistry, and
physics, arranging their relative statuses in nested hierarchical
models. This kind of model organization by levels was somewhat
arbitrary but useful, fitting certain properties of the data and
providing an economical synthesis of information. Such nested
hierarchy arrangements allow one to group a large number of taxonomic groups into fewer composite groups of higher rank, thereby
conveying the maximum amount of predictive information in the
minimum number of statements. The success of such schemes is
illustrated by the fact that they have spread to such diverse
fields as geology, palaeontology, anthropology, ecology, genetics,
art history, linguistics, lexicography psychology, and - archaeology, (Clarke 1968). The approach is quite versatile; on L'ile de
Bendor there is a museum with vine- and liqueur-bottles, and should
one want to, one could definitely develop a taxonomy for such
bottles. To make classifications as objective and repeatable as
possible there has recently been a trend towards use of numerical
measurements and methods in the description of entities. With
the publishing of "Principles of Numerical Taxonomy" by Robert
Sokal and Peter Sneath in 1963 a summary of the concepts became
widely available which has stimulated recent work in the field.
Later books (e.g., Jardine and Sibson 1971; Sneath and Sokal 1973)
have added to the general body of knowledge and further dissemi-
nated the basic ideas. The basic entity in numerical taxonomy
is the operational taxonomic unit - the OTU. In work with ancient
objects the OTU's may be artifacts, types, assemblages, or cul-
tures, which the researcher tries to relate in terms of their

lower-level entities or attributes (also called characters). The
level of measurement for such attributes is usually nominal or
ordinal. Any group of OTU's is called a taxon - in plural taxa.

By numerical taxonomy we will understand: the grouping
by numerical methods of taxonomic units into taxa on the
basis of their character states (Sneath and Sokal 1973,
p. 4).

To be able to "group by numerical methods" we must know how
to estimate resemblance. This brings us to the attribute matrix,
or A-matrix, a fundamental concept in numerical taxonomy. As an
illustrative example consider a cemetery where N gravesites have
been studied and described in terms of the presence or absence of
M types of pottery; the result of the study may then be condensed
in an A-matrix with N rows and M columns or what is equivalent N
points in an M dimensional space. The next step towards estimating resemblance between any two gravesites is to decide on how to
weight the M attributes. The answer to this problem may surprise
researchers familiar with traditional pattern recognition literature: in numerical taxonomy all attributes are usually given
equal weight (an alternative approach is described in Wong and Liu
1975, Sec. IV). The matter has been discussed by Sneath and Sokal
(Sneath and Sokal 1973, Section 3.9) who list 7 arguments in favor
of equal weighting, Argument no. 1 runs as follows "if it cannot
be decided how to weight the features, one must give them equal
weight - unless it is proposed to allocate weight on irrational
grounds". To estimate the taxonomic resemblance between two gravesites we must by way of a suitable distance-measure (or the opposite: a similarity-measure) express the difference between a
pair of rows as a one-digit statistic. Many possible one-digit
statistics with interesting properties have been discussed in the
literature (Sneath and Sokal 1973, Chapter 4), in the following
section on "Seriation" two such similarity-measures will be reported on. Having computed the $(N - 1)N/2$ possible similarities

(or what is the opposite: the distances) between pairs of the N gravesites the researcher can present the results in terms of an N by N symmetrical similarity matrix (also called resemblance matrix).

How can one use a similarity matrix to gain new insight into man past? This depends on what kind of relationships are under consideration. Often a researcher would want to apply cluster analysis techniques hoping to discover that his data are structured as interrelated clusters. When such a structure actually is revealed the next step for the researchers would be to discover the underlying reasons for this particular structure. Cluster analysis has received much attention in the literature (Sneath and Sokal 1973, pp. 201-245) and will not be discussed any further here. In other cases the chronological ordering of his finds (say, a set of gravesites) may be of concern to the researcher, if so seriation methods are in order. As seriation methods are not so familiar to the pattern recognition community the following section is devoted to this topic. Finally the aim of the researcher may be to obtain a two- or three-dimensional display illustrating the relative "closeness" of his finds (e.g. a set of gravesites). This aim may be achieved by some kind of factor analysis: principal components analysis, principal factor analysis, or multiple factor analysis (Harman 1967). These methods have been widely discussed in the pattern recognition literature, consequently we shall not give them more space here. Instead we will in a later section report on an alternative approach: multidimensional scaling.

IV. Seriation

Let our starting point be a matrix where each row indicates a particular collection of artifacts, e.g. the contents of a particular grave in a cemetary and each column indicates the quantity (relative or absolute) of some particular type of pottery found in each grave. Such matrices can be sizable! In his celebrated study from the 1880's, Flinders Petrie worked with 900 graves, the contents of each was sorted into 800 types of pottery plus objects of

other types. The decision on what pottery should be of the same
type and what should be of different types, i.e. the construction
of a typology for the objects and variety of objects is largely a
subject one. We assume that the archaeologist has the necessary
knowledge and flair to construct a workable typology (otherwise the
effort is doomed).

Assume that we have N gravesites and M members of our typology
then each grave may be illustrated by a point in M-dimensional
space. Rather than searching for clusters the seriation problem
is one of sequencing the N points in some proper manner. Usually
the objective is to establish a basis for a prehistoric chronology.
Should the N points tend to cluster strongly they will not be well
suited for seriation analysis.

Here, a simple example may be in order to get the basic concept of seriation across. Think of some future archaeologists
working in American junkyards from the fifties and sixties. Hopefully, the reader will agree that it should be possible to seriate
the excavated cars utilizing the dimensions of their tail fins,
their headlight arrangements, etc., as typology. Also, the reader
will hopefully agree that the very same archaeologists having
successfully seriated their American findings could excavate
European junkyards and seriate their findings there, using some of
their results from America - the reason being that the Detroit
designs influenced European carmakers to some extent and with some
delay.

4.1 The Petrie Concentration Principle

Let us for a moment consider a very simple numerical example.
An archaeologist has opened four graves, Y_1, Y_2, Y_3 and Y_4, and he
decides to describe each grave by the presence or absence of pottery of types X_1, X_2 and X_3. In Y_1, X_1 was present and X_2 and X_3
were absent; Y_1 is described by the binary code $(1,0,0)$. Assume
that Y_2, Y_3 and Y_4 may likewise be described as $(0,1,1)$, $(1,1,0)$

and (1,1,1). If so, the 4-by-3 attribute matrix below describes the four graves. An entry in the matrix will be referred to as a_{ij}. We assume in the following that each column contains at least one "1" and one "0".

	X_1	X_2	X_3
Y_1	1	0	0
Y_2	0	1	1
Y_3	1	1	0
Y_4	1	1	1

How similar are the findings in Y_1 and Y_2? To answer this question we need a measure of similarity, an MS. Many MSs have been proposed in the literature but let us choose an obvious candidate, one well suited for binary distances.

$$\text{Sim}(Y_u, Y_v) = \frac{1}{3} \sum_{t-1}^{3} \max \{a_{ut} \cdot a_{vt}, (1 - a_{ut}) \cdot (1 - a_{vt})\}$$

As Y_1 and Y_2 agree in none of the rows, $\text{Sim}(Y_1, Y_2) = 0$. A logical next step is to list all the similarities in a 4-by-4 matrix. The matrix is symmetrical and the diagonal consists of 4 "ones"; each of the 16 entries, b_{uv} has the meaning

$$b_{uv} = \text{Sim}(Y_u, Y_v)$$

	Y_1	Y_2	Y_3	Y_4
Y_1	1	0	2/3	1/3
Y_2	0	1	1/3	2/3
Y_3	2/3	1/3	1	2/3
Y_4	1/3	2/3	2/3	1

Now the order in which the four graves Y_1, Y_2, Y_3 and Y_4 were listed by the archaeologists may be assumed to be fairly arbitrary, therefore any permutation of $Y_1, \ldots, Y_4$ would be just as reasonable a listing. If we list the graves in the order Y_1, Y_3, Y_4, Y_2 the corresponding permutated similarity matrix takes the form

	Y_1	Y_3	Y_4	Y_2
Y_1	1	2/3	1/3	0
Y_3	2/3	1	2/3	1/3
Y_4	1/3	2/3	1	2/3
Y_2	0	1/3	2/3	1

The diagram below illustrates the inequalities between the $Sim(Y_u, Y_v)$-values in the permutated matrix.

The permutated matrix illustrates a case of <u>perfect seriation</u>; i.e. we have succeeded in reordering rows (and thereby also columns) in such a way as to place the highest similarities close to the principal diagonal of the matrix and having an orderly decrease in similarity values away from the diagonal.

If we rearrange the original attribute matrix according to the permutation we obtain the matrix below.

	X_1	X_2	X_3
Y_1	1	0	0
Y_3	1	1	0
Y_4	1	1	1
Y_2	0	1	1

A matrix where in each column all the "1s" occur consecutively is called a <u>Petrie</u>-matrix or P-matrix in honor of Flinders Petrie. Any permutation of a Petrie-matrix is called a pre-Petrie-matrix or pre-P-matrix. The permutation which transform a pre-Petrie-matrix into a Petrie-matrix must be found by an iterative algorithmic procedure since no analytical procedure is known, and a trial of all permutations usually will prove too expensive to carry out. In addition there are dangers of being trapped in local optima (Kendall 1963).

The matrix invites the construction of hypotheses about chronological developments. Based on the matrix one could surmise that Y_2 is the oldest grave from a period when only pottery of Types X_2 and X_3 were in use; the second oldest grave then becomes Y_4 which shows that X_1 has been introduced; the youngest but one

among the graves becomes Y_3 from which we learn that X_3 has gone
out of fashion; the youngest grave becomes Y_1 from which we learn
that by now also X_2 has been replaced. (The chronology could of
course be reversed making Y_1 the oldest, and Y_2 the youngest
grave). The interesting thing about the permutated attribute
matrix is that the ranges for the 1s in the columns have been reduced. X_1 is present in Y_1, Y_3 and Y_4, as the graves are listed
consecutively, the range for X_1 is $R_1 = 3$, likewise the ranges for
X_2 and X_3, R_2 and R_3, are seen to be 3 and 2. (Before the permutation the ranges were $R_1 = 4$, $R_2 = 3$, and $R_3 = 3$). If we take $\bar{R}$,
the average range, as a (rather unsophisticated) expression for
the ordering of the ensemble of graves in a communal way, we
notice that $\bar{R}$, thanks to the pertubation, has been reduced. Before the perturbation, $\bar{R}$ was $(4 + 3 + 3)/3 = 10/3$; now $\bar{R}$ is $(3 +
3 + 2)/3 = 8/3$, which turns out to be the smallest value achievable.
In most cases perfect seriation is not possible but it is still of
interest to find the permutation which minimizes $\bar{R}$ (or a similar
measure or ordering). A more sophisticated measure of ordering
(Kendall 1963) is $S(P)$ listed below; here N_j is the total number
of "1"s in column j and R_j is the range of the "1"s in column j.

$$S(P) = \sum_j N_j \log R_j$$

In the simple example above, the four graves were arranged
(by a suitable permutation) in a chronological meaningful order.
The principle applied is what Kendall (Kendall 1971) calls Petrie's
Concentration Principle. The principle asserts that:

> if the typology is "chronologically significant", and when
> the graves have been correctly ordered (or anti-ordered),
> then the "sequence-date"-ranges for the individual types
> will be found to have been individually (or in some communal
> way) minimized.

Petrie's Concentration Principle lies at the root of all
seriation efforts, but its implementation is complicated for two

reasons. First of all: what is understood by a typology being
"chronologically significant"? In certain cases the answer seems
obvious. When copper tools are more efficient than stone tools,
it seems a reasonable assumption that graves with copper tools are
younger than graves with stone tools. As copper tools are replaced by the even more efficient bronze tools, which in turn are
replaced by iron tools, we get a typology motivated by the desire
for efficiency; this was the idea of C. J. Thomsen and Worsaae.
A typology may also be motivated by the desire for decoration. If
crushed shell is added to the clay it becomes easier to decorate
the pottery before it is fired. It now seems reasonable to assume
that the more elaborately decorated pottery has been made after
the invention of the "additive" and the less decorated pottery
stems from an earlier age. In contradistinction to the two examples a change from one type of pottery decoration to another will
give us no clue as to which type of decoration was the earliest.
Often a typology may be confirmed by some consequence of the
seriation; e.g., having seriated 51 graves from the La Tene cemetery, Kendall (Kendall 1971, Figure 3) points out that the temporal sequencing illustrates how the earliest graves were located
in the North-East corner and how the cemetery gradually was ex-
panded towards the South-West.

The second reason why the Concentration Principle is complicated has to do with the problem of "Communal Minimization". Re-
calling that Petrie himself worked with 800 types of pottery and
900 graves it becomes clear that communal minimization - in the
strict sense - usually will not be achievable. We shall shortly
return to this problem area during the discussion of Abundance
Matrices. In closing a result should be mentioned; it only applies
to matrices where all entries are binary, "0" or "1".

We again consider N finds, each of which may be described
by an array of M binary digits as discussed in this section - or
what amounts to the same: a vertex on a (hyper-)cube in M-

438

dimensional space. Furthermore, let the origin be defined as the
vertex where all M coordinates are zeroes. If we generate an N-
by M-matrix two questions present themselves: (i) is there a
permutation of the N rows, which will give a perfect seriation;
i.e., is the matrix a pre-Petrie-matrix? (ii) If so, how do we
find the permutation?. The latter question is related to the
Travelling Salesman Problem, which will be discussed in the following section. The answer to the first problem will now be
briefly outlined, it makes use of the concept of a Hamiltonian
Circuit (Wilkinson 1971). Per definition a Hamiltonian Circuit
is a re-entrant path passing through each of the N vertices and the
origin precisely once; the minimum length for a Hamiltonian circuit
is exactly 2M. It may be shown that a necessary and sufficient
condition for a perfect seriation of the N rows to be possible is
that a re-entrant path of length 2M (a Hamiltonian Circuit) can be
established through the N vertices and the Origin, 0. The figure
below illustrates a Hamiltonian circuit for Y_1, Y_2, Y_3 and Y_4. A
Hamiltonian circuit may begin in 0 and pass through Y_1, Y_3, Y_4 and
Y_2 back to 0, the length being 2M = 6 units. We notice that Y_1,
Y_3, Y_4 and Y_2 is the sequence which after the permutation gave the
minimum value of $\bar{R}$ (Wilkinson 1971). A Hamiltonian circuit may be
traversed in either of two directions corresponding to the two
possible chronological orderings.

4.2 On Abundance Matrices

Clearly the description of a grave by an array of M binary
digits (illustrating the absence or presence of M types of artifacts) constitutes a rather drastic data reduction. If we instead
indicate the quantity observed (in relative or absolute measure)
of each artifact, we can still describe the grave by a point in
M-dimensional space but now the point is no longer restricted to
be located on one of the vertices of an M-dimensional (hyper-)
cube. If all N graves are described by their quantities of the M
artifacts, the result may be listed as a N-by-M-matrix. Such a

matrix is called an <u>Abundance Matrix</u> (Kendall 1971). An example
is shown below with 3 types of artifacts, M = 3, and 4 graves N = 4.

	X_1	X_2	X_3
Y_1	0,9	0,1	0,0
Y_2	0,0	0,2	0,8
Y_3	0,3	0,7	0,0
Y_4	0,1	0,5	0,4

As before our goal is to order the graves according to age.
Besides the ranking we would also like to get an idea about the
relative similarity (or closeness) of any pair of graves. Before
one can talk about closeness, we must decide on (i) the relative
weight given to each artifact (i.e. is X_2 more important than X_3
etc.?). Also, (ii) we must decide on what similarity measure to
use. The answers to the two questions should be provided by the
archaeologists (and not the mathematicians) as they call for flair
and experience in the field. To make things simple in our example,
let us assume (as is usually done) that all entries have equal
weight, i.e. all a_{ij}'s have the weight 1. Also let us use a similarity measure, SR, (introduced by Robinson (Robinson 1951)), which
is in particular good when each of the matrix-rows sum to unity
as $0 \leq SR \leq 1$.

$$SR(Y_u, Y_v) = 1 - \sum_{t=1}^{3} \frac{1}{2} \cdot |a_{ut} - a_{vt}|^p \qquad p > 1$$

In the following we will use p = 2 for the sake of simplicity.

Rather than work with the N-by-M-matrix it is at this point
more convenient to compute the $N(N - 1)/2$ similarities and list
the M-by-M similarity matrix. The SR-matrix for the example is
listed below

	Y_1	Y_2	Y_3	Y_4
Y_1	1	0.27	0.64	0.52
Y_2	0.27	1	0.51	0.87
Y_3	0.64	0.51	1	0.88
Y_4	0.52	0.87	0.88	1

If we permutate the Ys we can obtain the matrix below

	Y_1	Y_3	Y_4	Y_2
Y_1	1	0.64	0.52	0.27
Y_3	0.64	1	0.88	0.51
Y_4	0.52	0.88	1	0.87
Y_2	0.27	0.51	0.87	1

The permutated matrix has the property that all rows (and consequently all columns) are unimodel in the weak sense with a maximum at the diagonal. Such a matrix is called a Robinson-matrix, or R-matrix, in honor of W. S. Robinson who introduced the concept (Robinson 1951). An R-matrix has the property that the closer the Ys are the more similar the corresponding graves are. If a matrix by permutation can be made an R-matrix, it is called a pre-R-matrix. Only few matrices are R- and pre-R-matrices in the strict sense.

The impression that the ordering is chronologically significant is confirmed if we permutate the artifact matrix and order the graves as (Y_1, Y_3, Y_4, Y_2). We then arrive at the matrix below

	X_1	X_2	X_3
Y_1	0.9	0.1	0.0
Y_3	0.3	0.7	0.0
Y_4	0.1	0.5	0.4
Y_2	0.0	0.2	0.8

When we read any of the columns from top to bottom (or the other way), we see how the corresponding artifact got into fashion and later got out of fashion again. Whether the columns should be read from top to bottom or from bottom to top must be decided by the archaeologists.

When seriation is attempted one should be aware of two potential sources of error: oscillations in taste, and the Doppler-effect. Oscillations in taste are well exemplified (Clarke 1968, Figure 29) by English grandfather clocks; they were made in much the same simple style in the periods 1670-80 and 1800-50 whereas the trend in the intermediate period up until c. 1770 had been towards more elaborate decorations, at that time, however, the trend reversed itself. The Doppler-effect is illustrated by the familiar observation that it takes time for fashions (and other impulses) to diffuse from centers of fashion (and other kinds of culture) to outlying places (Clarke 1968, Figure 80).

V. Nonmetric Multidimensional Scaling

Again let us consider a typical problem and assume that we are concerned with N gravesites each of which is described by its quantities of M different kinds of pottery. In other words our information may be described by N points, each illustrating an OTU, in an an M-dimensional space (or by, what amounts to the same, an N-by-M A-matrix). For the sake of ease of inspection and representation the researcher will often want to place the N points in a space with a dimensionality of less than M- two or three dimensions is usually the goal; such a - usually drastic - reduction of dimensionality is called ordination. One possible way of reducing the dimensionality is to apply some form of factor analysis (Harman 1967; Sneath and Sokal 1973, pp. 245-249) to the data and only retain the three directions in M-dimensional space which together tell us most about how dissimilar (or similar) the N gravesites are. As such methods are familiar to researchers in the field of pattern recognition we will bypass them here and instead turn our attention to the most general ordination technique: nonmetric multidimensional scaling.

Nonmetric multidimensional scaling is carried out in the following manner. First, all the $N(N - 1)/2$ dissimilarities (or as many as are available) are ranked from the smallest to the largest value. Thus the basic similarity matrix may be a distance or a correlation matrix, or the matrix may only express rank orders of the dissimilarities as evaluated by a subjective observer. Secondly, a decision is taken to represent the N OTU's in a M'-dimensional space where the axis are called X_1, X_2,...,$X_{M'}$.M'

442

usually is one, two, or three and substantially less than M. The distances among the N points in M'-dimensional space, b'_{ij}, may be computed in a variety of ways, commonly as Minkowski metrics.

$$b'_{ij} = (\sum_{k=1}^{M'} |x_{ki} - x_{kj}|^r)^{1/r}$$

With $r \rightarrow \infty$ the Minkowski-metric becomes the "sup"-measure, and with $r = 1$ it becomes the Manhattan or city-block metric. With $r = 2$ it becomes the Euclidean metric which is the most widely used metric. If the locations of the N points in M'-dimensional space can be so arranged that the $N(N - 1)/2$ distances, b'_{ij}, are monotonically related to the original $N(N - 1)/2$ ordinal dis-similarities, b_{ij}, the ordination would be considered perfect. Only rarely will it be possible to achieve perfect ordination. We consequently need a measure of how well we have done, such a measure called S, "the measure of stress", has been developed by Kruskal (Kruskal 1964). The basic idea is the following. We rank the $N(N - 1)/2$ b'_{ij}-values and then we determine a set of $N(N - 1)/2$ "corrections", b''_{ij}, with the property that the $(b'_{ij} + b''_{ij})$-values have the same ranking as the b_{ij}-values. Clearly there are many possible sets of b''_{ij}-values, but we are only interested in the particular set, b^*_{ij}, for which the expression below has been minimized.

$$\sum_{i<j} (b''_{ij})^2 / \sum_{i<j} (b'_{ij})^2$$

The numerator of this expression is the familiar sum of squares of goodness of fit while its denominator is a scale factor to make stress estimates comparable. When the set of $N(N - 1)/2$ b^*_{ij}-values has been established the stress, S, is computed

$$S = (\sum_{i<j} (b^*_{ij})^2 / \sum_{i<j} (b'_{ij})^2)^{\frac{1}{2}}$$

At this point the reader may well ask: but how do I compute the set of b'_{ij}-values so that the stress has been minimized? The answer to this is that these operations may be carried out by the MDSCAL program developed by Kruskal (Kruskal 1964).

MDSCAL employs an iterative technique to minimize the stress for b_{ij} computed by any given Minkowski distance coefficient, and for any dimensionality M'. An important advantage of nonmetric multidimensional scaling is that it can consider dissimilarity matrices with missing or tied dissimilarity values.

If the similarities between utensils from the gravesites reflect changing patterns in taste and fashion <u>a multidimensional scaling of the data should reveal a chronologically significant ordering of the N points</u>. In other words, multidimensional scaling may be used in seriation studies. A number of papers on how the method has been applied in work with ancient objects may be found in Hodson et al. 1971. As an illustrative example the "Horse-Shoe Method" (Kendall 1971) should be mentioned. Here the N points are forced to lay in a two-dimensional plane. If the similarity matrix is (reasonably close to) a pre-R-matrix, the N points will fall on a bended line, the "horse-shoe". The order of the points along the line is the order which will (almost) change the matrix into an R-matrix.

Another way of looking at the problem is to say that each of the N points is "separated" from each of the other (N - 1) points by their similarity, the smaller the separation the greater the similarity. The ordering problem may now be seen as one of finding a path (the continuum) so that each of the N points is visited once and only once, while maximizing the sum of the (N - 1) similarities. If N is small an exhaustive search for the optimal ordering is possible - but that is rarely the case in practice. The similarity of this problem to the Traveling-Salesman Problem has been noted by several workers (Wilkinson 1971; Hubert and Schultz 1974) who have tried to use related techniques. Recently, very fast algorithms have been developed for solving the Traveling-Salesman Problem (Held and Karp 1971; Helbig Hansen and Krarup 1974), they may also be of value within this problem area. Two iterative methods by Gelfand (Gelfand 1971) are somewhat similar in nature.

VI.   Miscellaneous Applications

Any worker in the field of pattern recognition, who establishes connections with archaeologists, may get acquainted with problems where his experience and expertise may be useful. In this section we will mention some cases which illustrate this point.

6.1   Decipherment of Ancient Writings

Five thousand years ago writing began in Mesopotamia and Egypt; its beginnings were somewhat later in India and China, and later still in Europe. Clearly, it is of immense importance for the understanding of a civilization that the historians be able to read the records available. In 1822 J. -D. Champollion deciphered ancient Egyptian writing, and thereby made possible the first great step forward in Egyptian archaeology. In 1846 Henry Creswicke Rawlinson succeeded in deciphering the Mesopotamian cuneiform writing, an event which likewise was of great consequence to archaeology. Since then many other types of writing have been understood. Nevertheless, the writings of several civilizations this far have proven impervious to any effort of decipherment. Given a number of representative records it seems possible to use pattern recognition technique or artificial intelligence methods in such a "code breaking" effort.

6.2 The Akhenaten Temple Project

A project of an entirely different nature should be mentioned here. It was initiated by Ray Winfield Smith (Smith 1967; Smith 1970) in 1966 and has been the subject of a BBC educational TV program. Basically, the problem amounts to reconstructing the decorated walls of a temple when only 35,000 of the original 85,000 decorated blocks are available.

Briefly, what happened is the following. 1367 B.C. Amenophis IV together with his famous Queen Nefertiti inherited the throne of Egypt. This event took place in the hay-days of the New Kingdom; we get a glimpse of life at court from the tomb of his son-

445

in-law Tutankhamen. For political reasons Amenophis IV gave up
the numerous gods of the Egyptian pantheon and introduced monotheism - at the time a revolutionary concept. In 1363 B.C.
Amenophis IV introduced the adoration of the sun-disc, the "Aten".
In consequence of this, the King changed his name to Akhenaten and
moved the capital from Thebes to Tell el Amarna where he built a
temple in the honour of Aten. The temple was situated on the east
bank of the Nile, a vast complex of structures which may have extended more than a mile into the desert. After a reign of 17 years,
Akhenaten died in 1350 B.C., leaving behind him an empire in dis-
array. An irated priesthood reinstated the former numerous gods
and dismantled the only 20 year old temple. It is estimated that
about 250,000 blocks - a third of which were decorated - were used
to build the Aten temple. These blocks were in the following years
put to large-scale reuse in subsequent buildings in the area.
Since the turn of the century, numerous archaeological repair projects have brought more than 35,000 decorated blocks to light. The
blocks were stacked away in storehouses or just left in the open.
In 1966, Ray Winfield Smith initiated an effort to study and -
insofar as possible - to reconstruct the decorated temple walls.
To each of the blocks he assigned a nine-digit identification number. Then the block was photographed with its number. Next, the
block and its decorations were described in digital form, trans-
ferred to IBM punch cards and then to magnetic tape. The actual
matching of blocks is then performed by a question-answering system which rapidly scans the wealth of data. The digital coding
of the information on the polychrome blocks makes use of a priori
knowledge about the many scenes which are highly repetitive in
nature. It is for instance known that long sunrays terminating
in human hands extended across many of the reliefs; the presence
of part of a sunray, its color, and its angle with the horizon is
therefore important information. In total 16 different lists were
used to specify major type block decorations, one for sunrays, one

for figures (subdivided under kings, queens, princesses, priests, and so forth) and others for hieroglyphs, and for such categories as architectural details and defacements.

After a promising start the project was slowed down by political events in the Near East. However, as a first result one of the great reconstructed walls has been put on display in the new museum in Luxor. Had it not been for the computer-aided search for wall patterns we would not have been so familiar with the king who introduced monotheism.

6.3 Modern Tools in Archaeology

The application of aerial photography started during World War 1. At that time it was noticed that many pictures taken for military reconnaissance purposes revealed historical sites. This was in particularly true for pictures taken while the rising or setting sun made the shadows from even small obstacles appear long. Even if a site had been razed to the ground it might still show up as patterns in soil color or in the density of crop.

Archaeologists have also borrowed techniques from the geo-physical prospecting business. Patterns of changing electrical conductivity or magnetic disturbances in the soil are used as clues to hidden sites. When recognized in the ground burial chambers and the like may then be inspected and photographed by way of an inserted periscope. Use of mine detectors is commonplace even by amateurs (J. 1975).

Also at sea the archaeologists are active. After the scuba was developed by Jacques-Yves Cousteau underwater excavations have become possible. Cousteau's work at Le Grand Congloué near Marseille was the first such excavation.

VII. Epilogue

We live at a time when the very existence of humanity is threatened as we are regularly being reminded of by latter-day eschatologists (e.g. Mesarovic and Pestel 1974 and Epstein 1975). In this situation it seems natural to turn to the records of the past and see if any patterns may be detected which can be of guidance to us. The thought of using records of the past to gain new insight is familiar from the natural sciences and has often paid handsome dividends. The problem of detecting the patterns - if any - which determine the historical events is actually a generalization of the seriation problem. The problem has been attacked by a number of researchers most of which, unfortunately enough, arrived at the most diverse answers. Just from last century the following names could be mentioned: Karl Marx[*], Lord Acton[*], Oswald Spengler[*], and Arnold Toynbee[*].

The inherent difficulty with this kind of work with ancient objects is of course that though the researchers profess to talk about the same periods and events, they weigh the noisy evidence differently; a discussion of the patterns in history may be found in the article on "History, Philosophy of" Encyclopedia Britannica (vol. 8, pp. 961-965, 1974). Admittedly, it will be very difficult to apply pattern recognition techniques to the prediction of historical events but considering the importance of the problem even a partial success (and the mere discussion of the whole problem area) should be welcomed. (The easy thing for the reader is to claim that it cannot be done - but isn't this what most readers did say when they first heard about plans of roaming the lunar surface in a car, and in that undertaking the interests at stake were much smaller).

Modeling of socio-economic systems (Chen 1974; Proc. IEEE, March 1975, Special Issue on Social Systems engineering) has been achieved with some success and a rich variety of methodological approaches have been developed which may prove useful. But the basic weakness of such studies and of any study of world dynamics or Club-of Rome-type work is that the erratic behavior of a society under duress is ignored. Just think of the wisdom with which the industrialized nations handle their energy crisis and the under-developed nations take care of the population explosion. To

include the vagaries of groups of men some kind of pattern recognition effort is needed. The task is as difficult as it is urgent.
However, in closing let me point to one helpful fact. There is an
obvious place where such a pattern recognition study should be
initiated: Thucydides[*] account of the Peloponnesian War[*], 431
B.C. to 404 B.C. (Thucydides 1961). From the beginning of the war,
Thucydides, first and most famous recorder of contemporary history,
realized the significance of the events which were taking place
around him. He examined the day-to-day occurrences in an almost
clinical spirit with the express motivation that future genera-
tions should benefit from the experience of their predecessors.
We have here - in so far as it is possible - a truthful description
of events, a prerequisite for pattern recognition. Basically, the
war was an allout fight between Athens and Sparta while a huge
Asian empire, Persia, loomed large in the background. A number of
descriptors come to mind. Athens was a democracy, a wealthy and
hedonistic society spurred by the curiosity of its citizens. Based
on trade with the Mediterranean and Black Sea countries, its power
base was a strong navy and a well-filled treasury. Sparta was a
totalitarian state, a comparatively poor garrison state with a
hearty dislike for foreigners and foreign ideas, agriculture was
the principal source of income, its power base was a strong army.
Pattern recognition work with such ancient records calls for a
sophisticated interdisciplinary effort. But also the lay reader
may fiend food for thought in Thucydides' account: e.g. Pericles'
speech on the importance of Megara at the outbreak of the war is
the Domino Theory anticipated by 2400 years; also Pericles' funeral
oration, where Democracy is extoled as being the best kind of
government, may stir some readers (and be considered bunk by
others). Thucydides is not our only source, other authors have
also reported on their observations during the turbulent years;
foremost among these is Plato, pupil of Socrates and Aristotle's
teacher.

Having studied how, in this case, one event led to another, what options appeared to be open, and why decisions were made as they were, the interdisciplinary team could study later relevant periods in history. The next result should then be the acquisition of a data base (akin to a file of medical case stories) which could be studied with an eye to future decision making.

References

1. Chen, K. (editor, "Technology and Social Institutions", New York, IEEE Press, No. PC00315, 1974.

2. Clarke, D. L., "Analytical Archaeology", Methuen, London, 684 pp., 1968.

3. Daniel, Glyn, "From Worsaae to Childe: The Models of Prehistory", The Prehistoric Society, Vol. 37, 2, London, 1971.

4. Epstein, William, "The Proliferation of Nuclear Weapons", Scientific American, vol. 232, no. 4, pp. 18-33, April 1975.

5. Gelfand, Alan E., "Rapid Seriation Methods with Archaeological Applications", in Hodson et al., pp. 186-201, 1971.

6. Glob, P. V., "The Mound People: Danish Bronze-Age Man Preserved", Cornell University Press, 1974.

7. Harman, H. H., "Modern Factor Analysis", 2nd ed., University of Chicago Press, Chicago, 1967.

8. Helbig Hansen, K. and Krarup, J., "Improvements of the Held-Karp Algorithm for the Symmetric Traveling-Salesman Problem", Mathematical Programming 7, 1974.

9. Held, M. and Karp, R. M., "The Traveling-Salesman Problem and Minimum Spanning Trees, Part II", Mathematical Programming 1, pp. 6-25, 1971.

10. Hodson, F. R., Kendall, D. G., and Tautu, P. (eds.), "Mathematics in the Archaeological and Historical Sciences", Proc. of the Anglo-Romanian Conference, Mamaia, 1970. Edinburgh University Press, Edinburgh, 565 pp. , 1971.

11. Hubert, L. and Schultz, J., "Seriation and Quadratic Assignment", Personal communication.

12. Hymes, D. (ed.), "The Use of Computers in Anthropology", Mouton, La Hague, 558 pp., 1965.

13. J., A. K., "Tuned-in to Treasure", National Geographic School Bulletin, vol. 53, no. 30, p. 474, May 5, 1975.

14. Jardine, N. and Sibson, R., "Mathematical Taxonomy", Wiley, London, 286 pp., 1971.

15. Kendall, D. G., "A Statistical Approach to Flinders Petrie's Sequence Dating", Bull. Internat. Statist. Inst., 40, pp. 657-680, 1963.

16. Kendall, D. G., "Seriation from Abundance Matrices", in Hodson et al., pp. 215-252, 1971.

17. Kruskal, J. B., "Nonmetric Multidimensional Scaling: a Numerical Method", _Psychometrica_, 29, pp. 115-129, 1964.

18. Mesarovic, M. and Pestel, E., "Mankind at the Turning Point: the Second Report to the Club of Rome", London: Hutchinson, 1974.

19. Robinson, W. S., "A Method for Chronologically Ordering Archaeological Deposits", _American Antiquity,_ vol. 16, pp. 293-301, 1951.

20. Smith, Ray Winfield, "The Akhenaten Temple Project", Expedition, pp. 24-32, Fall 1967.

21. Smith, Ray Winfield, "Computer Helps Scholars Re-create an Egyptian Temple", _National Geographic Magazine_, vol. 138, pp. 634-655, November 1970.

22. Sneath, P. H. A. and Sokal, R. R., "Numerical Taxonomy", San Francisco: W. H. Freeman and Co., 1973.

23. Thucydides, "The Peloponnesian War", Translated by Rex Warner, Penguin Books, 1961.

24. Wauchope, Robert, "Lost Tribes and Sunken Continents", Chicago University Press, 1962.

25. Wilkinson, E. M., "Archaeological Seriation and the Traveling Salesman Problem", in Hodson et al., pp. 276-284, 1971.

26. Wong, A. K. C. and Liu, T. S., "Typicality, Diversity, and Feature Pattern of an Ensemble", _IEEE Trans. on Computers,_ vol. C-24, no. 2, pp. 158-181, February 1975.

ON THE APPLICATION OF FUZZY SET THEORY TO CLUSTER ANALYSIS

E. Backer

Laboratory for Information Theory
Department of Electrical Engineering
Delft University of Technology
Mekelweg 4, Delft-2208, The Netherlands

I. Introduction

In this paper we will concern ourselves with cluster problems in which the structure of the collection of objects is such that clusters can hardly be found. We will propose a cluster model which has been based upon some ideas of Fuzzy Set Theory.

The advantage of 'fuzzy' clustering over other methods should be particularly true in situations where the clusters to be detected are not compact and well separated. The proposed clustering model is not simply based upon distance similarities, but also takes into account the degree of contribution (belongingness) of each sample to a suggested category. Fuzzy sets as a theoretical basis for clustering were first suggested by Bellman, Kalaba and Zadeh [1]. Subsequently, various theories of fuzzy clustering were proposed by, among others, Gitman and Levine [2], Gitman [3], Ruspini [4], Dunn [5] and Bezdek [6]. In an interesting paper of Diday [7], the notion of 'strong' and 'weak' cluster 'pattern', in the sense of types of fuzzy sets, has been developed. The method presented in this paper is similar to that of Diday to the extent that obtained clusterings are characterized by means of some quantity representing the degree of structure.

In section IV, we start with a general definition for the measure of the amount of non-statistical <u>uncertainty</u> in making decisions about the assignment of sample points to a certain number of categories, in the setting of fuzzy set theory. With the help of this uncertainty measure we can define a <u>similarity function</u> which leads to a very useful quantity in clustering, <u>the amount of structure</u>.

In section V, the amount of structure of a fuzzy set will be defined. It will be shown that the greater the amount of structure the more valid the suggested partion is supposed to be with respect to the 'natural' grouping of the collection of objects.

In section VI, we will discuss the clustering algorithm. There, we propose a <u>repartition function</u> for improving the clustering in the sense of maximization of the total amount of structure.

Finally, some experimental results will be given.

II. Preliminaries

Since the development of the model presented in this paper is heavily based upon the algebraic framework of fuzzy set theory the following may serve as a brief introduction in the notation and mathematical background. A more rigorous and detailed treatment of this basic material is contained in Zadeh's paper [8].

<u>Definition</u>: Let X be a set of sample points. A fuzzy set A in X is characterized by a <u>membership function</u> $f_A(x)$ which associates with each sample point x in X a real number in the interval [0,1] such that the value of $f_A(x)$ represents the 'grade of membership' of x in A.

<u>Remark</u>: In consequence of this characterization an ordinary set is a special case of a fuzzy set, where $x \in A$ if $f_A(x) = 1$, and $x \in A$ if $f_A(x) = 0$.

<u>Definitions</u>: (i) The <u>complement</u> of a fuzzy set A is denoted as A' and its membership function is defined by $f_{A'}(x) = 1 - f_A(x)$, for all x X; (ii) a fuzzy set A is <u>contained</u> in B, or equivalently,

A is a subset of B if $f_A(x) \leq f_B(x)$, for all $x \in X$; (iii) the union of two fuzzy sets, $A \cup B$, is a fuzzy set defined by $f_{A \cup B}(x)=$ MAX$[f_A(x), f_B(x)]$, for all $x \in X$; (iv) the intersections of two fuzzy sets, $A \cap B$, is a fuzzy set defined by $f_{A \cap B}(x) = $ MIN$[f_A(x),$ $f_B(x)]$, for all $x \in X$.

Remark: If $f_A(x) + f_B(x) = 1$ for all $x \in X$, then

$$f_{A \cap B}(x) = \frac{1}{2} - \frac{1}{2}|f_A(x) - f_B(x)| \qquad (1)$$

In the discussion which follows, if $\{A_i\}$ is a set of k fuzzy sets, we assume

$$\sum_{i=1}^{k} f_{A_i}(x) \leq 1 \qquad \forall x \in X \qquad (2)$$

III.   The Clustering Problem

We state the clustering problem just briefly; for details, the reader is referred to the literature [9], [10], [11].

The problem can be characterized as follows: given a set of objects $X = [x_1, x_2, \ldots, x_j, \ldots, x_N]$, it is assumed that the properties of each object x_j are expressed as an n-dimensional vector, from which, in the majority of cases, a similarity function $s(x_i, x_j)$ is derived for every pair of points (x_i, x_j). For example, the Euclidean similarity measure is very popular, because of its simple interpretation in terms of proximity; it simply is based on: the smaller the distance the greater the similarity.

It is required to divide the set X into (often assumed to be given) exhaustive and disjoint categories C_i, $i = 1, 2, \ldots, k$, in such a way that members within each category in some sense, resemble more than members belonging to different categories. Further it is desired to obtain that partitioning, which minimizes a given criterion function. The way of partitioning a collection of objects into a number of categories depends highly on the nature of the similarity function. There are many ways of defining a similarity function, and the special type of similarity measure we discuss in the next section is only one possibility. However, this similarity measure appears to lead to a unified view of the 'fuzzy' clustering problem.

The intuistic model for this 'fuzzy' clustering, here, is the following: let the unknown structure of the data be represented by U(X). In reality U(X) is rather fuzzy in nature. The ultimate goal is to find a partition C(X) which represents the real structure U(X) as close as possible. The meaning of C(X) U(X), C(X) is representing U(X) very close, is specified once some criterion G has been selected.

Accordingly, we try to minimize the difference between U(X) and C(X). Now, let it be that our notion of structure can be represented by a set of membership functions of an induced set of fuzzy sets, given a partition C(X). The more the membership function is able to reflect the structure, the more the fuzzy structure F(X) matches the real structure U(X). For every object in the collection there may exist some confusion about the category-assignment due to the induced set of fuzzy sets. So, the decision about F(X) as a whole, resulting in C(X), is by no means trivial but bears a certain amount of uncertainty. This amount of uncertainty plays, as will be seen, a crucial role.

If C(X) is any partition, and $C^*(X)$ denotes that partition which induces a fuzzy structure $F^*(X)$ in such a way that the amount of structural uncertainty is minimal, then, to achieve $C^*(X)$ an algorithm is needed. The present algorithm of 'fuzzy' clustering is basically iterative. This means that we start with an arbitrary C(X) and try to improve the clustering in the sense of minimizing the structural uncertainty, by transferring objects from one cluster to another until no further improvement is available. The meaning of improvement is then completely specified once we have selected our criterion function G.

IV. A Measure of Uncertainty; Point Pair Similarity

Consider a fuzzy set A defined on the set of sample points X which is characterized by its membership function $f_A(x)$. We would like to have a definition for the amount of uncertainty

when a decision on sample point x should be taken about its assignment to some partition of X.

Definition 1: Let the decision rule be given by: if $f_A(x) \geq a$,
then $d_a(x) = 1$ and $x \in C_A$, else $d_a(x) = 0$ and $x \in C_{A'}$, with $a \in$
[0,1], then, $C_a(X) = (C_A, A_{A'} | d_a(x))$ represents a partition of X
with respect to fuzzy set A, given a decision function $d_a(x)$.

Remark: a does not depend on x.

Definition 2: The uncertainty in the decision $d_a(x)$ with respect
to fuzzy set A and sample point x can be represented by

$$i_x(A) = |f_A(x) - d_a(x)| \tag{3}$$

Remark: For $i_x(A)$ it is always true that $i_x(A) \geq 0$ and $i_x(A)|$
$(d_a(x)=1) = i_x(A)|(d_a(x)=0$.

In consequence of definition 2, it follows:

Definition 3: The average amount of uncertainty in mapping the
fuzzy set A on the partition $C_a(X) = (C_A, C_{A'} | d_a(x))$:

$$I_X(A) = \frac{1}{N} \sum_X |f_A(x) - d_a(x)| \tag{4}$$

where X is the set of sample points and N is the cardinality of X.

We indicate the special case $a = \frac{1}{2}$ by $d^*(x)$; consequently,
$C^*(X)$ and $I_X^*(A)$ will refer to this special case.

Three properties are very useful:

Property 1: $I_X^*(A) = \frac{1}{N} \sum_X |f_A(x) - d^*(x)| \tag{5}$

$$= \frac{1}{N} \sum_X \text{MIN} [f_A(x), f_{A'}(x)]$$

Property 2: $I_X^*(A\ B) = \frac{1}{N} \sum_X \text{MIN} [f_A(x), f_B(x)] \tag{6}$

Property 3: If $I_X(A.S) = \frac{1}{N} \sum_S |f_A(x) - d_a(x)|$ for $S \subset X \tag{7}$

then $I_X(A.S) + I_X(A.(X-S)) = I_X(A)$

Note: Proofs are omitted due to space limitations; for greater
detail, see [12].

As a consequence of the above properties it can be proved
that a partition $C^*(X) = (C_A, C_{A'} | d^*(x))$ is optimal to the extent

that the amount of uncertainty $I_X(A)$ is minimal; thus, we have the inequality

$$I_X(A) \geq I_X^*(A) \tag{8}$$

Next, we shall define a quantity which represents the degree of similarity in decision making about pairs of points in X. Roughly speaking such a quantity will be maximum (or minimum) if there is complete agreement in the way of decision making for each of the points of a given pair; on the contrary, the quantity will be minimum (or maximum) if the decision making for each of the points is completely opposite.

Intuitively, such a quantity is related to any quantity which represents the degree of statistical dependence.

If x, y ε X we set $f_A(x,y) = \frac{1}{2}(f_A(x)+f_A(y))$ (9)

Then, it follows:

$$i_{xy}(A) = |f_A(x,y) - d_a(x,y)| = MIN\ [f_A(x,y), f_{A'}(x,y)] \tag{10}$$

Now, we define a function $j_A(x:y)$ as follows:

Definition 4: The increase in the amount of uncertainty about the decision concerning fuzzy set A with respect to the less ambiguous variable in the case that a point pair (x,y) is taken into account instead of a single point, is defined as:

$$j_A(x:y) = i_{xy}(A) - MIN\ [i_x(A), i_y(A)] \tag{11}$$

It can easily be shown that

$$j_A(x:y) = \frac{1}{2}\ |f_A(x) - f_A(y)| \tag{12}$$

Thus, $j_A(x:y)$ represents also the degree of similarity in category-belongingness of a point pair (x,y).

Remark: The properties of j(x:y) are such that this quantity may serve very well as a point pair (dis)similarity function in a 'fuzzy' clustering technique. The behaviour of the function j( ) is completely specified once a rule of membership-assignment has been selected. In section VII, emphasis will be given to some local and global rules.

V. The Amount of Structure

We assume that an appropriate membership operator has been chosen, for all $x \in X$ and all categories (see section VII). Then, if x_i, x_j are two sample points in X, we define

$$s(x_i, x_j) = 1 - 2j(x_i : x_j) \qquad (13)$$

as a similarity function.

Since similarity and dissimilarity are obviously related as $s(x_i, x_j) = 1 - d(x_i, x_j)$, it follows that $d(x_i, x_j) = 2j(x_i : x_j)$ is a measure of dissimilarity between x_i and x_j.

In view of this dissimilarity measure we have:

Definition 5: $X_p = \{x_i \mid \underset{j}{\text{MAX}} \, d(x_i, x_j) \leq p\}$ \qquad (14)

as a prototype of a partition of X with respect to fuzzy set A.

Where $\quad p = \frac{1}{2} (\underset{i}{\text{MAX}} \, [f_A(x_i)] - \underset{j}{\text{MIN}} \, [f_A(x_j)])$ \qquad (15)

Then, the fuzzy set A is transformed into a partition $(X_p, X - X_p)$ according to an optimal ratio of the average 'within group' similarity and the average 'between group' similarity.

(Proof is omitted due to space limitation).

Definition 6: The average 'within group' similarity is given by

$$S_W(A.X_p) = 1 - \frac{2}{N_p(N_p - 1)} \sum_{x_i \in X_p} \sum_{x_j \in X_p} j_A(x_i : x_j) \qquad (16)$$

Definition 7: The average similarity between group and outside is given by

$$S_B(A.X_p) = 1 - \frac{2}{N_p(N - N_p)} \sum_{x_i \in X_p} \sum_{x_j \in (X - X_p)} j_A(x_i : x_j) \qquad (17)$$

Remark: If $(X - X_p) = \emptyset$, then $j( )$ is degenerated and should be set to zero.

Definition 8: The amount of structure of the fuzzy set A will be expressed as:

$$H(A.X_p) = 1 - \frac{S_B(A.X_p)}{S_W(A.X_p)} \qquad (18)$$

It is easily verified that $H(A.X_p)$ satisfies the following properties:

(i) $\quad 0 \leq H(A.X_p) \leq 1$ $\qquad\qquad$ (19)

(ii) $\quad H(A.X_p) = 0 \quad$ iff $\quad d(x_i,x_j) = 0$ for all $x_i, x_j \epsilon X$ $\qquad$ (20)

(iii) $H(A.X_p) = 1 \quad$ iff $\quad d(x_i,x_j) = 0$ for all $x_i, x_j \epsilon X_p$ $\qquad$ (21)

$\qquad\qquad$ and $d(x_i,x_k) = 1$ for all $x_i \epsilon X_p, x_k \epsilon (X-X_p)$

Maximum structure corresponds to $H(A.X_p) = 1$ and minimum when $H(A.X_p) = 0$.

Example: $\quad f_A^{(1)}(x)$ and $f_A^{(2)}(x)$ are two arbitrary membership functions of a fuzzy set A; both result in the same partition $(X_p, X-X_p)$.

In table I the numerical values for the 'within group' similarity, the similarity between group and outside, and the amount of structure are given for both cases.

TABLE I:	$W_W(A.X_p)$	$S_B(A.X_p)$	$H(A.X_p)$
(1)	0.96	0.83	0.05
(2)	0.82	0.68	0.17

VI. The Clustering Model

The clustering model is based upon the following criterion function

$$G = k - \sum_{i=1}^{k} H(A_i.X_{p_i}) \qquad\qquad (22)$$

The motivation for using G as a criterion is straight forward. If the amount of structure for every category is 1 (situation where data easily be grouped into k categories), the criterion G would take a value 0. In most practical situations $(H(A_i,X_{p_i}) < 1$ for every i which will result in G > 0. However, that partition which minimizes G is supposed to be the partition most closely to the 'natural' partition.

Consider further a single vector x_h. Assume x_h has been assigned to category C_i, then, we will determine the change in G as a result of a reclassification of x_h in, say C_j. In view of this we define

$$r(x_h,C_j) = H(A_j.X_{p_j}^+) - H(A_j.X_{p_j}) \qquad\qquad (23)$$

$X_{p_j}^+$ is the set of all elements contained in X_{p_j} <u>and</u> the element x_h. Likewise:

$$r(x_h, C_i) = H(A_i \cdot X_{p_i}) - H(A_i \cdot X_{p_i}^-) \qquad (24)$$

where $X_{p_i}^-$ is the set of all the elements contained in X_{p_i} <u>except</u> x_h. (23) and (24) represent the changes in G as a result of a reclassification of x_h. In the following possible situations the action should be specified as follows:

(i) $0 \le r(x_h, C_j) \le r(x_h, C_i)$: x_h remains classified in C_i,

(ii) $0 \le r(x_h, C_i) < r(x_h, C_j)$: add x_h to C_j and delete x_h from C_i,

(iii) $r(x_h, C_i) < 0 < r(x_h, C_j)$: add x_h to C_j and delete x_h from C_j,

(iv) $r(x_h, C_j) < 0 < r(x_h, C_i)$: x_h remains classified in C_i,

(v) $r(x_h, C_i) < r(x_h, C_j) < 0$: add x_h to C_j and delete x_h from C_i,

(vi) $r(x_h, C_j) < r(x_h, C_i) < 0$: x_h remains classified in C_i.

Consequently, we can found a <u>reclassification rule</u> like:

<u>If</u> $\underset{j \ne l}{MAX} [r(x_h, C_j)] = r(x_h, C_j) > r(x_h, C_i)$ $\qquad (25)$

<u>then</u> add x_h to C_j and delete x_h from C_i, <u>otherwise</u> x_h remains classified in C_i.

This rule must be employed for all x_h, $h = 1, 2, \ldots, N$. If there are no reclassifications the procedure is terminated, otherwise a new set of $f_{A_i}(x)$ should be assigned for all $x \in X$, $i = 1, 2, \ldots, k$.

The following example shows the behaviour of the reclassification rule applied on the same sample point, but from different points of view.

<u>Example</u>: In this example we evaluate two partitions which only differ in one sample point, say x_h. Figure 2 shows both points of view: a. x_h is an element of category II and we consider a reclassification from II to I, and b. x_h is an element of I and we consider a reclassification from I to II.

<u>Note</u>: the data has been taken from [13].

Table II presents the numerical evaluation of viewpoint a. and viewpoint b.

462

Table II:

a.

$S_W(I) = 0.79$ $S_W(II)= 0.86$ $S_B(I,II)=0.23$	$S_W(I^+) = 0.70$ $S_W(II^-)= 0.90$ $S_B(I^+,II^-)=0.25$	
$H(I) = 0.71$ $H(II) = 0.73$	$H(I^+) = 0.64$ $H(II^-) = 0.72$	$r(x_h,I)=H(I^+)-H(I)=-0.07$ $r(x_h,II)=H(II)-H(II^-)=0.01$
Since $r(x_h,I) < 0 < r(x_h,II)$, it follows: $\underline{x_h}$ $\underline{remains\ classi}$-$\underline{fied\ in\ II}$.		

b.

$S_W(I) = 0.81$ $S_W(II)= 0.81$ $S_B(I,II)=0.25$	$S_W(I^-) = 0.88$ $S_W(II^+)= 0.76$ $S_B(I^-,II^+)=0.25$	
$H(I) = 0.69$ $H(II) = 0.69$	$H(I^-) = 0.72$ $H(II^+) = 0.67$	$r(x_h,I)=H(I)-H(I^-)=-0.03$ $r(x_h,II)-H(II^+)-H(II)=-0.02$
Since $r(x_h,I) < r(x_h,II) < 0$, it follows: $\underline{add\ x_h\ to\ II\ and}$ $\underline{delete\ x_h\ from\ I}$.		

Note: Partition a. results from the basic Isodata clustering procedure, b. is a result of a min. squared error procedure; also, b.
results from the Jarvis-Patrick clustering algorithm. (see [11],
[14]).

In conclusion, partition a. should be considered more
natural' than b., though this decision is obviously very marginal.

VII. Membership Assignment

The procedure as described in the previous section demands
for an initial category-assignment. Therefore, we have the following possibilities: (i) the initial category-assignment is a
complete guess, (ii) the initial category-assignment results from
a simple 'hard' clustering model. This was the case in the previous example. However, the most important question is that of the
membership-assignment. This means that there should be some

membership operator (local or global) which assigns to every sample point a set of membership values in accordance with the set of fuzzy sets, contributing additional information for discriminating between categories. Figure 3 illustrates some local and global operators.

<u>Local operators:</u> (see Figure 3a.)

For : $X_j^{(s)} = \{x | d(x_j, x) \leq s\}$, $n^{(s)} = ||X_j^{(s)}||$, $n_I^{(s)}$ +

$$n_{II}^{(s)} = n^{(s)}$$

we have: $f_{A_I}(x_j) = n_I^{(s)} / n^{(s)}$

Likewise: $f_{A_I}(x_j) = \{MIN\limits_{x \epsilon (X-I)} [d(x, x_j)]\} / s$ for $d(x, x_j) \leq s$

$$= 1 \qquad\qquad\qquad \text{for } d(x, x_j) > s$$

<u>Global operator:</u> (see Figure 3b.)

$$f_{A_I}(x_j) = \frac{\sum\limits_{x \epsilon X} d^2(x, x_j) - \sum\limits_{x \epsilon I} d^2(x, x_j)}{\sum\limits_{x \epsilon X} d^2(x, x_j)} : \frac{1}{K-1}$$

In conclusion, the membership-assignment is very dependent of the nature of the membership operator. The choice of the operator determines the nature of the similarity function, and, consequently, the meaning of the preference of one way of partitioning over another.

VIII. Experimental Results

The data that we used in this experiment originates from two categories handwritten numerals, category "0" and category "3". Each numeral is represented by a 16-dimensional pattern vector. In order to visualize the structure of the set of sample points the Patrick-Fischer non-parametric two-dimensional mapping algorithm [15] has been applied.

Figure 4a and 4b show two clustering results, (1) and (2), in which 0 and 3 denote sample points from category "0" and "3" respectively. Consequently, A_1 and A_2 are the induced fuzzy sets, according to the number of categories taken into account (k=2). Both clusterings result in approximately the same (optimal) value of a classical performance measure.

Table III shows the evaluation of the suggested clusterings by means of the similarity function $j(x_i:x_j)$.

Note: In this experiment a nearest neighbor local operator has been used.

Table III:

A_1	A_2	A_1	A_2
$S_W(A_1.X_{P_1})=0.98$	$S_W(A_2.X_{P_2})=0.85$	$S_W(A_1.X_{P_1})=0.97$	$S_W(A_2.X_{P_2})=0.94$
$S_B(A_1.X_{P_1})=0.20$	$S_B(A_2.X_{P_2})=0.20$	$S_B(A_1.X_{P_1})=0.05$	$S_B(A_2.X_{P_2})=0.05$
$H(A_1.X_{P_1})=0.80$	$H(A_2.X_{P_2})=0.76$	$H(A_1.X_{P_1})=0.95$	$H(A_2.X_{P_2})=0.95$
$H_{total}^{(1)}=1.56$		$H_{total}^{(2)}=1.90$	

From this it follows that (2) should be considered as the most 'natural' partition, which is in complete accordance with the real categories they belong to.

Acknowledgements

The author wishes to thank Professor Y. Boxma (Delft University of Technology) for his advice and encouragement.

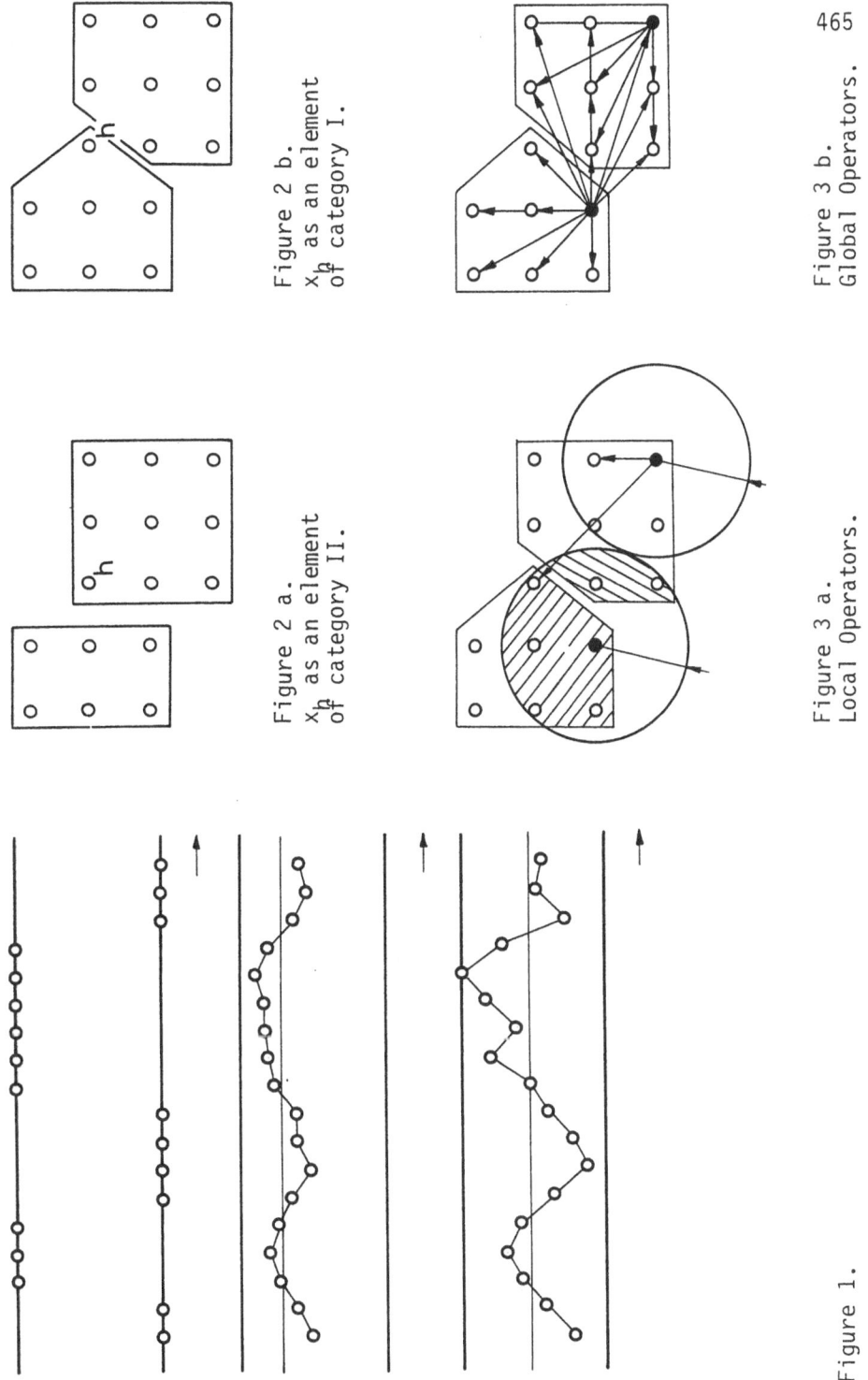

Figure 2 b.
x_h as an element
of category I.

Figure 3 b.
Global Operators.

Figure 2 a.
x_h as an element
of category II.

Figure 3 a.
Local Operators.

Figure 1.

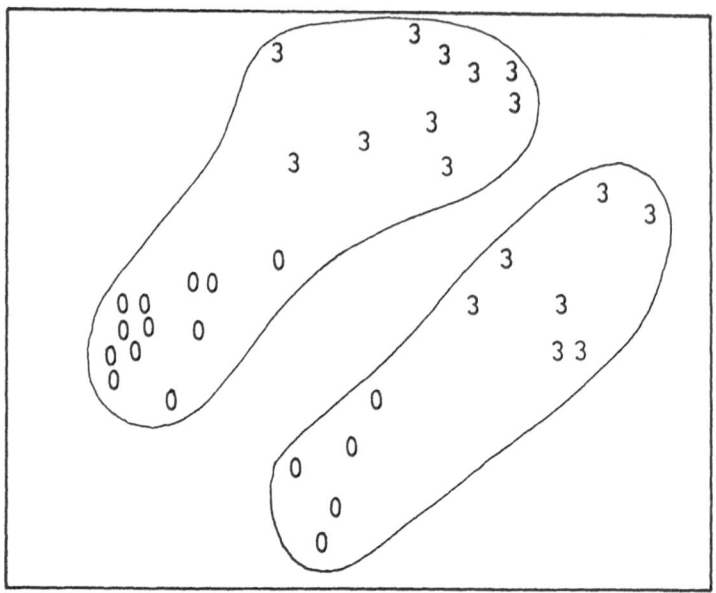

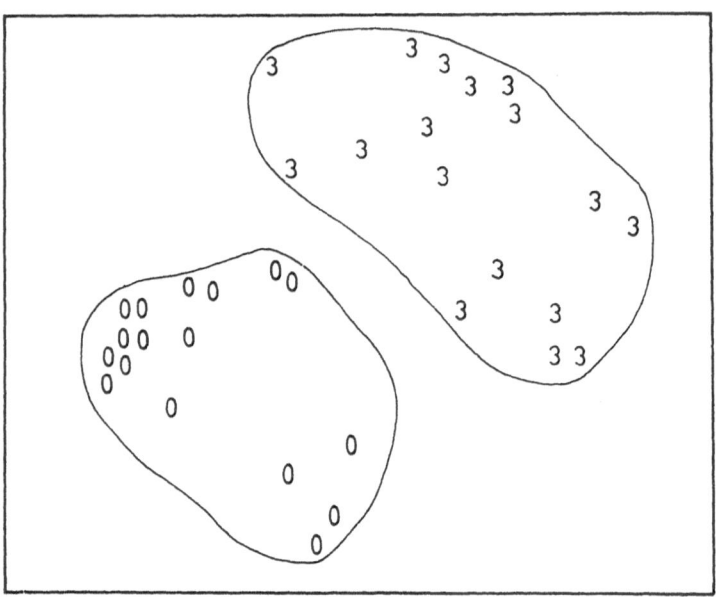

Figure 4.   Two Clustering Results.

References

1. Bellman, R., Kalaba, R., Zadeh, L., Abstraction and Pattern Classification, Journ. of Mathm. Analysis and Appl., Vol. 13, 1 (1966).

2. Gitman, I., Levine, M. D., An algorithm for detecting Uni-model Fuzzy Sets and its application as a Clustering Technique, IEEE Trans. on Comp., Vol. C-19, No. 7, 583 (1970).

3. Gitman, I., A parameter-free Clustering Model, Pattern Recognition, Vol. 4, 307 (1972).

4. Ruspini, H. R., Numerical methods for fuzzy clustering, Inf. Sci. 2, 319 (1970).

5. Dunn, J. C., A fuzzy relative of the ISODATA process and its use in detecting Compact Well-Separated Clusters, Journ. of Cybernetics, 3, 32 (1974).

6. Bezdek, J., Fuzzy Mathematics in Pattern Classification, Ph.D. Thesis, Cornell University (1973).

7. Diday, E., Optimization in Non-Hierarchical Clustering, Pattern Recognition, Vol. 6, 17 (1974).

8. Zadeh, L. A., Fuzzy Sets, Inf. Contr. 8, 338 (1965).

9. Watanabe, M. S., A Unified view of Clustering Algorithms, IFIP Cong. '71, Ljubljana, Booklet TA-2, 64 (1971).

10. Duda, R. O., Hart, P. E., Pattern Classification and Scene Analysis, John Wiley, (1973).

11. Tou, J. T., Gonzalez, R. C., Pattern Recognition Principles, Addison-Wesley Publ. Com. (1974).

12. Backer, E., A non-statistical type of uncertainty in fuzzy events, Trans. of the Colloquium on Inf. Theory, Keszthely, in press (1975).

13. Dubes, R., Jain, A. K., Clustering Techniques: The User's Dilemma, Technical Report TR 75-01, Dept. Comp. Sci., Michigan State Univ. (1975).

14. Jarvis, R. A., Patrick, E. A., Clustering using a similarity measure based on Shared Near Neighbors, IEEE Trans. on Comp., vol. C-22, 1025 (1973).

15. Patrick, E. A., Fischer II, F. P., Nonparametric Feature Selection, IEEE Trans. on Inf. Theory, Vol. IT-15, No. 5, 577 (1969).

THE ROLE OF THE ASSOCIATIVE PROCESSOR IN PATTERN RECOGNITION

Aaron B. Navarro

Synectics Corporation

I. Introduction

Many computer applications require identical operations on multiple sets of data. Present day digital computers accomplish these tasks through the use of sequential central processors capable of addressing only one datum at a time within any single data set.

One class of problems that has been resolved by such processors deals with the identification and location of small fixed binary patterns in large two-dimensional pixel arrays. However, this has proven to be very costly, primarily because of the large size of the pixel arrays and the extremely long execution times associated with the processing of these arrays. In the light of these potential difficulties, considerable attention has recently been directed to a new and promising approach provided by the appearance of the Associative Processor (AP). The AP provides a hardware realization of content addressability, parallel processing, unprecedented I/O capability, and seems well suited to data processing operations encountered in pattern recognition.

The work, presented in this paper, discusses the many AP capabilities and AP algorithms for finding well-defined discrete binary patterns in a two-dimensional pixel array. With these algorithms a time saving of several orders of magnitude is expected in solving the aforementioned pattern recognition problems.

II. Associative Processing

The term "associative", as used in describing the characteristics of this class of computer organization, predates modern computer technology and relates more closely to describing theories on human brain functions, e.g., recall by association. Modern computer-related usage of the adjective "associative" now refers to interrelationships between data elements rather than to the storage structure itself.

Thus, any machine capable of performing the operation aRb can be considered a relational machine (hence an associative one). However, some machines are designed to perform such operations in a more highly efficient manner. Two such machines are considered by this paper in addition to the conventional sequential processor. They are the parallel machine, and the "associative" processor (Figure 1). In reality the "associative" processor (AP) is simply a parallel machine with a special memory architecture called Content Addressable Memory (CAM). CAM enables access of memory by its contents rather than requiring conventional physical location addresses - either absolute or relative. In addition, the AP is able to perform parallel arithmetic and logical functions, as any parallel machine, on all or on a selected subset of words in its memory.

The AP has recently been implemented by Goodyear (the Goodyear Associative Processor (GAP) known as STARAN) and by Raytheon (the RAP).

Key to the understanding of unique AP capabilities are the concepts of search, mask, response store, bit slice, and word slice.

The CAM is organized as a two-dimensional array (e.g., 256 X 256 bits for STARAN) which may be addressed in a conventional fashion (the word or partial word known as a word slice) or in an orthogonal fashion (the bit slice). The addressabilities are shown in Figure 2. In bit slice processing the same bit in every word of the array is subject to identical and parallel processing as done to a word on a conventional machine.

The AP words may be divided into arbitrary fields, each field of size appropriate to its use and containing necessary information. Any field can participate in a "search" operation whereby a given bit configuration (key) is simultaneously related to the field contents for all words. Relations include EQ, GT, LT, etc. All word fields satisfying the search requirements cause a response bit to be raised. The summary of all such responses (positive and negative) is called a response store. The response store for this example is, in reality, a bit slice itself. This slice can and does participate in AP processing by masking memory word addresses that are to be active for further operations.

In addition to the array organization and response store, the AP, as any other parallel machine, has multiple processing elements (PE's). For the GAP, one PE per word is employed.

Collectively, the PE's provide the capability to:

o   operate on all or a selected subset of words in memory,

o   store the results of search, arithmetic, and logical operations,

o   logically combine data from successive operations.

Lastly, AP Input/Output may be accomplished in bit serial word parallel mode.

In summary, a substantial gain can thus be expected when the AP is applied to areas in which high parallelism exists or when relational operations are required.

III. Search Strategies

The following sections deal with the problem of finding all locations in a large N x N array at which are located a two-dimensional search pattern of m x m array elements (Figure 3).

The definitions and capabilities of sequential parallel, and associative machines from the introductory sections are used. Strategies for searching over more than one pattern are also given.

A. The Sequential Machine

The sequential machine is limited by its capability to process against only one information element at a time - be it a bit, byte, or word. In general, the location of a two-dimensional binary pattern of size m x m pixels in a large array of N x N pixels requires examining each of $(N - m + 1)^2$ pixels. If we assign the entity $S(N,m,P)$ equal to the number of searches needed to find P patterns of size m x m in an N x N array,

$$S_{SEQ}(N,m,P) = (N - m + 1)^2$$

The independence of S_{SEQ} with respect to P arises from the basic structure of the sequential processor. In order to determine if any single pattern exists, one can easily arrange the m^2 bits of the pattern (and the object being examined) into a one-dimensional bit string, thus allowing simple table look-up (or one can look at m bits at a time through a hierarchical decision tree whose branches are set by the desired patterns). It is this characteristic that has been exploited in the recognition algorithms currently available and under development.

B. The Associative Machine

In staying with the definitions of the introductory sections, the associative machine is primarily a partially parallel machine with content addressable memory. It is the characteristics of CAM that are of interest here - i.e., how CAM allows direct location of all memory cells containing the desired pattern.

Current CAM/AP architecture allows search in either of two dimensions, but not simultaneous search in both directions. A "row" of m bits in the pattern may be simultaneously compared to all slices of m bits in a N-bit column, in "m" bit-slice searches. This results in $(N - m + 1)$ x m searches to locate all positions in the N x N array that contain the pattern of m x 1 bits. As

each "row" of m bits in the m x m pattern may be different, m
such searches are required. Thus, a first estimate -

$$S_{AP} = P \, m^2 (N - m + 1)$$

As, at most 2^m "row" patterns need to be searched,

$$S_{AP} \leq 2^m \, m^2 (N - m + 1)$$

One would think that a few gains could be made by keeping track of
row pattern "hits" and by using these hits to direct fewer searches
on sequential row patterns. Such a saving is, in fact, quite small
as each row search covers N rows simultaneously. All N rows of a
m bit wide slice would need to be non-responsive before any sav-
ings could take place. Even then, as the search is so fast, little
is gained.

C. The Parallel/Relational Machine

It is quite clear that, at most, m^2 binary relation (operators) are required to uniquely specify a m x m binary pattern.
The simplicity of these operators (equality of elements, inequality
of elements, and state of an element) suggests that significantly
fewer relationships could be involved in developing a single relational representation for simultaneous searching of more than one
pattern. This concept reflects the physical principle of entropy.
The more one can specify rigid structure through detailed information, the lower the entropy.

The lowest entropy search is the search for a single unique
pattern. As one relaxes the maximal number of constraints needed
to specify a unique pattern, more patterns will fit the remaining
constraints. A simple case for this argument is the search for a
unique pattern or its inverse. Here, at most $m^2 - 1$ relationships
need to be specified; a simple inequality relation between the
neighborhood central point and its $m^2 - 1$ neighbors uniquely specifies $m^2 - 1$ pixels in terms of the center pixel. Inverting the
state of the center pixel inverts the state of the remaining $m^2 -
1$ pixels of the pattern thereby inverting the entire pattern.

Other examples are now under investigation for those groups of patterns (such as crosses, T's, and no junction cases) of specific interest to scene analysis and graphic processing. However, no matter what the application, the larger the number of patterns in a search class, the lower the number of operations required. To the best of the author's knowledge no relational machine is commercially available at this time. Such a machine would be able to simultaneously execute a process involving two (or more) relatively positioned array elements for all elements on the array. Mathematically, for elements A_i, at array positions $X_i = (X_i Y_i)$ and B_i at position $X_i + \Delta$, the machine would simultaneously execute $A_i R B_i$ for all i's in the array. Such an architecture is well within the state of the art and could be implemented if there is adequate demand.

For such a machine, the maximum number of operations necessary to locate and identify any of 2^m patterns in the N x N array is:

$$S_{REL} \leq m^2$$

It is, however, important to note that the Goodyear STARAN machine can also be employed in a relational manner. In this case only a bit slice at a time may be related to another bit slice for a limited number of operations (AND,XOR). The number of such operations to be performed depends upon the magnitude of Δ but will not exceed N. Thus, the number of operations is limited by:

$$S_{APR} \leq m^2 N$$

This indicates a potential reduction ratio $\dfrac{(N - m + 1)2^{-m}}{N}$ which, for N >> m approaches 2^{-m}.

IV. Algorithm Timing

A. The Sequential Processor

The algorithm to be presented has the flow chart of Figure 4.

To create the table address, one must string the bits of the neighbor states into a single word. Under best of cases with no I/0, and m smaller than a word size, m addresses must be accessed, the contents masked, and the bits shifted into place. Thus a minimum of 3m cycles are involved - this is highly dependent on machine instruction set depth. To this one adds the address calculation overhead and mask determination. Assuming a multi-register CPU with appropriate indexing, this may be accomplished in approximately 10 instructions. Also, one should add overhead of another $3m + 10$ instructions when word boundaries are crossed by the m pixel byte. This occurs in 100 $\frac{(m - 1)}{W}$ percent of the time. Assuming a 16-bit minicomputer and $m = 3$, another $\frac{3m+10}{8}$ instructions are involved. These numbers are conservative and represent only the innermost loop. Their sum is thus:

$$I = \frac{(15 + m)}{16} * (3m + 10) * (N - m + 1)^2$$

B. The Associative/Parallel Algorithm

A total of 3 instructions per bit slice is required for each slice in the m-pattern. Of these three, one is bookkeeping, one is a search command, and one is a store response store command. Additional bookkeeping to change the field of the common register is required every m searches. Therefore a total of $(3 + 3/m) * m$ instructions are required to search for an m-bit pattern. This procedure is reproduced m times to cover the full m^2 pattern and must be repeated $N - m + 1$ times to cover the array. Thus, for single pattern:

$$I_{single} = m^2 (N - m + 1) (3 + 3/m)$$

When a class of patterns is to be searched:

$$I_{class} = 2^m m^2 (N - m + 1) (3 + 3/m)$$

C. The Associative/Relational Algorithm

As applied to existing machinery, the parallel/relational algorithm cannot perform to its maximal potential. However, an approximate timing for an AP implementation of the algorithm can be obtained as follows.

W is the word size for a sequential processor.

For each bit slice, one must establish the field positions for both elements of a relation. This requires approximately 3 instructions. Three more instructions are utilized in manipulating the bit slice to align it for the relational process. The process itself takes one instruction, and the "AND"ing of the results back into an output bit slice takes two more instructions. An additional instruction is included for sequencing for a total of ten instructions. m^2 relations are to be computed for each bit slice (i.e., for each pixel in a bit slice) and N such slices must be processed. The total number of instructions is approximately:

$$I_{rel} \doteq 10m^2N$$

V. Analysis and Conclusions

All the fiven times reflect just the primary operations absolutely necessary for the searches and may therefore be considered as low values obtainable only by ideal machines. To these times, I/O time must be added to real world calculations on arrays larger than those provided by available hardware.

Despite these cautions, the relative magnitudes of the derived timings are expected to hold true. From these relative magnitudes it should become clear that the relational algorithm on the associative machine offers the best performance when one searches for multiple patterns; however, when a single pattern is involved, the associative/parallel algorithm provides the best performance.

The ratio of timings $I_{relational}/I_{associative}$, for N >> m becomes:

$$R \sim \frac{3.3m}{1 + m}$$

This is relatively constant as a function of m and is in the range of 3. Thus, errors of a few instruction counts in developing the relational timings could increase the advantage already given to the single pattern associative/parallel search for those cases involving search for a single pattern.

There is low sensitivity to errors in the ratio of $I_{relational}/I_{associative}$ for multiple pattern searches as the 2^m factor completely dominates. Thus for multiple pattern searches, the proper search strategy is relational.

Both ratios are basically independent of N (for N >> m) so that no change in advantage would be expected for larger arrays.

Lastly, it is quite clear that, even with an ideal sequential processor, the search times can be reduced by several orders of magnitude with an AP.

In summary, three techniques for identifying the existence of one or more two-dimensional patterns in a large two-dimensional pixel array have been presented and the timings for existing processors have been computed. The emergence of associative and parallel processing hardware clearly provides significant computational advantage when applied to the described pattern recognition problem.

VI. Acknowledgments

I wish to thank Synectics Corporation for supporting this work, and Barry K. Moritz for his contributions to this paper.

478

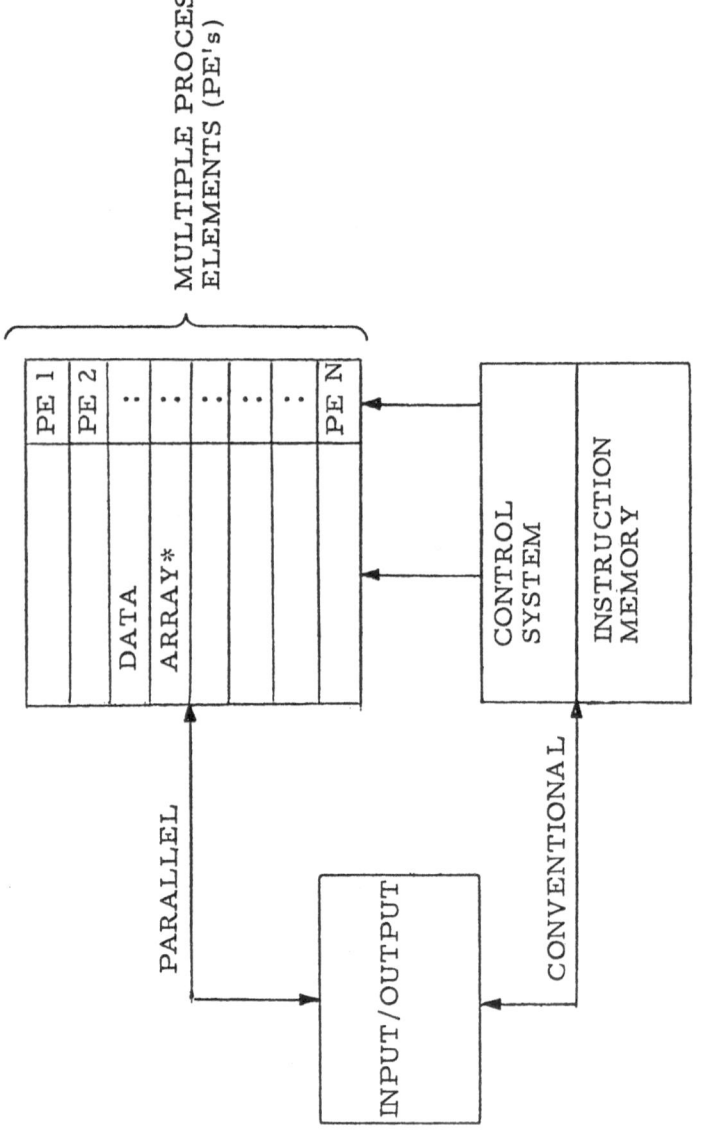

Figure 1. Parallel Machines and Associative Processors.

* CONTENT ADDRESSABLE FOR ASSOCIATIVE MACHINES

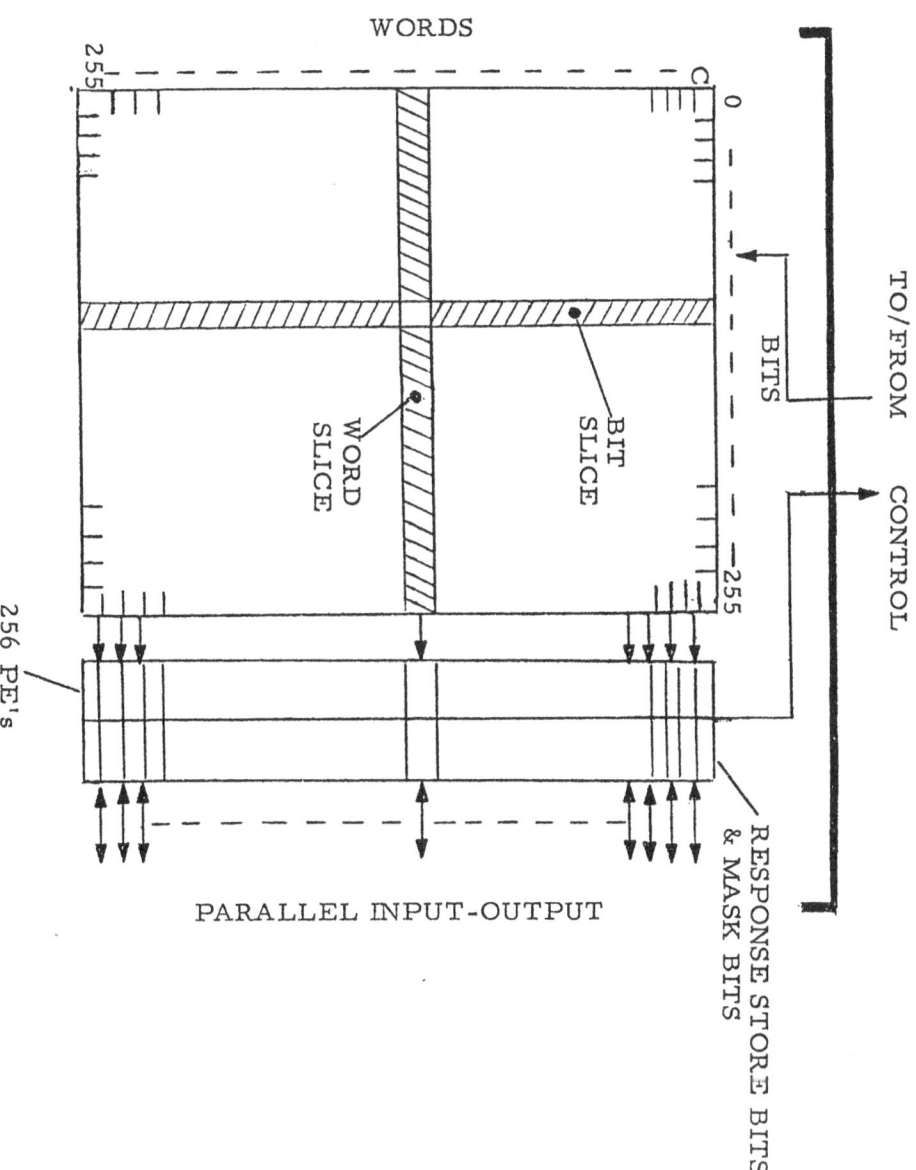

Figure 2.
Associative Processor Array (256 words x 256 bits per array).

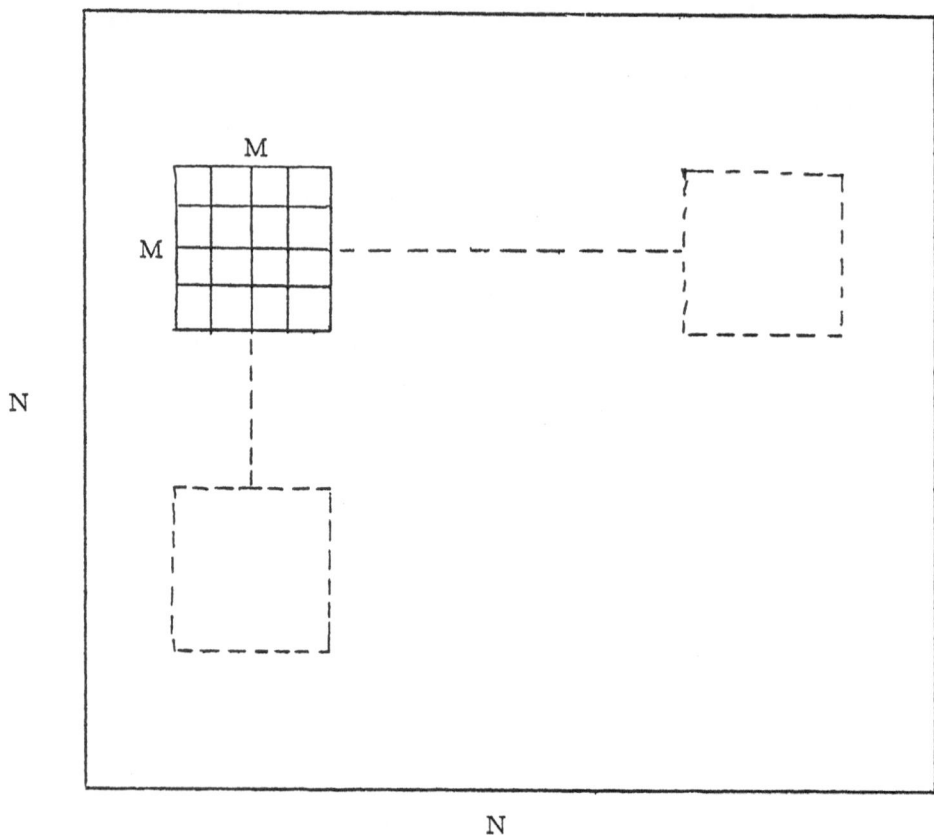

Figure 3.
Finding an M x M Binary Pattern in an N x N Binary Array.

References

1. Goodyear Aerospace Corp., User and Programming Manuals for STARAN, GER-15096, GER-15028.

2. Radosevic, R. G.,"Associative Array Processing Techniques Applied to Automated Cartography,"Goodyear Aerospace Corporation.

3. Rosenfeld, A., Picture Processing by Computer, Academic Press, 1969.

4. Yau, S. D., and Yang, C. C., "Pattern Recognition by Using an Associative Memory", IEEE Transactions on Electronic Computers, December 1966.

5. Deutch, E. S., "Thinning Algorithms on Rectangular, Hexagonal, and Triangular Arrays", CACM, September 1972.

6. Murthy, I. S. N., and Udupa, K. J., "A Search Algorithm for Skeletonization of Thick Patterns", Computer Graphics and Image Processing, 3, 1974.

7. Hilditch, C. J., "Linear Skeletons from Square Cupboards", Machine Intelligence, 4, 1969.

PERCEPTUAL PROCESSES IN READING AND WORD RECOGNITION

James F. Juola, Glen A. Taylor, and Chong S. Choe

University of Kansas

I. Introduction

The topic of this paper is the human information-processing system involved in reading and recognizing words. A model of perception is presented in which information from a visual display interacts with information retrieved from an observer's memory system to produce perceptual experience. Results from experiments on word and letter string perception are discussed which focus on how memory for past visual stimuli functions in interpreting current input. Of particular interest are comparisons of tasks which show facilitative effects of familiarity, structural regularity, and meaningfulness of the display versus tasks in which performance is insensitive to such manipulations. Task differences are used to discover ways, in the sequence of events that determines our visual experience, characteristics of words operate to facilitate perception.

Preparation of this paper was supported in part by funds from Biomedical Sciences Support Grant RR-07037 from tne National Institutes of Health and from Grant BMS74-12801 from the National Science Foundation. We thank Timothy Miller for his assistance and Carl McFarland and Michael Young for their comments on an earlier version of this paper.

This paper is about the perceptual and memory processes involved in normal, adult reading. Reading is an information-processing skill involving abstraction of meaning from arbitrary and conventional visual symbols. This skill obviously depends on information derived from the stimulus as well as that retrieved from the reader's memory system. The information conveyed by printed alphabetic languages is highly redundant. Some redundancy is due to semantic and syntactic constraints placed on words by the meaning and structure of the sentences in which they are embedded. Since the skilled reader is aware of such constraints, words in text can be identified with less attention to their visual representations than would be required if they were presented in isolation (Smith, 1971; Tulving and Gold, 1963). Redundancy also exists within words. This is reflected in the relative likelihoods with which letters occur independent of context. The latter constraints are generalized into orthographic rules that determine permissable letter sequences in words. Knowledge of these sources of information is internalized by the skilled reader and used in efficient reading. A major goal of reading research has been to determine how linguistic knowledge interacts with incoming visual information during reading.

It is assumed that literate adults have internalized representations of letters and words in memory, including information about their auditory and visual properties. Frequently occurring letter clusters such as syllables or spelling patterns might also have separate representations in memory (Gibson and Levin, 1975; Smith and Spoehr, 1974). How internal representations of letters, letter clusters, and words function in reading is a major topic of this paper. For now, let us describe these as possible candidates for perceptual units. Perceptual units can be thought of as permanent abstractions of commonly occurring stimuli that can be compared directly with unanalyzed information detected by the visual system. A match results in recognition

of the stimulus, although conscious experience of what is perceived might be determined by which memory units are activated
as much as by the stimulus itself. These issues will be recon-
sidered after a brief description of fundamental visual processes
in reading and word recognition. Some research in this area will
then be discussed that focuses on the problem of identifying the
appropriate units of analysis in word perception. Finally, we
will suggest how perceptual and memory systems might be integrated during reading.

II. A Model of Visual Processes in Reading

While reading, the eyes fixate a series of points as they
scan a line of text. Each fixation lasts for about 250 milliseconds followed by a 25 to 50 millisecond saccadic movement to
the next fixation point. Most fixations follow the linear order
of the text, but even in skilled readers about 15% are regressive
movements to earlier parts of the passage. Adult readers tend
to fixate every word or two, leading to the normal reading rate
of about 300 words per minute. We do not know how much visual
information is processed during an eye fixation, but research has
shown that very little useful information is available beyond the
immediate bounds of the word or small group of words being fix-
ated (Rayner, 1975). Thus, when a single word is presented in a
perception experiment, the visual processes involved are probably
similar to those operating during an eye fixation in reading.

When the image of a word is projected onto the retina,
brightness changes are channeled along neural pathways to the
visual cortex of the brain. We know about the form of information at this level from recordings of the activity in cortical
cells in cats, monkeys, and other animals. Single cells have
been found in the visual cortex that respond only to lines,
edges, or angles having specific orientations. As Smith and
Spoehr (1974) have pointed out, "these results are of great importance ... because line segments at a particular orientation

are very likely candidates for critical features of letters."
Thus the raw materials for the recognition of words are realized
physiologically. Learning to recognize letters and words presumably involves the development of internal categories defined
in terms of their critical features and the relations among these
features.

Figure 1 presents a schematic representation of the processes involved in visual perception. Information from the retina
is assumed to be registered in some central locus called the
"icon," which preserves a two-dimensional representation of the
stimulus as it was projected onto the retina. The icon is built
up within 100 milliseconds of stimulus onset, remains at maximum
resolution while the stimulus is on, and begins to decay after
the stimulus is turned off. Evidence from studies of brief visual displays indicates that some information is available in the
icon for several hundred milliseconds after the display has terminated (Sperling, 1960).

While information is represented in the icon, a visual image
is constructed that is based on iconic inputs as well as on activated visual codes from long-term memory. The visual image is
assumed to represent our conscious experience of "seeing". Thus
visual perception is an active, constructive process in which
contributions from memory are always present (cf. Neisser, 1967).
The involvement of memory in perception has been termed "interpretation" by some theorists in order to distinguish an earlier
"extraction" stage (Pachella, 1975; Smith and Spoehr, 1974).
The view is that critical features are first extracted from the
icon, and then they are compared with visual representations of
possible matching categories in memory. In word perception,
features extracted from the display might be compared directly
with stored visual codes, and when the best-matching unit is
selected, it is used to fill in the visual image. Since features
within letters and words are redundant, it is conceivable that

extraction and interpretation might be interactive processes combining to produce the conscious image (Henderson, in press).

III.   Empirical Research in Word Perception:

A Search for Units of Processing

Much of the research on word perception has been concerned with the issue of perceptual units. That is, the question of interest has been whether words are recognized as wholes or if they first must be broken down into smaller units such as syllables or individual letters which are recognized and then reassembled into words internally. Research concerned with determining the functional units in word perception can be traced at least to the time of Cattell (1886a,b). He determined that more letters could be reported from a brief visual display of words or short sentences than from strings of unrelated letters. Also, thresholds for identifying common words were shown to be about the same as those for single letters. From these data, Cattell argued that words are perceived as wholes, in much the same way that letters are.

More recently, evidence has been obtained for the existence of perceptual units intermediate between words and single letters. For example, Eleanor Gibson and her colleagues (Gibson, Pick, Osser, and Hammond, 1962) varied the orthographic acceptability of nonword letter strings and found that accuracy of report for a briefly displayed item increased with the regularity of its spelling. Gibson argued that these results implied the use of perceptual units larger than letters, but, since they affected the perceptability of nonwords, they are not integrated to the level of entire words. She termed these units "spelling patterns," which were originally defined as frequently-occurring letter clusters with an invariant pronunciation. Later research (Gibson, Shurcliff, and Yonas, 1970) demonstrated similar effects of spelling patterns among deaf and hearing observers, which led Gibson to lessen the emphasis on pronunciation or phonemic processing. Instead, spelling patterns are apparently functional in purely visual matches between their stored representations and features extracted from the display.

The report procedure has been criticized because of serious problems of interpretation inherent in the results (Baddeley, 1964; Smith and Spoehr, 1974). In this procedure, a visual display containing several letters is presented for a brief time, and the observer then reports as many letters seen as possible. There are many possible causes of an advantage for regularly-spelled strings. First, there are processes normally thought of as perceptual, such as extracting features from the icon and constructing a visual image in conjunction with matching information from memory. Both of these processes could be facilitated by the presence of familiar, frequently-occurring letter clusters in the display. The observer's task includes more than this, however, and the visual image needs to be maintained while individual letters are converted to names. Retention of several letter names also taxes memory capacity such that some of them might be forgotten before they can be reported. If the strings are clustered into units larger than individual letters, such as pronounceable syllables, a greater amount of information can be held in active memory (Miller, 1956). The possibility of chunking the strings into multi-letter units obviously increases with their orthographic regularity. A further problem is the response itself which is subject to biases whenever the observer is encouraged to produce as many lettersnames as possible. In this case, guesses are likely to conform to orthographic patterns, and thus are more likely to be correct when the strings themselves are orthographically regular.

It was not until 1969 that Reicher clearly demonstrated an advantage for words in perceptual processes. Reicher's experimental procedure is illustrated in Figure 2. On each trial a visual display of a four-letter word, an anagram of the word, or

a single letter was briefly flashed. The display was followed by
a masking field to destroy the iconic image along with a pair of
letter alternatives between which the observer was to choose. On
word trials, either alternative made an acceptable word when included in the appropriate display position. The objective was to
eliminate, or at least minimize, possible contamination of perceptual effects with those due to retention and response biases.
Reicher's results were clear: observers were more accurate in
picking the correct letter when words were displayed. There were
no significant differences in accuracy between nonword and single-
letter trials.

Whereas Reicher's experiment demonstrated that words are
more perceptible than nonwords, the question of which units are
responsible for this advantage was left unanswered. That is, his
words differed from the nonwords by being familiar visual units
as well as by containing regular spelling patterns, which the
anagrams generally did not. Recent research has focused on this
issue by comparing recognition performance for irregular letter
strings, orthographically regular and pronounceable strings
(pseudowords), and words. For example, Baron and Thurston (1973)
found a difference between pseudowords and unpronounceable strings
using a procedure similar to Reicher's. One implication of this
result is that words might owe their perceptual superiority to
the presence of subunits such as spelling patterns. Therefore
Cattell's early claim that words are more perceptible than random
letter strings because they are processed as wholes could be
false; words might be processed more efficiently only because
they contain more familiar letter clusters. Cattell's judgment
was soon vidicated, however, as Juola, Leavitt, and Choe (1974)
and Manelis (1974) demonstrated the perceptual superiority of
words over pseudowords using Reicher's procedure. In a slightly
different task, Choe (1975) required observers to determine
whether or not a briefly presented stimulus matched a four-letter

target string that was shown either before or after the stimulus display. Again, observers were consistently more accurate in responding to words than pseudowords.

The conclusion to be reached with respect to recognition is that words are indeed more perceptible than orthographically regular and pronounceable pseudowords. Factors crucial to obtaining a word superiority effect appear to include the use of common words and limited practice with the set of pseudowords. Repeated visual experience with a small set of pseudowords can apparently eliminate their perceptual disadvantage relative to words (Baron and Thurston, 1973; Taylor and Chabot, in preparation), perhaps through the development of internal representations which are functionally equivalent to those for words. Subsequent research has been aimed at identifying the locus of the word superiority effect as it normally occurs in perception.

Some attempts have been made to simplify the recognition task to make it even less susceptible to influences of non-perceptual processes. For example, Eichelman (1970) presented pairs of letter strings simultaneously, one types above the other, and observers had to decide whether they were the same or different. Responses were faster when the two strings were words than when they were nonwords. Further studies have examined the roles of degree of wordness and amount of practice with the stimuli. The results have been similar to the previous findings involving recognition accuracy in that matches were found faster for words than for pseudowords, which were in turn faster than those for irregular nonwords. Differences in response speed for these three types of items decreased gradually with practice (Barron and Pittenger, 1974).

Whereas the simultaneous judgment task results in similar word superiority effects to those obtained in recognition, some problems of interpretation remain. The fact that both items are presented at the same time makes it difficult to determine at

what level their internal representations are compared. Some of
these problems can be eliminated by changing the same-different
task from one involving simultaneous presentations of two letter
strings to a task involving successive presentations. In several
experiments using this procedure, Taylor, Miller, and Juola (1975)
presented word and pseudoword displays in either all upper or all
lower case letters or in various mixtures of type cases. These
manipulations were designed to assess the status of single letters, letter clusters, syllables, and whole-word units in perception.

In the first experiment, target words were presented in intact form (all upper or all lower case) followed by an intact or
disrupted test word. The two words were the same item on 75% of
the trials, although their letter cases never matched. Examples
of the stimuli and the data from "same" trials are presented in
Figure 3. The time to make a same judgment increased substantially with the introduction of any case disruptions, indicating that
words have functional integrity as perceptual units. The fact
that response time continued to increase with the number of case
alternations suggests that if the whole-word unit was disturbed,
multi-letter units were functional, and these units were themselves disrupted more often as case alternations increased. Had
single letters been the only perceptual units relevant in this
task, no substantial differences in mean response time between
any of the intact or case alternate conditions would have been
expected. In addition, it was found that syllabic structure did
not interact with the effects of case alternations. That is, two-
syllable words were judged as rapidly when case alternations oc-
curred within syllables as when they were consistent with syllable boundaries. This result implies that syllables were not
functional visual units.

In a second experiment, words and pseudowords were used on
separate trials, and the data are also presented in Figure 3.

Again there was a significant increase in decision time with increasing numbers of case alternations, but there were no significant differences in the effects of alternations on words and pseudowords. The distinct advantage for intact words found in the first experiment was not replicated. These data imply that the perceptual units relevant for matching words and pseudowords can be the same, and that these units are undetermined, multi-letter clusters. Apparently the inclusion of pseudowords in the second experiment discouraged the use of a whole-word strategy and thus led to the lack of any advantage for intact word displays. Similar strategy effects in a recognition task involving pseudowords and irregular nonwords have been reported by Aderman and Smith (1971). In their study, observers could not make use of intermediate units to facilitate perception unless they expected spelling regularities in the display.

Thus the results from successive judgment tasks are consistent with those showing word superiority effects in simultaneous matching and in recognition. These findings offer convergent evidence that words are more perceptible than pseudowords or irregular letter strings. Unfortunately, the locus of the word advantage cannot be determined from these studies alone. That is, it is possible that words are superior to nonwords in terms of the representation of information in the icon, the abstraction of features from the icon, or the interpretation of iconic information. Although the successive judgment task has been used to eliminate some problems inherent in simultaneous matching, it apparently has problems of its own. These primarily involve possible word advantages in non-perceptual processes such as retention of visual information about the target and the comparison process itself.

A final experimental procedure to be considered resolves some of these issues and leads to an interpretation of word perception that is consistent with the results discussed here. This task

involves the use of a small set of targets that is of the same form
on all trials, and the nature of the test stimuli is the only
variable manipulated. Results using this procedure have shown
word advantages over pseudowords in some cases but not in others,
depending on methodological details. A word advantage has been
found when a different pair of target letters is presented on
every trial (Juola, Leavitt, and Choe, 1974; Reicher, 1969). However, when a small set of targets is fixed and searched for in a
succession of displays, no word superiority is found (Bjork and
Estes, 1973; Estes, Bjork, and Skaar, 1974; Juola, Choe, and
Leavitt, 1974; Massaro, 1973). This difference could be due to
differential processing strategies adopted by the observers in
the two cases. With a constantly changing set of targets, the
best strategy might be to attempt to recognize the display string
before searching its image for the presence of a target. On the
other hand, sufficient practice with a small set of targets could
lead to the adoption of a detection strategy. In this case, a
critical set of features could be smaller than that necessary for
recognition to occur. The lack of a word advantage in detection
indicates that neither the resolution of the iconic information
nor the rate of feature extraction from it differs for words and
other letter strings. Word advantages in other tasks are thus
apparently due to interpretive processes that involve activation
of visual units in memory and the use of them to construct visual
images. Word advantages also can exist in other comparison, retention, and response processes that often contribute to performance in visual information-processing tasks.

IV. Conclusions

The results from research on word perception have been discussed with respect to two issues. One concerns the type of
memory units that are compared with incoming visual information.
The other concerns when and how, in the sequence of events that
determines our visual experience, these units come into play.

Both of these issues were considered in terms of a model of visual perception that can be summarized as follows: Perception begins with the formation of an iconic image of the stimulus. The icon consists of uncategorized features in structured relationships to one another that reflect brightness and contour information in the display. Features are extracted from the icon as long as it is active in memory. This extraction process simultaneously activates perceptual units in relation to the number of their features detected in the icon. Which units can be activated depends, to some extent, on the processing strategy of the observer, as attention can be channeled to certain units depending on what is expected. When a specific unit is selected, it contributes to the formation of a visual image, and thus to what is consciously seen. Words owe their perceptual advantages to the matching and activation of larger visual units than those available for pseudo-words or irregular letter strings. In general, the fewer units that are needed to construct the visual image, the more rapidly and accurately it is formed.

These perceptual processes are assumed to be similar whether one is reading words in a book or viewing briefly-exposed words in a tachistoscope. Recognizing words apparently involves a direct match between visual information extracted from the stimulus and visual representations stored in memory. In reading, information processed at any time determines expectations about what is to follow. These expectations consequently can facilitate perception by narrowing the set of possible alternatives. Yet recognizing words is only a small part of the processes involved in reading for comprehension. Understanding printed text involves integrating information available from several eye fixations and interpreting it with respect to the representation of meaning in memory. In order to develop a model of the reading process, several elaborations of the simple perceptual model shown in Figure 1 would have to be undertaken. These would be necessary to explain (1) how word recognition is involved in the access of word meanings, (2) how information from previous eye fixations is maintained and integrated into phrases and sentences, and (3) how syntactic and semantic knowledge operates on this information to realize an internal representation whose meaning is consistent with that intended by the writer. Although some authors maintain that reading for meaning is analogous to recognizing words (i.e., visual information could be matched directly with units of meaning, Smith, 1971), it is clear that extending the present methods to understanding reading will be a longer and more arduous task than uncovering the fundamental processes involved in word recognition.

496

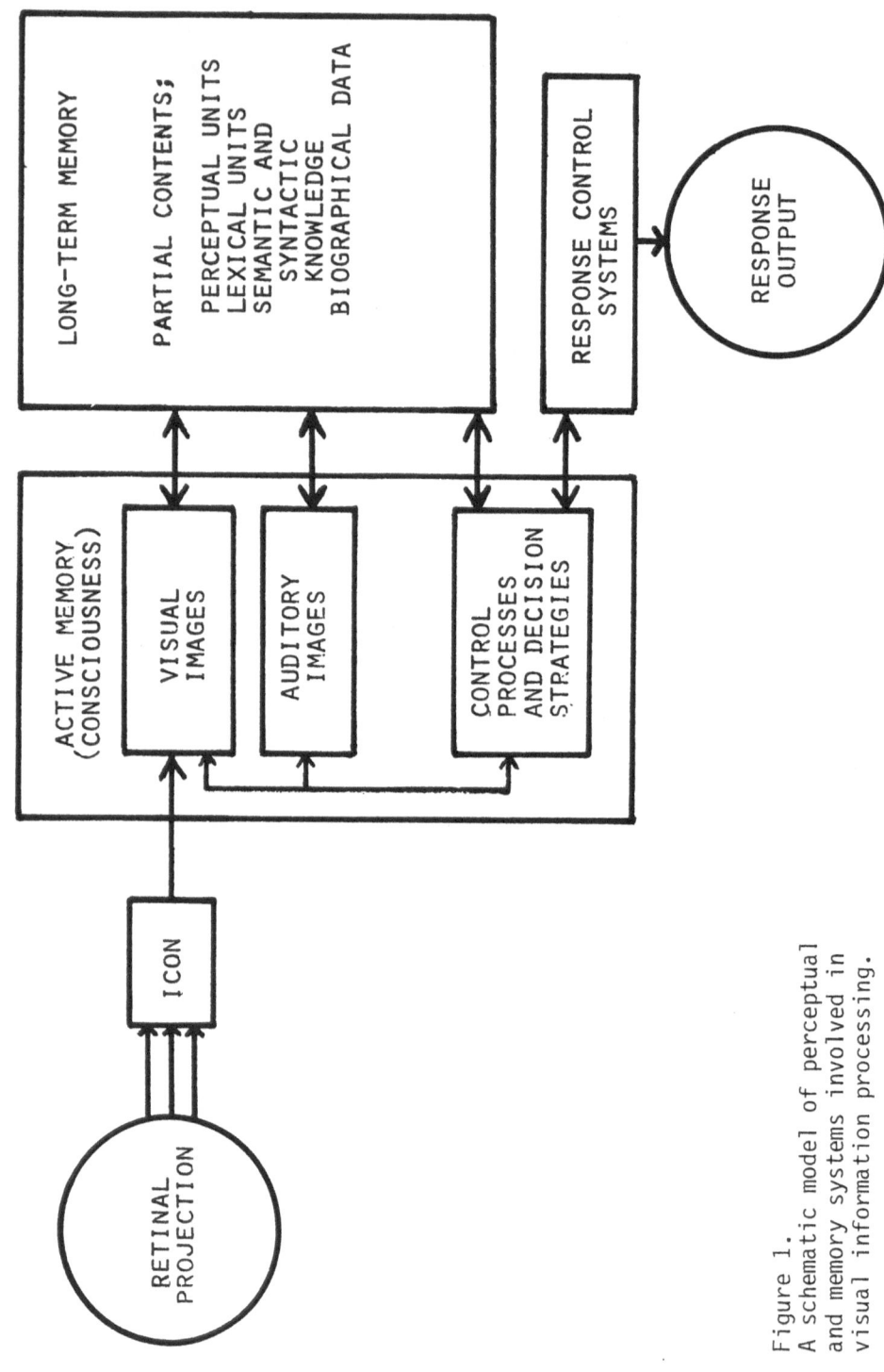

Figure 1.
A schematic model of perceptual
and memory systems involved in
visual information processing.

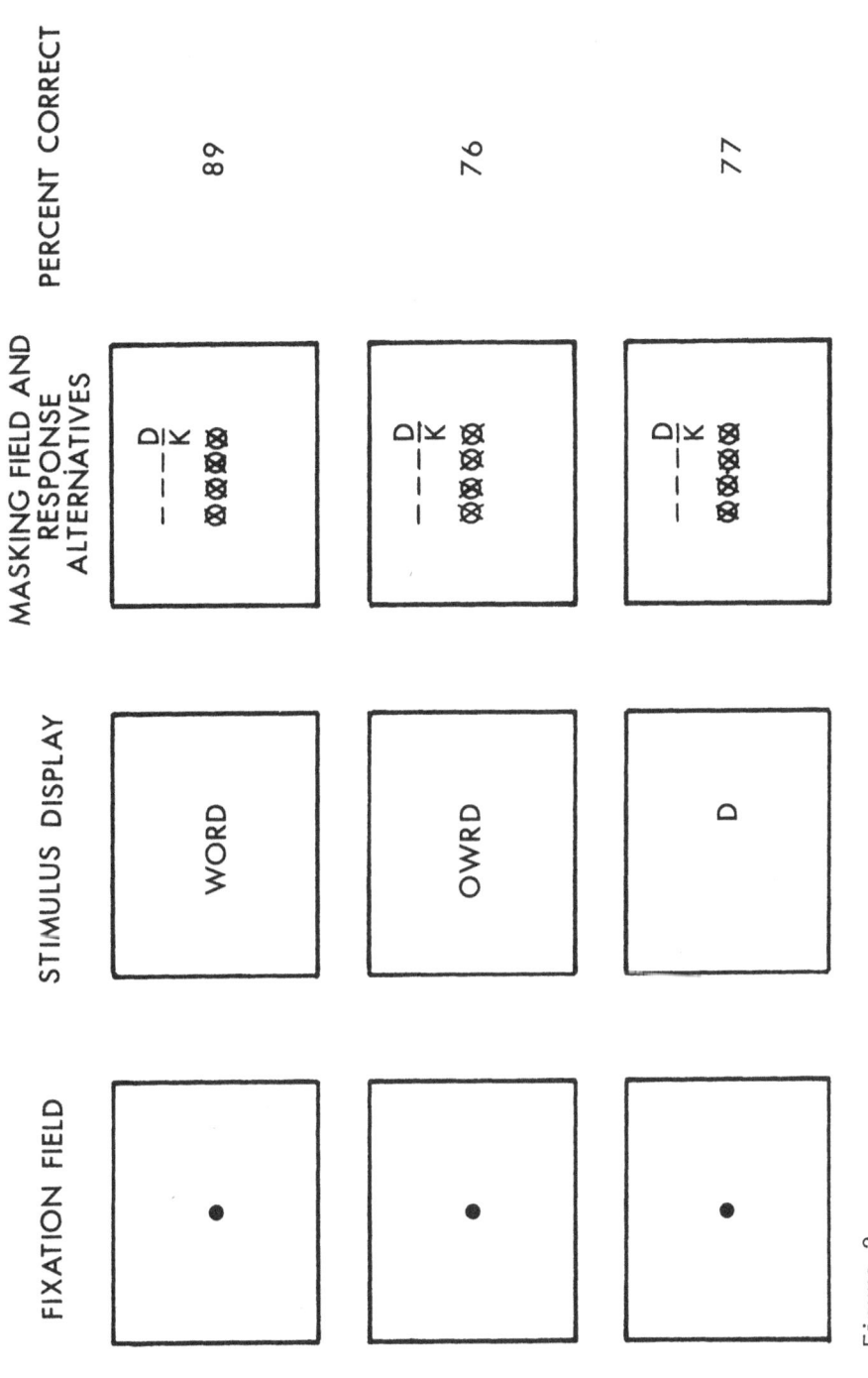

Figure 2.
Examples of stimuli and the results from a perceptual recognition experiment by Reicher (1969).

498

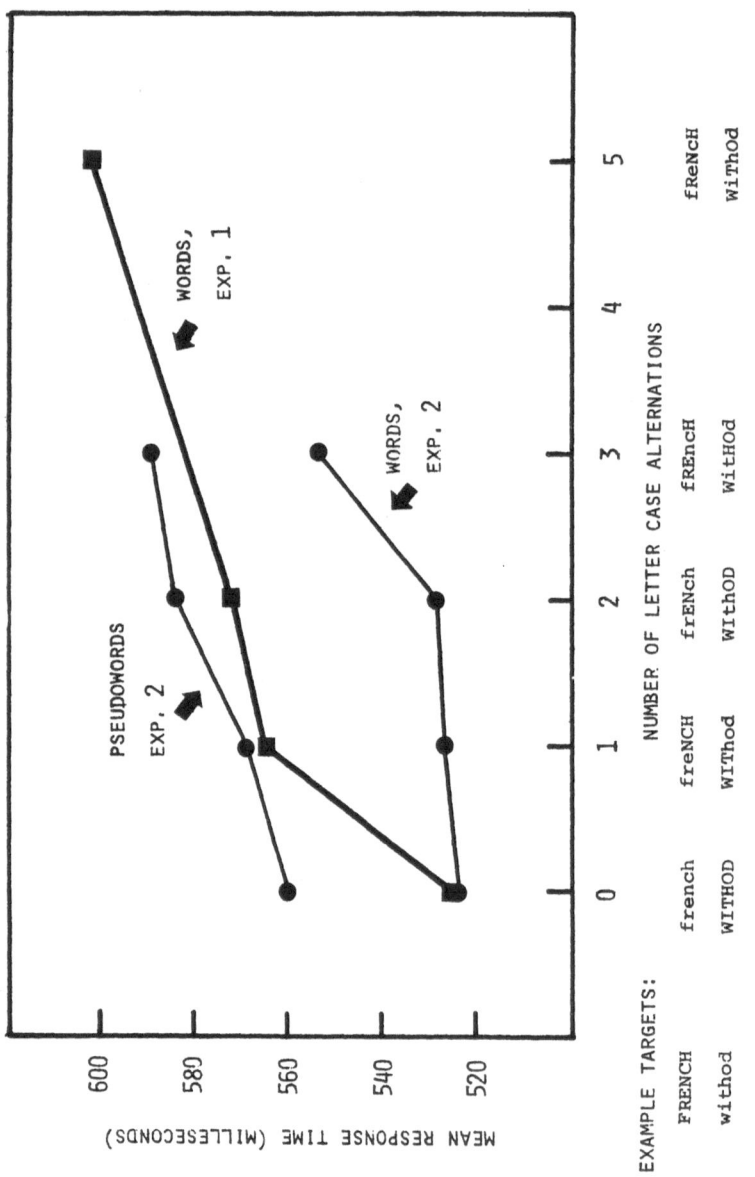

Figure 3.
Mean response time for judging a test string of letters to be the same as a target string plotted as a function of the number of letter case alternations in the test string.
In experiment 1, all letter strings were words, and both words and pseudowords were used in experiment 2 (Taylor, Miller, and Juola, 1975).

References

1. Aderman, D., & Smith, E. E. Expectancy as a determinant of functional units in perceptual recognition. Cognitive Psychology, 1971, 2, 117-129.

2. Baddeley, A. D. Immediate memory and the "perception" of letter sequences. Quarterly Journal of Experimental Psychology, 1964, 16, 364-367.

3. Baron, J., & Thurston, I. An analysis of the word-superiority effect. Cognitive Psychology, 1973, 1, 217-223.

4. Barron, R. W., & Pittenger, J. B. The effect of orthographic structure and lexical meaning on "same-different" judgments. Quarterly Journal of Experimental Psychology, 1974, 26, 566-581.

5. Bjork, E. L., & Estes, W. K. Letter identification in relation to linguistic context and masking conditions. Memory & Cognition, 1973, 1, 217-223.

6. Cattell, J. M. The time it takes to see and name objects. Mind, 1886, 11, 63-66 (a).

7. Cattell, J. M. The time taken up by cerebral operations. Mind, 1886, 11, 220-242, 377-387, 524-538 (b).

8. Choe, C. S. The effect of set and meaningfulness on word perception. Unpublished doctoral dissertation, University of Kansas, 1975.

9. Eichelman, W. H. Familiarity effects in the simultaneous matching task. Journal of Experimental Psychology, 1970, 86, 275-282.

10. Estes, W. K., Bjork, E. L., & Skaar, E. Detection of single letters and letters in words with changing vs unchanging mask characters. Bulletin of the Psychonomic Society, 1974, 3, 201-203.

11. Gibson, E. J., & Levin, H. The psychology of reading. Cambridge, Mass.: The MIT Press, 1975.

12. Gibson, E. J., Pick, A., Osser, H., & Hammond, M. The role of grapheme-phoneme correspondences in the perception of words. American Journal of Psychology, 1962, 75, 554-570.

13. Gibson, E. J., Schurcliff, A., & Yonas, A. Utilization of spelling patterns by deaf and hearing subjects. In H. Levin and J. P. Williams (Eds.), Basic studies on reading. New York: Basic Books, 1970.

500

14. Henderson, L. Word recognition. In N. S. Sutherland (Ed.), _Tutorial essays in experimental psychology_. Potomac, Md.: Erlbaum Press, in press.

15. Hubel, D. H., & Wiesel, T. N. Receptive fields, binocular interaction and functional architecture in the cat's visual cortex. _Journal of Physiology_, 1962, _160_, 106-154.

16. Hubel, D. H., & Wiesel, T. N. Shape and arrangement of columns of cat's striate cortex. _Journal of Physiology_, 1963, 165, 559-568.

17. Hubel, D. H., & Wiesel, T. N. Receptive fields and functional architecture of monkey striate cortex. _Journal of Physiology_, 1965, _195_, 215-243.

18. Juola, J. F., Choe, C. S., & Leavitt, D. D. A reanalysis of the word-superiority effect. Paper presented at the annual meeting of the Psychonomic Society, Boston, Mass., 1974.

19. Juola, J. F., Leavitt, D. D., & Choe, C. S. Letter identification in word, nonword, and single letter displays. _Bulletin of the Psychonomic Society_, 1974, _4_, 278-280.

20. Manelis, L. The effect of meaningfulness in tachistoscopic word perception. _Perception & Psychophysics_, 1974, _16_, 182-192.

21. Massaro, D. W. Perception of letters, words, and nonwords. _Journal of Experimental Psychology_, 1973, _100_, 349-353.

22. Miller, G. A. The magical number seven, plus or minus two: Some limits on our capacity for processing information. _Psychological Review_, 1956, _63_, 81-97.

23. Neisser, U. _Cognitive Psychology._ New York: Appleton-Century-Crofts, 1967.

24. Pachella, R. G. The effects of set on the tachistoscopic recognition of pictures. In P. M. A. Rabbitt and S. Dornic (Eds.), _Attention and performance V_. New York: Academic Press, 1975.

25. Rayner, K. The perceptual span and peripheral cues in reading. _Cognitive Psychology_, 1975, _7_, 65-81.

26. Reicher, G. M. Perceptual recognition as a function of meaningfulness of stimulus material. _Journal of Experimental Psychology_, 1969, _81_, 275-280.

27. Smith, E. E., & Spoehr, K. T. The perception of printed English: A theoretical perspective. In B. H. Kantowitz (Ed.), <u>Human information processing: Tutorials in performance.</u> Potomac, Md.: Erlbaum Press, 1974.

28. Smith, F. <u>Understanding reading</u>. New York: Holt, Rinehard, & Winston, 1971.

29. Sperling, G. The information in brief visual displays. <u>Psychological Monographs</u>, 1960, <u>74</u>, No. 498, 1-29.

30. Taylor, G. A., & Chabot, R. Differential backward masking of letters and words by masks of varying orthographic structure. In preparation.

31. Taylor, G. A., Miller, T. J., & Juola, J. F. Isolating the units of visual word perception. Paper presented at the annual meeting of the Psychonomic Society, Denver, Colo., 1975.

32. Tulving, E., & Gold, C. Stimulus information and contextual information as determinants of tachistoscopic recognition of words. <u>Journal of Experimental Psychology</u>, 1963, <u>66</u>, 319-327.